WILLS AND ESTATE RECORDS

OF

McMINN COUNTY, TENNESSEE

1820-1870

Researched, Compiled, and Edited

by

REBA BAYLESS BOYER

This volume was reproduced from
an 1964 edition located in the
publishers private library,
Greenville, South Carolina

Please direct all Correspondence & Orders to:

Southern Historical Press, Inc.
PO Box 1267
375 W Broad Street
Southern Historical Press, Inc.
Greenville, S.C. 29602-1267

FOREWORD

This volume of Wills and Estate Records of McMinn County, Tennessee, 1820-1870, is the third in the series of publications contemplated by the Historical Projects Committee of the McMinn County Chapter, East Tennessee Historical Society, the first volume being the McMinn County, Tennessee, United States Census, 1850, transcribed in 1961, and the second volume being the Marriage Records of McMinn County, Tennessee, 1820-1870, published in 1964.

McMinn County, Tennessee, was formed from lands ceded to the United States by the Cherokee Indians. The Act of Organization was passed November 1819 and the County Court was organized March 1820.

The material in this volume is taken from three major sources: the Will Books, the County Court and Circuit Court records, and the Chancery Court files and record books. The Will Books were completely abstracted, with notation of every entry. The County Court and Circuit Court records were searched, but only pertinent facts, which are not in the Will Books, were included. The Chancery Court references give only a brief outline of the family information contained in the voluminous papers.

The Will Books are identified by letters. I have abstracted Will Books A, B, C, D, E, F, and part of G. An index to the remainder of the Wills entered in Will Book G, probated after 1870, is to be found on a separate page in this volume.

The County Court and Circuit Court books are not numbered or lettered, but identified only by dates. To save space I have given each book a number.

The Chancery Court lawsuits are numbered. At several periods, the clerk began again at number one, so that we find from one to four lawsuits with the same number.

The individual books and records researched are as follows, with the abbreviations used in this volume:

WILL BOOKS

WB A   1819-1830. Indexed. The first Will is that of James Cunningham, proven June 1820. The last entry, filed 9 September 1830, begins on page 223 and is continued to Book B.

WB B   1830-1838. Indexed. Page one is a continuation of Book A. The last numbered page is 302, March 1838. There are several unnumbered pages at end of book dated 1834.

WB C   1838-1841. Originally indexed, but only one page of index is now remaining. Pages 1-19, 22-47, and 348-351 are now missing. Page 20 is dated 2 June 1838. Page 347 is dated 1 March 1841. Pages 22-47 and 348-351 were copied by the Works Progress Administration, Historical Works Project, Mrs. Penelope Johnson Allen, State Supervisor, to whom I am greatly indebted for copies of the missing pages.

WB D   1841-1849. Indexed. Pages 1 to 596 dated from 2 March 1841 to 2 January 1849.

WB E   1849-1856. Indexed. Pages 1 to 572 dated from 23 January 1849 to 12 October 1856.

WB F   1856-1862. Indexed. Pages 1 to 478 dated from 20 October 1856 to 30 October 1862.

WB G   1863-1893. Indexed. In the Court Minute Book 1864-1868, pages 15-16, 3 October 1864, is the following entry: "Affidavit of R. M. Fisher Clerk of County Court of McMinn Co. that the Record Book, the Will Book G, the tax Book for 1863, the Marriage Record, and the Revenue Docket have all been destroyed or carried off by the Public enemy of the Country... Clerk authorized to open and substitute other books." The present book, pages 1 to 480, is dated from 23 July 1863 to September 1893. The above affidavit clearly shows that many Wills that were recorded from 30 October 1862 to 3 October 1864 in the original Will Book G are not in the records.

COUNTY COURT AND CIRCUIT COURT BOOKS

CR1   1820-1829. Minutes of the Court of Pleas and Quarter Sessions. Indexed. Pages 1 to 445 dated from March 1820, the organization of the Court, to 2 June 1829.

CR2   1824-1831. Minutes of the Court of Pleas and Quarter Sessions. Not indexed. Pages 1 to 540 dated from 7 June 1824 to 6 June 1831.

CR3   1829-1836. Minutes of the Court of Pleas and Quarter Sessions. Not indexed. Pages 1 to 482 dated from June 1829 to 10 March 1836. This book is composed entirely of State and Civil Cases and is not a minute book in the strict sense of the word.

CR4   1831-1841. County Court Minutes. Not indexed. Pages 1 to 557 dated from 7 June 1831 to 2 August 1841.

CR5   1841-1849. County Court Minutes. Not indexed. Pages 1 to 555 dated from 6 September 1841 to 2 October 1849.

CR6   1850-1857. County Court Minutes. Not indexed. Pages not numbered. Pages missing at front and back, and some missing in body of book. The remaining pages are dated from September 1850 to January 1857.

CR7   1857-1861. County Court Minutes. Not indexed. Pages 1 to 565 dated from 6 April 1857 to 2 September 1861.

CR8   1861-1863. County Court Minutes. This book, without covers and with many missing and torn pages, was found in May 1965, after having been missing for many years. The pages were originally numbered, but many numbers are now torn off. The remaining pages are dated from October 1861 to November 1863.

CR9   1864-1868. County Court Minutes. Indexed. Pages 1 to 480 are dated from 5 September 1864 to 6 July 1868.

CR10   1868-1873. County Court Minutes. Indexed. Pages 1 to 483 dated from 3 August 1868 to 21 April 1873.

CR11   1866-1876. Administrators and Executors Settlements. Indexed.
         Pages 1 to 360 dated from 29 October 1866 to 2 March 1876.
         This book was also found as CR8, above.

CR12   1852-1855. Circuit Court State and Civil Minute Book. Index-
         ed. Pages 1 to 420 dated from 16 Apr 1852 to 18 August 1855.
         The following Judges of the Third Judicial Circuit sign the
         Minutes: E. Alexander, April 1852 and April 1854; John L.
         Goodall, August 1852 and December 1854; Charles F. Keith,
         December 1852 to August 1853; John C. Gaut, December 1853,
         August 1854, and April 1855; Robert H. Hynds in interchange
         with John C. Gaut, August 1855.

CR13   1860-1865. Circuit Court State and Civil Minute Book, Fourth
         Judicial District at Athens. Not indexed. Covers and pages
         1-20 are missing. Pages 21 to 480 dated from 10 December 1860
         to 22 December 1865. The following Judges sign the Minutes:
         John C. Gaut, December 1860 to December 1864, with exception
         of April 1861 when George W. Brown is Judge; George W. Bridges,
         August 1865 to December 1865. No Court from May 1863 to
         August 1864. No Judge present in April 1865. This book was
         also found as CR8, above.

CR14   1867-1868. Circuit Court Minutes. Indexed. Pages 1 to 560
         dated from 8 April 1867 to 15 December 1868. The following
         Judges sign the Minutes: James P. Swann in interchange with
         Wm. L. Adams, 8 April 1867 to 15 April 1867; Wm. L. Adams,
         15 April 1867 to 15 December 1868, with D.C. Trewitt taking
         the bench on several occasions in April and August 1868 and
         N. A. Patterson taking the bench in April 1868.

CR15   1868-1872. Circuit Court Minutes. Indexed. Pages 1 to 640
         dated from 15 December 1868 to 12 December 1872. The follow-
         ing Judges sign the Minutes: Wm. L. Adams, December 1868,
         April, August, and December 1869, April and August 1870; James
         P. Swann in interchange with Wm. L. Adams, several days in
         April and August 1869; John B. Hoyl, December 1870, April,
         August, and December 1871, April, August, and December 1872;
         D. M. Key, several days in December 1870; T. Nixon Van Dyke
         for one day in August 1871.

CR16   1834-1867. County Court Execution Docket. Not indexed.
         Pages 1 to 197 dated from September 1834 to December 1867.
         Pages 198 to 261 are blank. Page 262 is description of James
         Roberts, a free man of color, who was emancipated by the Will
         of George Roberts. Pages 263 to 265 are blank. Pages 266 to
         270 contain signatures of those receiving Acts and Journals
         of the Legislature.

CR17   1857-1888. Justice of Peace Docket. Not indexed. Front
         pages are missing. Justices are T. P. Duggan, B. E. Cass,
         W. H. C. Thompson, and Hugh Duggan.

The County Court Clerks, with their years of service, follow:

         1820 to 1826.   Young Colville.
         1826 to 1836.   Arch. R. Turk, with Deputy Clerks W. P. Turk,
                         William Sherrill, Saml. H. Jorden, and Samuel
                         Workman.
         1836 to 1840.   John B. Jackson, with Deputy Clerk D. D. Haymes.
         1840 to 1844.   Thos. Vaughan, with Deputy Clerk S. Workman.

1844 to 1848.   James C. Carlock, with Deputy Clerks A. Slover
                and John L. Bridges.
1848 to 1852.   Geo. W. Mayo, with Deputy Clerk Thos. Vaughan.
1852 to 1855.   Thos. Vaughan, with Deputy Clerks Robert Y.
                Vaughan and John M. Vaughan.
1855.   John M. Vaughan.
1855 to 1864.   Wm. George, with Deputy Clerk W. T. Blackwell.
1864 to 1866.   R. M. Fisher.
1866 to 1870.   Thos. Hale, with Deputy Clerks W. G. Horton,
                John Slover, Jr., Lon Blizard, and James Howard.
1870.   Lon Blizard.

CHANCERY COURT FILES AND RECORDS

CC   followed by the appropriate number of the lawsuit, with date
        of filing. In several instances, additional information from
        the Chancery Court Execution Dockets, et cetera, has been in-
        cluded. It would have been impractical, in this volume, to
        abstract these lawsuits completely. The researcher must bear
        in mind that these cases sometimes continued for many years,
        and that conflicting testimony was often given by the various
        witnesses.

I have adhered to the spelling and wording as used in the original
sources as far as was practical. I have listed all places of residence other than McMinn County, Tennessee, when given in the original.
If the name of a county is given without the name of the State, then
it is understood that the said county is in Tennessee. Punctuation
has been purposely kept to a minimum.

                            Reba Bayless Boyer

McMinn County
Athens, Tennessee
May 1966

INDEX OF WILLS IN WILL BOOK G, PROBATED AFTER 1870,
WITH DATE OF PROBATE WHEN STATED

Adair, John 1889
Alexander, W.W.
Armstrong, Samuel 1882
Arnel, H.A.
Avens, Wesley
Ballew, Harriett A. 1886
Ballew, Mary L. 1886
Barb, A. 1871
Barnett, C.A. 1890
Bayless, J.J. 1890
Beaver, David W. 1885
Bledsaw, Martin 1879
Bonine, Jacob
Bradford, Wesley 1879
Briant, William H. 1884
Bridges, James G. 1883
Brock, Terry 1875
Burk, Ellen 1884
Burn, N.M. 1892
Buttram, M.K.
Cameron, Edmond D. 1891
Carlock, James C.
Cate, Gideon
Cate, Greenberry 1873
Cate, Mary
Chesnutt, Raleigh
Chesnutt, W.S.
Clark, Anderson 1879
Clark, Indiana 1890
Cleage, Alexander 1875
Coffee, James
Cooper, G.W. 1892
Crabtree, Thomas, Sr.
Crabtree, Thomas and Easter
Crockett, William A. 1879
Crouch, L.W.
Crow, A.H.
Cunningham, Moses
Davis, Morgan 1881
Deatherage, Parthena 1889
Dodson, Levi B. 1893
Dodson, Nimrod
Dodson, S.B.
Elliott, John 1889
Ellis, Ransom A.
Forrest, John M. 1875
Foster, C.A.
Fox, J.H. 1892
Frank, Wiley 1886
Fyffe, Helen M. 1876
Gaston, Hattie H. 1890

Gaston, Joseph D.
Gaston, Wesley
Gettys, James 1879
Gibson, Matthew R.
Goddard, Thornton C. 1884
Griffin, Young H.
Hackler, Robert 1889
Hagey, J. Clark 1888
Hamilton, Charles
Hamilton, James
Helm, Merideth A. 1879
Henderson, James M. 1892
Hicks, George M. 1893
Hill, J.T. 1896
Hoyl, Lawson 1872
Hurst, Mrs. Elizabeth H. 1893
Hutsell, John A.
Jack, William M. 1892
Jerkins, Laura A. 1878
Johnson, Elizabeth 1885
Johnson, Uriel
Joines, John H. 1886
Keith, Alexander H.
Keith, Thomas L. 1893
Kelly, S.E. 1883
King, C.L. 1892
Kingsley, Nathaniel W.
Kyker, W.F. 1892
Lambert, Tenison
Landsberry, Mary Jane 1876
Lane, D.H. 1886
Lane, John F. 1882
Lane, Russell
Lane, Sarah 1871
Lasater, William
Lattimore, Thomas 1890
Lawson, Tyre
Lee, Susan 1884
Lockmiller, Elijah 1880
Lowery, J.H.
Lowry, James
Luttrell, Sarah Frances 1883
McAdoo, Richard A.
McCameron, Elizabeth C. 1883
McGaughey, Martha 1891
McKeldin, Emily 1890
McNabb, Albon
McNabb, Taylor 1876
Manis, George W. 1887
Martin, Mrs. Emma J. 1883
May, Cordie N. 1884

May, Dr. Milton R.
Mayfield, Pearson B., Jr. 1883
Mayfield, Thomas B. 1872
Mayfield, Williams, Jr.
Mayo, Margaret T. 1890
Melton, John N. 1889
Melton, Nathan 1882
Melton, Silas R. 1879
Merideth, Martha Ann
Middleton, John J. 1882
Monday, Mrs. J.M.C. 1892
Munsey, Mary J.
Orton, Charles 1871
Patterson, Sarah
Payne, Margaret J. 1882
Peak, Bluford 1884
Pearce, David 1885
Plank, Hyram
Powers, Robert S. 1891
Prigmore, Thomas 1872
Pugh, Sarah J. 1884
Rentfro, Eliza L. 1888
Reynolds, Humphrey 1872
Reynolds, Robert
Rice, Margaret
Roberts, Benjamin
Robert, Fanny 1893
Russell, Thomas J. 1885
Sellers, William B. 1893
Sharp, John F.
Shell, C. 1893
Shelton, James 1879
Shelton, John E.
Sherer, William 1890
Shults, Mary O. 1893
Simpson, John
Slover, John F.
Small, A.G.
Spence (Spencer), William
Spradling, Richard 1889
Sullins, Timothy 1885
Swaffer, John 1881
Swaffer (Swafford), Thomas M. 1886
Swaffor (Swafford), John L.M. 1891
Swaffor (Swafford), Nancy A. 1890
Terry, William
Thurman, William 1879
Torbert, John 1882
Turley, William A. 1880
Turner, Hashur H. 1871
Varnell, D.N.
Wallis, M.L.
Wamac, Alexander 1874
Weeks, David W.
Whiteside, W.F.
Williams, J.B.
Winters, William 1891

Woody, Nancy H. 1880
Yoder, Eli 1891

ADAMS
    CR4 292, 5 Dec 1836. Hannah Grogin allowed $25 for keeping two
      orphans, Letty and Stephen Adams, for year 1837.
    CR4 425, 4 Feb 1839. David Adams an orphan bound to Hiram Ingram.
    CR4 460, 7 Oct 1839. Burow Buckner released from Apprentice Bond
      of Stephen W. Adams.
    CR4 502, 6 Jul 1840. Letty Adams orphan girl aged 10 last May
      bound to Isham Julian.

ADAMS, JOHN Q.
    CR8, 5 Jan 1863. Court pays for coffin for John Q. Adams, a
      Volunteer.

AGNEW, JANE
    WB G 210, Will exec. 1 Oct 1866; to Penelope Blizard when she
      reaches 21 or marries. Exec: A. Blizard. Wit: John F.
      Slover, Wm. G. Horton.
    CR9 218, 7 Jan 1867. Will proven.

AHL, BENJAMIN
    WB G 182, Will exec. 25 Dec 1865; to dau. Frances B. Ahl; dau.
      Mary Standafer already advanced her share; $1 each to daus.
      Nancy Swaffer, Lucy Liner, and sons John R., B.J., and Danl. W.
      Ahl. Exec: A.J. Standifer. Wit: John Jenkins, C.E. Walsh.
    CR9 172, 6 Aug 1866. Will proven.

ALEXANDER
    CR4 326, 7 Aug 1837. Sheriff ordered to bring in orphan Wm.
      Alexander from house of Abraham Cook.

ALEY, JONES
    CR5 294, 6 Jul 1846. Court pays for coffin for pauper.

ALLEN, ELIZABETH
    CR6, 6 Jan 1851. Court pays for shroud for pauper.

ALLEN, JOHN
    WB D 416, 8 Jan 1847. Comm. Uriel Johnston, James Gaut, and Isam
      Julian set apart year's support for dau. Nancy.
    WB D 416, 4 Jan 1847; 417, 1 Feb 1847; 537, 17 Jun 1848. Invt.,
      Acct. of sales, and Sett. by Chas. T. Thornton, Adm.
    WB E 149, 11 Mar 1851. Final sett.; paid $70.13 each to heirs
      Saml. Edgman, William and Hannah Cook, Nancy Allen, John A.
      D____am, William Farmer; $35.06½ each to heirs John T., and
      Milton Wilson; $14.02½ each to heirs Jonathan, Hiram, John D.,
      and Wm. Allen, and Wm. Lain.

ALLEN, JOHNATHAN
    WB A 210-212, Jun 1830. Invt. and Sale by Wm. Maples, Adm.;
      buyers include Sarah E., Ananias, and John Allen, Jr.
    WB B 81, 5 Jun 1832. Sett. by Wm. Maples and Sarah Allen, Adms.
    CR2 424, 1 Mar 1830. Robt. Cowan, James Gaut, and Saml. Hardy
      app. Comm. to lay off year's support for widow Sarah E.

ANDERSON
    CR5 28, 7 Feb 1842. James Anderson, orphan aged 7, bound to
      Absalom Beck.

ANDERSON, ALLEN G.
    CR9 342, 2 Dec 1867; and 353, 6 Jan 1868. John N. Anderson app.
      Adm. and Comm. app. to lay off year's support for widow Lely
      and family.

CR 144, filed 20 Sep 1867. Allen Anderson died May 1867 leaving
widow Letitia and children Thomas, John M., Sarah A. wife of
Joseph Hendrix, Saml. H., Rhoda J., Lewis, and James, last three
being minors.

ANDERSON, CLARK
  CR15 257, 11 Apr 1870. Martha A. Meredith, Adminx., for the use
  of Harriet B. Anderson, widow, and Laura C., Tilley, and Robt.
  D. Anderson, children.
  CR15 274, 13 Apr 1870. The State VS Thos. and Andrew J. Crawford
  and Wiley H. Warren for murder of dec'd on 29 Jan 1870.
  CR15 362, 15 Dec 1870. Burge VS Crawford. Since institution of
  suit there has been born unto Clark Anderson, dec'd, and his
  wife Harriet R. another child named Grace.

ANDERSON, ISAAC
  WB D 246, 16 Oct 1844; 246-248, 2 Dec 1844; and 420, 12 Nov 1846.
  Comm. John Arnwine, Neley Chrisman, and Henry Matlock set apart
  year's support for widow Jane and family. Invt., Sale, and Sett.
  by Alexander and Wm. M. Biggs, Adms.; buyers include Robt., M.D.,
  and Amanda J. Anderson.

ANDERSON, SARAH M.
  WB G 236, Will exec. 9 Aug 1870, prob. Oct 1870. Testatrix is a
  widow; to her son and only heir Geo. Christopher Anderson, who
  is to remain with her mother Catharine Crow; advice to both son
  and mother; Exec. and Gdn. to son: John R. Howard, Sr., and in
  case of his refusal or death, bro. C.C. Crow to serve. Wit:
  Emoline T. Wilson, Wm. W. Alexander.
  CR10 249, 4 Oct 1870. M.D. Anderson app. Adm. with Will annexed
  and C.C. Crow app. Gdn.

ANDERSON, WILLIAM H.
  CR9 52, 5 Jun 1865. Sarah M. Anderson app. Adminx.

ARMSTRONG, ANDREW
  WB D 361, Will exec. 4 Mar 1846, recorded 6 Apr 1846; to wife Mary
  Ann; Uriel Johnston to be Gdn. of three children, Malinda Jane,
  Wm. Baker, and Sarah Catherine. Exec: bro. John Armstrong.
  Wit: Raleigh Chesnutt, John A. Gouldy.
  WB D 362, 4 May 1846; 414, 7 Dec 1846; 536, 3 Jun 1848. Acct. of
  Sales, Invt., and Sett. by Exec.
  WB D 534, 6 May 1848; E 102, 6 May 1850; 191, 6 May 1851; 278,
  6 May 1852. Sett. by Cary Armstrong, Gdn.
  WB E 320, 1 Dec 1851. Invt. of sale held 8 Oct 1851 by Exec. with
  no sale to widow.
  WB E 362, 22 Dec 1853. Final sett. by Exec.; receipt of David
  Cantrell, Gdn., for balance of acct.
  WB E 366, 2 Apr 1853. Sett. by Gdn.
  WB E 400, 17 Nov 1854. Sett. by Rebecca Armstrong, Exec. of Carey
  Armstrong, dec'd, Gdn.; receipt of David Cantrell, Gdn., for
  total amount.
  WB E 416, no date; 425, 30 Apr 1855; 509, 14 Apr 1856. Sett. by
  Gdn.
  WB F 63, 7 Apr 1857. Sett. by Gdn.; receipt from Jane Smith for
  1/3 of sum.
  WB F 172, 7 Apr 1858; 261(1), 7 Apr 1859. Sett. by same Gdn.
  WB F 363, 7 Jan 1861. Sett. by J.C. Carlock, Gdn.

WB G 166, no date. Final sett. by same (by his wife), Gdn. of Sarah C. Armstrong who was a minor heir; receipts in full to heirs J.A. Smith and W.B. Armstrong for all funds; Gdn. is chargeable 1 Mar 1866.

ARMSTRONG, CARY
  WB E 384, Will exec. 15 Jul 1854, proven 6 Nov 1854; to wife Rebecca and children. Exec: wife. Wit: W.C. Vaughan, R. Stubblefield.
  CC 234, filed 11 Dec 1855. Cary Armstrong died Aug 1854 leaving widow Rebecca, who was dau. of John Morris, and children: Sarah, wife of George Snoddy; Robert; Wm.; Jackson; and Taylor, all minors.

ARMSTRONG, JOHN
  CR6, 5 Sep 1853. Moses Sweeny app. Adm.
  WB E 333, 20 Sep 1853; 342, 7 Nov 1853; 560, 27 Aug 1856. Comm. James Sloop, James Neill, and John W. Davis lay off year's support for widow and family. Invt., Sale, and Sett. by Adm.
  CR6, 3 Jan 1854. Petition to sell slaves. Moses Sweeny, Adm., VS Elizabeth Armstrong, widow, Sarah and George W. Culpeper, Amanda and Francis Pearce, Catharine, Priscilla, Elizabeth, and Louisa Armstrong, heirs, the last two being minors.
  WB F 158, 27 Feb 1858. Sett. by Francis M. Pearce, Gdn.
  WB F 380, 29 Jan 1861. Sett. by Benj. Wells, Gdn.
  WB F 425, 23 Nov 1861. Sett. by same Gdn.; balance paid to the ward who is married.

ARMSTRONG, PRISCILLA
  WB E 567, 16 Aug 1856; 571, 19 Sep 1857; F 242, 26 Nov 1858. Sett., Invt., and final report by Elizabeth Armstrong, Adminx.; vouchers "shares &C" of $83.19½ each to Sarah wife of Geo. W. Culpeper; Elizabeth Armstrong, Sr.; Catharine wife of Wm. Moore; Amanda wife of Francis M. Pearce; and Elizabeth Armstrong, Jr., and $116.19½ to Benj. Wells, Gdn.

ARMSTRONG, SAMUEL M.
  CR2 207, 8 Mar 1827. Benj. D. Armstrong app. Adm.
  WB A 136-138, 17 Mar 1827. Sale; 4 Jun 1828 Adm. makes sett. with Court Comm. A.D. Keys, J.K. Brown, O.G. Murrell.

ARMSTRONG, SARAH
  WB F 38-40, no date. Invt. and Sale by C.A. Armstrong, Adm. See also WILLIAM ARMSTRONG.

ARMSTRONG, THOMAS
  WB D 131, 3 Apr 1843; 142, 5 Jun 1843; 278, 29 Apr 1845. Invt., Sale, and Sett. by Moses Sweeny, Adm.
  WB D 141, 28 Mar 1843. Comm. Joel Triplet, Gideon Cate, and Uriel Johnston set apart year's support for widow Nancy.
  WB D 504, 14 Feb 1848. Sett.; receipts of heirs James, Clinton, and Wm. Armstrong, Bannister Collier, Wm. John, and E. Goode.

ARMSTRONG, WILLIAM
  CR6, 7 Jan 1856. Allen Armstrong app. Adm.
  WB E 526, 7 Jul 1856. Invt. by C. Allen Armstrong, Adm.; all personal property turned over to widow Sarah.
  CR6, 30 Nov 1856. Petition to sell land by Adm. and Gdn. of Thomas, Mogamery, Francis, David, and Joseph Armstrong, minor heirs.

WB F 339-341, 29 Aug 1860. Sett. by Adm. of Wm. and Sarah Armstrong; payments for schooling for Francis, tuition 1857 and 1859 for Magancy Armstrong, to Magana Risdom by Gdn. 1859 and 1860, to Jane Armstrong for board of Thomas and Joseph Armstrong, and account for David Armstrong.

WB F 360, 28 Nov 1860. Sett. by Saml. Armstrong, Gdn., who is charged with amounts in favor of Fremers, Joseph, and D. Armstrong.

ARMSTRONG, WILLIAM, SR.

WB E 284, Will exec. 19 Dec 1850, proven 6 Dec 1852; to sons Samuel and Wm. P.; to dau. Sarah Armstrong; to granddau. Louisiana. Execs: Saml. and Wm. P. Armstrong. Wit: Thos. Vaughan, John Simpson.

ARNOLD, DANIEL (colored)

WB G 165 and 219, Will exec. 20 Jan 1866; to son Prince Arnold; to grandchildren John, Mollie, and Rufus Arnold and any other child which son Prince may have by present wife Parthena, the three above-named being children of theirs. Exec: Oswell Liner. Gdn. of Legatees: Wm. L. McKnight. Wit: G.M. McKnight, David Weeks. Signed by mark.

CR9 142, 2 Apr 1866. Will proven.

CR9 378, 2 Mar 1868. Ordered that Will be recorded second time as there is an error.

CR10 115, 7 Jun 1869. Prince Arnold contests validity of Will.

CC 163, filed 7 Mar 1868. Daniel Arnold, a man of color, died about 1 Feb 1866.

ARNWINE, ALBARTIS (ALBARTAS)

WB F 92, 5 Oct 1857; 100, 7 Dec 1857; 327, 29 Dec 1859. List of notes and accts., Invt., and Sett. by Henry and J.W. Matlock, Adms.

WB F 161, 26 Mar 1858; 267, 18 May 1859; 335, 18 May 1860; 411, 18 May 1861; 471, 18 May 1862. Sett. by Sarah Arnwine, Gdn. to Thos. and M.F. Arnwine, minor children.

CC 286, filed 18 Feb 1858. Albartis Arnwine died June 1857 leaving widow Sarah and children Thomas W.L. and Fleming M.M. Arnwine, minors.

ARNWINE, JOHN

WB F 301, Will exec. 21 Mar 1858, Codicil 9 Dec 1858. "I have bequeathed" to James and Mary Forest, Sterlin and Ann Lewis, John and Elizabeth Moore, Wellington and Manila Rothwell, Isaiah and Nancy Garrison, Allen and Martha Dotson (this on 22 Feb 1853); "I bequeath" to son Marshal Arnwine and to my within named daughters; "I have bequeathed to William Albert in full as my book will show Chrisley Foster and his children as the Receipts will show in full". Wit: Silas G. Latham, James M. and Lang R. Dodd, and C.W. Rutledge. Codicil: "I deeded to my son Albartis Arnwine 319 acres of land to his heirs their portion in full of my Estate". Codicil 9 Dec 1858: "with the exception of Brother Albartises Estate in texas"; "my claim in Texas to go to my six son-in-laws and Fosters two children namely Elizabeth Ann and Sarah Isabel now the wives of Wm. and John Buttram"; "owing to the death of my wife". Wit: James M. Dodd and C.W. Rutledge.

CR7 315, 6 Jun 1859. Will produced and held up for confirmation.

CR7 332, 5 Jul 1859. Objection to Will made by James Forest, Sterlin Lewis, Wellington H. Rothwell, and I.S. Garrison who contest said paper; referred to Circuit Court.

CR7 373, 2 Jan 1860. Will proven by two witnesses. Will had been sent back by Circuit Court for registration.

ASH, HUGH B.
  CC 298, filed 2 Aug 1858. Hugh B. Ash, son of Robert Ash, died leaving widow, now the wife of _____ Pettigrew, and children, all over 21 and nonresidents: Wm. J., Thos. J., Robert B., Mary A., and Martha.

ASH, JAMES R.
  CC 298, filed 2 Aug 1858. James R. Ash, son of Robert Ash, died Aug 1856 leaving his second wife Elizabeth and a son by first wife, Wm. B. Ash.

ASH, ROBERT
  WB F 199, Will exec. 26 Jan 1857, proven Oct 1858; already given lands to grandson Wm. B. Ash; to lawful heirs, ¼ to oldest son, ¼ to Mary A. Firestone, ¼ to heirs of H.B. Ash, ¼ to grandson Wm. B. Ash. Wit: James C. Carlock, Larkin Wells.
  WB F 222; Acct. of sale held 14 Oct 1858.

ASHLY, WILEY
  CR7 474, 2 Oct 1860 and 487, 5 Nov 1860. Court to pay Howel Ashly for furnishing pauper's coffin; order rescinded.

ATCHLEY, McCAMPBELL
  CR6, 1 Nov 1852. Pleasant M. Miller of Meigs Co. app. Adm.
  WB E 302, 7 Feb 1853. Invt. of sale by Adm.
  WB E 303, not dated. Comm. Silas Mynatt, James Pearce, and James Bonner set apart year's support for widow and family.
  CC 198, filed 14 Jan 1854. McCampbell Atchley died leaving widow Lydia and children: Mary wife of Henderson John (Mary in McMinn and husband in Ill.), James, Noah, Pleasant, Elizabeth, and Nancy Atchley, all minors except Mary.

ATKINSON (ATKISON), EDWARD
  WB A 68-70, 29 Aug 1822. Sale by Ann and John Atkinson, Adms.
  WB B 256, July Court 1837. Report by James Atkison, Gdn to John Atkison, Sally Asbery Millia Belinda Campbell James Ann Combs and Fany Atkison, minor heirs. /No punctuation./ "have receipts on said heirs nine of Them".
  WB C 72, 15 Nov 1838. Report by same Gdn. Receipts from heirs Barnabas Thornhill, Camel B. Atkinson, John Combs, John Atkinson, John Erwin, James Atkinson, John McMinn, Asburry Atkinson, James Blackborn.
  WB C 187, 15 Nov 1839. Final report by same Gdn.

ATKINSON, JOHN
  CR4 507, 7 Sep 1840. James and Asbury Atkinson app. Adms.
  WB C 325-333, no date. Invt. of Sale by Adms. Buyers include James, A., and Campbell B. Atkinson.
  WB C Loose unnumbered sheets. Add. Sett. by Adms. 22 Sep 1842.
  WB D 60, 10 Aug 1841. Report by Ezekiel Bonner, Gdn.
  WB D 114, 22 Oct 1842. Sett. by same Gdn. "schooling for Nat & Lafayett Atkinson".
  WB D 115, 22 Sep 1842. Sett. by same Adms.
  WB D 133, 3 Apr 1843. Report by same Gdn.
  WB D 185, 6 Nov 1843. Sett. by same Gdn., receipts for schooling for Nat. and Vilena Atkinson.
  WB D 187, 4 Mar 1844; WB D 198, 8 Apr 1844. Sett. by same Gdn.

WB D 214, 31 Jul 1844. Final report by same Gdn.; receipt of
Asberry A. Atkinson, new Gdn., for total sum.
WB D 268, 14 Feb 1845; WB D 353, 12 Feb 1846; WB D 426-428, 12
Feb 1847; WB D 507, 12 Feb 1848; WB E 24, 12 Feb 1849; WB E 95,
12 Feb 1850; WB E 154, Feb 1851; WB E 236, 12 Feb 1852. Sett.
by Gdn. and Adms.
WB E 315, 7 Apr 1853. Sett. by Gdn. Voucher for tuition for
Nat. L. Atkinson at Hiwassee College.
WB E 345, 23 Dec 1853. Sett. by Gdn. for Nat L. Atkinson.
WB E 377, 7 Apr 1854. Sett. by Gdn. for Vilena Atkinson.

ATKINSON (ATKERSON), WILLIAM
WB A 12, no date and no signatures. Invt.
CR2 182, 4 Dec 1826. Supp. Invt. filed.

ATLEE, EDWIN A.
CR10 113, 3 May 1869. John L. and E. A. Atlee, Jr., app. Adms.
CR10 126, 2 Aug 1869. Report by Comm. assigning dower in lands
to widow Delilah G. /p. 128 is interesting plat of dower7.
CR10 171, 7 Feb 1870. P. C. Wilson resigns as Adm.
CR11 191, 4 Nov 1870. Sett. by John L. Atlee, Adm.
CC 288, filed 9 May 1871. Edwin A. Atlee, Sr., died 16 Apr 1869
leaving the following children: Amelia V. wife of Alexander F.
Cox of Tex.; Anna E. wife of John S. McCampbell of Tex.; S.C.
widow of _____ Luter; Mary P. wife of N.T. Ayers of Ohio;
Dr. John L.; Edwin A., Jr.; B.G.; Letitia S. wife of P.C. Wilson;
Margaretta S. wife of Thos. M. Coleman of Tex. By Nov Term 1871
Letitia S. and P.C. Wilson are both dead leaving children: Mary
E., Fanny G., Henry L.P., all minors under 14. Margaretta S.
Coleman dies by May Term 1872 leaving children Thomas and Anna,
minors.

AUTRY (ARTERY), REDERICK
CR6, 3 Dec 1855. James Bryan and John Rigans app. Adms.
WB E 492, 4 Feb 1856. Invt. of sale by Adms.
CC 271, filed 20 Apr 1857. Reddick Autry died Sep 1855 leaving
widow Jane (who is granddaughter of Jane Riggins, dec'd) and
minor children: Joseph, Rebecca, Hiley, William, Richard, Mary,
and Elizabeth.
CR9 276, June 1867. Jane Ortery app. Gdn. of Elizabeth Ortery her
own minor heir and Thomas Pugh and Jackson Ortery, grandchildren.

AVENS, WESTLEY
CR13 356, 24 Aug 1865. A. P. McClatchy VS Westley Avens - Death of
defendant is suggested and proven.

AYRES, DAVID B.
CR2 229, 3 Sep 1827. Susannah Ayers app. Gdn. of Salina P. Thorp,
Joseph C., Daniel R., Susan J., and James W. Ayres, minor heirs.

BAILES, JAMES
CR6, 5 Sep 1853. Robert A. Anderson app. Gdn. for Mary Jane
Bailes, minor heir.

BAILEY, ANDREW
WB A 150, Will exec. 28 Nov 1828; to wife Lucy; to sons Wesly,
Hayman; to daus. Jane, Charity, and Polly. Execs: wife Lucy
and son Wesly. Wit: Saml. Workman, Jane McClachy.
CR2 350, 4 Mar 1829. Will proven.
WB A 176, 1829. Invt. by Execs.

BAILEY, NANCY
  CR2 383, 7 Sep 1829. Will proven by Samuel McConnell and continued
  for further probate.

BAIN (BAYNE), SAMUEL R.
  CR7 341, 5 Sep 1859. R.J. Patty app. Adm.
  WB F 293, not dated. Comm. Robert Cochran, Wm. L. Dodson, and
  M.C. Derick set apart year's support for widow and family.
  WB F 293, 27 Sep 1859. Acct. of sale by Adm.
  WB F 422, 25 Oct 1861. Sett. by same Adm.; 27 Apr 1864 Amanda E.
  Bain receipt for balance /interlined/.
  CC 73, filed 27 Dec 1859. Samuel R. Bain died Jul 1859 intestate
  leaving widow Elizabeth and minor children: Clementine, Sarah
  J., Elmina, James R., and Nancy T. Bain, all of McMinn Co.

BAKER, ALEXANDER
  WB E 20, Will exec. 4 Feb 1847; to wife Pruda; to daus. Martha
  Armstrong, Susanah Coats, Pallissam Baker, Azzeezam Hail; to
  little dau. Sarah Catherine Baker and to Mareazean Wammac, when
  they come of age; to sons Andrew and Champenas; to three young-
  est sons Wilson, Morris, and Eli D. Exec: Jonathan Thomas.
  Wit: Jonithan Thomas, Wm. Albert. Signed by mark.
  CR5 509, 5 Feb 1849. Will proven.
  WB E 36, 5 May 1849. Comm. John Howell, R. Spradling, and Wm.
  Albert set apart year's support for widow.
  WB E 43, 4 Jun 1849; 259, 17 Jun 1852. Invt., Sale, and Sett. by
  Exec.

BAKER, ANDREW J.
  CR4 513, 8 Sep 1840. Mary Baker app. Adminx.
  WB C 289, 19 Sep 1840. Comm. Oliver Dodson, Thomas Duckworth,
  and Christian Peters set apart year's support for widow Mary.
  WB C 350, no date. Invt.
  WB D 163, 30 Oct 1843. Sett. of Adminx., made by Jeremiah F.
  Strange.

BAKER, ELIZABETH MAYFIELD HILL HUDGENS
  CC 283, filed 6 Mar 1870. Elizabeth, dau. of Penelope Mayfield,
  dec'd, died between Feb 1853 and 1857. She had children as fol-
  lows: son Jesse Hill by her first husband; Eliza and Williams
  Hudgens by her second husband. Her third husband was John Baker.
  Her dau. Eliza Hudgens married Wm. Smith 1857 when she was about
  15. Wm. Smith died about 1860-61. The children of Eliza Hudgens
  Smith are Wm. B. and Sarah E. Smith, minors.

BAKER, GEORGE W.
  CR6, 2 Feb 1852. Allen Haley, James H. Melton, and F.M. Lusk app.
  Comm. to lay off year's support for widow Artemissa.
  WB E 207, 1 Mar 1852. Invt and Sale held 27 Feb 1852 by Joseph
  Grier, Adm.
  WB E 235, 21 Feb 1852. Report by above Comm.
  WB E 406, 18 Jan 1855. Sett. by Adm.

BAKER, JOHN
  WB F 444, 4 Nov 1861. Comm. Oliver Dodson, Wm. L. Dodson, and
  Chas. Cate lay off year's support for widow Mary.
  CC 229, filed 15 Nov 1869. John Baker died about Sep 1861 leaving
  widow Mary, who has since married Elbert Brock, and children:
  Callaway of Roane Co.; Elizabeth and Sarah, minors, of Roane Co.;

Hamilton; Joe; James; Mary wife of Solomon Bogart; Emeline wife
of Elbert McGinty; Catherine wife of R. Cobb.

BAKER, NATHANIEL
CR2 180, 4 Dec 1826. Will partly proven by James Walker.

BAKER, WILLIAM
CR2 111, 5 Dec 1825. Daniel Pearce app. Adm., the widow consent-
ing, and also app. Gdn. of John and Delila Baker, minors under 14.
CR2 307, 1 Sep 1828. John and Delilah Baker, over 14, choose Daniel
Pearce as Gdn.
CR2 364-365, 1 Jun 1829. Arthur Baker, minor over 14, chooses David
H. Dicky as Gdn. Dicky app. Gdn. for James and Andrew Baker,
minors under 14.

BALL
CR7 505, Jan. 1861. L.L. Ball app. Gdn. for his own minor children,
John R., Jas. P., and John H. Ball.

BALL, LEVEN (LEAVEN) L.
WB G 176-177, Will exec. 16 Mar 1864, Codicil 27 Dec 1864; to wife
Lucinda; to son John K. $150 and if he die without issue money to
be divided between E.E. Weir and John H. Ball; to son James P.
$1150 and if he die without issue money to be divided among John
K. Ball, E.E. Weir, and John H. Ball; to Sarah Hedington and her
heirs. Exec: W.H. Ballew or W.G. Horton. Wit. to Will: T.B.
and W.L. Mayfield. Wit. to Codicil: T.B. and Wms. Mayfield.
WB G 194, no date. Comm. T.B. Mayfield, Humphrey Reynolds, and
William Mayfield set apart year's support for widow.
CR9 164, 4 Jun 1866. Will proven.
CR11 159, 3 Sep 1869. Sett. by James K.P. Ball, Adm.

BALLEW, ABRAHAM J.
CC 117, filed 20 Jan 1851. Abraham J. Ballew died 24 Aug 1844,
without wife or child, being unmarried, leaving mother and
father William and Frances Ballew, and the following bros. and
sisters: John H. who died about 1846 also unmarried, William H.,
David W., Eliza E., Mary L., and Harriet A. Ballew, and Elizabeth
E. wife of Thomas B. Mayfield. Elizabeth E. Mayfield died after
her bro. Abraham died, leaving husband and five children, namely,
Elizabeth Frances, Louisa Penelope, Mary Letitia, Emeline Elvira,
and William Mayfield, all minors. The said Wm. Mayfield has
died, unmarried, since his mother died.

BALLEW, WILLIAM
WB E 107, Will exec. 29 Aug 1849, proven 2 Sep 1850; to wife
Francis; to dau. Eliza Emeline, interest on money placed in
hands of Wm. H. Ballew for her use; to children of dau. Elizabeth
Elvira Mayfield: Elizabeth Francis, Louisa Penelope, Mary Letitia,
and Elvira Emeline; to children William Henry, David Washington,
Mary Louisa, and Harriet Adelia. Execs: sons Wm. Henry and
David Washington Ballew. Wit: James Forrest, Wm. L. Rice.
WB E 108, Oct 1850; 121, 5 Nov 1850. Invt. and Acct. of sale.
CR6, 3 Dec 1850. Widow Francis petitions Court to enter on record
her dissent to the Will.
WB E 305, 1 Feb 1853. Sett. by Execs.; Devisees Wm. H., David,
Mary L., and Harriet A. Ballew make division of slaves among
themselves, reserving two as joint property during the lifetime
of their mother, to take care of and wait upon her in her old age.

BALLINGER, JACOB and MARY
CR6, 6 Jan 1851. Court pays E.L. Kirksey for making coffins for Jacob Ballinger and wife Mary, paupers, in year 1850.

BARKSDALE, NATHAN and JOHNATHAN
CR6, 3 Dec 1855. Richard Rothwell app. Gdn. to minor heirs.
WB E 509, 7 Apr 1856. Report by same, Gdn. to minor heirs of Nathan Barksdale, dec'd; received all funds from estate of Johnathan Barksdale, dec'd.
CR7 82, 7 Dec 1857. Richard Rothwell Gdn. to Arametha A. and Andrew J. Barksdale, minor heirs.
WB F 71, 7 Apr 1857; 177, 7 Apr 1858. Sett. by Gdn.
WB F 261(2), 7 Apr 1859. Sett. by same Gdn.; "allowed gdn. for travel expense from Athens Tenn to Albemarle Co Va".
WB F 361, 7 Nov 1860. Sett. by same Gdn.; John F. Hannah's receipt for total amount.

BARNETT, DAVID
WB D 89, 6 Jul 1842. Report by Elisha White, Gdn. to John, Jesse, Elizabeth, William, Narcissa, Daniel J., Nancy C., and Martha White, minor heirs.
WB D 226, no date. Report by same Gdn.; receipts for equal amounts from John White, M and Maddux, Jesse White, J.F. and N. Benton, and D.J. White.
WB D 388, 29 Aug 1846. Sett. by same, Gdn. to his minor children who are heirs of David Barnett, dec'd; receipts in full from Nancy C. and Martha White.

BARNETT, JAMES M.
CC 273, filed 1 Dec 1870. James M. Barnett died about 1847 leaving widow Elizabeth M. and children: W.C., Charles A., Stephen S., Nancy S. wife of G.W. Bogart, Margaret E. wife of H.B. Burns, Mary C. widow of Patrick Wilson, and Frances J. wife of Joseph F. Wilson of Lewis Co., Mo.

BARNETT, WILLIAM
WB D 483-484, Will exec. 29 Dec 1846; to wife Mary; to children James M., John W., Wm. H., Saml. H., and Robt. C. Barnett, Polly Williams, and Sally M. Hale. Execs: sons John W. and Wm. H. Wit: Isom Julian and Israel C. Smith. Signed by mark.
CR5 381, 4 Oct 1847. Will proven by Israel C. Smith.

BASSWELL, WILLIAM
CR4 475, 6 Jan 1840. Court pays for shroud and coffin.

BATES, WILLIAM
CR5 188, 7 Oct 1844. Calvin H. Senter app. Adm. of James Senter, dec'd, William Bates the late Adm. having departed this life.

BAYSINGER (BASINGER), MICHAEL
CR7 496, 3 Dec 1860. L.P. Baysinger app. Adm.
WB F 367, no date. Comm. Jos. H. Melton, Allen Haley, and C.A. Pickens lay off year's support for four minor heirs.
WB F 394, 8 Feb 1861; 472, 30 Oct 1862. Invt. and sett. by Adm.

BEAN, AARON
CR10 161, 3 Jan 1870. C.H. Bean app. Adm.

BEASLEY, JOHN J.
CC 60, filed 25 Aug 1860. John J. Beasley dies during the lawsuit by Aug 1861, leaving widow Rebecca Ann and children: Susan Ann,

Elizabeth, Matilda, Theodore, John William, and Rufus.
WB F 447, 22 Feb 1862. Invt. by Rebecca Beasley, Adminx.

BEAVERS, MARY
WB G 181. Will exec. 31 May 1866; to son John B. Cobb; to dau.
M.C.A., wife of Isaac Benson "to compensate her for so kindly
taking care of me in my advanced age & feeble health"; to grandson John C. Gilbreath of Ore. "if there be as much as five
thousand dollars collected from estate of my father Samuel McJunkin
of S. C."; to Julia C. wife of Chas. W. Rice of Ark. Exec: son-
in-law Isaac Benson. Wit: James Parkerson, James Steed.
CR9 171, 6 Aug 1866. Will proven.
CR11 140, 1 Jul 1868. Power of Atty. from Chas. W. Rice and wife
Juliet C. of Benton Co., Ark., to P.B. Mayfield of Cleveland,
Tenn., to collect from Isaac Benson, Exec., their share of estate
of Mary Beavers, mother of said Juliet C. Rice, or from the
estate of Mary Beavers' father and mother, Samuel and Sarah
McJunkins (McJenkins), late of Greenville Dist., S.C., and to
turn over such funds to Standwik H. Mayfield.

BEELER, JOHN
CR5 50, 4 Jul 1842. Samuel Beeler app. Adm.
WB D 93, 1 Aug 1842. Invt. of debts due the estate in State of
Tenn.

BELLOWS, M.R.
CR7 176, 3 May 1858. James Parkerson app. Adm.
WB F 213, 4 Oct 1858. Invt. by Adm.
WB F 253, no date. Comm. C.W. Rice, G.C. Bradford, and L.C. Rentfro
lay off year's support for widow S.J.

BENNETT, JOHN
CC 260, filed 8 Sep 1870. Lawson VS Atkinson. Power of Atty. 1851
to Jeremiah Bennett of White Co., Tenn., from Matthew Curry and
wife Elizabeth and Isaac Bennett of Hancock Co., Ill, David and
Rachel Bennett of McDonough Co., Ill., heirs at law of John
Bennett late of McMinn Co. Power of Atty. 15 Sep 1850 to Jeremiah
Bennett from Jesse K. Miller and wife Eliza, formerly Eliza
Bennett (dau. of John Bennett) of Dallas Co., Iowa.

BIGHAM, ANDREW
CR4 193, 2 Jun 1834. John Camp app. Adm.
WB B 147, 27 Jun 1834; 170, 2 Mar 1835. Invt., Sale, and Add.
Invt. by Adm.; buyers include Matilda, Polly, Levicy, and David
Bigham.

BISHOP, JOSEPH
CR9 82, 2 Oct 1865. John B. Kennedy app. Gdn. of Isaac Bishop,
minor.
CR9 148, 2 Apr 1866. John B. Kennedy resigns as Gdn. of Isaac
Bishop. John B. Kennedy app. Gdn. of Eliza Jane and Isaac
Bishop, minor heirs.
WB G 213, 16 Nov 1866. Sett. by same, Gdn. of Isaac Bishop.
CR9 315, 7 Oct 1867. Dan Carpenter app. Gdn. of Isaac Bishop.

BISHOP, ROBERT
CC 351, filed 5 Nov 1872. Robert Bishop died Apr 1870 leaving bro.
J.M. Bishop and widow Sarah and children: Elizabeth A., Sampson
C., and R.M., all minors.

BISHOP, THOMAS
  CR5 46, 6 Jun 1842. Isaac Wallin app. Adm.
  WB D 98, 1 Aug 1842. Invt. of sale by Adm.; Hannah Bishop the only
  buyer.

BISHOP, THOMAS
  CC 243, filed 6 May 1870. Thomas Bishop died 1863 leaving widow
  Nancy and children: James C., Robert T., Sarah D., John M.P.,
  and Elizabeth, all minors. Robert Bishop, dec'd, was bro. to
  Thomas Bishop.
  CR10 213, 6 Jun 1870. Sampson and Robert Bishop VS Nancy, James
  C., Rob. T., Sarah D., John M.P., and Elizabeth Bishop, the last
  five being minors. Petition to sell land.
  CR10 235-237, 5 Sep 1870. Plat of land assigned by Comm.; 1/3 to
  Sampson Bishop, 1/3 to Robert Bishop, and 1/3 to Nancy Bishop,
  widow, and the five minor children.

BLACKBURN, JAMES
  WB G 25, Will exec. 1 Jun 1861; to wife Mary; to two children
  Parthenia Artelessa Blackburn and James De Witt Clinton Black-
  burn, minors and children of Mary. Exec: John Rogers. Wit:
  A.J. Dodson, F.A. Pettitt.
  CR9 23, 7 Nov 1864. Will proven.

BLACKBURN, JESSE R.
  WB G 57-59, 3 Apr 1865. Invt. by R.G. Blackburn, Adm.; includes
  notes bad and doubtful dating back to 1833.
  WB G 167, 30 Apr 1866. Sale by Robert G. Blackburn, Adm.
  CC 226, filed 10 Nov 1869. Jesse R. Blackburn died Dec 1864
  leaving widow Mary and children: Susan A. wife of Thomas A.
  Cass, Melinda E. widow of G.C. Duggan, Margaret A., Eliza E.
  wife of R.E. Martin, and R. G. Blackburn.

BLACKBURN, SAMUEL
  WB B 176, Will exec. 9 Nov 1834, proven June 1835; to wife Margaret; to six children: James, Robert, Jesse, Levina, Mose,
  and John. Execs: sons James and Robert. Wit: Isom Julian,
  Peter Airhart.

BLACKWELL, JULIUS W.
  CR14 214, 20 Aug 1867. State of Tenn. VS Wm. H. Ballew et al;
  Death of J.W. Blackwell one of defendants is suggested and not
  denied.
  CC 81, filed 25 Nov 1867. Children of Julius W. Blackwell and
  wife, both dec'd, are: Ada or Addie wife of _____ McCulla of
  Knoxville; Helen, dec'd, wife of John L. Bridges, dec'd (whose
  children are Julius B. and John E. Bridges both minors over 14
  of Atlanta); and Wm.T. Blackwell, dec'd. Ada McCulla, Julius
  B. and John E. Bridges are the only living descendants of
  Julius W. Blackwell.
  CR9 349, 6 Jan 1868. Invt. by J. Grubb, Adm.

BLACKWELL, WILLIAM T.
  CR14 437, 17 Apr 1868. Ada McCulla VS J.B. and John E. Bridges,
  minors, and John F. Slover and A.H. Keith. Petition for sale
  of house and lot for distribution. A.H. Keith sold house to
  Blackwell. Slover is Gdn. of minors.

BLAIR, JAMES
  CR1 327, 3 Jun 1828. Wm. Blair VS John Armstrong, James Johnston,

and John Blair, Execs.

BLAIR or BLAIN, MARY M.
  CR15 160, 12 Aug 1869. Wm. F. Johnson, Adm., VS E.T.&Ga. R.R. Co.

BOLDING, JOHN
  CR4 384, 1 Oct 1838. Thomas Smart app. Gdn. to Wm. and Joseph B.
  Smart, minor heirs. /Name of dec'd not given here./
  WB D 89, Jul 1842. Report by same Gdn.; receipts from minors for
  their full shares; witnesses John McGaughy and Jacob Vanzant.

BOND, PETER
  WB A 192, Will exec. 13 May 1829; to wife Joana; to children until
  youngest child be of age. Execs: Amon and Benjamin Bond. Wit:
  John W. and Wm. H. Barnett. Signed by mark.
  CR2 408, 8 Dec 1829 and CR2 411, 9 Dec 1829. Will proven.
  CR5 69, 6 Sep 1842. Elizabeth Bond, 16, chooses Samuel Wilson as
  Gdn.
  WB D 213, 17 Jul 1844; 369, 15 Apr 1846. Sett. by Samuel Wilson
  Gdn. to the minor heir.
  CR5 331, 4 Jan 1847. Saml. Wilson released as Gdn.

BONNER, EZEKIEL
  WB D 395-399, Will exec. 3 Sep 1845; to wife Mourning "she being
  present and such being her wishes"; to sons James and Moses; to
  daus. Margaret Graves, Elizabeth McDowell, and Vinny Atkinson;
  to granddau. Parilee wife of John Gregory; to grandson Thomas
  Greenville Bonner son of dau. Margaret Graves; to grandchildren
  Nat. L. and Vilena Atkinson children of dau. Rebecca Atkinson,
  dec'd; to grandchildren Jemima and Mourning Womack children of
  dau. Sally Womack, dec'd. Execs: Wm. Cowan and Levin L. Ball.
  Wit: Tho. J. Campbell and Emanuel Hany. Codicil "added imme-
  diately after executing the same" but dated 3 Aug 1845.
  CR5 308, 5 Oct 1846. Will proven. Execs. named refuse to serve.
  Widow, legatees, and next of kin refuse to serve. James McNabb
  app. Adm. with Will annexed.
  WB D 405-411, 4 Dec 1846. Invt. and sale by Adm.; includes note
  for collection on James Cooly of Ga. but it is said he lives
  Ala.
  WB D 412, 7 Nov 1846. Comm. Jo McCulley, E. Haney, and Wm.
  McKamy set apart year's support for widow Mourning.
  WB D 429, 502, 503, 584 dating from 1 Mar 1847 to 2 Jan 1849.
  Settlements by Adm.; by John Wammack Gdn. to his minor children;
  by James Bonner Gdn. to Thos. Greenville Bonner; by James Bonner
  Gdn. to Vilena and Nat. L. Atkinson minor heirs of Jno. Atkinson,
  dec'd, so far as the estate of Ezekiel Bonner is concerned.
  WB E 17, 23 Jan 1849. Sett. by Adm.; paid to heirs Moses and James
  Bonner, John McDowell, James Atkinson, John Gregory, and Mourning
  Bonner, widow; paid John Wamack, Gdn.; paid James Bonner, Gdn.
  WB E 24, 25, 77, 93, 103, 149, 151, dating from 15 Feb 1849 to
  2 Jan 1851. Sett. by same Gdns. and Adm.
  WB E 162, 5 May 1851. Sett. by Tapley Gregory, present Gdn. to
  Thos. G. Bonner.
  WB E 202, 2 Jan 1852. Sett. by John Wamack, Gdn. to Gemima Ada-
  line and Mourning Elizabeth Wamack; final payment to Peter Cate
  and wife Gemima Adline Cate, heirs.
  WB E 205, 209, 304, 313, 330, 354, 367, 368, 407, 488, and WB F 44,
  152, 262, dating from 15 Feb 1852 to 6 May 1859. Sett. by same

Gdns. On 24 Apr 1854 (E 368) Thos. G. Bonner's receipt for
total amount. On 6 May 1859 (F 262) Mourning E. Wamack of lawful age receives her funds.
WB E - Loose sheet of paper not registered in book, dated 9 Jan
1855. Final Sett. by James Bonner, Gdn. to Velina W. Atkinson;
receipt of E.W. and V.W. King, heirs, for balance in acct.

BONNER, JAMES
WB F 316, 10 Jan 1860. Comm. Wm. McKamy, Stephen Hill, and I.B.
Haney lay off year's support for widow and family.
CR7 381, 5 Mar 1860. John Gregory app. Gdn. to James B., Calvin,
Parallee, and George F. Bonner, minor heirs. Anna Bonner, widow,
files petition for dower in lands.
WB F 367-371, 22 Nov. 1860. Invt. and sale by James Gregory, Adm.
WB F 403, 1 Jul 1861. Report by John Gregory, Gdn.
WB F 403, 17 Mar 1862. Sett. by James Gregory, Adm. of estate of
John Gregory, dec'd, who was Gdn.
WB G 69, 29 Jun 1865 and 188, 12 Jul 1866. Sett. by Adm.
WB G 192, 1 Sep 1866. Sett. by Joseph McCulley, Gdn. of James
Polk, Calvin S., Paralee, and Franklin Bonner, reporting from
1862.
CC 65, filed abt. 30 Jun 1866; CC 87, filed 17 Sep 1866; CC 137,
filed 23 Aug 1867. James Bonner died leaving widow Anna and
children, viz: Sarah, wife of Joseph Walker of Mo.; Elizabeth,
wife of James Gregory; Mary, wife of Elmore Brock of White Co.,
Tenn.; Martha, wife of John Weir of Ark.; Margaret, wife of John
E. Hutsell; Ezekiel; James P.; Calvin; Parallee, wife of John
Shearer; and George Francis, a minor.

BOOKOUT, JESSE
CR5 359, 5 Jul 1847. Coroner paid for holding inquest on 14 Jun
1847.

BOON, ELIZABETH
CR5 121, 4 Sep 1843. David Moss app. Adm.
WB D 166-168, 4 Dec 1843. Invt. of sale by Adm.; buyers include
Sarah, Daniel, Israel, John, and Allen Boon.
WB D 313, 29 Aug 1845. James C. Carlock, Clerk, makes pro rata
sett. of estate between Allen Boon, Adm. of David Moss who was
Adm. of Elizabeth Boon, and the creditors.

BOON (BOONE), ISRAEL
CR4 467, 4 Nov 1839. David Moss and Allen Boon app. Adms.
WB C 213-215, Feb 1840. Invt. of sale by Adms.
CR4 471, 2 Dec 1839. Comm. Samuel Hardy, James Gaut, and Chas. T.
Thornton lay off year's support for widow Elizabeth and children.
WB D 41, 2 Nov 1841. Sett. by Adms.
WB D 295, 2 May 1845. Sett. by Allen Boon, Adm.; receipts in full
from the heirs /not named7, including his own.
CC 57, filed 21 Aug 1848. Cansler VS Cansler; Israel Boone died
Sep 1839.

BOON (BOONE), JESSEE
WB A 196-197, Will exec. 23 Nov 1829; to wife Sarah; to sons
Israel and Johnithan; to Johnithan Wilson, Smith Coffey, Wm.
Coffey, Wm. Gragg, Marvel (Mavel) Coffey, Daniel Boon. Execs:
Israel Boon, Asbury M. Coffey. Wit: A.M. Coffey, John Thompson,
Johnithan Allen.
CR2 409, 8 Dec 1829 and 412, 11 Dec 1829. Will proven.

WB B 186-188, 9 Sep 1835. Invt. of sale 1 Sep 1835 by A.M. Coffey, one of Execs.

BOWERMAN, JAMES
CR10 151, 1 Nov 1869. Will proven by Phillip Rawlings, J.H. and C. Walsh. See also Sarah and James Bowerman.

BOWERMAN, JOHN
CR6, 6 Jan 1857. M. Bowerman app. Adm.

BOWERMAN, SARAH and JAMES
CR10 150, 1 Nov 1869. Report of sale by J.M. Bigham, Adm.

BOWLING, SIDNEY
CR2 480 and 483, 6 Dec 1830. Joseph Cobb, Saml. McConnell, and Henry Bradford app. Comm. to lay off year's support for widow Denitha. Wm. Logan app. Adm.

BOYD, FRANCIS
WB F 68-69 and repeated 88-89, Will exec. 7 May 1857, proven Jul 1857; to wife Polly "land in Grainger Co. whereon Pleasant Smith & Jonathan Wade now live"; to dau. Mary Jane; to only son Thomas Jefferson; dau. and son to live with mother free of charge until dau. marries and son comes of age; "the proceeds of the store". Exec: Joseph McCulley. Wit: John Crawford, Wm. George. Advisory to the Executor (follows second registration of the Will): "My special friend Milton Shields will settle between me and the heirs of Henry Boyd Deceased with Doctor Samuel Shields surviving Executor. Milton Shields will make settlement with John C. Tate & Co. he having a perfect knowledge of all these affairs at the Panther Springs Grainger County Tenn...... if it should become necessary to employ other Counsel Judge Robert Barton of Jefferson who is my friend will attend to it.... The Evidences of debt due F. & H. Boyd are at Athens and panther springs all the books are at Athens. I mean the settled account between us."
WB F 108-147, 1 Jan 1858; 294, 25 Oct 1859; 361, 25 Oct 1860; 404, 15 Apr 1859. Invt. by Exec., Sett. by Mary Boyd, Gdn. of Thos. J. Boyd, and Invt. of sale.
WB F 417, 25 Oct 1861. Sett. by Gdn.; paid for board for Thos. J. at Mossy Creek.
WB G 161, 12 Mar 1866. Sett. by same, Gdn. of her minor son.

BRADFORD, F. R.
WB G 218, Will exec. 6 Nov 1863; to two bros. Henry and Fielding Bradford. Wit: A. Coldwell, C.L. King.
CR9 344, 2 Dec 1867. Will proven.

BRADFORD, JAMES F.
CR12 29, 9 Aug 1852. Resolutions passed by the members of the Athens Bar: Col. James F. Bradford departed this life at his residence in vicinity of Athens on Sat. 17th Inst...born Jefferson Co., Tenn., 11 July 1801...bereft of his father at an early age...responsibility of widowed Mother and large family of brothers and sisters, he being the oldest then at home... at the first setting of the Hiwassee District he commenced study of law under direction of Hon. Chas. F. Keith at the present site of the Town of Athens...admitted to bar in 1823... elected to Legislature of Tenn. in 1833 but returned to private practice...stricken by attack of apoplexy on Friday.

WB E 273, 18 Sep 1852. Comm. Uriel Johnston, James Neill, and Hugh P. Wilson set apart year's support for family "taking into consideration the number of the family which is in all 25 persons".

WB E 285-296, 6 Dec 1852. Invt. and sales by Mrs. Nancy Bradford, Adminx., includes list of books in law library; partnership of Bradford & Dodson.

WB E 454, 23 Aug 1855. Add. Invt. by same Adminx.

CC 13, filed 9 Jun 1855. James F. Bradford died 17 Jul 1852 leaving widow Nancy, who is dead by Nov 1867 when suit is reinstated, and children, viz: Chas. K. over 21 in 1855; Mary who becomes 21 by 22 Aug 1856; Cornelia, dec'd, a minor without issue; James F., Jr., William C., Henry, and Fielding, all minors in 1855; John D. and Franklin, both minors in 1855 and dec'd by Nov 1867.

BRADLEY, WILLIAM

CR4 219, 2 Mar 1835. Susan Bradley app. Adminx.

WB B 178, Jun 1835. Report by Comm. John Arnwine, Henry Matlock, and James Small setting apart year's support to widow.

WB B 178, 21 Mar 1835. Invt. of sale by Adminx. "A list of property given to Wm. Bradley's children": to Malenda Christian, Agnes West, Elizabeth Baker, Susan Orr. Buyers include John Bradley, John Christian, Josiah Orr.

WB C 43, 8 Sep 1838. Sett. by same Adminx.

BRANDON, JOHN

WB A 208-209, Will exec. 6 Apr 1830; to wife Anna; to sons Hiram, Calvin (a minor), Joseph, Jefferson, William; to daus. Tamsy, Jane, and Polly (a minor). Execs: wife Anna and friend Philip Fry. Wit: Isaac Lane and Peter Reagan. Signed by mark.

CR2 449, 7 Jun 1830. Will proven.

CR3 80, 8 Jun 1830. John B. Cate and wife Tamsey formerly Tamsey Brandon VS Hiram, Calvin, Joseph, Jefferson, William, Jane, Polly, and Anna Brandon and Phillip Fry. John B. Cate and wife Tamsey, one of the heirs, suggest to the Court that John Brandon was not of sound mind when making Will; trial ordered.

CR3 118. Plaintiffs agree with the assent of the Court that a non suit be entered.

WB E 39, 21 Mar 1849. Sett. by Phillip Fry, one of Execs.; paid heirs J.B. Cate and wife, James Brandon, Eli Wells and wife Polly; reports that Anna Brandon, Execx., paid over to heirs Wm., Hiram, Jane, and Calvin Brandon such property as was bequeathed to them.

BRANNOM, JOHN and MARTHA

CR9 87, 6 Nov 1865. Isaiah and Martha Brannom, orphan children of John and Martha Brannom, dec'd, bound to John Hix.

BRANNON

CR4 284, 3 Oct 1836. Patience Lawson app. Gdn. to Jane Brannon, minor heir.

BREWER, LEWIS

CR6, 6 Jan 1857. P.W. Brewer app. Adm.

WB F 46-48, no date. Invt.

WB F 248, 21 Dec 1858. Sett.; equal payments to Calvin Shoemak and wife, L.B. Baysinger and wife, and Jane H. Brewer, leaving same amount due James Brewer a minor.

BRIANT, JOHN G.
   CR7 429, Apr 1860. Coroner's jury of inquest finds that deceased
   came to his death on 26 Mar 1860 by a fall from his horse.
   CC 91, filed 6 Oct 1866. John G. Briant died 27 Mar 1860 leaving
   no wife or child and the following as his only bros. and sisters:
   twin bro. Louis F.; Wm. H.; Mathew S.; Martha M. wife of W.A.
   Nelson; Elizabeth J. wife of Wm. Foster; Esther C. wife of J.C.
   Pennington of Monroe Co.; Mary I. a minor under 21 who by 23 Nov
   1867 is wife of P. Cleveland. In 1839 Wm. F. Briant deeded land
   to Louis F. and John G. Briant. In 1866 Esther C. and J.C.
   Pennington give receipt to A.D. Briant for their share of lands
   of John G. Briant, dec'd, it being a part of the lands on which
   A.D. Briant now lives.

BRIANT, WILLIAM F.
   WB A 253, Will exec. 15 Apr 1840. "The undersigned Testator being
   almost destitute of property"; to three sons and four daus.; to
   son Allison D. Briant; to granddau. Betsy Baker; to grandson
   Wm. H. Briant who is son to Allison Briant and his wife Ann.
   Exec: Allison D. Briant. Wit: A. and John Winkle.
   CR4 500, 4 May 1840. Will proven by Abraham and John Winkle.

BRIDGES, HELEN E.
   CC 188, filed 25 May 1853. Helen E., dec'd, was wife of John L.
   Bridges, dau. of Julius W. and Mahala D. Blackwell, and niece
   of Adaline A. Blackwell of Knoxville. Helen E. Bridges was
   alive in Feb 1851. Her minor children are Julius B. and John
   E. Bridges.

BRINLEY (BRINDLEY, BRINLEE), STEPHEN
   WB D 216, Will exec 30 Jan 1843. Wife Sarah to have entire estate
   and at her death she may will it to whom she pleases. Execs:
   W. Cowan and John Poe. Wit: Saml. and Chas. McNelly. Signed
   by mark.
   CR5 182, 5 Aug 1844. Will proven. Execs. refuse to serve and
   Court app. Wm. T. McCallie.
   WB D 376, 3 Aug 1846. Sett. by Adm.; no personal property.

BRIT, MARY
   CR7 272, 3 Jan 1859. Court pays for coffin and shroud for pauper.

BROCK, ELBERT
   WB E 333, 1 Oct 1853. Comm. John Jack, Thomas Everton, and E.T.
   Kirksey lay off year's support for widow Mary and family.
   WB E 403, 25 Nov 1854. Invt. by J. Jack, Adm.
   WB E 418, no date. Widow Mary is assigned land as dower.
   CR6, 1 Jan 1855. John Jack, Adm. VS Mary Brock, widow, and Andrew
   J. and Margaret E. Brock, the latter an infant, heirs. Petition
   to sell land.
   WB F 50, 2 Jan 1857. Pro rata sett.; paid for obtaining grant to
   land.
   CC 233, filed 14 Dec 1869. Elbert Brock died Sep 1853 leaving
   widow Mary (alive in 1869) and only children: Lucinda or Lucy
   (who died after her father without issue and who was wife of
   S.H. Thompson); Andrew Jackson; Isaac (who died 23 Dec 1848,
   who married 10 Apr 1848 Mary Jane Saunders, and who left one
   child Margaret Elizabeth, born 5 Jun 1849, who by 22 May 1871
   has married Ben Phillips).

BROCK, ISAAC
  CR6, 2 Apr. 1855. John J. Dixon app. Gdn. to minor heirs.
  See also ELBERT BROCK.

BROCK, W.M.
  CC 233, filed 14 Dec 1869. W.M. Brock died leaving wife Eliza
    (who has since married Elihu Kelley) and three children: Elmira,
    Tennessee, and Buchanan.

BROOKSHIRE
  CR5 41, 2 May 1842. Jesse Brookshire, orphan aged 15 years and 3
    months, bound to Wm. Armstrong.

BROOM, MELUS
  WB D 400, no date. Comm. D. Dorsey, Oliver Dodson, and Joel
    Triplet list property.
  CR5 309, 5 Oct 1846. Above Comm. app. to lay off year's support
    for widow Polly.

BROWDER, EDMOND
  WB F 465-468, no date. Invt. of sale and notes by Henry Rice, Adm.
  WB G 60, 11 May 1865. Sett. by C.L. Rice, Adm. of Henry Rice,
    dec'd, and Adm. De Bonus Non of Edmund Browder.
  WB G 188, 7 Jul 1866. Sett. by same Adm.
  CC 39, filed 6 Dec 1865. Edmund Browder died 6 Sep. 1861 leaving
    children, viz: Matthew, born 26 Sep 1805, now of De Kalb Co.,
    Ala.; Lavinia, born 10 Dec 1806, wife of Jesse Grissam; Deborah,
    born 30 Jul 1809, wife of Jesse Samples; Sally, born 1 Dec 1810
    and died 24 Oct 1823; John Wesley, born 17 Mar 1812, who died
    before lawsuit is filed, leaving widow Jane and two children,
    Edmund and Marline, wife of Napoleon Bradford; Darius, born
    30 Oct 1813, now of De Kalb Co., Ala.; Martha or Patey, born
    7 May 1815, who dies by Nov. 1871 and is wife of Wm. Callahan,
    non-residents; Celia (Selah, Selia), born 14 Nov 1816, wife of
    Jonathan Johns of Knox Co.; Lovana, born 12 Jul 1818, wife of
    Elijah Grisham; Talitha (Delitha, Tallitha), born 30 Sep 1819,
    wife of Wm. Bolin; Calvin, born 2 Nov 1820; Samuel D., born 16
    Apr 1822, now of Bradley Co.; Robert F., born 22 Sep 1823, died
    May 1873, married Arminda C. Erwin; Albert, born 17 Jul 1825;
    Catherine, born 27 Aug 1828 and died 7 May 1830.

BROWDER, JOSEPH
  CR9 3 and 5, 5 Sep 1864. Simeon Browder app. Adm. Comm. app.
    to lay off year's support for widow Ellen and family.
  WB G 23, 3 Oct 1864 and 110, 29 Sep 1865. Invt. and sale by Adm.
  CR9 352, 6 Jan 1868. Wm. R. Smith app. Gdn. of Julie Browder,
    minor heir.
  CR11 151, 5 Feb 1869. Sett. by Adm.; equal payments to J.F.
    Browder, M.E. Vanzant, and W.R. Smith, Gdn.
  CC 273, filed 1 Dec 1870. Joseph Browder died about 1863 leaving
    heirs John F. of Ga., Simeon E. of Polk Co., Julia a minor,
    Mary wife of Isaac Denton.

BROWN, A. BROOKS
  WB F 309-310, Verbal Will exec. 23 Jan 1860. "Statement of J.W.
    Blackwell and Wm. W. Alexander as to the last Will and Testament
    of A.B. Brown, dec'd, reduced to writing by Wm. W. Alexander one
    of the witnesses Tuesday the 24th day of January A. D. 1860"; the
    witnesses, of Athens, were at the death bed of A. Brooks Brown

on the morning of the 23rd Jan 1860; to Daniel Bledsoe and wife
Margaret Bledsoe for caring for him during his illness; balance
to his "recognized natural son George Brown of Blount Co., Tenn."
Wit: Wm. G. Horton and Jas. C. Calhoun.
CR7 376, 6 Feb 1860. Will proven. Court satisfied that the widow
could not be conveniently found. Jesse Brown, bro. of dec'd,
appears and offers no objection to the Will.
CR7 380, 7 Feb 1860. Jury of inquest finds that A.B. Brown being
alone on 23 Jan 1860 did shoot himself with a shotgun loaded with
buckshot from the effects of which he died this the 24 Jan 1860.
WB F 336, 16 Mar 1860. Invt. by Jas. H. Hornsby, Adm., with Will
annexed. A partnership existed between dec'd and H.H. Rider.
WB F 448, 7 Mar 1862. Final sett.; receipt for balance from heir
George Brown.

BROWN, JOHN
CR3 392, 1 Sep 1834. Wm. L. Tate, Adm. VS Zacariah Keith.

BROWN, JONATHAN
WB A 176 and 198, no date. Invt. by Sarah and Aron B. Brown, Adms.
CR2 365, 1 Jun 1829. Sarah and Aron B. Brown app. Adms.
CR2 392, 10 Sep 1829. John Austin and Joel K. Brown app. Comm. to
lay off year's support for widow Sarah.
See also SARAH BROWN

BROWN, J.W.
WB G 234-235, Will exec. 13 Jul 1870, probated Sep 1870; to wife
N.K.; to minor heirs R.N.; H.L.; M.M.; N.K.; J.W.; and M.L.
Brown; to legal heirs; if granddau. Ady Brock dies before reach-
ing 21, her portion to legal heirs; to John Rogers, about 10
acres adjoining his own land. Execs: James Parkison, Esq.,
J.H. Lowry. Wit: Wm. Combs, J.A. Owens.
CR10 304, Jul 1871. Petition of W.C. and Winfield S. Brown and
Kinner Brown, widow and legatees, to set aside Will; ordered
that Will be set aside; appealed to Circuit Court.
CC 207, filed 9 Jun 1871. J.W. Brown died leaving children Wm. C.,
Windfield S., and three minors by his first wife who is long
since dead, and three minor children by his surviving widow,
N. Kinner Brown. Complainants claim that Testator was insane at
time will was made.

BROWN, MARY D.
CR9 375, 2 Mar 1868. Report of sale by C.F. Gibson, Adm.

BROWN, SARAH
CC 59, filed 21 Aug 1860. Sarah Brown died a short time after
buying a lot in Athens on 4 Jun 1834 leaving children by her
first husband Robert Green, viz: Phebe Green of McMinn Co. and
Hannah Green of Meigs Co.; also leaving children by her second
husband Jonathan Brown, viz: Jessee of Rhea Co.; Sarah, Noama,
and Isaac who live in the West; Abraham of Mo.; Joseph who died
without heirs; Aaron B. who died with a wife living in Ark. and
no legitimate children /See A. Brooks Brown/.
CC 31, filed 16 Oct 1865. Sarah Brown died about 1839 leaving
children as given above. All the children by Brown, except
Jessee, have died without lawful issue.

BRYAN, F.P.
CR7 378, 6 Feb 1860. T.S. Denson app. Adm.

WB F 327, no date. Comm. Wm. Rogers, B.C. Hul<u>tern</u>, and C.H. Senter set apart year's support from the accts. and notes for widow Mary Ann and family.

BRYAN (BRYANT), WILLIAM B.
CR4 458, 7 Oct 1839. Robert M. Newman and James Bryant app. Adms.
CR4 467, 8 Oct 1839. Chas. W. McDonald and Chas. Cate app. Gdns. to Mary, Emaline, Thomas, Mariah, Allin, and·Wm. Bryant, minor heirs, and are chosen Gdns. by Pleasant and Peter who are of age to choose for themselves.
WB C 178, Nov 1839. Comm. John McGaughey, John Crawford, and Chas. W. McDonald set apart year's support for heirs.
WB C 279-285, 5 Oct 1840. Invt. of sale and Sett. by Adms.
CR4 519, 5 Oct 1840. James Bryan and Robt. M. Newman released as Adms. and James Bryan app. Adm.
WB D 133, no date. Report by Pleasant Bryan and Wm. Rucker, Gdns. to minor heirs.
WB D 137, 25 Feb 1843. Sett. by James Bryan, Adm.
WB D 146, no date. Report by Chas. Cate and Chas. W. McDonald, Gdns.; receipts from Mary, Emeline, Allen, Thomas, Wm., and Nancy M.
WB D 215, 6 Jul 1844. Sett. by Pleasant Bryan, Gdn.; vouchers for Emeline, Mary, Thomas and Allen.
WB D 226, 5 Sep 1844 and 307, 6 Jul 1845. Sett. by Adm. and Gdn.
WB D 374, 3 Aug 1846. Sett. by Peter L. Bryan, Gdn., successor to P.B. Bryan; heirs are Emeline, Nancy, Allen, Thomas, and Wm.
WB D 375, 6 Jul 1846. Sett. by Pleasant B. Bryan, former Gdn.; paid equal amounts to James C., Peter L., and P.B. Bryan.
WB D 439-448, 23 Mar 1847 and 524-525. Sett. by Peter L. Bryan, Gdn.; heirs are Emeline, Nancy, Allen, Thomas, and Wm.
WB E 45, 22 Mar 1849. Sett. by same Gdn.; final payment to heir Emeline (Emily).
WB E 91, 23 Mar 1850. Sett. by Gdn., Nancy Mariah is an heir.
WB E 163, 264, 329, 371, 431, 521; WB F 72, dated from 23 Mar 1851 to 7 Mar 1857. Settlements and final sett. by Gdn.; William paid in full (1851); heir Nancy paid in full (1853); Thos. G. paid in full (1855); Allen paid in full (1857).

BRYANT (BRYAN, BRIANT), RICHARD A.
WB B 137, 3 Mar 1834. Invt., 10 Dec 1833, and Sale, 21 Dec 1833, by Moses Cunningham and Amon Bond, Adms.
WB C 100, 5 Jan 1839. Sett. by Adms.; receipt from Katharine Briant.
WB D 570, 11 Sep 1848. Sett. by Moses Cunningham, one of Adms.; paid Mrs. C. Bryant, widow.
CC 56, filed 21 Aug 1848. Richard A. Bryan died about Nov 1833 leaving heirs: George A., Robert, Washington, John, William, Lewis, Richard, Maria, Elizabeth (now dead without issue), Alexander (now dead without issue), and Mary Bryan (now wife of Henry Kinser).

BUCKNER, JAMES
CR8, 5 Jan 1863. Will proven by E. Brock and Geo. M. Moore, the two subscribing witnesses. James Buckner and E. Maynor who were app. Execs. in the Will, qualify and make bond. /No will is on record./

BUCKNER, JAMES
>WB G 75-84, 29 Jul 1865. Invt. by G.D. Buckner, Adm.; interesting list of a dentist's Accounts Receivable; charges for gold, tin, bone, and paste plugs, extractions, silver plates; also charge to Wm. Stephenson for 438 gals. whiskey, 18 Apr 1862; C.W. Rice charged 1851-1852 for cash expended in building Cave Spring Mill and in 1856 for cash expended in building steam mill at Riceville.
>WB G 102-104, 2 Sep 1865. Report of sale held 18 Aug 1865.
>CC 141, filed 6 Sep 1867 and CC 409, filed 10 Nov 1874. Dr. James Buckner died 17 Jun 1864 leaving widow who died 17 Sep 1864 and children: G.D. of Bedford Co., Tenn.; William A., who died after his father died leaving children Laura and William Buckner; James M. of Washington Co., Tenn., 1867, and of Texas, 1874; E.A. (Bettie) wife of J.A. Owens who married after her father died and is of Texas, 1874; D. Lafayette of Sullivan Co., Tenn., 1867, and of Bedford Co., 1874; Nan Sue Alice and Crayton Tennessee, minors of Meigs Co.

BUCKNER, NANCY E.
>CR7 193, 3 Jul 1858. J.R. Buckner and C.B. Newman app. Gdns. to J.A., H.C., T.J., Wm. L., and Burrow J. Buckner, minors.
>WB F 189, 30 Jul 1858 and 280, 3 Sep 1859. Sett. by Gdns.
>WB F 347, 3 Sep 1860. Sett. by Gdns.; receipt from John A. Buckner for about 1/6 of funds.
>WB F 415, 3 Sep 1861. Sett. by Gdns.
>CR7 471, 2 Oct 1860. Petition to sell land. James R. and John A. Buckner VS Isaac H. Lewis and wife Myriam, Henry C., Thos. J., Zachary T., Wm. L., and Burrow Buckner, the last five minors by their Gdn. ad litum C.B. Newman.
>CC 44, filed 26 Jan 1866. Robert Newman and James Buckner, Sr., were grandfathers of the minor heirs. In 1866, John A. Buckner, age 27, deposes that he is one of heirs and is bro. to James R. Buckner.

BULLINGTON, ROBERT
>CR6, 4 Apr 1853. Coroner paid for holding inquest over the body.

BUNCH, ANDERSON
>CR10 55, 7 Sep 1868. Alexander Wamack app. Gdn. of minor heirs.
>CR10 483, May 1873. W. Gettys app. Gdn. of Mary A. and Martin A. Bunch, minor heirs.

BUNCH, JOSEPH
>CR7 226, 6 Sep 1858. John Massey app. Adm.
>WB F 247, 3 Jan 1859. Invt. by Adm.

BUNCH, NANCY
>CR4 508, 7 Sep 1840. Martin Bunch app. Adm.
>WB C 334-336, 4 Jan 1841. Invt. of sale; buyers include Micajah, Lambert, Jancy, Martin, Joseph, and James Bunch.
>WB D 172, 3 Sep 1842. Sett. by Adm.; receipts from Charity, Micajah, Martin, Green, Daniel, and Lambert Bunch, not identified as heirs.
>WB D 209, 29 Jun 1844. Sett. by Adm.; receipts from Charity and Francis Fharris, Gincy Bunch, and Mary Farless.

BUNCH, PAUL
>CR4 485, 2 Mar 1840. Nancy and Micajah Bunch app. Adms.
>WB C 245-248, 6 Apr 1840. Invt. and Sale by Nancy and Lambert

Bunch, Adms.
WB C 248, 6 Mar 1840. Comm. L.L. Ball, Hardy S. Morris, and Benj.
Newton lay off year's support for widow Nancy and family.
WB D 171, 3 Sep 1842. Sett. by Lambert Bunch, surviving Adm.;
receipts from Martin, Joseph, and Lambert Bunch, no relationship
stated; "property purchased by the widow who has since died".
WB D 210, 29 Jun 1844. Sett. by Adm.; receipts from Lively Taylor,
Paul and Joseph Bunch, no relationship stated.

BURCH (BERCH, BIRCH), THOMAS
CR2 448 and 452, 7 Jun 1830. Thos. Cate app. Adm. John Miller,
Joab Hill, and John Neil app. Comm. to lay off year's support
for widow Sarah.
WB A 216, 8 Sep 1830. Sale by Adm.
CR4 59, 5 Mar 1832. Sarah Burch app. Gdn. of her own child, Ava
Elizabeth Burch, minor
CR4 137, 4 Mar 1833. Zachariah Rose app. Gdn. for Ava E. Burch.
Sarah Burch, former Gdn., released.
WB B 141, 2 Jun 1834. Add. invt.
WB B 142, Jun 1834. Account of sett. between adms. of estates of
Wm. Burch and Thomas Burch, dec'd, made 28 Nov 1833, with Wm.
Dodson, John Simmons, and Nathaniel Smith as Arbiters. "On the
subject of the account of Thomas Burch of the $104 against his
fathers Estate as that was proven by Elizabeth and Henry Burch
two of the four heirs of said Estate....thirty six dollars paid
to George W. Burch as he was at that time a minor....agreed by
all parties that Henry L. Burch receive out of estate of Wm.
Burch deceased....pay to Mrs. Aron Davis". Agreement signed by
Thomas Cate, George W. Burch, H.L. Burch, Zacheriah Rose, and
Aron Davis.
WB B 171-172, Sett. 2 Jun 1835 filed by Thomas Cate, Adm. with
John Miller and Elijah Hurst. Report includes proven account
and note against estate of Wm. Birch dec'd and undivided piece
of land in Claiborne Co.
WB C 86(1), 1 Dec 1838. Final sett. by Adm.
WB C 101, 5 Dec 1838; WB D 76, 5 Dec 1841 and 145, 5 Dec 1842.
Sett. by Zachariah Rose, Gdn. to Elizabeth Burch, minor heir.
WB D 266, 5 Dec 1844. Sett. by Gdn.; "rec'd a note for $100
which was willed to her by her grand Father Thomas Cate".
WB D 401, 5 Dec 1845. Sett. by Gdn.
WB D 500, 15 Jan 1848. Sett. by Gdn.; "Ward's receipt filed in
full, James H. Birch & A.E. Burch his wife"; signed Zachariah
Rose, Gdn. to A.E. Birch.

BURCH (BIRCH), WILLIAM
CR2 325, 2 Dec 1828 and 328, 3 Dec 1828. Thos. Burch app. Adm.;
Henry Birch, minor orphan over 14, chooses Elijah Hurst as Gdn.;
George Birch chooses John Neil as Gdn.
WB A 155, 1 Jan 1829 and 156-162, 3 Mar 1829. Invt. and Sale.
WB A 220, 1 Jul 1830. Comm. John Miller and Joab Hill report on
how far Thomas Burch, Adm. of Wm. Burch, dec'd, has administered
on said estate.
WB B 67, 5 Sep 1831. Final report by Gdn.; Comm. Jos. Minze and
Henry Matlock settle with John Neil, Gdn. of George Burch, who
has arrived at age of 21.
WB B 68, 21 Jun 1831. Comm. John Miller and Joab Hill settle with
Thomas Cate, Adm.; division of estate among four heirs: Elizabeth

Davis (formerly Elizabeth Burch, the widow), Henry and George Burch, and the heirs of Thomas Burch, dec'd.
WB C 85, 1 Dec 1838. Final sett. by Thomas Cate, Adm.; receipts from Henry, George, and Sarah Burch and A. Davis, heirs.
See also THOMAS BURCH.

BURGER, JOHN
CR2 134, 6 Mar 1826. Susanah Burger app. Adminx.

BURK, WILLIAM PINCKNEY
CR6, 3 Jan 1854. Margaret A. Burk app. Gdn. of Wm. H. Burk, minor.
CR6, 2 Jan 1855. Hugh P. Wilson app. Gdn. of William Henry Burk, minor.
WB E 527, 7 Apr 1856. Sale by H.P. Wilson, Adm.; buyers include Wm. and Ross Burk.

BURNS, ELIZA
CR7 189, 7 Jun 1858. C.W. Cobb app. Adm.

BURNS, JOHN
CR8, 5 Jan 1863. Court pays for coffin for pauper.

BURNS, WILLIAM
WB G 223, Will exec. 12 Oct 1864, Codicil 8 Feb 1869; of Town of Athens; to wife Rebecca, all estate. Exec: M.L. Phillips. Wit: F.M. Kilgore, Nat C. Jones, T. Richmond. Codicil: Loretta Ward wife of B.L. Ward may live upon premises where I now live during lifetime of wife provided she remain separate from her husband; $5 to sister Artemesa Burns; $5 to Wm. Warren; Theodore Richmond to act as Exec. with M.L. Phillips. Wit: Wm. H. Briant, Thos. Coldwell.
CR10 100, 5 Apr 1869. Will proven by Nat C. Jones, T. Richmond, and Thos. Caldwell who saw W.H. Briant sign as witness.
CR11 274, 11 Apr 1873. Sett. by M.L. Phillips, one of Execs.; stand charged with Invt. of Drugs and Drug Store in Invt. Bk. p. 169.

BUTTRAM, HIEL
WB G 217, Will, not dated; to Jacob M. Buttram one-half of land on which I live if he pay for it in four years; to daughters; $50 to educate grandson Jackson Wattenbarger, son of dau. Jane Wattenbarger; $20 to Nancy Ann Wattenbarger to make her equal with other heirs in way of horses which have been given them; $200 for building house of worship for Methodist Episcopal Church on or near ground where old church stands near my house. Execs: John G. and Moses K. Buttram. Wit: Joseph and Thomas Mortin.
CR9 351, 6 Jan 1868. Election to fill out unexpired term of Hiel Buttram, dec'd, Trustee of McMinn Co.
CR9 353 and 360, 6 Jan 1868. Will proven by Thomas Morton who swears that the other witness, Joseph Morton, is old and can not appear.
CR11 292, 15 Dec 1873. Sett. by Execs.; receipts of $256.21 each from Christopher Wattenbarger, Sarah Richardson, Jacob M. Buttram, Julia M. Foster, Alfred Carroll and wife, Chrisley Foster and wife, James G. Buttram, and Peter Wattenbarger; receipt from Jacob M. Buttram, Gdn.; Execs. have not filed receipts for their interest in estate.

BUTTRAM, JACOB
WB E 465, Will exec. 23 Sep 1855; $100 each to daus. Lavena Williams,

Temperance Hurt, Prudence Moorland, Margaret Keeton, Julia
Malissa Fields, Mary Wan, and to lawful heirs of Nancy Keith;
balance of estate to be divided between above named heirs and
sons Hile and Larkin Buttram and lawful heirs of Noah Buttram,
dec'd. Exec: son Hile. Wit: Moses Buttram, Uriah Shipley,
and Miles M.c.uistion.
CR6, 5 Nov 1855. Will proven by Moses Buttram and Miles H.
McCuistion.
WB E 470-473, 3 Dec 1855 and 3 Mar 1856. Invt. of sales and list
of notes.
WB F 165, 11 Mar 1858. Sett. by Exec.; paid daus. as given above;
paid $45 each to Heil Buttram and the heirs of Larkin Buttram,
dec'd; paid $3.50 each to Noah Buttram, P.A. Scrogans, and Julia
A. Scrogans.

BUTTRAM, JAMES
CR4 354, 5 Mar 1838. Joel Triplet app. Adm.
WB C 165, 1839. Sett. by Adm.; cash paid to Andrew Buttram.

BUTTRAM, LARKIN
WB F 157, 26 Feb 1858. Comm. John F. Shearman, James Wilson, and
Greenbery Cate lay off year's support for widow Rebecca and
family.
CR7 80, 7 Dec 1857. Comm. report that five of the children of
widow Rebecca are children of a former husband and have a separate estate and a regular Gdn. and that the other two are
children of Larkin Buttram by a former wife and do not ask an
allowance, therefore Comm. to lay off year's support for Rebecca
alone.
CC 277, filed 16 Dec 1857. Rebecca, widow of Robert W. Hamilton,
married Larkin Buttram in Meigs Co. about 1855. Larkin died
8 Sep 1857 leaving widow Rebecca and following children by a
former wife: Nancy, wife of Joseph Sliger of Oregon Territory;
Sarah, wife of Andrew Foster; Mary; Elizabeth; William; Jane
Sliger, dec'd, who had children Elizabeth Ann, Joseph, William,
Jacob, and Sarah.
WB F 178-182, 22 May 1858 and 296, 15 Oct 1859. Invt. of sale
(22 Oct 1857) and Sett. by Wm. Buttram, Adm.
WB F 300, no date. Report by Andrew Foster, Gdn. of Elizabeth C.
Buttram, a minor. Report by Christopher Sliger, Gdn. of his own
minor children, to wit, Elizabeth N., Jasper, William, Jacob,
and Sarah.
WB F 353, 12 Oct 1860; 365, 3 Dec 1860; 424, 3 Dec 1861; 441,
12 Oct 1861; WB G 40, 3 Dec 1864. Sett. by the above Gdns.
WB G 84, 2 Aug 1865. Final sett. by Andrew Foster, Gdn.; receipt
in full from Elizabeth C. Buttram by her husband Joseph Tuggle.

CAGE, MARY
CR6, 7 Jul 1851. A.B. Brown paid by Court for making coffin for
Mary Cage, a pauper, in Dec 1850.

CALDWELL, JOSEPH P.
WB E 438, Will exec. 23 Jun 1853; to wife Sarah; to dau. Mary C.
Couch; proceeds from sale of farm to be equally divided among
Wm. B., Solomon M., and Robert R. Caldwell, Elizabeth Gee, the
heirs of Martha Hayes, Mary C. Couch, Jane Thompson, and Lucinda
Critinden. Exec: Samuel W. Thompson. Wit: John M. and Jesse
A. Dodson.

CR6, 6 Aug 1855. Will proven.

WB E 457, 22 Sep 1855. Invt. and sale; sold land warrant issued for services of sd. Caldwell in War of 1812.

WB E 458, 1 Oct 1855. Add. invt.; includes coffin and burial for Mrs. Caldwell.

WB F 49, 28 Feb 1857. Final sett. by John M. Dodson and S.W. Thompson, Execs.; receipts from Wm. B., Lucinda, R.B., and S.M. Caldwell, Elizabeth Gee, Mary Couch, and S.W. Thompson for $31.15 each; receipts from J.C., Samuel P., and W.H. Hays, Talitha Aly, and Julian Stansbury for $6.50 each.

CALHOUN (CALHOON), WILLIAM

CR4 371, 2 Jul 1838. Thos. L. Hoyle app. Adm.

WB C 42-43, Sep 1838. Sale held 26 Jul 1838 by Adm.; buyers include James (one Tomahawk .12½), John, and Jordan Calhoun.

CR4 392, 1 Oct 1838. Sheriff ordered to bring Mary Calhoun, an orphan child of Wm. Calhoun, into Court to be disposed as the law directs.

WB E 259, 1 Aug 1840; WB D 279, 4 Mar 1845; 388, 4 Mar 1846; 510, 29 Jan 1848. Sett. by Adm.

WB E 153, 26 Jan 1851. Sett. by Adm.; paid J. Foster and wife, heirs.

WB E 405, 9 Jan 1855. Sett. by Adm.; receipt of James C. Calhoun for total amount.

CALLAHAN, JOHN NELSON

CR4 535, 4 Jan 1841. John Callahan of Kentucky, app. Adm.

WB C 347, 1 Mar 1841. Invt. of sale by Henry Goforth, agent for John Callahan, Adm.

CALLOWAY, GRACE S.

CR6, 7 Nov 1853. R.J.F. Calloway app. Adm.

WB E 347-349, 2 Jan 1854. Invt. of sale by Adm.; buyers include Mrs. Calloway.

WB E 493, 28 Feb 1856. Sett. by Adm.; receipt of N.T. Callaway "for division".

CALWELL

WB E, loose scrap of paper. "This the 21st of Dec. 1855 Wm. George Clk. Marion Calwell, Honey Creek PO, Mcdonal Co. Mo."

CAMERON, ARCHIBALD

WB B 87-88, Will exec. 24 Feb 1832, proven Sep 1832; to seven children: Polly, Betsy, William, Daniel Edmon, John, James, and Israel, when youngest son Israel comes of age. Execs: John Douglass and Thomas P. Wells. Wit: Reece Pickens, Joel Gregg. Signed by mark.

WB D 432-434, 1 Mar 1847. Invt. taken 20 Aug 1846 and Acct. of Sales held 3 Sep 1846, by Execs.

WB E 222, 18 Mar 1852. Final sett. by Execs.; equal payments to heirs B.S. Culpeper, E.D., James, Wm. O., John, and Israel S. Cameron, and John W. Spearman for his wife.

CAMP, JOHN

Cr5 243, 1 Sep 1845. John Hambright app. Adm.

WB D 339-343, 3 Nov 1845. Invt. and Sale by Adm.

WB D 344, 25 Sep 1845. Comm. A.P. McClatchey, Wm. McKamy, and Wm. T. McCallie set apart year's support for widow.

WB D 499, 16 Sep 1847 and 513, 18 Jan 1848. Sett. by Adm.

WB E 566, 11 Aug 1856. Final sett. by Adm.; vouchers for various amounts to heirs of Mary Camp (paid 1848); to Gdn. of minor heirs (paid 1848); vouchers for $20.71 each to Sterling P. Camp, Jas. Knox, and Wm. P. Caldwell; voucher for $82.84 to Mary A. Camp.

CC 236, filed 18 Apr 1870. John Camp died about 1840 leaving as his only heirs Sterling P. Camp, now of Ill.; T.J. Camp; J.B. Camp; Mary /sic7 A. wife of James Knox; C.T. wife of Dr. W.P. Caldwell; M.J. wife of George P. Billingsly, last five of Bradley Co., Tenn.

CC 257, filed 5 Sep 1870. John Camp, Sr., died leaving widow Mary who is still living. His children are Nancy A. wife of James M. Knox; Elizabeth T. wife of Wm. P. Caldwell; Mary J. wife of George Billingsly; Thomas J.; and John B. Camp, all of Bradley Co.; Sterling Camp, now dec'd, leaving widow Semantha H. and minor children: Thomas B., John R., Wm. S., Benj. F., and Anna K., all of McDonough Co., Ill.

CAMP, STERLING

WB E 157-158, Will exec. 28 Sep 1848, proven 2 Jun 1851; to wife; to dau. Mary Bates and her heirs, $700 all of which I have paid; to dau. Sarah McKnight, $700 all of which I have paid; to dau. Margaret Porter, $700 none of which is paid; to son John, $700 which I paid him in his lifetime; to son William, $700 all of which I have paid him in cash; to son Thomas, $700 paid in land; to dau. Keziah Hambright and her heirs, $700 all of which I have paid; to dau. Margaret Porter, part of farm after wife's death. Execs: son Thomas and grandson Sterling Parkison Camp, either one or jointly. Wit: Wm. M. Scarbrough, Wm. S. McKnight.

WB E 198, 2 Feb 1852 and 313, 11 Mar 1853. Invt. and sale and add. invt. by John Hambright, Adm. with Will annexed.

WB E 344, 7 Nov 1853. Sett. by Adm.; receipt of Anna Camp, widow.

WB E 566, 11 Aug 1856. Final sett. by same Adm.; vouchers of $467.88 each to Kiziah Hambright, Sarah McKnight, Margaret Porter, William Camp, Thomas Camp, Mary Bates, and the heirs of John Camp, dec'd.

CC 149, filed 7 Feb 1852. Sterling Camp's children as named in Will. Keziah is wife of John Hambright. Margaret is wife of Wm. C. Porter. Thomas is of Ill. William is of Bradley Co. Son John Camp's children are Nancy A. wife of James Knox, Sterling Parkinson Camp of Ill., and Elizabeth T., Mary Jane, Thomas J., and John D. Camp, all minors.

CAMPBELL

CR16 133, Dec 1856. Exparte Petition for partition of slaves - Caroline R., Margaret L., and Henrietta M. Campbell.

CC 16, filed 17 Feb 1857. Exparte petition, T. Nixon Van Dyke, Gdn. of Henrietta M. Campbell. Henrietta is granddau. of Dr. Wm. H. Deaderick with whom she is living. Mrs. Caroline R. Sample is sister to Henrietta and when she married she moved to Charleston, S. C.

CAMPBELL

CR6, 2 Feb 1852. Edward Robeson app. Gdn. to Sarah M. Campbell, minor.

CAMPBELL, GALAWAY

CR7 356, 7 Nov 1859. Isham Dennis app. Adm.

WB F 301, 3 Dec 1859 and 414, 5 Aug 1861. Invt. and sett. by Adm.; only asset is a note on Mathew Campbell.

CAMPBELL, JOHN
WB A 17-18, no date. No signatures; Invt.

CAMPBELL, JOHN
CR4 454, 2 Sep 1839. Chas. Delday app. Gdn. to Daniel and James Campbell and is chosen Gdn. by John and Katharine Campbell, minor heirs.

CAMPBELL, MATHEW
CR6, 3 Jul 1854. Jury of inquest finds that on 2 May 1854 Gallaway Campbell did murder Mathew Campbell with a chisel.
CR12 272, 18 Aug 1854. The State VS Gallaway Campbell. Grand Jury Indictment; Mathew Campbell stabbed on 2 May 1854 and died 3 May 1854.

CAMPBELL, THOMAS J.
WB E 140, Will exec. 27 Feb 1838; "of Athens"; all estate to wife Sally L., "believing that she will do justice so far as in her lies towards the several children she has borne me". Exec: wife. No witnesses.
WB E 142, 12 Nov 1851. Comm. R. C. Jackson, James S. Bridges, and Jas. B. Taylor, app. Aug Term 1850, lay off year's support for widow.
WB E 155-157, 7 Apr 1851. Invt. by Thos. J. Campbell, Jr., Adm. with Will annexed.
CC 179, filed before 23 Feb 1853 (original bill not dated). Thomas J. Campbell died after 23 Nov 1847 leaving widow Sally, who has since died, and children: Louisa P. wife of Wm. W. Anderson; Richard B.; Mary L. wife of D.C. McMillan, all of Hamilton Co.; Thomas J., Jr., of McMinn Co.; Clinton of La.; and granddau. Sarah Waterhouse of Ga., a minor.

CAN____, WILLIAM
CR2 494, 7 Dec 1830. Will partly proven by Wm. Stamper and held for further probate.

CANSLER
WB E 113, 5 Oct 1850. Sett. by Jefferson C. Cansler, Gdn. to his idiot bro. Wm. N. Cansler; received cash from S.C. belonging equally to him and to his sd. bro.

CANSLER (CANCILOR, CANSELER), NATHANIEL H.
WB A 217-220, 8 May 1830. Invt. and Sale, by Wm. Cancilor, Adm.; buyers include Polly, John, and Wm. Cancilor.
CR2 458, 8 Jun 1830. Alexander Stinson, Henry Bradford, and Saml. McConnell app. Comm. to lay off year's support for widow.
CR2 468, 6 Sep 1830. Henry Bradford reports that the other two app. Comm. failed to appear and that he with Wm. Lea and Asberry M. Coffey proceeded to lay off year's support for widow Polly.
CR4 101, 3 Sep 1832. Edward Elms app. Gdn. for Patsy and Henderson Cansler, minor orphans.
WB B 130, 6 Mar. 1833. Comm. Saml. McConnell, John Hill, and Wm. Lee settle with Adm.
WB C 223, 26 Feb 1840. Report by Edward Elms, Gdn. to Nathaniel Cansler, minor heir, for years 1834-1840.
WB D 42, 26 Feb 1841. Sett. by same Gdn.

CANSLER (CANSELER), WILLIAM, SR.
  WB C 79-80, 30 Nov 1838. Sett. by Wm. and John Cansler, Adms.
  WB C 202, 30 Nov 1839; WB D 34, 30 Nov 1840; 76, 30 Nov 1841; 146,
    30 Nov 1842; Sett. by John Cansler, Adm.
  WB D 225, 23 Sep 1844. Sett. by John and Wm. Canserler, Jr., Adms.;
    Vouchers of John W. and Wm. N. Canseler, debtors to Wm. Canseler
    for boarding; vouchers of Thos. W. and Carroll Canseler, debtors
    to Wm. Canseler for cash paid
  CC 57, filed 21 Aug 1848. Wm. Cansler died May 1835 leaving heirs:
    Jefferson C., John M., Thomas H., and Wm. Nelson Cansler.

CANTRELL (CANTERELL), DAVID
  CR7 338, 5 Sep 1859. Reynolds Cantrell app. Adm.
  CR7 350, 3 Oct 1859. Petition to sell lands. Reynolds, Rebecca W.,
    and Malcomb Cantrell, S.P. Hale and wife Elmina VS C.B. Newman
    and wife Clementine, and Alice E., Martha A., Margaret M., and
    Mary M. Cantrell, and Miranda A., Felix M., and Sarah A. Hoyle,
    minors by Gdn. ad litum C.R. Hoyl. There are eight living heirs
    and dau. Adeline Hoyle left three children who are named in peti-
    tion, making nine shares in all; petitioner Rebecca W. is entitled
    to dower.
  WB F 287-290, 5 Oct 1859. Invt. by Adm.
  WB G 154, 5 Feb 1866. Report by Rebecca W. Cantrell, Gdn. of minor
    heirs; nothing has ever come into her hands.
  CR10 61, 5 Oct 1868. Power of Atty. from Reynolds Cantrell of
    Bartow Co., Ga., to Stephen P. Hale of Madisonville, Monroe Co.,
    Tenn., to act as Adm.

CANTRELL, GABRIEL
  WB E 70, 3 Dec 1849. Comm. D.A. Cobbs, Saml. Firestone, and Joseph
    Cobbs set apart year's support for widow.
  WB E 76, 7 Jan 1850. Invt. and Acct. of Sale by L.E. Cantrell and
    J.C. Carlock, Adms.
  WB E 220, 23 Mar 1852. Sett.
  CC 114, filed 18 Feb 1867. Gabriel Cantrell died 1849 leaving
    widow Nancy, now of Mo., and children: L.E., who died in Oct
    1860; Wm. J.; Thomas H.; James R.; Robert F.; Charles M.; Felix
    G.; Sarah J.; Hezekiah C.; Benj. D.; Joseph P. (last three
    minors over 14); and Mary E., wife of John D. Caskey. The last
    six are of Mo. Son L.E. Cantrell died leaving widow Sarah Ann
    and children: Robert P., John D., Mary T., Thomas J., and Emmet
    Cantrell, all minors under 14.

CANTRELL (CANTERELL), L.E.
  WB F 351-352, Will exec. 17 Oct 1860, proven Nov 1860; to wife
    Sarah Ann; "I will & desire that my Executors" bring suit for
    partition of lands of father Gabriel Cantrell, dec'd; "I having
    bought my Mother Nancy Cantrell's interest in the same and the
    interest of the following named brothers of mine heirs of Gabriel
    Cantrell To wit William J., Thomas H., James R., Robert L., and
    M.A. Cantrell, the following named brothers and sisters of mine
    and heirs of Gabriel Cantrell deceased are minors from which I
    have not bought their interest, to wit Felix G., Mary E., Sarah
    J., Hezekiah C., Benjamin D., and Joseph P. Cantrell"; about
    three acres around Father's grave to be left for family burying
    ground; "until my children arrive at the age of majority"; wife's
    uncle Joseph Lattimore. Execs: wife and esteemed friend and
    uncle Joseph Lattimore. Wit: J.B. Cobb, C.R. Hoyl, J.R. Ware.

WB F 366. Acct. of sale.
CR7 484, 5 Nov 1860. Wm. Burk app. to serve as Sheriff, because of death of L.E. Cantrell, former Sheriff.

CARAGIN, MARY
CR8, 6 Jan 1862. Court pays for coffin for pauper.

CARDEN, LARKIN
CR17-56, 13 Jan 1868. Jorden, J., and L. Carden, Execs. VS J.H. Knight and Thos. Elliott.

CARDWELL, HAZY
WB G 70-74, 5 Aug 1865. Invt. and Acct. of sales held 23 Dec 1864 by Timothy Sullins, Adm.
WB G 125, 20 Oct 1865. Report by Lazarus Dodson, Gdn. to minor children of Hazy Cardwell who was former Gdn. and who received additional amounts Jan 1860 and Sep 1861.
WB G 197, 28 Sep 1866. Sett. by same Adm.

CARLOCK, ASA L.
CR9 158, 7 May 1866. L.H. Carlock app. Gdn. to James M., A.H., John L., A.J., and S.R. Carlock, minor heirs.

CARLOCK, ISAAC N.
CR9 283, 1 Jul 1867. Comm. app. to lay off year's support for widow and family for year 1866. Nancy M. Carlock app. Adminx.
CR10 91, 1 Feb 1869. John L. Smith app. Gdn. of minor heirs.

CARNEY, RHODA
CR5 289, 4 May 1846. Sheriff ordered to bring in George W. Carney, son, to be dealt with as the Court may order.
CR5 293, 6 Jul 1846. Moses A. Cass paid for furnishing provisions and funeral expenses for the widow Carney and daughter.

CARRUTH (CAROUTH), JAMES
WB A 142-143, Will exec. 21 Feb 1828; to aged father John Carruth; to only bro. Walter Carruth; to five sisters, Peggy, Ann, and Tilly Carruth, Sarah Egnew, and Cinthy Nicholson; to Atliff Griffen, minor son of Jonas Griffen. Exec: bro. Walter. Wit: Saml. McConnell, Nathl. H. Cansler.
CR2 293, 3 Jun 1828. Will proven.

CARSON, WILLIAM
CR2 171, 4 Sep 1826. Nancy Carson app. Adminx.
CR4 259 and 262, 6 Jun 1836. Application being made for guardian to Eliza McCartny Addison Commadore Perry minor heirs of William Carson William Alexander Carson who is of age to choose for himself the Court appointed Nancy Carson as guardian to Eliza McCartny Addison Commadore Perry who entered into bond and security approved by the Court. /Note: this is copied as written except that inserted above the first line at "Eliza" there is written: "Katharine Jane Isabella Miller". No punctuation or spaces in entry./
CR4 262, 6 Jun 1836. Power of Atty. from Nancy and Wm. A. Carson to Joseph Newman acknowledged by makers and certified to Washington Co., Ill.

CARTER, AMOS
CR4 359, 5 Mar 1838. Invt. returned by Robert Carter and James Cold, Adms.

CARTER, CHARLES, SR.
   WB D 23-24, Will exec. 17 Jul 1841; to children Charles, Samuel,
   Josiah, and William Carter, Nancy McSpadden, and Susannah wife
   of Daniel Lowry. Execs: Abraham Barb, Daniel Lowry. Wit:
   John Grubb, Wm. Terry, and Andrew Pangle. Signed by mark.
   CR4 556, 2 Aug 1841. Will proven.
   WB D 26-30, 6 Sep 1841; 47-48, 1 Nov 1841; 164-166, 4 Dec 1843.
   Invt. of sales; Add. Invt.; Invt. of slaves; and Sett. by Execs.
   WB D 231, 1 Nov 1844; 384, 7 Sep 1846. Sett. and Add. Invt. by
   Daniel Lowry, one of Execs.

CARTER, G. J.
   CR8, Nov 1861. Henderson Carter app. Adm.

CARTER, HENDERSON
   CR14 479, 10 Aug 1868. Henderson Carter VS Jackson Grubb. The
   death of plaintiff is suggested and admitted. S.M. Carter and
   H.M. Simpson have been app. Adms.

CARTER, JESSE
   WB E 82-84, 25 Jan 1850. Acct. of sale and Invt. by James Sewell,
   Adm.; personal property in Monroe Co.
   WB E 88, 11 Jan 1850. Comm. John Neill, Philip Fry, and D.F.
   Jameson set apart year's provisions for widow Susan and family.
   WB E 197, 10 Mar 1852. Sett. by same Adm.; paid equal amounts to
   heirs Peter, James, Henderson, John, and Lewis M. Carter, Margaret
   Trim, and Levi Pressley.

CARTER, LEROY C.
   CR4 329, 4 Sep 1837. James Cole and Robert Carter app. Adms.
   WB B 263, Sep 1837; 265-268, no date; 302, Mar 1838. Invt., Sale,
   Add. Invt. by Adms.; buyers include William, Robert, and Polly
   Carter.
   WB C 166, 7 Mar 1839. Comm. James T. Reid, Wm. W. Anderson, and
   John McGaughey app. by Court to prorate assets among the debtors.
   WB C 226, 27 Feb 1840. Sett. by Robert Carter, one of Adms.

CARTER, RANDOLPH
   CR4 323, 3 Jul 1837. Petition. Randolph Carter lately died in-
   testate without issue or widow; Amos Carter is a brother and
   Wm. Mouldin is the husband of one of the sisters.
   WB B 277-282, Jan 1838; 283-286, Feb 1838; C 149, 19 Jul 1839.
   Invt., Add. Invt., and Sett. by Amos Carter and Wm. Moulden,
   Adms.
   WB D 77-80, 13 Apr 1842. Sett. by Adms.; receipts from heirs Wm.
   Mouldin and G.J. Washam; receipts from the following who appear
   to be heirs: Adam and Franky Shipe, James M. Carter Gdn. for
   Jackson Carter, Peter, Amos, Martin B., H.H., Winston, James M.,
   W.H., J.A., and Amos Carter, J.W. and J.H. Bounds, and Amos
   Carter, Gdn.   "there is $1053.00 in hands of administrator be-
   longing to James Chambers husband of Jane Carter who is absent
   the administrator knows not where".
   WB D 348, 7 Jan 1846. Sett. by Wm. Molden, one of Adms.; receipts
   from Amos, Wm. H., James M., and Martin B. Carter, Amos Carter
   Gdn. of J.S. and G.W. Chandler with no relationship stated; Adm.
   still holds share of James Chambers.

CARTER, SUSANNAH
   CR9 72, 4 Sep 1865. H.M. Simpson app. Adm.

WB G 136, 23 Nov 1865. Sale by Adm.; buyers include Henderson and James Carter.

CARTRIGHT, JOHN
CR4 509, 7 Sep 1840. Catharine Cartright, John Harrel, and Martin M. Hix app. Adms.
WB C 275, 19 Sep 1840; 298, 7 Dec 1840. Invt. of sale and Add. invt. of sale by Adms.; buyers include Catharine and Lemuel Cartright; accts. include one for David Cartright's Estate.
WB D 127, 4 Mar 1843. Sett. by Martin M. Hix and John Harrel, Adms.
CR4 523, 5 Oct 1840. Abraham Barb, John W. Barnett, and Wm. Lee lay off year's support for widow Catharine

CASADA, REUBEN
CR5 329, 4 Jan 1847. Benj. Wells app. Adm.
WB D 461, 22 May 1847. Invt. by Adm.; it appears from report that Manuel Parkison was former Adm.
WB E 38, 31 Mar 1849; 72, no date; and 178, 12 Apr 1851. Sett. by Adm.

CASADA, WESLEY
CR4 540, 5 Apr 1841. John Gaston app. Gdn. to John W.P. Cassada, minor orphan and heir.
WB D 201, 3 Jun 1844. Report by Gdn.; "there has been an administrator appointed in the State of Georgia".

CASSADA, DAVID
CR5 512, 5 Feb 1849. Benj. Wells app. Adm.
WB E 37, no date. Invt. by Adm.; includes note on Reuben Cassada.

CASTEEL
CR4 292, 5 Dec 1836. Orphan boy named William Casteel aged 13 bound to John McDonnell.

CASTEEL, ALEXANDER
CC 236, filed 18 Apr 1870. Alexander Casteel of McMinn Co. died about 1867 leaving children Joseph, Madison, Sarah wife of Lewis Erwin, Amanda M. wife of James G. Ricks, Paralee R. wife of Christopher C. Ricks, and Elizabeth wife of James Brown of Ill.

CASTEEL, EDMOND
CR2 505, 7 Mar 1831. Elizabeth and Barney Casteel app. Adms.
CR2 538, 6 Jun 1831. A paper purporting to be a copy of the last Will was partly proven by Hesekiah Randolph who says that it is a copy of the original Will in substance and that original Will was lost out of his possession and that he had his doubts whether said Casteel was at time of making and signing Will of sound mind, though he had heard him frequently say previous to that time that it was the way he intended to dispose of his property; continued for further probate. Petition of Michael Lower, Security for Barney and Betsey Casteel, Adms., that said Adms. are making waste with said estate and asks Court to demand surrender of said estate.
CR4 10, 8 Jun 1831. Ordered that Saml. Yates and Michael Lower take into their possession all of the estate and take care of it until further orders.
CR4 26, 6 Sep 1831. Ordered that a paper purporting to be the copy of Will of Edmond Casteel, dec'd, be given back to the widow and that all proceedings quashed as the parties have all agreed and come to a compromise.

CC 228, filed 25 May 1855. L.M. Stansbury and wife Melissa and
James Casteel VS Pearson Elliott et al. Complainants charge that
Edmond Casteel made will attested by Hezekiah Randolph and Wm.
Fairbanks, but said will was fradulently removed and never probated. Edmund Casteel died 1829-1834 leaving widow Elizabeth as
his last wife, and children: Abraham, Willis, Nancy, Barney of
Union Co., Ga., Morris of Ala., Mary wife of John Jackson of Ky.
(above seem to be by former wife), Melissa Ann wife of L.M. Stansbury of Roane Co., and James Casteel of Anderson Co. (these two
by Elizabeth). Melissa Ann was about one year old when father
died. /There is much family information in the depositions in
this case./

CATE, CHARLES
  WB A 59-61, Will exec. 18 Jul 1824; to wife Lucy; to James, Thomas
  Jefferson, Amos, and William after they come of age; to Rachel,
  Magdalena, Elijah, and Sally Cate, Martha Liles, Lucy Vandyke.
  Execs: wife Lucy and son Elijah. Wit: Joab Hill, Elijah Hurst,
  Wm. Terry.
  CR2 22, 6 Sep 1824 and 33, 6 Dec 1824. Will proven.
  WB C 98, 15 Dec 1838. Sett. by Elijah Cate, one of Execs., for
  years since 1824.

CATE, JEMIMA
  CR10 89, 1 Feb 1869. Sett. by P.B. Cate, Gdn. of his own minor
  heirs.
  CC 393, filed 18 Feb 1874. Lyle VS Shelton. Jemima Cate died
  leaving husband Peter B. Cate, who died soon after Jan 1872, and
  children: John H., W.T., R.F., S.B., and Joseph H. Cate, all
  minors. Peter B. Cate was app. Gdn. in Meigs Co. before Feb
  1868 and in McMinn Co. in June 1865.

CATE, SIMEON
  CR4 529, 4 Jan 1841. John Miller, John McGaughy, and John Crawford
  app. Comm. to lay off year's support for widow Polly.
  CR5 25, 3 Jan 1842. John Neil app. Gdn. to John, Eliza, Osker, and
  Parshall Cate, minor orphans.
  WB D 87, 5 Jul 1842. Sett. by Gdn.; "has nothing in his hands nor
  never has had of said Estate".

CATE, WILLIAM
  CR4 458, 7 Oct 1839. Chas. Cate and Chas. W. McDonald app. Adms.
  WB C 177, 1 Nov 1839. Comm. Saml. Kelly, Oswell Phillips, and
  Pleasant Barn set apart year's support for widow Elizabeth and
  family.
  WB C 196-200, Jan 1840. Invt. and Sale; buyers include Simeon,
  George, and John E. Cate, and the widow.
  WB D 95, 15 Jun 1842 and 213, 20 Jul 1844. Sett. by Chas. W.
  McDonald, one of Adms.
  CR12 16, 17 Apr 1852. Petition to sell land and petition for
  Dower: Elizabeth Cate, widow; Joseph Zigler and wife Mary;
  Ann; Alfred; John; Peter; Thomas J. Cate; and Wm., Charles, and
  Jacob Cate by their Gdn. Thos. J. Cate.

CAVES, GEORGE
  CR6, Jul 1855. Coffin furnished for dec'd, a pauper.

CHAMBERS, EDMUND
  CR4 295, 2 Jan 1837. Sheriff ordered to bring into Court the
  minor orphans.

CHAPMAN (CHAPMON), EDMUND (EDMOND) W.
  CR4 259, 6 Jun 1836. Lemuel Chapman app. Gdn. to Jane and Syntha
    Chapman, minor heirs, and is chosen Gdn. by Coleman, John and
    Ma_____ who are of age to choose for themselves.
  WB B 257, Jul 1837. Report by Gdn.; "paid five of said heirs";
    "expences going to South Carolina".
  WB C 26, 4 Jun 1838. Sett. by Gdn. of Coleman, John, Jane, and
    Cyntha Chapman, minor heirs; has paid one of heirs.
  WB C 40, 6 Aug 1838. Sett. by same Gdn.; receipts from heirs
    Wilson Chapman, Nancy Chapman, and Elzy Triplet by his wife, heir.
  WB C 162, 6 Aug 1839 and 301, 6 Aug 1840. Reports by same Gdn.
  CR5 176, 1 Jul 1844. Lemuel Chapman, Gdn. to Wiley, John, Ann,
    Madison, Syntha, and Jane Chapman, makes bond.
  WB D 307, 20 Aug 1845. Report by Gdn.; receipts in full "dated
    some three years before the last settlement" and all for equal
    amounts from Elizabeth Jane, Wiley, Cyntha, Madison, and John H.
    Chapman, and James Farmer.

CHAPMAN, LEMUEL
  CR5 468, 4 Sep 1848. Wilson Chapman app. Adm.
  WB D 569, 20 Sep 1848. Comm. Charles T. Thornton, Wm. Lee, and
    George Reynolds set apart year's support for widow Martha.
  WB D 594-596, 30 Oct 1848. Invt. and Sales by Adm.; in an "exhibit
    of business of estate in Georgia" are the following entries:
    bacon deposited with Elisha Perryman of Putnam Co., Ga.; note on
    Francis M. Allen of Social Circle, Walton Co., Ga.; note on
    Richard B. Kearney of same; bacon deposited with Wm. Wiggins of
    Polk Co., Tenn.
  WB E 145-147, 7 Feb 1851. Sett. by Adm.; paid one note Union Univ.;
    paid expenses for trip to procure title to lands and collect
    money in Ga.
  CC 103, filed 31 Jul 1850. Lemuel Chapman died 1848 leaving widow
    Martha and minor children Lemuel H., Mary Anne, Sarah Jane,
    Josephine, and John W.

CHARLES
  CR9 452, 6 Jul 1868. James M. Charles app. Gdn. of Oliver D.,
    John E., and James D. Charles, minors.
  CR10 102, 5 Apr 1869. James M. Charles resigns as Gdn. of his own
    minor children as nothing has come into his hands; John M. Dodson
    app. Gdn.

CHRISTIAN, LEWIS
  CR5 545, 6 Aug 1849. Wm. F. Keith app. Adm.

CHURCH, SETH
  CR6, 6 Dec 1852. Richard C. Jackson, Wm. H. Ballew, and Wm. P.H.
    McDermott app. Comm. to lay off year's support for widow.

CLEAVELAND, R.R.
  CR14 545, 14 Dec 1868. F.K. Berry Adm. and S.G. Cleaveland Adminx.
    VS Wiley Franks - Debt.

CLINE, D. ANTHONY
  CR9 160, 4 Jun 1866. Wm. B. Armstrong app. Gdn. of Nancy, David
    B., and Caroline Cline, minor children under 14.
  CR10 111, May 1869. Sett. by same Gdn.

COATS, JAMES T.
  CR2 242, 8 Sep 1827. William Hogan app. Adm.

COATS, WILLIAM
  CR7 360, 5 Dec 1859. Wm. N. Coats app. Adm.
  WB F 336, 19 Dec 1859. Comm. James Gregory, Sterling Lewis, and
    Tyry Lawson lay off year's support for widow and family
  WB F 374, 6 Feb 1860. Invt. and sale by Adm.; buyers include
    Louisa and J.J. Coats.
  CR8, 5 Jan 1863. Mrs. Eliza A. Coats app. Adm. John Hart and
    James Gregory with County Surveyor app. to allot dower out of
    the lands to widow Eliza A.
  CR8, 2 Feb 1863. Eliza A. Coats app. Gdn. of her own minor children.
  CR9 86, 3 Oct 1865. Eliza A. Coats resigns as Gdn.
  CC 217, filed 6 Sep 1869. Butler VS Price. Louisa Coats, widow,
    formerly Louisa Butler, is one of complainants.
  CC 677, filed 17 Mar 1880. Goodman VS Thomas. Wm. Coats died
    1860 /sic/ leaving widow Louiza A. and children: W.N., who died
    1863 unmarried; Mary S. Marlow; Julia Price; Jasper J., whose
    wife is Elizabeth; Sarah Clark; Rachel, wife of John Goodman of
    Obion Co., Tenn.; Louiza T. (aged about 33), wife of T.J. Blank-
    enship of Independence Co., Ark.; Margaret (about 21), wife of
    J.H. Irwin of Sharp Co., Ark.; Henry, who died 1864, married but
    without issue and his wife has long since again remarried.

COBB
  CR9 284, 1 Jul 1867. J.B. Cobb app. Gdn. of his own minor heirs,
    John A., Joseph L., James C., and James B. Cobb.

COBB, B.P.
  CR13 180, 3 Nov 1862. The State VS B.P. Cobb - Murder. The Atty.
    Gen. suggests death of defendant and it is admitted.

COBB, D.J.
  CR7 79, 7 Dec 1857. Joseph R. Wear app. Adm.
  WB F 160, 1 Mar 1858. Sale by Adm.

COBB (COBBS), JOHN
  WB B 220-221, Will exec. 10 Sep 1836, proven Jan 1837; to wife Mary;
    to son John B. or Berry, under age; to the four girls, Julett,
    Angelina, Nancy, and Harriett. (These five are called the chil-
    dren). Wife agrees. Execs: father Joseph Cobbs, David A. Cobbs,
    and Jessey Mayfield. Wit: James Hawkins, Hiram Yancey, Jonathan
    Whitten. Signed John Cobbs, Mary Cobbs.
  CR4 284, 3 Oct 1836. On this day was presented a paper writing pur-
    porting to be the last will and testament of John Cobb, deceased,
    for probate, and thereupon came Juliet, Angelina, Nancy, and
    Hariett Cobb by their next friend David A. Cobb and contested
    the validity of the same so offered for probate....certified to
    Circuit Court.
  CR4 295, 2 Jan 1837. Jury finds that Will is legal and certifies
    it to County Court for recording. Court appoints Mary Cobb as
    Gdn. to John Berry, Juliet Caroline Mary M. Katharine Nancy Jane
    Adaline Harriet R. Imandra Edaline /sic/, minor heirs.
  WB B 225-230, Feb 1837 and C 61, 3 Nov 1838. Invt.; property dis-
    bursed to widow Mary; Invt. of sale; and Sett. by Robt. W.
    McClary, Adm.
  WB C 159, 25 Apr 1839. Report by Mary Cobbs, Gdn. to John,
    Angelina C., Juliet C., Nancy, and Harriet Cobbs.
  WB C 231, 3 Nov 1839 and D 3, 14 Apr 1841. Sett. by Adm.; Spencer
    and Mary Beavers, Gdns. to minor heirs.

WB D 71, 18 May 1842. Sett. by Adm.; teste: J.P. McClary.

COBB (COBBS), JOSEPH, SR.
WB C 265-267, Will exec. 7 Jan 1840; Joseph Cobb, Farmer; to wife
Mary; to son David A. Cobbs; to grandson Joseph Cobbs Junior, son
of David A. Cobbs; to son Joseph Cobbs; to grandson David Cobbs,
son of Joseph Cobbs; to dau. Mary, wife of John Cox; to Rizzy,
Wm., and Joseph, children of dau. Mary; to dau. Rizzy, wife of
Saml. Firestone; to all my children, namely: David A., John,
and Joseph Cobbs, Rizzy Firestone, and Mary Cox; to grandchildren
Nancy, Harriet, John B., Juliet, and Angeline, children of son
John. Execs: sons David A. and Joseph. Wit: Henry Bradford
and Evan Jones. Signed Joseph Cobb.
CR4 507 and 510, 3 Aug 1840 and 7 Sep 1840. Will proven by Henry
Bradford. Subpoena for witness Evan Jones returned endorsed not
to be found in this county. Thomas W. Marston and Wm. Mulky
swear that signature is genuine.
CC 264, filed 12 Jan 1857. Joseph Cobb left widow Mary who died
8 Nov 1856; dau. Rizzy is named Arispa; dau. Mary died after her
father and before her mother; son John is dead; son Joseph's
children are David (now dead, who was of full age and left bros.
and sisters of full and half blood), Martha, Mary, and another
daughter. Dau. Mary Cox, dec'd, left children, viz: Joseph
Cox died Jan 1852, a minor; Arispa Cox, died after bro. Joseph,
wife of John E. Hickox, who left son Horace Hickox, a minor; Wm.
Cox who reaches full age soon after Bill is filed; and Susan Cox,
wife of Philmer W. Green of Bradley Co. Nancy and Harriet Cobb,
daus. of son John, dec'd, are both now dead leaving heirs.

COBB, MARY
See JOSEPH COBB, SR.

COBBS
CR7 119, 1 Mar 1858. Joseph Cobbs app. Gdn. to Nancy D., Margaret
T., Susan C., Josephine, and C.E. Cobbs, his own minor children.

COCHRAN, DESON LOT ALLEN
CR17 58, 15 Feb 1868. Allen Cochran, Adm. VS A.A. and J.M. Cass.

COCHRAN, WILLIAM ALLEN
CR9 71, 4 Sep 1865. Uriel Johnston app. Adm.
WB G 109, 30 Sep 1865. Invt. and Sale by Adm.; notes on J.A. and
Mary A. Cochran.
WB G 119, no date. Comm. J.M. Jackson, Nathan Kelley, and James
Neill set apart year's provisions for widow and family.
CR9 77, 2 Oct 1865. Mary A. Cochran app. Gdn. for her own minor
children.

COFER, JAMES
CR9 171, 6 Aug 1866. Elizia Cofer app. Adminx.

COFFEE, POLLY
WB D 107, Will exec. 20 Jul 1842; "Dear brother & Sister"; sister
Jane to raise daughter; father Benjamin Roberts; to dau. Eliza-
beth. Wit: Jefferson and Jane Dixon, Robert Mansell, and Wm.
S. Roberts. Signed by mark.
CR5 66, 5 Sep 1842. Will proven.
WB D 119, 6 Feb 1843. Invt. and Sale by Benj. Roberts, Exec.;
buyers include James Coffey, Benjamin, Henry M., Thomas M., and
Thomas C. Roberts.

WB D 222, 24 Aug 1844. Sett. by Exec.; "said Executor has the receipt of J.L. Dickerson, Guardian which the Executor says is in full".

COFFMAN, G.P.F.
 CR6, 5 Nov 1855. Elizabeth Coffman app. Adminx.
 WB E 469, 28 Nov 1855. Comm. John Whitesides, Wm. R. Elder, and H. McNabb lay off year's support to widow Elizabeth and family.
 WB E 482, 14 Jan 1856. Invt. of sale; buyers include Margaret and Green Coffman; six notes on Albert Lyle of Chattanooga executed for a house in that town; note on Albert Coffman.
 CC 266, filed 23 Jan 1857. G.P.F. Coffman died in 1855 leaving widow Elizabeth, who is the dau. of David Wear, and minor children: Margaret N., Isaac G., Martha J., Mary E., Wm. B., Sarah R.E.

COLEY, SALLY
 WB A 71-73, Will exec. 9 Mar 1807, probated Goochland Co., Va., on 19 Sep 1808, and copied by Wm. Miller, C.G.C. 10 Jul 1825; to slaves Lucy and her children, all minors; to sister Nancy Coley; to James Coley, son of Peggy Coley, provided he comes into this County in the course of two years after my decease; to Wm. Coley, son of Molly Coley; to Molly, Frank, Betsy, and Peggy Coley. Execs: Chas. Massie and Wm. Turner (who refuse to qualify). Wit: Pleasant Turner, Robt. and Hazard Singleton.
 WB A 74; James Coley's Freedom Papers, (A boy of color). Dated 20 Feb 1809 and admitted to record in Hawkins Co., Tenn., May 1810 by Richard Mitchell, Clk., who is certified by Jacob Hackney, Chrm. of Ct. of Pleas of Hawkins Co., 27 Sep 1824.

COLLINS, E.B.
 CR15 168, 13 Aug 1869. T.B. Boyd, Adm., VS Mary A. Reagan, Adminx. of James A. Reagan.

COLLINS, ELIZABETH
 CR10 198, 4 Apr 1870. Court to pay for having grave dug.

COLLINS, SUSANNAH
 CR2 271, 4 Mar 1828. Court makes appropriation for support of Ann and John Collins, orphan children, for year 1828, payable to Wm. Gibbs.

COLLINS, TERRY
 CR9 220, 7 Jan 1867. Joseph Bunch app. Gdn. to Joseph, Noah, Abraham, and Troy Collins.
 CR10 211, 6 Jun 1870. Sett. by same Gdn.

COLVILLE, GEORGE
 WB E 421-422, Will exec. 10 Aug 1853; to son George, land warrant for serving U.S. in Wayne's War and the family Bible; to son-in-law Joseph C. Weir, the home farm provided he pay son George $231 "it being the amount of cost and expenses paid by me on account of the Chancery suit with the heirs of Young Colville deceased"; to dau. Sarah Weir; to grandson Saml. Colville, Botta's History in 2 vols.; "my two faithful slaves Joshua and Anthony" both to be freed or live with either of children or grandchildren if they choose that in preference to being colonized in Liberia. Exec: son George. Wit: Saml. Workman, Richard Morgan, and Pleasant Jones.

COLVILLE, SAMUEL
    CR2 475, 7 Sep 1830. Geo. Colville, Sr. and Jr. app. Adm.
    WB B 65, 6 Sep 1831. Invt. of sale by Adms.; note collected from
      davisson and Joseh /sic/ Colville.
    CR4 73, 6 Mar 1832. Catherine Colville, over 14, chooses Geo.
      Colville, Jr., as Gdn.
    CR3 223, 9 Mar 1832. Crawford & Murrell VS the Adms.; Writs of
      Scire facias issue to Joel K. Brown and Betsy his wife late
      Betsy Colville, Sally, George, Catharine, Warner Elmore, Bath-
      ialine, and Amanda M. Colville, Spencer Beavers and wife Rutha
      late Rutha Colville, heirs at law.
    CR3 246, 8 Jun 1832. Court app. Spencer Beavers Gdn. ad litem of
      Warren E., Bathialine, and Amanda M. Colville.

COLVILLE, YOUNG
    CR1 255, 5 Dec 1826. Office of Clerk vacant by the death of Young
      Colville, former Clerk.
    WB A 84-92, no date. Invt. of Sale held 1 Jan 1827 by Saml.
      Colville and Nutty Colville, Adm. and Adminx.
    CR1 336, 4 Jun 1828. Nutty Colville widow. Act of Assembly passed
      at Nashville on 22 Oct 1827 entitled, An Act for the relief of
      the widow & Heirs of Young Colville, dec'd. Court appoints John
      Walker and John McDowell Gdns. for Warner Elmore, Bethialine, and
      Amanda Murrell Colville, heirs.
    WB B 9-11, 26 Oct 1830. Invt. of Young Colville unadministered at
      time of death of Samuel Colville, so far as has come into hands
      of Nutty Colville and Saml. H. Jordan, Adm., in place of Saml.
      Colville.

COOKE, GEORGE W.
    WB E 419-421, Will exec. 3 Mar 1855; to wife Sarah Jane; "to raise
      educate and provide for each of my children". Execs: wife and
      bro. James B. Cooke. Wit: R.F. and H.C. Cooke.
    CR6, 7 May 1855. Will proven.

COOKE (COOK), JACOB
    CR5 42 and 43, 2 May 1842. Joel Culpepper app. Adm. Zechariah
      Keith, John Scarborough, and John Poe app. Comm. to lay off year's
      support for widow Nancy.
    WB D 68, 6 May 1842 and 119, 6 Feb 1843. Invt. and Sale by Adm.;
      Nancy, Catharine, and Mary Cook are principal buyers.
    WB F 42, 12 Jul 1856. Sett. by same Adm.

COOKE, JOHN A.
    WB E 71, 8 Jan 1850. Invt. and Sale held 26 Dec 1849 by C.R. Hoyl,
      Adm.; received cash from Execs. of Wm. H. Cooke, dec'd, a part of
      estate due dec'd.
    WB E 257, Jun 1852. Final sett. by Adm.; vouchers for eleven
      receipts from legatees, not named.
    WB E 262, 2 Aug 1852. Report by C.R. Hoyl Gdn. of minor heirs of
      his former wife Sarah M. Hoyl, dec'd; received of estate of John
      A. Cooke and from estate of Wm. H. Cooke.
    For further reports, see WILLIAM H. COOKE.

COOKE, MATTHIAS
    CR3 35, 11 Sep 1829. Joseph Robison and Wm. S. McEwen VS Matthias
      Cooke; death of defendant is suggested.
    CR3 38, 8 Dec 1829. Above suit revived against heirs, to wit, Rily,
      Charity, John, Saml., Betsey, George, and Peter Cook.

CR3 45, 9 Dec 1829. Amon Bond app. Gdn. to heirs pendente lite.

COOKE, THOMAS J.
CR15 265, 13 Apr 1870. The State VS D.H. Dickey - Murder. D.H. Dickey killed with a knife Thomas J. Cooke on 15 Feb 1870. Wm. G. Cooke prosecutor.

COOKE, WILLIAM H.
WB D 576-578, Will exec. 1 Oct 1848; to wife Mary; to children George W., Robert F., Hezekiah C., James B., and John A. Cooke, Nancy W. Thompson, Eliza Kimbrough, Clarissa Cooper, Elmira Cooper, Miranda Hoyl, Ataline Carson, Susan Chatten; Wm. H.C. Thompson (dau. Nancy W. Thompson's oldest son) to receive nothing; "as a part of the amount going to Clarissa Cooper the field ad- joining Thomas Cooper"; to Baptist Church one acre of land to include the meeting house of Conesauga Bapt. Church; to the pub- lic ten acres of land for a public burying ground; "$160 of the money owing me by Henry J. Brock be remitted to him". Execs: sons Robert F. and George W. Wit: David A. Cobbs, B.S. Cul- peper, and L.E. Cantrell.
CR5 488, 6 Nov 1848. Will proven.
WB E 26-33, 5 Mar 1849. Acct. of sale held 5 Dec 1848.
WB E 52, 255, 262, 304, 363, 425, WB F 79, 330, 419, WB G 17, dated from about 1849 to 1864; various reports by Execs. and by C.R. Hoyl, Gdn. to his own minor children (see JOHN A. COOKE).
CC 507, not dated. Wm. H. Cooke died 9 Oct 1848 leaving children Robert F. of Monroe Co.; Nancy W. wife of Daniel Thompson; Eliza wife of Duke W. Kimbrough; Claressa wife of Thomas Cooper; Elmira widow of James Cooper; Attaline wife of James Carson of Bradley Co.; Sarah M. (who died 28 May 1850) wife of Caleb R. Hoyl (their children are Clinton D., Putnam W., Mary B.J., David, and Susan, all minors); Susan wife of John D. Chattin of Rhea Co.; John A. (died 19 Nov 1849 without issue); Hezekiah C.; George W.; and James B.

COOKE, HEZEKIAH C.
WB F 258, 27 Feb 1859. Comm. M.L. Philips, James Melton, and F.M. Lusk set apart year's provisions for widow Mary and family.
WB F 268-279, 18 Mar 1859. Invt. by J.B. and R.F. Cooke, Adms.
WB G 183, 3 Aug 1866. Sett. by R.F. Cooke, Adm.
CC 82, filed 16 Jul 1859. Hezekiah C. Cooke died about 24 Jan 1859 leaving widow Mary and children: Robert F., Wm. H., John B., Mary J., Eliza E., James B., and Hezekiah C., the last four minors.

COONS, G.W.
CR10 216, 4 Jul 1870. In Tax delinquents for 1869 G.W. Coons is listed as dec'd.

COOPER, ELMIRA
CR6, 2 Oct 1854. Geo. W. and Hezekiah C. Cooke app. Adms.
WB E 393-399, 6 Nov 1854; F 45, 31 Jan 1857; 326, 29 May 1860. Invt. and sale by Adms., Sett. by H.C. Cooke, Adm., and final sett. by R.F. Cooke, Gdn. Receipts in full from heirs Wm. B. and J.W. Cooper and D.C. Cooper wife of Thomas Biggs.
CC 82, filed 16 Jul 1859. Elmira Cooper was sister to Hezekiah Cooke. Elmira's children, all minors at time of her death: Mary V. wife of Jesse M. Cobb, Clarinda wife of Thomas Biggs, William, and James Cooper. All are of age now except James who

will reach lawful age in Apr next.

COOPER, HENRY

WB B 162, Will exec. 24 Oct 1834, probated Dec 1834; to wife Eliza;
to two children Elmira and William Philip Cooper. Execs. and
Gdns. to children: friends Thomas and Bennet Cooper and Wm. H.
Cook. Wit: R.J. and G.W. Cook.

WB B 240, 27 Mar 1837. Sett. of Adms. with Comm. J.C. Carlock,
G.C. Cantrell, and Benjamin W. Patty. One item is paid to Eliza
Kimbro, late Eliza Cooper, widow and relict of said Henry Cooper,
dec'd.

WB C 96, 3 Dec 1838. Sett. by Wm. H. Cook one of Execs.; voucher
to Duke W. Kimbro and wife Eliza, widow of Henry Cooper.

WB D 390, 21 Nov 1845; 462, 21 Nov 1846; 506, 25 Nov 1847; E 45,
11 Jun 1849; 152, 14 Mar 1851. Sett. by Exec.

WB E 110, 11 Jun 1850. Sett. by Duke W. Kimbrough, Gdn. to Wm. P.
and Elmira Cooper.

WB E 188, 11 Jun 1851. Sett. by Gdn.; paid expenses at Clinton
School for heir Wm. P. Cooper.

WB E 278, 1 Jun 1852. Sett. by Gdn.; receipt of Thos. Cooper, Gdn.
of Wm. P. Cooper for full amount.

WB E 346, 7 Dec 1853. Final sett. by Gdn.; receipt of Wm. A.
Dugan who has intermarried with Elmira Cooper.

COOPER, JAMES

CR5 30, 8 Feb 1842. Thomas Cooper app. Adm.

CR5 34, 4 Apr 1842. Willie Laseter, Obed Patty, Sr., and John W.
Barnett app. Comm. to lay off year's support for widow Elmira.

WB D 68, 6 Jun 1842; 173, 15 Dec 1843; 280, 25 Apr 1845; 387,
25 Apr 1846; 502, 26 Feb 1848. Invt. of sale and Sett. by Adm.;
Sett. by G.W. Cooke, one of Gdns. of minor heirs.

CR6, 2 Oct 1854. Petition to sell land: Jesse M. Cobb and wife
Mary V. VS Clarenda, William, and James Cooper, minor heirs of
James and Elmira Cooper, dec'd.

COOPER, PHILIP

WB C 91-93, Will exec. Oct 1838, probated Dec 1838; to wife
Clarrenday; to dau. Lucinda; to sons Bennett, Henry, Thomas, and
James Cooper; to daus. Jincy Boyd and Sally Patty; Jincy Boyd is
dead and her share to go to her children; Henry Cooper is dead
and his share to go to his two children. Execs: Bennett Cooper
and Benjamin Patty. Wit: C. Sanders, Joseph Hamilton, George
Reynolds, and Lewis Hail. Signed by mark.

WB C 110, Jan 1839; 179, Oct 1839; 311, no date. Invt., Sale, and
Add. Invt.

WB C 337, 28 Jan 1841. Sett. by Benj. W. Patty, one of Execs.;
vouchers include legatees Benj. W. Patty, Drucinda Cooper, Bennett Boyd, and J.L. McClary.

WB D 347, 30 Nov 1845; F 250, 23 Oct 1858. Sett., Invt., and Sale.

WB F - Loose sheet of paper, not dated, not registered in book.
Sett. by Benjamin Patty, Exec.; three heirs entitled to $36 each;
balance in estate $8051.50 /in pencil this figure is divided by
seven to get "one share" and "Due B.W. & Sarah Patty"_7.

COPELAND, SOLOMON

CR 2 138, 7 Mar 1826. John Copeland app. Adm.

COUCH, JONATHAN

WB D 422, 20 Jan 1847 and 525, 17 Mar 1848. Sett. by Chas. W.

Rice, Gdn. to minors; "there being eight children who are equally
interested"; "amount due the five minor children".
WB E 103, 17 May 1850. Sett. by Gdn.; paid heirs Rachel and Celia
Couch; bought articles for David and Robert Couch, minors.
WB E 354, 17 Jan 1854. Sett. by Gdn.; receipt from Jonathan Couch.

COUCH, JOSEPH
WB D 43, 6 Oct 1841. Comm. David Smith, Wm. Randolph, and Nathaniel
Crittenden lay off year's support for widow Mary; Jont. Couch
agrees.
WB D 46, 1 Nov 1841 and 154, 25 Sep 1843. Invt. of sale and Sett.
by Allen Ware (Wear), Adm.

COWAN, JAMES W.
CR2 116, 6 Dec 1825. Robert Cowan app. Gdn. to Nancy Jane Cowan,
minor orphan.

COX, JOSEPH
CR6, 5 Jan 1857. P.W. Green app. Adm.

COX, MARY
CR6, 6 Jan 1857. P.W. Green app. Adm.

CRAIG, ALEXANDER
WB A 32, Will exec. 16 May 1823; to wife Susannah Craig; to the
children. Exec: Saml. Logan of Rhea Co., Tenn., and Saml.
Craig. Wit: Elisha Price, Samuel Craig.
WB A 67, no date. Invt. filed by Execs.

CRAWFORD, ELIZA ANN
See JOHN CRAWFORD.

CRAWFORD, JOHN
WB F 428-430, Will exec. 17 Sep 1846, proven May 1862; to wife
Eliza Ann; to dau. Amanda Hawk; to minor children John, Hugh,
Thomas, Eliza Ann, and Elinor Orregon Crawford, and one that is
yet unborn. Execs: Francis Boyd and James C. Carlock. Wit:
James Mayo, Edmund Roberts.
CR8, 6 May 1862. Will proven by Edmund Roberts; one of the persons
named as Exec. has died and the other not appearing, he is order-
ed to appear and qualify or resign.
CR8, 2 Jun 1862. J.C. Carlock app. Exec.
CR9 377, 2 Mar 1868. Ordered that Invt. be spread of record.
The Will Book that it should have been recorded in has been lost
or mislaid.
CR11 251, 13 May 1872. Final sett. by Exec.; paid $2000 each to
seven heirs, namely, P.A. Bradford and wife, John, A.J., Hugh,
and Thomas Crawford, W.W. Grubb and wife, and W.H. Briant and
wife.
CC 88, filed 21 Sep 1866. John Crawford died leaving widow Eliza
Ann and children: John; Andrew, a minor; Ellen O., who marries
W.W. Grubb of Ringgold, Ga., during the lawsuit by 28 Nov 1866;
Hugh; Thomas; Eliza Ann, wife of Wm. H. Briant; and Amanda, wife
of Patton A. Bradford.
CC 206, filed 15 May 1869. John Crawford died Mar 1862.
CC 256, filed 6 Sep 1870. Grubb VS Carlock. Widow Eliza Ann died
1 Jan 1868. Dau. Amanda was the widow Hawk when she married
Bradford. W.W. Grubb is of Monroe Co. Son John is of Atlanta.

CRAWFORD, SOLOMON
    CR5 546, 6 Aug 1849. Susan Crawford app. Gdn. to minor heirs.
CRISP, JOHN
    CR5 28, 7 Feb 1842. Amon Bond app. Adm.
    WB D 67, 4 Jun 1842. Invt. by Adm.
CROCKETT, DAVID
    CR8, 3 Feb 1862. C.B. Newman app. Adm.
    WB F 445, no date. Comm. Wm. Newman, John K. Jackson, and Joseph
    Copeland lay off year's support for widow and family.
    WB F 456. Invt. sold 21 Feb 1862 by Adm.; buyers include John,
    Wm. A., J.H., Rebecca, and Thos. Crockett.
    CC 37, filed 30 Nov 1865. David Crockett died 26 Jan 1862 leaving
    widow Lucinda and children: Josiah, Wm. A., Eliza J. Elliott a
    widow whose son is Thomas J. Elliott a minor, Elvira C. wife of
    G.W. Clayton, Sarah P., Rebecca E., Thomas J., Margaret E.,
    Ailsey J., John Z.T., Narcissa L., and Susan A., the last five
    being minors.
    CR9 231, 4 Feb 1867. Sett. by James Russell, Adm.
    CR9 371, 3 Feb 1868. Chas. Cate app. Gdn. of Louisa and Susan A.,
    minor heirs.
CROCKETT, JOHN
    WB E 357-358, Will exec. 30 Jan 1854; to dau. Sarah Crockett; to
    grandson James Crockett that now lives with me; dau. Sarah and
    grandson James to live on and hold home farm as their own until
    son William Crockett's youngest child is 21, then farm to be
    sold and money divided among all heirs; all personal property to
    be divided between two daughters Sarah Crockett and Rebecca
    Cantrell and David Crockett and grandson James Crockett. Execs:
    son-in-law David Cantrell and Nelson M. Crockett. Wit: Wm.
    Newman, John Thompson, Lemuel H. Thompson. Signed by mark.
    CR6, 6 Mar 1854. Will proven; Execs. named being absent, David
    Crockett app. Exec.
    WB E 370, 5 Jun 1854. Invt. of sale.
    WB F 59, 28 Mar 1857. Sett. by Exec.; equal amounts paid in 1855
    to R.W. Cantrell, N.M. Crockett Gdn., Sarah, and David Crockett.
    CC 140, filed 4 Sep 1867. Complainant Nelson G. Crockett of Ga.
    is a grandson of John Crockett, dec'd. The children of John
    Crockett are as follows: Sarah, unmarried; Rebecca, widow of
    David Cantrell, dec'd; James and David who have both died since
    father died; Elizabeth Crockett, dec'd before her father, whose
    son is Wm. H. Crockett of Mo.; Margaret Newman, dec'd before her
    father; Jane, dec'd before her father, wife of George O. Patty;
    John A. and William both dec'd before their father. The young-
    est child of son William arrived at age of twenty-one several
    years ago; both Execs. have long since died; Orator Nelson G.
    Crockett has bought seven of the nine interests in said land and
    transfers it to Sarah Crockett and Rebecca Cantrell.
    The grandchildren of John Crockett, dec'd, are as follows: Obed
    of Ark., William and Eliza of Polk Co., Elizabeth wife of John
    Davis of Ga., who are children of son James Crockett; William A.
    of Ohio, J.H., L.J., Sarah G., R.E. wife of Col. McCrary, T.P.,
    M.E. wife of Taylor Rutherford, Alsey S. wife of David Vaughn
    of Monroe Co., A.C. wife of George Clayton, John Z.S., Louisa N.,
    and Susan A. who are children of son David Crockett; Mahala wife
    of Dr. John A. Long, Sarah wife of Alexander Culton of Bradley

Co., Clinton now dec'd, Emeline dec'd wife of Dimmon Dorsey, Nancy dec'd wife of Burrell Buckner, Rebecca dec'd wife of McCamy Dorsey, who are children of daughter Margaret Newman; Elizabeth wife of Wm. Rutherford and Margaret wife of Alexander McBroom, who are children of daughter Jane Patty; David R. of Roane Co., Wm. S. and James W. of Wright Co., Mo., John C. of Roane Co., Margaret Sharp said to be of Missouri, Sarah P. wife of G.M. Dennis of Wright Co., Mo., who are children of son John A. Crockett; James dec'd, John H. of Polk Co., and Martha wife of Wm. Couch of Polk Co., who are children of son William Crockett. The great grandchildren of John Crockett, dec'd, are listed as follows: Clinton Newman's children are Margaret wife of Wm. Armstrong, Alice, Mary, Spencer, David, Robert Lafayette, and Mac Newman. Emeline Newman Dorsey's children are Mandeville, Nic, Thomas, Eliza, and Mary Dorsey, all of Mo. Nancy Newman Buckner's children are Robert, John, Taylor, and Wm. Buckner of McMinn Co. and Miram wife of Isaac Lewis of Meigs Co. Rebecca Newman Dorsey's children are Julius B., Rufus, Allison, Lafayette, and Hariet Dorsey, all of McMinn Co.

CROCKETT, JOHN A.
  CR6, 4 Apr 1853. Nelson M. Crockett app. Adm.
  WB E 314, 9 Apr 1853. Comm. John K. Jackson, James Chesnutt, and Uriel Johnston set apart year's support for widow Nancy and family, there being seven in family.
  WB E 314, 2 May 1853. Invt. of sale by Adm.

CROCKETT, WILLIAM
  CR6, 3 Apr 1854. Robt. M. Newman app. Gdn. of James H. Crockett.
  CR6, 3 Sep 1854. Nelson M. Crockett app. Gdn. to James H. Crockett, minor heir of William Crockett, dec'd, in room of Robt. M. Newman, dec'd.
  WB E 528, 2 Aug 1856. Report by Gdn.

CROMWELL, OLIVER
  CR2 380, 7 Sep 1829. Patience Cromwell app. Adminx.
  WB A 175 (2), no date. Invt. by Adminx.
  WB B 8, 3 Oct 1829. Invt. of sale; buyers include Patience and John B. Cromwell.
  WB B 83, 21 Apr 1832. Comm. Hamilton Bradford, Samuel McConnell, and H.C. Bradford settle with Adminx.

CROW, ISAAC
  CR9 5, 6 Sep 1864. M.D. Anderson app. Adm.
  CR9 199, 5 Nov 1866. C.C. Crow app. Gdn. of minor heirs.
  WB G 18, no date. Invt. and Sale by Adm.
  WB G 107, 4 Sep 1865. Comm. L. Dodson and B. Wells on 13 Sep 1864 set apart year's provisions for Mrs. Catharine Crow and family.
  WB G 207, 21 Sep 1866. Sett. by Adm.

CROW, JOHN
  WB A 107-108, Will exec. 16 Oct 1827; to wife; to sons Benjamin and Robert; to daus. Sally (a minor), Nancy Taylor, Rachel Taylor, Peggy Hammon, Polly, Hannah, Cressa. Execs: Benjamin and Robert Crow. Wit: Micah Sellers, William Golden. Signed by mark.
  CR2 244, 3 Dec 1827. Will proven.

CRUISE, GILBERT
  CR4 309, 3 Apr 1837. Jesse H. Benton, Andrew Hutsell, and John
  McMahan app. Comm. to lay off year's support for widow.

CRUTCHFIELD, THOMAS
  CC 70, filed 9 Apr 1849. Thomas Crutchfield VS Drury P. Armstrong,
  Adm. of Wm. Park, dec'd. In Record Book A, p.48, 20 Aug 1850,
  the death of Thomas Crutchfield is suggested and the suit is revived in name of Wm. and Thos. Crutchfield, Execs.
  CC 206, filed 21 Apr 1854. Tipton VS Callaway. Thomas Crutchfield
  died leaving widow Sarah and children William and Thomas of Hamilton Co., and Mary Jane wife of J.H. Lumpkin of Ga.

CRYE, WILLIAM
  CR4 297, 2 Jan 1837. Jesse Anderson and John Madarus make oath
  that they were well acquainted with William Crye a Revolutionary
  Pensioner and that he departed this life in the County of McMinn
  on 30 Aug 1835 leaving widow Sarah.

CULTON, JAMES
  CR8 156, 6 Apr 1863. Will proven by Chas. Staples and John A.
  Thompson, the subscribing witnesses. M.D. Anderson the Exec.
  named in the Will declines to serve. Alex. Culton of Bradley
  Co. and R.M. McClatchey of McMinn app. Adms. with Will annexed.

CUNNINGHAM, JAMES
  WB A 1-3, Will exec. 7 Sep 18__, Codicil 1 Dec 1819; to wife Peggy;
  to daus. Susannah Young, Charlott Matilday, Amanda Fitsallen,
  Corinia Mirinda Albana; to sons Moses, Marchel W., Pleasant Theo-
  dor. Execs: wife Peggy and son Moses. Wit: Robert Ferguson,
  James Anderson.
  CR1 5, 5 Jun 1820. Will proven.
  CC 50, filed 24 Jun 1848. Children of James and Margaret Cunningham: Moses aged 48 in 1849; Marshall W. whose wife was a sister
  to Eveline the widow of Pleasant T.; Pleasant T. who died Sep
  1834 in Mo. where he had moved with family in 1833-34 (leaving
  widow Eveline and children Pleasant T., Jr., aged 18 in 1852, and
  Sarah wife of McMinn Dodson); Corinna wife of James Lowry. Pleasant and Eveline were married about 1830. Pleasant T., Jr., is
  anxious to move to Oregon with his mother Eveline and her family.
  Margaret Cunningham, wife of James, took possession of land in
  McMinn Co. in 1821 and in 1823-24 petitioned Legislature to grant
  the land to her at $1.25 per acre. She was a midwife and rode as
  a midwife until about 1837. She died in 1847 at age 84. James
  died owning land in Blount Co.

CUNNINGHAM, MARGARET
  See JAMES CUNNINGHAM.

CUNNINGHAM, PLEASANT T.
  CR4 455, 2 Sep 1839. Marshall W. Cunningham app. Gdn. to minor
  heirs.
  CR5 59, 6 Jul 1842. Same, Gdn. to Sarah and Pleasant Cunningham.
  WB D 201, Jun 1844; 210, 25 Jun 1844; 336, 25 Jun 1845; 402, 25
  Jun 1846; 505, 29 Feb 1848. Settlements by same Gdn.; paid widow
  and minor heirs for coffee, etc.

CUNNINGHAM, WILLIAM HENRY, SR.
  WB D 272-273, Will exec. 1 Aug 1843; to wife Magdalene, one half
  of plantation next to Trouts; to son Jesse, land on which I

settled him in Knox Co.; to granddaus. Harriet Theodosia Adaline
and Maranda James Caranda, daus. of son James, dec'd, the land on
which I settled their father in Knox Co.; to two sons John and
Wm. H.; son Wilie Houston has already received money; to son
Thomas W., land "reserving Mount Harmony meeting house with a lot
fourteen by seven poles square ... said house and lot I give ...
to the Methodist Episcopal Church"; to dau. Charlotte; to four
daus. Nancy Reagan, Polly Goddard, Betsy Pickle, and Gincy Patton;
to children not herein specified. Execs: sons-in-law Jonathan
Pickle and Wm. Patton. Wit: Saml. M. Johnson, Zenas A. Edwards,
and James Lowry, Jr. Signed by mark.
CR5 219, 3 Mar 1845 and 222, 7 Apr 1845. Will proven.
WB D 274, 7 Apr 1845; 282, 7 May 1845; 389, 7 Sep 1846; 394, 22 Sep
  1846. Invt., Sett., Add. Invt., and Add. Acct. of Sale by Execs.
WB D 395, 5 Oct 1846. Undivided property of which Charlotte McSpadden is to have half when collected; filed by Exec.
WB D 441, 29 Mar 1847. Sett. by Execs.; receipts of heirs Nancy
  Reagan, Polly Goddard, Betsy Pickle, and Gincy Patton.
WB D 506, 29 Feb 1848. Sett.; payments to Nancy Reagan, to Polly
  and Thornton C. Goddard, and equal amounts retained by the Execs.
  as their share.

CURD, RICHARD
WB D 318-320, 2 Sep 1845; 321-323, 6 Oct 1845; 345-346, 5 Nov 1845.
  Invt., Sale, and Add. Sales, filed by John W. Barnett and Chas.
  T. Thornton, Adms.
WB D 357, 28 Jan 1846. Comm. Uriel Johnston, James Gaut, and
  Samuel Hardy allot year's support to widow Susan and her child
  James H.
WB D 418, 18 Dec 1846. Sett. by Wm. P. Copeland, Gdn. to Benjamin,
  Mary, and Joseph Curd, minor heirs.
WB D 484, 18 Oct 1847. Same Comm. set apart year's support to three
  minor heirs, Benjamin, Mary, and Joseph.
WB D 491, 3 Dec 1847. Sett. by J.W. Barnett, Adm.
WB D 522, 7 Mar 1848. Sett. by Wm. P. Copeland, Gdn.; allowance to
  Gdn. for keeping two of the children up to this time; did not
  board Benjamin.
WB E 21, 3 Dec 1848; 23, 24 Feb 1849; 92, 24 Feb 1850; 94, 3 Dec
  1849. Settlements by Adm. and Gdn.
WB E 110, 19 Aug 1850. Final sett. by Adm.; paid W.P. Copeland Gdn.
  of Mary Curd now Mary Longley, Benjamin and Joseph Curd, heirs;
  paid heirs W.P. Copeland, Squire North; paid Susan Curd widow;
  paid Susan Curd as Gdn. of Jas. H. Curd; all receiving same amount.
WB E 144, 24 Feb 1851; 196, 24 Feb 1852; 308, 7 Mar 1853. Sett. by
  Gdn.
CR6, 7 Mar 1853. Same Gdn. has permission to remove his Gdnship.
  to Polk Co.
CR12 24, 19 Apr 1852. Wm. P. Copeland and wife and other heirs VS
  James H. Curd by his Gdn. Susan Curd, Robert M. Newman, and
  others. On 16 Sep 1843, one Simeon Eldridge by and with the consent of the said Richard Curd now deceased conveyed to one Benjamin Eldridge in trust for the benefit of the children of the
  said Richard Curd of his first marriage being the grandchildren
  of the said Simeon Eldridge....

CURTIS, JOHN
WB D 253, Will exec. 15 Jul 1844; to wife Dolly. Wit: John

Jenkins, A. Hanks. Signed by mark.
CR5 207, 6 Jan 1845. Dolly Curtis app. Adminx.

DARNELL, JOSHUA
CR10 216, 4 Jul 1870. Marked "dec'd" in list of tax delinquents
for 1869.

DAUGHERTY, JOHN
WB E 317, Will exec. 13 Jun 1849; to daus. Mary H. Daugherty,
Sarah Bradford, Cleninda Mitchell, and Julian Parkison. Exec:
David Bradford. Wit: John Jenkins, Allen Haley.
CR6, 4 Apr and 2 May 1853. Will proven and David Bradford of Polk
Co. app. Exec.

DAUGHERTY, MARY H.
WB G 238, Noncupative Will exec. 25 Sep 1870, proven 7 Nov 1870;
to the heirs of David Bradford, viz: Mary Jane Casaday, Sarah
Clarinda, Hannah Ann, Nancy Elizabeth, and Lucinda Virginia
Bradford, the land where said David Bradford now lives; to James
Mitchell, desk and fall leaf table. Attest: John Jenkins,
A. Slack.

DAVIS, ALFRED
CR9 67, 7 Aug 1865. Mary Davis app. Adminx.
CR9 70, 4 Sep 1865. Mrs. Mary Davis Adminx. resigns and Comm.
app. to lay off dower to her as widow.
CC 306, filed 10 Nov 1871. Norvell VS Davis. Alfred Davis died
4 Feb 1865 leaving widow Mary and children Emilia wife of John
Baker of Meigs Co. and Rachel wife of John F. Norvell. Widow
Mary denies that Emelia and Rachel are the only children of
Alfred Davis, dec'd. She asserts that son William was alive
when father died and was living in Wilmington, N.C., on 10 Mar
1865 and is still living so far as she knows.

DAVIS, JAMES R.
CR4 431, 4 Mar 1839. Isaac Davis app. Adm.
WB C 140, Jun 1839. Invt. filed by Isaac Davis, Adm.

DAVIS, ROBERT
CR5 204, 3 Dec 1844. Marked "dead" in list of Tax Delinquents for
1844.

DAVIS (DAVICE), WILLIAM
CR2 431, 2 Mar 1830. Nancy and Anthony Davis app. Adms.
CR2 452, 7 Jun 1830. Henry Smith, Wm. Brown, and Caswell Jarna-
gin app. Comm. to lay off year's support for widow Nancy.
CR2 488, 6 Dec 1830. John F., James A., and Francis M. Davis,
minors over 14, choose Jackson Smith as Gdn.
WB A 218-219, no date. Invt. by Adms.
WB B 170, 4 Mar 1835 and 198, 1 Aug 1836. Reports by Jackson
Smith, Gdn. to Frances M. Davis, minor heir.
CR4 327, 7 Aug 1837. Wm. Lowry, Elijah Hurst, and Uriel Johnson
app. Comm. to settle with Gdn. to F.M. Davis now F.M. Potts, heir.

DEADERICK, DAVID
CR4 314, 1 May 1837. It appearing to the satisfaction of the Court
that David Deaderick son of Dr. William H. Deaderick of McMinn
County departed this life on 23 Mar 1837 without wife or issue
and ..... that Penelope S. Campbell aged 26 years wife of Victor
Moreau Campbell, Eliza Ann Van Dyke aged 23 years wife of Tho.

Nixon Van Dyke, Joseph H. Deaderick aged 18 years, Margretta A. Deaderick aged 16 years, Frances N. Deaderick aged 13 years, Thomas S. Deaderick aged 11 years, Robert H. Deaderick aged 9 years, William H. Deaderick, Jr., aged 5 years, and Alexander H. Deaderick aged 3 years are the heirs at law and distributees; William H. Deaderick app. Gdn. to the last seven named; Onslow G. Murrell app. Adm.

WB B 257. Report to July Court 1837 by Adm.

WB D 88, 4 Jul 1842; 203, 1 Jun 1844; 306, 1 Jun 1845; 368, 1 Jun 1846, 493, 21 Jun 1847. Reports by Wm. H. Deaderick, Gdn. to his own minor children.

DEADERICK, WILLIAM H.

WB F 148-151, Will exec. 24 Sep 1857, Codicil 12 Oct 1857, proven Feb 1858; to wife Lois; wife Lois to board son Alexander as he now boards with me without charge until 1 Apr 1858 and same for granddau. Henrietta M. Campbell until she arrives at age of 18; to dau. Anne Eliza Van Dyke; to dau. Mary, free from control of any person she may marry; to three sons Robert, Thomas, and William; to son Alexander "the silver spoons which came from Mr. Hamilton"; to three granddaus. Caroline R. Samples, Margaret L., and Henrietta M. Campbell; to son Robert, all my medical books; to son Joseph; to dau. Margaretta Bridges; to children of Anne Eliza Van Dyke when they arrive at age of 21 or marry, money to be "expended in the purchase for said children of one dozen silver teaspoons, a half dozen silver table spoons, a half dozen silver tumblers, and a silver soup ladle for each of said children except Penelope who is to get a half dozen silver tumblers". Exec: son Alexander H. Wit: Wm. W. Alexander, James Turner.

CR7 114, 1 Feb 1858. Will proven and Exec. named qualifies.

CC 305, filed 23 Nov 1858 and 70, filed 19 Dec 1859. Wm. H. Deaderick died Oct 1857. Additional information on children and grandchildren is as follows: Eliza A. is wife of T. Nixon Van Dyke; Mary McK. is wife of Uriah L. York; sons Joseph, Thomas, and William are of Texas; son Robert H. is of Calif.; the daughter who was mother of the Campbell grandchildren was Penelope H., dec'd; granddaughter Margaret Letitia Campbell is the wife of J.H. Hale; Penelope Campbell's daughter Caroline R. Samples is now dead leaving minor son Wm. C. Sample who is summoned from Sumner Co.; dau. Margaretta A., wife of John L. Bridges, is now dead leaving Wm. D. Bridges as her only child. In Supp. Bill filed 13 Nov 1860, son Alexander H. has died since the land was sold on 2 Jun 1860.

CR7 486 and 488, 5 Nov 1860. U.L. York app. Adm. de bonis non. John L. Bridges app. Gdn. for his own minor child Wm. D. Bridges.

DEAN

CR5 46, 6 Jun 1842 and 50, 4 Jul 1842. James A. Dean, aged 12 or 13, and Thomas A. Dean, aged 4, orphans, bound to John Gaston; William Calvin Dean, age 16, bound to James Steed.

DEAN, AARON

CR5 255, 3 Nov 1845. Thomas Dean app. Adm.

WB D 357, 5 Jan 1846. Sale by Adm.; buyers include David, James, and Susannah Dean.

WB D 446, 11 Nov 1845. Comm. Wm. S. Calloway, Elijah Cate, and

James Wilson set apart year's support for widow Susannah.
WB D 447, 30 Apr 1847. James C. Carlock, Clk., makes pro rata
sett. between Adm. and creditors.

DEAN, FREDERICK
CR14 319, 13 Dec 1867. Death suggested and admitted in Court.

DEARMOND, JOHN
WB E 563, Will and Codicil exec. 7 Jun 1856; to John M. Dearmond a
minor son of Wm. B. Dearmond, 80 acres of land; $1 each to daus.
Easther and Adeline; 25 acres of land to son Thos. B. Dearmond.
Wit: J. Jack, J.J. Elliott. Signed by mark.

DEBORD, GEORGE
CR5 511, 5 Feb 1849. Wm. McKamy app. Gdn. to Mahal An Debord,
minor.
WB E 95, 18 Feb 1850; 190, 15 Feb 1851; F254, 18 Feb 1859; 394,
18 Feb 1861; 441, 18 Feb 1862. Settlements by Gdn.
CR8 143, 6 Apr 1863. Settlement which is made by Wm. P. McKamy,
Gdn. of minor heirs, ordered to be spread of record and the same
paid over to the Treas. of McMinn Co., the parties being unknown.

DENNIS, JOHN
CR2 245, 3 Dec 1827. James Dennis app. Adm.
WB A 112, 6 Dec 1827. Invt. of personal estate, by Adm.
WB A 123-124, no date. Sale. In list are James, Allen, Isham,
and Nancy Dennis.

DENNIS, OREN (OWEN)
WB G 27, 10 Oct 1863. Sale at his late residence by W.P. Cate, Adm.
CC 57, filed 18 Apr 1866. Orren Dennis, son of Allen Dennis, married Virginia Cate 22 Dec 1861 when he was 24, was conscripted
into Confederate Army, and died 24 Mar 1863 leaving the widow and
one dau. Lou Emma, and bros. and sisters Allen, Jr., age 26 in
1866 and Mark age 23 in 1866, both in Confederate Army with Orren,
Matilda age 25 in 1866, and others. Widow marries Lee Arwood
during the lawsuit.
CR9 372 and 375, 3 Feb 1868. Lee Arwood app. Gdn. of Lou Emma
Dennis, minor heir.

DENTON, ABRAHAM
CR9 372, 3 Feb 1868. Isaac Denton app. Adm.
CC 250, filed 18 Jun 1870. Abraham Denton died 1863.

DERRICK, CORNELIUS
CR6, 7 Jun 1852. Saml. Wilson app. Adm.
WB E 260, 5 Jul 1852. Invt. by Adm.
WB E 343, 24 Nov 1853. Report by same Adm. "not being able to come
to the Clerk's office".

DERRICK, JACOB L.
CR5 446, 1 May 1848. E.P. Bloom app. Adm.
WB D 558, 4 Sep 1848. Report of sale held 27 May 1848 at house of
Cornelius Derrick, Chestue Creek, McMinn Co., by Adm.
WB E 228, 29 Mar 1852. Sett.

DERRICK (DERICK), MICHAEL
WB C 186, Will exec. 4 Aug 1839, probated Oct 1839; to wife Elizabeth; equal division among children except that share of Magdalene Burger be divided into four parts, one part to her and three
parts to her children, Absalem, William, and Elizabeth; to

grandson Absalem Glossup. Execs: sons John and Cornelius.
Wit: A. Barb, Wm. Lee.
CR4 456 and 465, 7 and 8 Oct 1839. Will proven.
WB C 253-255, 1 Jun 1840. Sale; Jacob L. Derrick is a buyer.
WB D 151, 16 Aug 1843. Sett.; vouchers to heirs E.P. Bloom, George
Burger, and Michael C. Derrick.
WB D 297, 24 Mar 1845. Sett.; receipts for various amounts from
heirs Wm. H., J.L., John, A.G., Jonathan, Cornelius, and Michael
C. Derrick, G. Cantrell, John J. Parker, D.J. Firestone, E.P.
Bloom, George Burger, and Jonathan Derrick for minor heirs of
Joseph McMinn.

DICKEY, SAMUEL
WB C 192-193, Will exec. 19 Apr 1836, recorded Jan Court 1840; to
wife; to youngest son Samuel H.; to two single daus. Rebecca L.
and Nancy M.; to balance of heirs, James M., John F., David H.,
Elizabeth M. Elkins, Anny Gamble, and Polly Fox; wife's legacy
left her in N.C. by her sister Ann Houston. Execs: David H.
and Samuel H. Dickey. Wit: Abraham Fox, Saml. H. Dickey.

DITMORE, JOHN
WB B 59, Will exec. 19 Jun 1830; to companion and wife Liza; to
six sons, Verg and Edward H John Vivian Goleh Henry frances
Ditmore /as written, no punctuation7; to three daus., Mary L ye
Emaline /sic7 lot in Town of Collumbus, McMinn Co.; money com-
ing from John Ditmore of S.C. Wit: Samuel Yates, James B.
Jackson.
CR2 534, 6 Jun 1831 and CR4 9, 8 Jun 1831. Will proven.

DIVINE, JOHN
CR5 377, 4 Oct 1847. Thomas L. Hoyl app. Adm.
WB D 485, 22 Oct 1847. Comm. J.C. Carlock, John Hoyle, and G.W.
Kirksey set apart year's support for minor heirs; E.P. Bloom,
J.P.
WB D 518-520, 4 Mar 1848. Invt., Accts. Due, and Sale.
WB E 114, 16 Sep 1850. Sett. by Adm.; paid heirs John, Gemima,
Sarah, and Ebenezer Divine; paid Ebenezer Divine, Gdn. for minor
heirs; paid for provisions furnished the widow.
WB E 221, 21 Mar 1852. Sett.
CC 283, filed 14 Nov 1857. Ebenezer, William B., Sarah, and Mary
Divine VS Jephtha Smith and wife Jane, Margaret and John Divine,
John Samples and wife, Robert Smith et al. /Original Bill miss-
ing. Incomplete file. Information in Exec. Docket B and Record
Book B.7 Feb 1860: John H. Gouldy app. Gdn. ad litem of James,
Mary Jane, Matthew, and Jesse Samples, minor heirs of Jemima
Samples. The complainants and defendants own the land. Jane
Smith, Margaret and John Divine did not answer the publication.
Clerk & Master instructed to report number and names of heirs.
John Divine died leaving eleven heirs and distributees, Ebenezer
and Sarah and others not named. In 1850 Ebenezer and Sarah
Divine sold their undivided interest in land to John Samples who
assigned it to Robert Smith.

DIXON
CR4 550, 5 Jul 1841. Edom Dixon, minor orphan aged 6 years last
Jun 15th, bound to Wm. O. Barnett to learn the farming business.

DIXON, ELI, JR.
CR7 338, 5 Sep 1859. James Forest, H.L. Shults, and Wm. L. Rice

app. Comm. to lay off year's support for widow and children.
WB F 295, no date. Above Comm. make report.
CR7 345, 3 Oct 1859. James Wilson and Eli Dixon, Adms., allowed
six months to report inventory, it consisting of leather in tan.
CR7 347, 3 Oct 1859. M.L. Philips and David Neil app. Comm. with
County Surveyor to lay off dower to widow Malissa Dixon.
WB F 371, 5 Nov 1859. Sale.
CR10 209, 2 May 1870. Adms. of James Wilson find papers belonging
to estate of Eli Dickson, Jr. James Wilson and Eli Dickson, Sr.,
are both dead; D.M. McReynolds app. Adm.

DIXON, ELI, SR.
CR9 54, 5 Jun 1865. F.M. Rowan of Monroe Co. app. Adm.
WB G 70, 3 Jul 1865. Invt.
WB G 88, 27 Jul 1865. Comm. James Forrest, W.L. Rice, and Isaac
Stalcup lay off year's provisions for widow and family.
WB G 135, 28 Nov 1865. Sale.
CC 136, filed 9 Aug 1867. Eli Dixon died Jan 1865 leaving widow
Charity and children: Miriam wife of Thomas Matlock of Texas,
Sarah E. wife of F.M. Rowan of Monroe Co., John H. of Ill.,
Texas and Oregon Dixon minors of McMinn Co.
CR11 281, 26 Sep 1873. Sett.

DOAN (DONE)
CR4 120, 3 Dec 1832. Ira Done app. Gdn. for Absolem and M.J.
Done, minor orphans.

DOCKERY, WILLIAM
CR5 550, 1 Oct 1849. Thomas J. Hoyl app. Adm.
CR16 114, Oct 1850. Same Adm. VS Sarah Ann Dockery widow, Emelia
and Henry Dockery, heirs, and James C. Carlock, Gdn. ad litem of
minor heirs.

DODD
CR5 471, 4 Sep 1848 and 482, 2 Oct 1848. James H. Dodd, an orphan
aged 14, and Sarah Jane Dodd, an orphan aged about 12, bound to
John A. Rowles.

DODD, JOHN, SR.
WB E 403-404, Will exec. 2 Jan 1839 /probated about Jan 1855_7; to
wife Levina; to children Levina, James, Mary Ann, John, Elizabeth
B., and Lang R. Execs: wife Levina and son James M. Wit: John
and Albartis Arnwine.
WB E 466, no date. Invt. by James M. Dodd, Exec.
WB F 299, no date. Report by Lang R. Dodd, Gdn. to John, Mary, and
Elizabeth Dodd, Idiots of John Dodd, dec'd.
WB F 359, 17 Nov 1860. Sett. by same Gdn.; paid Jas. M. Dodd trav-
eling expense to Va. and back.

DODD, LANG R.
CR9 91, 6 Nov 1865. L.R. Dodd, now dec'd, who was Gdn. of John,
Mary, and Elizabeth Dodd, heirs of John Dodd.

DODSON (DOTSON), ALLEN
CR8 137 and 141, 2 Mar 1863. W.H. Rothwell app. Adm. James Carter,
Joseph Barnette, and Jas. Willson app. Comm. to lay off year's
support for widow and family.
CR8 149, 6 Apr 1863. Wellington H. Rothwell, Adm. VS Martha Dodson
widow and others; ordered that A. Caldwell, Esq., be app. Gdn. ad
litum for minor children, to wit, Eliza J., Nancy A., and John

Dodson.

WB G 47-50, 18 Feb 1865. Sale held 13 Mar and 2 May 1863 by Adm.; "as per Inventory returned heretofore and which said Inventory is believed to have been destroyed by the Wheeler raid in August 1864".

CC 34, filed 17 Nov 1865. Amended Bill filed 27 Feb 1873. Allen Dodson died Feb 1863 leaving widow Martha and children: Jane wife of Pryor Dobbs (she dies by Nov 1867 without issue), Nancy wife of Franklin Wallis, and John, a minor.

CR9 292, 5 Aug 1867. J.F. Wallis app. Gdn. of John Dodson, minor heir.

DODSON, DAVID

CR2 177, 6 Sep 1826. William and Frances Dodson app. Adms.

CR2 299, 1 Sep 1828. Wyley Laseter, Wm. Lea, and Wm. Killingsworth app. Comm. to settle with Wm. Dodson, Adm.

WB D 364, 7 Apr 1846. Report by Wm. L. Dodson, Adm.; receipts in full from heirs Alfred, James, and Mary Jane Dodson, William and Nancy Martin, Elizabeth Dodson wife of Addison Jenkins; "heretofore he made a Settlement with Commissioners appointed by the County Court".

DODSON, WILFORD

WB F 184-185, Will not dated, proven Jul 1858; to wife Lusina Jane; to children Melville P. and Mary D.; bro. A.J. Dodson to be Gdn. of the two children until they reach 21. Execs: bros. A.J. and E.A. Dodson. Wit: C.W. Rice, A.P. Bradford.

WB F 228-239, 5 Oct 1858. Invt. of the open accts. on the Book of the firm of W. & A.J. Dodson up to 1 Jul 1858.

WB F 258, no date. Comm. Wm. S. Calaway, J. Atkins, and John G. Hale set apart year's support for widow and family.

CR9 218, 7 Jan 1867. Lucina J. Dodson app. Gdn. of Mary D. Dodson, her own minor heir.

CR10 370, May 1872. Report by Lucina J. Porter, formerly Dodson, Gdn. of her own minor child.

DORSEY, DIMMON

CR4 281, 5 Sep 1836. Thos. Wakefield and John Duckworth app. Adms. Joel Triplet, Frederick Haile, and Oliver Dodson app. Comm. to lay off year's support for widow.

CR4 293, 6 Dec 1836. Application being made for Gdn. to Elisha Sarah Betsey Ann Thomas Woodward Nancy Adaline Martha and McCajah Dorsey, minor heirs; Thomas Wakefield and Thomas Duckworth chosen by Nancy Adaline Martha and McCajah who are of age to choose for themselves and are app. as Gdns. for Elijah Sarah Betsey Ann and Thomas Woodward /written without punctuation/.

CR4 293, 6 Dec 1836. Oliver Dodson, Robert Stephenson, Martin Casady, Wm. H. Cook, and Robt. Newman app. Comm. to allot dower in land to Elizabeth (Betsey) Dorsey, widow.

WB B 211-215, Nov 1836; 252, Jun 1837; 294, 20 Dec 1837; WB C 76, 24 Nov 1838. Invt. of sale and reports filed by Adms. and Gdns.

WB C 77, 24 Nov 1838. Report by Gdns.; paid to Elizabeth and Nancy Dorsey, heirs; a dress for Martha Dorsey; tuition for Sarah Dorsey.

WB C 211, 4 Feb 1840. Report by Gdn.; paid to Micajah Dorsey, Richard T. Goode, and George Gaut, heirs.

WB D 42, 4 Feb 1841 and 94, 4 Aug 1842. Sett. by Thos. Duckworth, Gdn.

WB D 203, Apr 1844. Sett. by Gideon Cate, successor to Thos. Duckworth as Gdn.; undivided land belonging to seven heirs and note belonging exclusively to minor heirs.

WB D 211, 19 Jun 1844; 310, 19 Jun 1845; 371, 19 Jun 1846. Sett. by same Gdn.

WB D 514, 29 Jan 1848. Sett. by Elisha Dorsey, successor to Gideon Cate as Gdn.; wards are Sarah D. and Elizabeth Ann Dorsey.

WB E 64, 2 Oct 1849. Sett. by Gdn.; acct. of Sarah D. Dorsey fully settled.

DORSEY, JOHN

WB C 182-183, Oct 1839. Invt. by Dimmon Dorsey and John C. Gautt, Adms.

WB C 219, 28 Dec 1839. Report by Comm. Robert Stephenson, Samuel Hardy, and Oliver Dodson setting apart year's support for widow Mahalia and family; sworn to before John McGaughey.

WB C 236-238, Mar 1840 and WB D 39, 26 Oct 1841. Sale and sett. by Adms.

WB D 198, 9 Apr 1844. Sett.; receipts from Mahala Dorsey, widow and Gdn. for Salina Jane Dorsey and James Alexander Dorsey, heirs; Wit: Jesse H. and James Gaut.

WB D 202, 3 Jun 1844. Report by same Gdn.; has provided for heirs since 21 Sep 1839.

DOUGLASS

/Note: Name of deceased is never given in these reports but is probably Nancy Dickson Bishop Douglass./

WB D 251, no date. Report by John Douglass, Gdn. to his minor children.

WB D 349, 19 Jan 1846. Sett. by Gdn.; "Amount allowed Guardian for making 3 trips to S. Carolina for cash & for all services as Guardian 15.00".

WB D 419, 19 Jan 1847. Sett. by Gdn.

WB D 511, 19 Jan 1848. Sett. by Gdn.; receipt in full from heir Hugh Douglass.

WB E 18, 19 Jan 1849. Sett.; paid heirs R.C. and S.R. Rhodes.

WB E 78, 19 Jan 1850. Sett.; paid heirs Caswell and Nancy Matilda Lee.

WB E 148, 19 Jan 1851; 209, 19 Jan 1852; 304, 19 Jan 1853; 355, 19 Jan 1854; 405, 19 Jan 1855; 489, 19 Jan 1856. Settlements by Gdn.

WB F 44, 19 Jan 1857. Sett.; voucher for 1/3 of amount to Wm. M. Cass and wife Julia and 1/3 to Elizabeth Douglass.

WB F 152, 19 Jan 1858; 260(1), 19 Jan 1859; 313, 19 Jan 1860. Sett.

DOUGLASS (DOUGLAS), ELIZABETH

WB C 39, Will exec. 16 Oct 1837, proven Sep 1838; to son John Douglas, Mary Jones, and Lettice Bolding to make them equal with James and Wm. Douglas, then rest of estate to be divided equally among children. Wit: Christopher Huffaker, Wm. L. Bolding. Signed by mark.

CR4 379, 3 Sep 1838. Will proven by the two witnesses, who are app. Execs.

DOUGLASS (DOUGLAS), HUGH D.

CR8, 8 Jul 1862. M.A. Cass app. Adm.

CR8, 1 Jun 1863. John A. Gouldy app. Gdn. of minor heirs, to wit, John, Mary, and Sarah Douglas.

DOUGLASS (DOUGLAS), JOHN
   CR8, 4 May 1863. Wm. Douglas and Jas. H. Rucker, citizens of
      Bradley Co., app. Adms.
   CR8 163, 4 May 1863. J.F. Benton, E.W. Carlock, and J.F. Strange
      app. Comm. to lay off year's support for widow Julia A.
   WB G 25. Acct. of sale of rents of farm sold 5 Sep 1863 by Adms.
   CC 20, filed 27 Jun 1863 and consolidated with No. 163, filed
      4 Feb 1867. Chancery Court in McMinn County was suspended after
      Federals had taken possession from about 10 Sep 1863 to 1864 or
      1865. Confederate Notes were accepted by Bank of Tenn. up to
      5 Sep 1863. John Douglass died 7 Apr 1863 leaving widow Julia
      now of Monroe Co. who dies during the lawsuit by 23 Aug 1865 and
      the following children: William of S.C. and later of McMinn Co.;
      Eliza C. wife of James Rucker of Bradley Co.; Sarah R. wife of
      William Rhodes of Calif.; Elizabeth J. wife of Ezekiel Bates of
      Bradley Co.; Nancy M. wife of Joseph Smith of Polk Co.; Julia A.
      wife of Wm. Cass; Hugh D., dec'd, whose children are John, Mary
      Jane, and Sarah, all minors; Mary L., dec'd, wife of Asahel
      Carlock, whose children are James M., Adelia H., John L., Amelia
      J., Sarah E., and Lemuel C.H., Carlock, all minors of Missouri.
      Ezekiel Bates and Joseph Smith die during the lawsuit by Aug 1865
      and Asahel Carlock dies by 1869.
   CR11 153, 15 Feb 1869. Sett. by Adms.; paid unequal amounts to
      L.L. Carlock, Wm. Cass, Jane Bates, and Matilda Smith.
   CR10 283, Apr 1871. Court pays for holding inquest over body of
      John Douglass in 1863.
   CR11 331, 31 May 1875. Sett. by James H. Rucker, one of Adms.;
      there are eight heirs: John A. Gouldy Gdn. of Hugh Douglass'
      heirs, Nancy M. Smith, E.J. Bates, L.L. Carlock Gdn. of minor
      heirs of Mary Carlock, J.H. and E.C. Rucker, Sarah Rhoads,
      /blank space in record/.

DOUGLASS, NANCY DICKSON BISHOP
   CC 83, filed 22 Dec 1849. Asahel Carlock and wife Mary formerly
      Douglass of Polk Co., Mo., Ezekiel Bates and wife Jane formerly
      Douglass of Bradley Co., Wm. Rhodes and wife Sarah R. formerly
      Douglass, Caswell Lea and wife Matilda formerly Douglass, all of
      McMinn Co. VS John Douglass and William, Hugh D., Julia Ann,
      Dorcas, John E., and Elizabeth Caroline Douglass. About 18___
      John Douglass now of Polk Co. married in S. C. Nancy Dickson
      Bishop, dau. of Nicholas Bishop. Copy, 1846, of deed of gift of
      slave girl and her increase dated 26 Feb 1817 from Nicholas to
      dau. Nancy and her heirs. Nancy died about 18___ leaving above
      named Oratrixes and other named children, William of Anderson
      Dist., S.C., Hugh D. of McMinn Co., all of whom are of lawful
      age, and minors, to wit, Julia Ann, Dorcas, John E., and Eliza
      Caroline Douglass of Polk Co. John Douglass (the father) holds
      slaves. Petition for distribution.

DOUGLASS, ROBERT
   WB B 259-260, Will exec. 27 Jun 1837, probated 7 Aug 1837; to wife
      Elizabeth; to oldest son James; to younger son William R.; to
      son John; to Maryan dau. of son Wm. R.; to dau. Polly Jones; to
      Robert Jones son of Polly and Richard Jones; to dau. Letticia
      Bolding; money due me in Va. Execs: sons James and Wm. Wit:
      Lewis Payne, Wm. L. Bolding.
   WB B 265, 4 Sep 1837. Invt. by J.S. Douglass, Exec.

WB C 26, 21 Jun 1838. Sett. by Execs.; received from the Execs. of
James Douglass, dec'd, in Campbell Co., Va., in April.
WB D 96, 3 Jun 1842. Sett. by Execs.; paid James Douglass for two
trips to Campbell Co., Va.; paid Wm. L. and Lettice Bolding for
the benefit of Robert and Elizabeth Douglass while sick.

DOWING, CHARLES
CR4 372, 2 Jul 1838. Appropriation of $5 to John McCartney acting
as Coroner in the case of the dead body of Charles Dowing a part
Cherokee as supposed.

DUCKWORTH, JOHN
CR5 1, 6 Sep 1841. Thos. Duckworth app. Adm.
WB D 56, 13 Sep 1841. Comm. Oliver Dodson, James M. Hemphill, and
James Gaut set apart year's support to widow Ann.
WB D 65-67, 3 Jan 1842 and 169, 23 Nov 1843. Invt. of sale and
sett. by Adm.

DUCKWORTH, MARY
CR8 150, 6 Apr 1863. Henry Sloop paid for taking care of Mary
Duckworth, dec'd, a pauper.

DUCKWORTH, THOMAS N.
WB G 162, 28 Mar 1866. Sale by W.A. Duckworth, Adm.
WB G 163, no date. Comm. Wm. S. Edgeman, Andrew McRoberts, and
Wm. Dorsey set apart year's support for widow and family.
CR9 265, 6 May 1867. Mary Duckworth widow of Thos. N. who died
7 Jan 1866. Wm. A. Duckworth, Henry and Mary C. Eblin are only
heirs.
CC 135, filed 23 Jul 1867. Wm. A. Duckworth and Mary C. now Mary
C. Eblin are children by former wife. Widow Mary has dau. Eliza,
wife of Wm. Reynolds.

DUGAN, G.C.
CC 119, filed 12 Apr 1867. John C. McMahan VS Allen Ware, W.A.
Dugan, G.C. Dugan, and Jessee Wilson. Defendant G.C. Dugan dies
during lawsuit by 1868.

DUGGER, DANIEL D.
WB F 437-438, Will exec. 25 Aug 1861, proven Jul 1862; to wife
Matilda, land where I live in Buckhorn Valley, McMinn Co., until
youngest child comes of age; to son Joseph Alex Dugger "and any
other male child my said wife may be delivered of during my Life
or after my death if it Shall appear that it is my Child"; to
daus. Sarah Jane Mary Elizabeth Martha Ann Celia Catharine and
Isabella /no punctuation/; to son Daniel Dugger. Exec: wife.
Wit: James Guffey, C.V. Orten, J.B. Williams.
CR9 113, 5 Mar 1866. John Orton and M.G. McNabb released as
Securities for Mrs. Matilda Reed (formerly Matilda Dugger, wife
of Daniel D. Dugger, dec'd) as Execx. of sd. Dugger.

DUNN, JOSEPH
CR5 305, 7 Sep 1846. Nancy Dunn app. Gdn. to Wm. E. Dunn, minor
heir.

DYER, JOHN
WB E 70, 3 Dec 1849. Comm. James Small, Bogan Cash, and Wm. L.
Pearson set apart year's support to widow Charity and family.
WB E 72, 7 Jan 1850; 80, 18 Jan 1850; 152, 27 Mar 1851. Invt.,
Sale, and Sett. by Sterling L. Turner, Adm.

EATON, WILLIAM
  CR5 198, 2 Dec 1844. Henry Walker app. Adm.
  WB D 243, 17 Dec 1844. Comm. Chas. Staples, Wm. Grubb, and John
  McDonald set apart year's support for widow Jane and family.
  WB D 243, Jan 1845. Invt. of sale by Adm.
  WB D 421, 7 Dec 1846. James C. Carlock, Clk., makes pro rata sett.
  between Adm. and creditors.

EBLIN
  CR1 427, 6 Mar 1829. Wm. and John Eblin, Execs. VS Reubin White.

EDDINGTON, JAMES H.
  CR5 194, 7 Oct 1844. M.C. Hawk, Richard Settles, and C.P. Owens
  app. Comm. to lay off year's support for widow Fanny.

EDGEMAN, THOMAS
  WB F 373, 14 Aug 1860. Comm. Robt. N. McEwen, Andrew Hutsell, and
  John Crews set apart year's support for widow and family.
  WB F 376-377, no date. Sale by Wm. S. Edgeman, Adm.
  CC 290, filed 8 Jul 1861. Original suit dismissed in Feb 1865
  under the general rule dismissing all causes instituted while
  the State ignored her relations to the general Government. Suit
  reinstated 1869. Thomas Edgeman died 14 Jul 1860 leaving widow
  Nancy and children, to wit, William E. of Roane Co.; Margaret
  wife of Aaron Matthews; Thomas; Simeon; Gideon of unsound mind;
  John; George, dec'd, whose children are Margaret and Thomas;
  Mary Woolsey, dec'd, whose children are James, Margaret, and
  Thomas A. Woolsey; Catharine Sparks, dec'd, whose children are
  Samuel J., Susan, Martha, Jane, Thomas N., James, Talitha G.,
  and John E. Sparks, all minors of Ark.; and Philemon Edgeman of
  Ark.
  CR10 257, 5 Dec 1870. J.T. Lane resigns as Gdn. as heirs are all
  of lawful age.

EDWARD, DEBBY
  CR4 274, 4 Jul 1836. James Hays app. Adm.
  WB B 198, Sep 1836. Invt. by Adm.
  CR4 329, 4 Sep 1837. Jesse H. Benton app. Gdn. to Lindsey Edward,
  minor.

EDWARDS, S.J.
  CR14 57, 13 Apr 1867. W.M. Edwards Adm. VS M.A. Cass and F.M.
  Rowan, Adms. of Eli Dixon.

ELDER, JAMES
  WB G 203, 22 Sep 1866. Invt. and sale by R.A. McAdoo, Adm.
  WB G 208, Sep 1866. Comm. S.S. Morgan, Stephen Hill, and Silas
  Mynatt lay off year's support for widow and family.
  WB G 215, 17 Aug 1867. Sett. and sale by Adm.
  CR9 292, 319, 325, 337, Aug to Nov 1867. Petition for sale of
  land. R.A. McAdoo and S.W. Royston, Adms. VS Nancy Stephenson,
  Mary Dennis, Jacob, John, Daniel, Sarah W., Robert, Mark, Lou,
  and Crayton Elder, the last seven being minors. Mary Elder app.
  Gdn. of Craton Elder her own minor son. Elizia C. Elder app.
  Gdn. of Daniel, John, Sarah, Robert, Loutisia and Mark Elder,
  her own minor heirs.
  CR11 174, 14 Dec 1869. Sett. by Adm.; payments of various amounts
  to the following unidentified persons: Eliza C., Mary, Jacob,
  J.F., and James Elder, Wm. Stephenson and wife, M. Denis and

wife, Eliza C. Elder as Gdn., James Stephenson and wife, James Denis, M. Dennis, and Mary Elder as Gdn.

ELDER, ROBERT
CR9 442, 4 May 1868. Thomas Caldwell app. Adm.
CR9 448, 1 Jun 1868. Petition of Jacob Elder, bro. of Robert who died about 20 Aug 1863 leaving widow Eliza and children Daniel, John Franklin, Sarah Wills, Robert, Mark, and Luticia Elder, all minors with mother Eliza as Gdn.

ELDRIDGE, BENJAMIN
CR14 319, 13 Dec 1867. The death is suggested and proven in Court.
CR9 352, 6 Jan 1868. John T. Jones and John H. Eldridge app. Adms.
CR9 435, 6 Apr 1868. R.J. Patty app. Gdn. of Tennessee and Martha Eldridge, minor heirs.
CR9 441, 4 May 1868. Comm. app. to lay off year's support for widow.

ELDRIDGE, JAMES
CR9 52, 5 Jun 1865. Wm. L. McKnight app. Gdn. of minor heirs.

ELDRIDGE, MALISA M.
CR10 89, 1 Feb 1869. Sett. by W.S. McKnight, Gdn. to Eliza M., Mary, and Wm. M. Eldridge, minor heirs.

ELDRIDGE, SIMEON
CR6, 7 Jul 1851. A paper purporting to be the last Will is presented and Thomas Eldridge makes objection; referred to Circuit Court.
CR6, 1 Sep 1851. Thomas J. Russell having been nominated Exec. in the Will, declines to serve.
CR12 15, 17 Apr 1852. Contested Will: Thomas Russell, Exec. VS Thomas Eldridge, John and Simeon Browder, and others. Jury finds for the Plaintiff, that the paper purporting to be the last Will is the last Will; all papers including the original Will to be sent back to County Court; p. 17, defendants are refused new trial and they appeal to Supreme Court.
CR6, 5 Nov 1855. Wm. H. Ballew and Wm. L. Rice app. Adms.; Supreme Court of Tenn. ruled Sep 1855 that Will was not legal.
WB E 489-491, 4 Feb 1856. Acct. of sale by Adms.; cash belonging to estate handed over by Benjamin Eldridge.
WB F 297, 3 Nov 1859. Add. Invt. arising from hire of slaves which were in hands of John Jones and John Eldridge of Roane Co. and which came to hands of Adms. by order of Chancery Court at Cleveland.
WB F 337, no date. Add. Invt.

ELKINS, JOHN
CR2 430, 2 Mar 1830. Daniel Newman app. Adm.
WB A 209. Invt. Jun 1830 by Adm.; "negro woman Mima who has been taken off by John Cam____ who married the widow Elkins as well as every other article of property".

ELLIS, EZEKIEL
CR10 138, 6 Sep 1869. E.Z. Williams, R.A. and M.L. Ellis app. Adms.; widow requests dower and year's support.
CR10 140, 4 Oct 1869. Dower to widow Margaret.
CR10 436, Dec 1872. R.A. Ellis et al VS James H. Ellis et al. Defendants James H., John R., Ezekiel A., George W., Jerry, Jr., and William Ellis, Margaret J. and John Gardner, John T. Williams

N.J. and J.M. Forrest are all nonresidents of Tenn.; p. 440, Jan
1873: defendants William and Jerry Ellis, Jr., John E., Robert
B., Margaret E., and John T. Williams are minors; John E.,
Robert B., and Margaret E. Williams are of McMinn Co.; p. 442:
David Tunnell and wife Sarah are also defendants.
CR11 327, 29 May 1875. Sett. by Adms.; receipts as follows: D.H.
and Sarah T. Tunnell for ½ share, M.A. Woolsey for 3 shares,
J.M. and Nancy Forrest for 1 share, R.A. Ellis for 4 shares,
M.L. Ellis for 2 shares, E.Z. Williams Gdn. for 1 share, R.A.
Ellis by Power of Atty. for Jno. T. Williams and _____ Ellis,
R.A. Ellis by Power of Atty. for J.R., J.H., G.W., and Jeremiah
B. Ellis, Jno. M. and Margaret ____iner and Ezekiel A. Ellis.

ELSOM, ELIZABETH
CR5 534, 2 Jul 1849. R.A. McAdoo paid for taking care of Elizabeth
Elsom a pauper four weeks and for furnishing coffin and funeral
expenses.

EMBERSON, ALLEN
CR4 550, 5 Jul 1841. Court pays for coffin and shroud to bury
Allen Emberson, who was poor.

EMERSON
CR9 62, 7 Aug 1865. Sarah E. Emerson app. Gdn. of Wm. Henry Emerson.

EMMETT, GEORGE W.
CR5 310, 5 Oct 1846. Daniel Casteel app. Adm.
WB D 404, 7 Dec 1846. Invt. by Adm.

ERWIN, ISAAC
CC 239, filed 22 Apr 1870. Isaac Erwin died during late war in
Miss. leaving widow Ann and one child, Isaac R. Erwin, Jr., a
minor. Wm. B. Erwin is bro. to the dec'd.

ERWIN, WILLIAM
CR10 154, 6 Dec 1869. Simeon Graves and Samuel Perrin with E.L.
Miller, County Surveyor, to lay off dower to widow Elizabeth.
CR10 170, 7 Feb 1870. Elizabeth Erwin widow VS Heirs; report of
above Comm.; plat of land included.

ESSMAN, THOMAS
CR2 47, 10 Dec 1824. John Essman app. Adm. and files Invt.

ETTER, F.W.
WB F 156, Will exec. 20 Oct 1857, proven Mar 1858; all estate to
wife Sarah Ann and "Ediot" dau. Elizabeth, and at their death to
be equally divided among the legal heirs. Execs: sons Valentine,
George W., and Lemuel. Wit: Jess Dodson, John Swafford, and
Jas. Parkerson.
CR9 64, 7 Aug 1865. Lemuel Etter app. Gdn. of Sarah E. Etter.

ETTER, VALENTINE
CR9 279, 1 Jul 1867. Report by Lemuel Etter, Gdn. of minor heirs.

EVANS, SAMUEL, SR.
CR6, 3 Nov 1851. Samuel Snoddy app. Adm.
WB E 203, 5 Jan 1852 and 382, 15 May 1854. Invt. and final sett.
by Adm.
CR6, 5 Mar 1855. Samuel Evans app. Adm.; West B. Mizell and Samuel
Mizell make statement that Samuel Evans, dec'd, late a Revolution-
ary Pensioner of the U.S. at rate of $96 per annum, died 26 Aug

1851 in McMinn Co., Tenn., leaving following children surviving him to wit Samuel Evans, Harris Evans, Nancy Mizell, Esther Davis.

EVERTON, ALEXANDER
CR9 64, 7 Aug 1865. V.H. Jack app. Adm.
WB G 107, 13 Sep 1865. Comm. Elihu Kelley, Chas. Daugherty, and B.E. Cass lay off year's support for widow Caroline and family.
WB G 109, 29 Sep 1865. Invt. by Adm.
CR13 429, 15 Dec 1865. Vincent H. Jack Adm. VS Caroline Everton widow, Mary H., Thomas K., Elizabeth R., John H., Martha A., and James C. Everton, minor heirs; petition to sell land.

FAIN
CR10 117, 7 Jun 1869. Jane Fain app. Gdn. of her own minor heirs.

FELKER, MRS.
CR5 52, 4 Jul 1842. Joseph Sallee paid for making coffin in year 1839.

FENDER, MICHAEL
CR14 493, 12 Aug 1868. Charly Owen, Adm. VS Benjamin and M.G. Hensley; Debt; filed 1 Nov 1867.

FENELL, JAMES B.
CR5 549, 1 Oct 1849. Ann Fenell, widow of James B. Fenell, one of the Securities of Nelson and Polly Lawson, Adms. of Isom Lawson, dec'd, and Geo. W. Fenell, Adm. and Adminx. of James B. Fenell, dec'd, petition Court to require the Lawsons to give other security.

FIELD (FIELDS), JOSEPH
WB B 118-119, Will exec. 15 Jan 1833; to wife Letta; to sons Joel, Thomas, and John; to dau. Souehama. Execs: sons Beeson and John. Wit: John Foster, Wm. Dotson.
CR4 135, 4 Mar 1833 and 159, 3 Jun 1833. Will proven.
WB B 156, 5 Dec 1834. Invt. of sale.
WB B 178, 27 May 1835. Execs. make sett. with Comm. John Foster, Wm. Dotson, and Hartwell Ivey.

FIRESTONE, EVE
WB A 172, Will exec. 1 Sep 1828; all estate to son Matthias; daus. Eve Calfleash, Kitty Long, Mary Rice, Susannah Dingledine, Elizabeth Lamparter otherwise Elizabeth Johns, and sons Nicholas and John to receive nothing. Exec: son Matthias. Wit: Saml. McConnel, G. Cantrell. Signed by mark.
CR2 369, 2 Jun 1829. Will proven.

FIRESTONE, MATHIAS
WB E 89, Will exec. 21 Apr 1850; to wife Polly; two children Mary Ann and Mathias to be sent to school; to sons William, Samuel, John, and David; to rest of heirs, Alfred Firestone, James Douglass and wife Elizabeth, and the heirs of Joseph and Sarah Cobb (who are Martha, David, Mary, and Sarah); the Execs. to build house at Winton Spring for widow and my two children. Execs: son Samuel and E.P. Bloom. Wit: Uriel Johnston, Saml. Patterson.
WB E 104-106, 16 May 1850; 143, 6 Jan 1851; 223, 29 Mar 1852. Acct. of sales and Sett. by Execs.
WB E 224, 29 Mar 1852. Sett. by James C. Firestone, Gdn.; has

placed the two children in care of Saml. Firestone for last two
years.
WB E 309, 9 Feb 1853; 347, 17 Dec 1853; WB F 31, 28 Nov 1856; 242,
28 Nov 1858. Sett. by Execs., by Gdn., and by Samuel Firestone,
present Gdn.
WB F 255, 4 Jan 1859 and 321, 10 Apr 1860. Sett. by D.A. Cobbs,
Special Comm. app. Apr 1853 to receive purchase money and col-
lect the notes exec. by Saml. Firestone for the purchase of
lands belonging to estate.
WB F 322, 3 May 1860. Sett. by same Gdn.
CC 183, filed 2 Oct 1868. Matthias Firestone died leaving second
wife Polly who died 26 May 1850 and their children Mary Ann and
Matthias, Jr., and following children by former wife: Samuel,
John of Ark., William of Ala., Alfred of Ga., Elizabeth wife of
James Douglass of Mo., and Sarah dec'd wife of Joseph Cobb.
Dau. Mary Ann, wife of John Cross of Washington Co., Ark., married first Archibald Miles Benton, bro. of John Benton. Son
Matthias, Jr., was killed about 1862 at age 18. Son Samuel has
died recently leaving children: J.C. of Ala., Persha or Portia
wife of Thomas Martin, Mary wife of Jesse Givens of Ga., Telitha
wife of John Brandon of Ga., Sarah wife of Jesse Purdy of Texas,
Permilia wife of James Peal of Ga., and S. Polk residence unknown. The children of dau. Sarah Cobb, dec'd, are Martha wife
of Joseph Ware dec'd, David dec'd without issue, Mary wife of
John G. Mayfield of Polk Co., and Sarah Cobb.

FIRESTONE, SAMUEL
CR10 58, 5 Oct 1868. James A. Smith app. Adm.
CR11 71, 22 Feb 1869. Adm. reports that nothing has ever come
into his hands.
See also MATHIAS FIRESTONE.

FIRESTONE, WILLIAM
CR4 249, 8 Mar 1836. Sarah Firestone app. Gdn. to Mathias, Nancy,
and Sarah Ann Firestone.
WB B 247, Apr 1837; WB C 147, 8 Apr 1839; 312, Dec 1840; WB D 70,
8 Apr 1842; 290, 16 Jun 1845; 383, 16 Jun 1846; and 484, 16 Jun
1847. Sett. by Gdn.
CR5 389, 6 Dec 1847. Gdn. states that two of her children have
arrived at full age and live in Ala.; enters into bond as Gdn.
to Sarah Ann.

FISHER, CHRISTIAN
CR5 447 and 448, 1 May 1848. Mordicia Rucker app. Adm. James E.
Rucker, Allen Dennis, and James C. Bryan app. Comm. to lay off
year's support for widow Mary /sic/.
CR5 452, 5 Jun 1848. Above order rescinded and Comm. notified.
WB D 550, 7 Aug 1848. Invt. by Mordacia Rucker.
CC 59, filed 8 Sep 1848. In 1839 Christian Fisher, a foreigner,
had just come to this country and could scarcely speak a word in
English. He left papers written in German. He died in 184 /sic/
leaving widow Rebecca who has since married Charles Wincher and
minor children Margaret, Elizabeth, and John Henry Fisher.

FISHER, EMANUEL
CR9 160, 7 May 1866. Jacob P. Bryant app. Adm.

FITE, PETER
CR5 137, 1 Jan 1844. David Cantrell and Peter Fite, executors

named in a paper purporting to be the last Will of Peter Fite, dec'd, offer said paper for probate; Came Elias Fite and Lewis Pearce, two of the heirs at law, enter their dissent; all further proceedings continued until next session of Court; David Cantrell and Elias P. Bloom app. Adms. pendente lite.

WB D 193-197, 1 Apr 1844 and 355, 11 Feb 1846. Report of sale and Sett. by E.P. Bloom, one of Adms.

WB D 464, 11 Feb 1847. Sett.; receipts of heirs Henry, Peter, Jacob, and Elias Fite, Lewis Pierce, John Simpson, and John Murrah, all equal amounts.

CC 172, filed 7 Dec 1852. Peter Fite left heirs, viz: Henry of McMinn Co.; Christine Pierce and husband of Bradley Co.; Jacob residence unknown; Mary Murray and husband of Ill.; Peter of Ga.; Rachel Simpson and husband of McMinn Co.; and Elias Fite of Ill.

FLINN, WILLIAM
CR4 453, 5 Aug 1839. Kennedy Lonigan app. Adm.

FLOYD, ELIZABETH
CR5 294, 6 Jul 1846. Court pays for coffin for pauper.

FORBANK, JAMES
CR7 319, 4 Jul 1859. Jury of inquest reports that James Forbank being alone on 27 Jun 1859 did hang himself.

FORBES, ALEXANDER
CR2 263, 3 Mar 1828. James Forbes app. Adm.
WB A 140-141 and 147-148, no date and no signatures. Invt. and Sett. Names listed include Thomas, James, and Sarah Forbes.

FORE, A.P.
WB C 263-265, Will exec. 4 May 1839, recorded Sep Session 1840; to wife Nancy; to dau. Sarah Ann Penelope, a minor. Execs: much esteemed friends W.P.H. McDermott and Dr. Wm. H. Deadrick. Wit: Penelope E. Irvine, Robert T. Rentfroe.
CR4 506, 3 Aug 1840 and 511, 7 Sep 1840. Will proven.
CR4 512, 8 Sep 1840. Execs. refuse to serve and widow Nancy app. Adminx.
WB C 276-278, 5 Oct 1840. Invt.

FORE, NANCY
CR7 210, 6 Jul 1858. A.H. Keith app. Adm.
CC 46, filed 18 Jan 1859. Mrs. Nancy Fore died 21 Jun 1858.
See also PENELOPE IRWIN.

FORREST, JAMES
CC 253, filed 9 Aug 1870. James Forrest died 1869-70, before Bill filed, leaving heirs Alburtus, John M., and Wm. H.
CR10 253, 7 Nov 1870. A. Forrest app. Adm. of Wm. Yearwood in place of James Forrest, dec'd.

FOSTER, ANDREW
WB F 154, 9 Jan 1858. Comm. Thomas Prigmore, Heil Buttram, and A.D. Brient set apart year's support for widow Elizabeth.
WB F 166-168, 5 Apr 1858; 246, 3 Jan 1859; 318, 24 Mar 1860; 328, 24 Mar 1860; 418, 24 Mar 1861; 442, 24 Mar 1862; WB G 182, 1 Aug 1866. Invt. and Sale and Sett. by Wm. Foster, Adm., and Sett. by Wm. and Bettie Foster, Gdns.
CR7 158, 5 Apr 1858. Wm. and Bettie Foster, Gdns. to John H.C.,

Mary, Alvis, William J.F., Nancy E., and Margaret F. Foster, minor orphans.

FOSTER, SIMPSON W.
  CR8 134, 2 Feb 1863. Wm. H. Bryant app. Gdn. for minor heirs, to wit, Susan Jane, Mary Minerva, Margaret Virginia, Tennessee Caroline, Catharine Callafornia, Nancy Elizabeth, and Artey Simpson Foster. Wm. S. Foster of Polk Co., Tenn., app. Adm.
  CR8 149, 6 Apr 1863. W.D. Prather and Henry Sloop with County Surveyor allot dower in lands to widow Amanda.

FOSTER, THOMAS
  CR5 325, 7 Dec 1846. Listed as dead in Tax Delinquents for 1846.

FOX, ABRAHAM, SR.
  CC 89, filed 25 Sep 1866. Abraham Fox, Sr., died intestate leaving children: Anderson of Mo.; Nancy wife of Thompson Sanders of Ky.; Sarah McCormack; Mary wife of George Scott; Amanda wife of Daniel White of Ga.; Jacob; Abraham, Jr.; Elizabeth Coe; and Irelle Fox. Son Jacob has died since father died leaving children Williamson, David, and Rebecca dec'd wife of Martin Gold, dec'd, whose children are Wm. and Parilee Gold of Bradley Co. Son Abraham, Jr., has died since father died leaving widow Caroline and children, Malinda wife of Asa J. Howell, Josephine wife of Ransom Wammack, Caroline, John, and Samuel, minors. Dau. Elizabeth has died since father died leaving children, Wesley and Wm. Coe minors of Polk Co. Son Irelle has died since his father died leaving children, Levi, Mary Caroline, and Nancy Ann, minors of Roane Co.

FOX, JACOB
  WB C 51, 1 Oct 1838. Report by John McCartney and Abram Fox, Gdns. for Rebecca and Louisa Fox, minor heirs. Widow is entitled to dower in land.

FRANKLIN, BENJAMIN
  WB E 434, 7 Jul 1855. Comm. D.W. Prather, Wm. Burk, and D.D. Davis lay off year's support for widow Nancy.
  WB F 441, 14 Aug 1855 and 169-171, 9 Apr 1858. Invt. of sale and Sett. by Moses Sweeney, Adm.
  CC 262, filed 5 Dec 1856. (This file contains copy of Will of Robt. Franklin exec. 19 Apr 1825 and probated 11 Jul 1831 in Campbell Co., Va.) Benjamin Franklin, son of Robert, died in McMinn Co. in May 1855 leaving widow Nancy and children: Jane, Lucy who married Joseph H. Walker, Martha Susan who married Wm. H. Staples, Mary dec'd wife of John Hughes, and John R. Franklin, a minor. The children of Mary Franklin Hughes, dec'd, are Elizabeth wife of Isaac Pearce and minors Nancy, James, Martha, John, Jr., all of Bradley Co. Benjamin Franklin moved from Campbell Co., Va., to McMinn Co. bringing with him his idiot bro. Robert who is now living with the widow.

FRANKLIN, DAVID
  CR5 203, 3 Dec 1844. Listed as dead in Tax Delinquents for 1844.

FRANKLIN, EDMUND (EDWARD)
  CR4 31, 7 Sep 1831. James Wilson app. Adm.
  WB D 31, 7 Jul 1841. Invt. of sale held Oct 1831 by Adm.; buyers include Elizabeth Franklin; vouchers for years 1832-1835 against heirs, not named.

GAMBLE, WILLIAM P.
    CR5 382, 4 Oct 1847. Saml. H. Jordan app. Adm.

GARRISON (GARISON), ROBERT
    WB G 191, Will exec. 17 Oct 1865; to wife Rachel; to dau. Ollif
    Brandon; to Nancy Garison, wife of J.S. Garrison; to J.S. and
    Elizabeth Garrison. Exec: J.S. Garrison. Wit: A.D. Bryant,
    M.L. Wallis. Signed by mark.
    CR9 173, 6 Aug 1866. Will proven.

GASTON, JOSEPH
    CC 161, filed 5 Jul 1852. Joseph Gaston died 29 Jul 1851 leaving
    six children: Mitchell, Wesley, Josiah D., Sarah M., John of
    Ky., and Elizabeth who has married Wm. Smith of Hamilton Co.

GAULLING or GAULLENY, JOHN
    CR2 92, 5 Sep 1825. Daniel Kelly app. Adm.

GEORGE, WILLIAM
    CR9 90, 6 Nov 1865. P.H. George app. Adm.
    WB G 129, 4 Dec 1865. Invt. by Powell H. George, Adm.
    WB G 195, 31 Aug 1866. Comm. Wm. H. Howard, Wm. G. Horton, and
    A.H. Crow lay off year's support for widow and family.
    WB G 209, no date. Invt. by same Adm.; Mary George widow.

GIBBS, WILLIAM
    CR2 291, 2 Jun 1828. Ordered that the allowance heretofore made
    to Wm. Gibbs for support of two orphan children of Susannah
    Collins, dec'd, be paid to the widow of said Gibbs.

GIBSON
    CR10 257, 5 Dec 1870. T.F. Gibson app. Gdn. of his own minor
    heir Susan Gibson.

GIBSON, GEORGE
    CR8 139 and 142, 2 Mar 1863. C.F. Gibson app. Adm.; Plumly
    McGrew, E.Z. Williams, and John Scarborough app. Comm. to lay off
    year's support for widow and family.
    CC 122, filed 29 Apr 1863; 11, filed 20 Feb 1865; 261, filed 10 Sep
    1870. George Gibson started to Ky. to escape Rebel Conscription,
    was captured, and died in a hospital in Knoxville in Spring of
    1863. He left widow Barbara and three minor children, Elias,
    Timothy, and Charles. Charles F. and Joseph W. Gibson are bros.
    to George, dec'd. By May 1868 widow Barbary B. has married Wm.
    Crittenden.

GIBSON, JOHN
    WB D 134, 8 Mar 1843. Comm. Charles P. Owen, M.C. Hawk, and B.
    Brock lay off year's support for widow Rebecca.

GIBSON, LOUISA P.
    CR10 213, 6 Jun 1870. E.P. Gibson app. Adm.

GIE, SAMUEL
    CR15 217, 15 Dec 1869. W.L. Dodson VS Elizabeth Gie, Adminx. De
    Son Tort. Debt. Summons issued 17 Nov 1868.

GILBREATH (GALBREATH), JOSEPH
    CR2 243 and 244, 3 Dec 1827. Thomas Galbreath app. Gdn. of Eliza-
    beth, Mary, James, Sarah, Margaret, Samuel, and Joseph Galbreath,
    orphan minor heirs. Wm. Gilbreath app. Adm. Robert W. McCleary,
    Joseph Cobbs, and Wm. Phillips app. Comm. to lay off year's

support for widow Elizabeth

WB A 113, no date. Invt. by Adm.; one item is due from estate of John Gilbreath.

WB A 126-128, 6 Mar 1828. Acct. of sale.

CR2 384, 7 Sep 1829. Widow Elizabeth is app. Gdn. of her own minor children, James, Sarah Jane, Samuel L., and Joseph.

CR2 442, 5 Mar 1830. Petition. Joseph Gilbreath died 15 Sep 1827. Thomas Gilbreath, Gdn. to Mary, Elizabeth, and Peggy Ann, minor heirs.

WB B 72-74, Dec 1831. Report by Thomas Gilbreath, Gdn.

WB B 140, 3 Mar 1834. Sett.; Comm. Robt. W. McClary, D.A. and John Cobbs settle with Wm Gilbreath, Adm.; paid to Elizabeth for herself and as Gdn.; paid Hugh Reevely as Gdn. for Peggy Ann, a minor.

WB B 169, 2 Mar 1835 and 182, 7 Mar 1836. Reports by Hugh Reavely, Gdn.

WB B 236, 6 Mar 1837. Report by Hugh Reavely, Gdn. "to the Estate of Peggy Ann Gilbreath".

WB B 249, May Court 1837. Report by Elizabeth Gilbreath, Gdn. to her children James L., Sarah J., Samuel, and Joseph Gilbreath, minor heirs. She has in her possession five young negroes in which said minors have four sevenths undivided interest.

GILLY, SAMUEL

CR6, 2 Apr 1855. Coroner's jury rules that death came on 24 Nov 1854 by voluntarily hanging himself.

GIVINS, JOHN W.

CR6, 4 Feb 1856. W.L. Lafferty app. Adm.

WB E 511-514, 23 Feb 1856. Invt., Accts. Due, and Acct. of Sale by Adm. of estate of Dr. John W. Givins.

GLAZE (GLASE), HENRY

CR4 338, 7 Nov 1837. William Cate and George W. Martin app. Adms.

CR4 340, 4 Dec 1837. Russell Lane, Philip Fry, and Elijah Hurst app. Comm. to lay off year's support for widow Susan.

WB B 274, Jan 1838 and 290, Feb 1838. Invt. and Sale by Adms.; buyers include Susan, Henry, and John Glaze.

WB C 305-307, no date. Sett.

GODARD

CR7 194, 5 Jul 1858. Hugh Godard app. Gdn. to Mary E., S.J., Jas. B., and F.P. Goddard, his own minor children.

GOODWIN, WILLIAM

CR8, 6 Jul 1863. Court pays Daniel Horton for boarding deceased in case of small pox and Philip Neat for digging grave.

GRAHAM, ANSON B.

CC 69, filed 17 Dec 1859. Gibson VS Deaderick. Anson B. Graham was a citizen of McMinn Co. 15 Dec 1856 and is now deceased.

GRAHAM, JOHN

CR5 28, 7 Feb 1842. Pleasant Crew app. Adm.

WB D 57-60, 2 May 1842. Invt. of sale by Adm.; notes on David R. Graham.

GRANT, ISAAC G.

CR15 42, 17 Dec 1868. W.R. Grubb VS R.H. Abbott, Adm. of Isaac G. Grant.

GRAVES, CHRISTOPHER
  WB C 66, 5 Nov 1838 and 102-105, Jan 1839. Invt. and Sale by Union
    Graves, Adm.
  WB D 449, 8 Apr 1847. Sett. by same Adm.
  CC 245, filed 16 Apr 1856. Christopher Graves died leaving widow
    Nancy who is still living.
  CC 169, filed 20 Apr 1868. Christopher Graves died in the fall of
    1838 leaving the following children: Union; Simeon who dies dur-
    ing the lawsuit (1871); Vilena who married at age 23 to Jacob
    Sharp; Jacob, dec'd, without wife or child; Lucinda married to
    Wm. Smart of Ark.; Christopher; Elizabeth married to Isaac Smart;
    and Nancy married to John McInturf.

GRAVES, ELIZA
  CC 2, filed 7 Dec 1866; CC 37, filed 28 Jan 1869; CC 342, filed 7
    Sep 1872. Eliza, dau. of James Shelton of Bradley Co., widow of
    Edward Sharp who died in Bradley Co. in 1847, and wife of Simeon
    Graves, died leaving husband Simeon Graves and children: Nancy
    age 15, Elizabeth age 13, Cindy age 11, Lewis age 9, Daniel age
    7, Catherine age 5, Vilena age 4, and Simeon age 1 (all ages in
    Dec 1866). Eliza and first husband Edward Sharp had two chil-
    dren, Napoleon and Edward, Jr., who both died in Bradley Co.,
    intestate, and unmarried, in 1864. /Dau. Nancy is not in the
    list of children in CC 37./

GRAVES, HENRY M.
  CR6, 7 Apr 1851. Joseph B. Fitzgerald app. Gdn. for Thomas,
    Alvira, Sarah, and Clementine Graves.
  WB E 225; Gdn. Sett.; Sparta, 9 Dec 1851: G.G. Dibrell Clerk of
    White Co. Court certifies that D. and T. Snodgrass, Execs.
    paid to the Gdn. for the minor heirs.
  WB E 273, 18 Sep 1852. Sett. by Gdn.
  WB E 362, 18 Sep 1853. Sett. by Gdn.; receipt of heir J.T. Graves
    for amount which appears to be his final share; paid for school-
    ing for P.C. Graves; paid for Alvina Graves.

GRAVES, WILLIAM
  WB D 368, 7 May 1846. Comm. A. Slover, J. McGaughy, and John Craw-
    ford set apart year's support for widow Margaret A.C. and family.
  WB D 379-383, 6 Jul 1846; E 49, 1 Jun 1849; 271, no date. Invt.
    and sale held 1 and 6 Jun 1846, sett., and final sett. by widow
    and A.D. Keys, Adms.
  CR6, 2 Feb 1852. Donald M. Hood of Cass Co., Ga., app. Gdn. for
    minor heirs, Clara C. and George A. Graves, and receives permis-
    sion of Court to remove slaves to Ga.
  CR6, 4 Oct 1852. Petition: Donald M. Hood, a citizen of Gordon
    Co., Ga., states that sometime in 1845 Wm. Graves died leaving
    Margaret A. his widow and Clarissa C. and George Arthur Graves
    as his minor children, that the estate was settled according to
    law, that said widow has since intermarried with Moses Cunning-
    ham, and that a plot of ground in Athens reserved as a home for
    widow and minors was no longer needed as such. Hood, the Peti-
    tioner, is an uncle of said minors.
  WB E 285, 6 Dec 1852. Comm. Moses Cunningham, appointed by County
    Court, sells house and lot in Athens belonging to estate.
  WB F 280, 24 Aug 1859. Sett. by Jas. T. Lane, Gdn. of the two
    minors; paid expenses of four trips to Cassville, Ga.
  WB F 360, 3 Sep 1860; 414, 3 Sep 1861. Sett. by same Gdn.

WB F 416, 21 Mar 1861. Sett. by Moses Cunningham, Comm. to sell lots; paid Margaret Cunningham her interest.

GRAVES, WILLIAM
CR7 465, 4 Sep 1860. Jas S. Russell app. Adm. /Note: This deceased and the preceding one may be the same person.7

GREEN, B.F.
CR9 238, 4 Feb 1867. Amanda J. Green app. Adminx.

GREEN, CLARICY
CR10 130, 2 Aug 1869. Robt. Johnson app. Adm.
CR10 149, 1 Nov 1869. Report by Robert Johnson (Colored) Gdn. of minor heirs.

GREEN, GEORGE W.
CR9 15, 3 Oct 1864. Phebe Green app. Gdn. of Wm. Green, minor heir.

GREEN, JAMES S.
CR7 42, 6 Jul 1857. Josephine M. and John P. Green, minors over 14, choose John W. Hoyl as Gdn. and he is app. Gdn. to Samuel A., Mary O., David H., Andrew F., and Parthenia M. Green who are under 14.
WB F 186, 5 Jul 1858; 271, 5 Jul 1859; 331, 5 Jul 1860. Sett. by Gdn.
WB F 473, 3 Jul 1861. Sett. by same, Gdn. to Josephine M. Green who has married Isaac Lowry, John P., A.F., Mary, David H., and Parthence M. Green.
WB F 473, 5 Oct 1862. Sett. by Gdn.; Court allows sum to Gdn. for services and he gives same to wards; balance paid over to J.C. Carlock, Thos. J. Russell, and C.R. Hoyl, Gdns. appointed in his stead.
CR8, 6 Oct 1862. Petition to resign guardianship: John W. Hoyl, Gdn. VS John P., A.F., Mary O., David H., and Parthenia M. Green and Josephine Lowry, minor heirs. John W. Hoyl makes the following report: Settlement with John McSpadden, Adm. de bonis non of James S. Green, dec'd, of Decalb Co., Ala.; executed refunding bond for the share of Samuel A. Green, son of James S. Green, who left Ala. about 1852 or 1853 and has not been heard from since about 1854; this share of Samuel A. Green, the missing heir, is distributed to the other heirs, who execute refunding bonds.
WB G 89, 7 Aug 1865. Sett. by Thomas J. Russell, Gdn. to A.F. and Parthenia M. Green.
WB G 141, 5 Jan 1866. Sett. by Jas. C. Carlock, Gdn. to Mary O. and David H. Green; Mary O. receives half of funds.
CR9 384, 6 Apr 1868. Sett. by James C. Carlock, Gdn. to David H. Green.
CR10 277, 3 Apr 1871. Receipt from Parthena M. wife of W.J. Curtis for her full share.
CC 253, filed 9 Aug 1870. Andrew Felix Green, son of James S. Green, dec'd, was born 25 Jul 1849. He lived with Thos. A. Russell from about 1857 to 1866 and is a nephew of Russell's wife, a nephew of Caleb R. Hoyl, and a nephew of J.C. Carlock, James S. Green's wife was a sister to J.C. Carlock's wife. Alex. Green aged 58 in 1871 is a brother to James S. Green, dec'd.

GREEN, JANE
   CR7 430, Apr 1860. Coroner's jury of inquest finds that Jane
      Green came to her death on 14 Mar 1860 by accidentally burning.
   CR8, 7 Jul 1862. Court pays for coffin for pauper.

GREEN, PHEBE
   CR10 176, 7 Mar 1870. J.M. Black and T.J. Latham app. Adms.
   CR11 269, 3 May 1873. Sett. by T.J. Latham, one of Adms.; received
      on Pension.
   CC 450, filed 26 Feb 1876. Pheba Green died 1 Mar 1870 leaving
      children: Wm. H. of Aydlotte, Benton Co., Ind.; Sarah wife of
      James Frank; Elmina wife of Silas Latham (who has son Thos. J.);
      Benjamin Franklin and Asbury who went West 20-25 years ago and
      are believed dead; Lurana (Rainy) McCall, dec'd. The children
      of dau. Lurana McCall, dec'd, are Margaret wife of Carrick
      McCain of Mo.; A. Frank McCall of Stockton, Cedar Co., Mo.;
      Mary Ann wife of Anderson McCain of Meigs Co.; Wm. McCall of
      Meigs Co.; Harriet wife of James White of Meigs Co.; Enoch
      McCall of Roane Co.; and Sarah Shahan, dec'd, wife of Taylor
      Shahan.

GREEN, ROBERT
   See SARAH BROWN

GREEN, WILLIAM JACKSON
   CR10 220, 4 Jul 1870. Liddia Green app. Adminx.
   CC 267, filed 27 Oct 1870. Wm. J. Green died in McMinn Co. 14
      Apr 1870 leaving wife Lydia and children, all minors: Mary J.,
      Nancy E., Wm. Henry, John D., Lydia J., James J., and Martha C.
      Mrs. Crabtree is aunt to children.

GREGG, NELSON
   CR10 175, 7 Mar 1870. Frank Triplett app. Adm.
   CC 265, filed 11 Oct 1870. Nelson Gregg died intestate in Indiana
      about 1865 leaving widow Elizabeth of McMinn Co. who died Sep
      1869 and children: Marsena H., Mary Frances, Alcy, Caroline,
      and James Gregg, all of McMinn Co. and last four are minors.
   CR10 359, Apr 1872. A. Slack app. Gdn. of Mary F., Alcy V., Ann
      E.C., and James Gregg and William Strange.
   CR11 276, 30 May 1873. Sett. by Adm.; receipt from Mary F. Gregg
      and A. Slack, Gdn.

GREGORY, JOHN
   CR8, 4 Nov 1861. James Gregory app. Adm.
   WB F 445, 18 Nov 1861. Comm. P.A. Bradford, Wm. P. Varnell, and
      John F. Sharp lay off year's support for widow and family.
   WB F 450, no date; WB G 169, 7 Apr 1866. Sett. by Adm.
   CR8, 3 Feb 1862. Petition to sell negroes: James Gregory Adm.
      VS Parilee Gregory, widow, and minor heirs to wit Malissa A.,
      James L., Taply J., William R., Sarah J., John H.K., and Jona-
      than (Jathan) A.

GREGORY, TAPLEY
   WB F 97, 9 Oct 1857. Comm. Mark Dennis, Tubal Zigler, and B.T.
      Zigler allow a year's provisions for widow and family.
   CR7 77, 7 Dec 1857. Eleanor Gregory VS Jonathan Gregory. The
      marriage of petitioner Eleanor Gregory with Wm. Burk is ad-
      mitted.
   WB F 105, 6 Jan 1858. Invt. and Sale by James Gregory, Adm.

WB F 291, 22 Sep 1859. Final sett. by Adm.; amount due heirs R.M.
Hambrick and wife Martha, Jesse Rucker and wife Marinda, Benjamin
Gregory, James E. and Elizabeth Rucker, Wm. B. and Sarah Erwin,
John Gregory, Jathan Gregory, Alfred and Mary Cate, Wm. and Ellen
Burk, and James Gregory.

GRIFFITH, JOHN
CR2 279, 5 Mar 1828. James Hickey app. Adm.
WB A 153, no date. Schedule of Estate, filed by Adm.; land sold
5 Mar 1829 by consent of most of the heirs; land on Waldings
ridge Bledsoe Co.; land in Marion Co.; horse taken possession of
by Benj. Griffith at death of John Griffith and taken by Wm.
Griffith Sr., father of John Griffith, dec'd, and now in possession of Wm. S. Griffith of Marion Co.

GRIGG, JOEL
WB D 291-292, Will exec. 22 Jul 1844; to wife Eunice; to children
Jesse R., Samuel, John R., Nelson, Robert W., Joseph E., Eunice,
Ann Blackwell, Sarah Harris, Mabel Queener, Martha Blackwell,
Mary Williams when she comes of age; "younger children as they
come of age". Execs: Nelson Grigg and Silvester Blackwell.
Wit: Samuel Patterson and Wm. Mulkey.
CR5 235, 2 Jun 1845. Will proven by Saml. Patterson. Handwriting
of Wm. Mulkey proven.

GRILLS, HARRIETT W.
CR6, 5 Jan 1857. Stark D. Grills VS Wm. G. Grills and others.
Judgment pro confesso entered against the following adult defend-
ants: Martha L., Margaret J., and Amanda E. Grills, and Samuel
L. Knox and wife. James Baker app. Gdn. for minor defendants.
WB F 37, 3 Mar 1857; 192, 3 Mar 1858. Sett. by M.L. Philips Gdn.
to minor heirs; paid Dr. Hall's medical bill for Sidney Grills.
CR7 292, 7 Mar 1859. Stark D. Grills VS Wm. G., Martha L., and
Margaret J. Grills, Samuel L. Knox and wife Mary E., adult heirs,
and Thomas J., Sidney L., Emeline E., Jasper E., and Dicy A.
Grills, minors.
WB F 305, 20 Dec 1859. Sett. by Gdn. to John J., S.L., Eliza E.,
Dicy, and Jos. Grills; paid one fifth of funds to Thos. J.
Grills.
WB G 105, 25 Aug 1865. Sett. by Gdn. to Thos. J., S.L., Eliza E.,
Dicy, and Joseph Grills; receipt in full from Saml. Knox, Gdn.
to Joseph A. and Emeline E. Grills for one half of funds.

GRISHAM, JAMES W.
WB F 475, Will exec. 10 Jan 1861; all estate to bro. Eligah;
"interest in Texas lands and land claims coming to the widow and
heirs of Christopher Winters Dec'd now being managed by Milton
P. Jarnagin". Exec: said brother. Wit: James H. Hornsby and
L.R. Hurst.
CR8, 4 Oct 1862. Will proven.

GRISHAM, JESSE
WB E 253-254, Will exec. 8 May 1852, proven 7 Jun 1852; all estate
to wife Mary Jane except saddle and hat to nephew Jesse Grisham.
Exec: Mary Jane Grisham. Wit: Edmund Roberts, John Ereckson.

GRISHAM, JOHN M.
CR6, 8 Apr 1856. Benjamin Wells and Thos. Grisham app. Adms.
WB E 510-511, not dated; 515-519, 2 Jun 1856; WB F 57, 6 Apr 1857.

Invt., notes and accts. due, Invt. of sale, and Add. Invt. by
Adms.
CC 242, filed 8 Apr 1856. John Grisham recently died in McMinn
Co. without legitimate issue. His bro. James W. of Troup Co.,
Ga., is entitled to one eighth of property.
CR6, 1 Dec 1856. Petition to sell land. Thos. Grisham and Benj.
Wells, Adms., and Thomas Grisham in his own right, James W.
and Eligah Grisham, Elizabeth McCrary and husband Robert, Mary
Ann Pharless and husband Samuel VS Martin Van___ Grisham, Joseph
Grisham, Jane Wyrick and husband Oscar, heirs and distributees.
WB F 251-253, 31 Dec 1858. Final sett. by Adm.

GRISHAM, THOMAS
CR2 472, 6 Sep 1830. John Grisham app. Gdn. for Meshack, John,
and James Grisham, minor orphans.

GRISHAM, WILLIAM T.
WB B 7-8, Will exec. 20 Jun 1829; to bro. Henry Hale Grisham.
Execs: father John Grisham and trusty friend John S. Wilson.
Wit: Robartis Love, Obiah Seay, Pleasant Chitwood, Robert W.
Hamilton.
CR2 484, 6 Dec 1830. Will proven.

GRUBB
CR7 112, 1 Feb 1858. Jackson Grubb app. Gdn. to Virginia, William,
Emma, John, and Frances Grubb, his own minor children.

GRUBB, ALLEN BURD
WB A 37-40, Will exec. 21 Nov 1821; "I Burd Grubb alias Allen Burd
Grubb now residing in Blount County and State of Tennessee"; to
sons Nelson Byers Grubb and Joseph Bates Grubb; Execs: friend
John McGhee of Blount Co., Tenn., Joseph Rogers and David McNair,
both residing near the River Tennessee and within bounds of
Cherokee Nation. Execs. to receive from bro. Henry Bates Grubb
interest on debt until guardians are appointed for the two sons;
house and lots in town of Calhounsville, Tennessee; amount of
Joseph Burd's bond; Joseph Burd shall not be required to pay
principle of bond except in five equal yearly installments.
Wit: Saml. Love, Math. W. McGhee, Mary M. Love. Codicil to
Will: John L. McCarty to replace David McNair as an executor.
CR2 2, 7 Jun 1824. Will proven by Saml. Love and Matthew W.
McGhee. Codicil proven by Matthew W. McGhee and Young Colville.
WB A 65-67, no date. Invt. by John L. McCarty and Joseph Rogers,
Execs.
WB A 131-135, 31 Jan 1828. Add. invt. Certified by Comm. Wm.
Smedley, James S. Bridges, Jas. G. Williams.

GRUBB, WILLIAM
WB D 349, 4 Feb 1846. Comm. C.L. King, John McDonald, and Allen
Ware lay off year's support for widow.
WB D 358-360, 2 Mar 1846. Invt. and sale by M.D. Anderson, Adm.;
buyers include Mahaly, James, and John Grubb.
WB D 508, 3 Feb 1848. Sett. by Martin D. Anderson, Adm.

GUDGER, WILLIAM
CR9 238, 4 Feb 1867. W.A. Gudger and Hugh Reynolds app. Adms.

CR9 244, 4 Mar 1867. Comm. app. to lay off year's support for
Nancy and family.

GUFFEY, JOSEPH A.
  CC 204, filed 13 Apr 1869. Joseph A. Guffey died May 1862 leaving
  as only heirs wife Mary C. and child Nancy S., now age 10. Mary
  and Joseph were married about 1860. Mary had inherited ¼ interest in lands of her father in McMinn Co. She wants to move
  to her people in one of western states.

HACKLER, GEORGE, SR.
  CC 53, filed 21 Aug 1860. George Hackler, Sr., died about 1847 in
  McMinn Co. leaving fourteen children: Betsey who is helpless;
  Henry; Polly of unsound mind; Robert; Susan wife of James Craw-
  ford, all of McMinn Co.; John of Roane Co.; Jacob a nonresident;
  Peggy wife of Nathaniel Louder of Mo.; Catherine Honeycutt of
  Mo.; George H., Jr., of Ill.; Christly of Ark.; Thomas of Texas;
  Hiram of Mo.; Charity who has died without issue.

HALE, FREDERICK
  CR2 50, 7 Mar 1825. Will proven by Benjamin Isbell, Wm. Majors,
  and Moses Cunningham; George and Samuel Hale qualify as Execs.

HALE, HENRY H.
  WB G 237, Will exec. 8 Sep 1870, probated Nov 1870; "I desire my
  body decently burried in the north corner of my Garden by the
  Masonic Brotherhood. I wish all notified and requested to
  attend and especially Major Jackson, Isaac Benson, Capt. Jaques,
  O.P. Rogan and all other special friends connected with the
  road." To wife Eliza A. all estate until son Robert D. becomes
  21, then equal division with him, but all to son if she marry
  again; to son Charles D., the son by first wife, $100 to be ap-
  plied to his education, provided he come to receive it. Exec:
  bro. John G. Hale. Test: J.W. Rentfro, A.S. Robinson.
  CR10 254, 7 Nov 1870. Will proven; John G. Hale declines to serve
  as Exec.; S.D. Standfield app. Adm.; widow Eliza A. records her
  dissent to Will; asks for dower; is app. Gdn. of her minor son
  Robert H. Hale, son of dec'd.
  CC 313, filed 6 Jan 1872. Henry H. Hale, son of Archibald Hale,
  died 18 Sep 1870 leaving family as named in Will. Son Charles
  D. was born 1862, is a grandson and ward of Wm. P. Simmons,
  and lives in Jasper Co., Mo. Son Robert D. died 15 Sep 1871.

HALE, JAMES
  CR2 243 and 244, 3 Dec 1827. Thos. F. Bible app. Gdn. for Wm. C.,
  Jane, Christopher P., Minerva, Martial C., and James Hail,
  minors. Henry Mesimore app. Adm.
  CR2 261, 3 Mar 1828. Wm. E. Derrick, Wm. Cunningham, and Isaac
  Lowry app. Comm. to lay off year's support for widow Catharine.
  WB A 124-126, no date. Invt. and Sale by Adm.
  CR2 403, 7 Dec 1829. Catharine Hale, widow, app. Gdn. of her own
  children as named above.

HALE, THOMAS
  WB G 230, Will exec. 6 Dec 1869, probated Feb 1870; body to be
  decently buried in grave yard near residence; all estate to be
  sold and money to be put on interest for benefit of son Ernest;
  wife Fannie to have custody of child with power to use funds for
  his education as long as she remains a widow and prior to son's

majority, when funds are to be turned over to him with his stepmother receiving her full share, one-half if she desires it; if
she marries then son, stepfather and mother to decide whether he
live with them; if this not agreeable or wife dies then Execs.
and bros. Henry H. and John G. Hale of McMinn Co. with James S.
Mopin my wife's bro. of Bedford Co. to settle with wife and provide for son; if son dies then remaining property to be divided
by law. Test: W.W. Alexander and James Steed.
CR10 172, 7 Feb 1870. Will proven.

HALEY, ALLEN
  WB G 30-31, Will exec. 16 Aug 1864; to niece Susan L. Rice, one-
  third of property; to nephews Robert, John C., and Allen Rice,
  Susan's part if she die before marriage; to Margaret A. and
  Nimrod Dodson, 2/3 of property; Aunt Myma to have her support on
  farm so long as she see proper to remain on same; the graveyard
  on premises to be for use of neighborhood. Execs: Nimrod
  Dodson and Robert Rice. Attest: David Bradford, John Jenkins.
  CR9 27, 5 Dec 1864. Will proven.
  WB G 34-38, no date. Invt. and unsettled blacksmith accounts
  filed by Execs., J.R. Rice and Nimrod Dodson.

HALL, O.P.
  CR10 354, Mar 1872. A.F. Keith app. Adm.
  CC 367, filed 24 Mar 1873. O.P. Hall died 25 Jan 1870 leaving
  widow Amanda (who was the widow of Ellis M. Riggs) and children:
  Parker S. Hall, son by a former wife, and Alonza P. Hall, a
  minor son by Amanda.

HAMBRIGHT, JOHN, SR.
  WB A 203-205, Will exec. 25 Aug 1829; to wife Nancy; to three daus.
  Jane, Elizabeth, and Polly Hambright; to sons Frederick, Benjamin;
  Gevin Robeson, John, and Amos Hambright; "having assisted son
  Frederick Hambright when he first took to himself a wife";
  "having assisted son Benjamin Hambright in paying for a piece of
  land in Knox County". Execs: friends Peter Hambright, Jese W.
  Edington. Wit: Peter Hambright, William Smeadly, Starling Camp.
  CR2 418, 1 Mar 1830. Will proven by Wm. Smedley and Sterling Camp;
  Jesse W. Edington app. Exec.

HAMBRIGHT, NANCY
  CR5 221, 7 Apr 1845. Wm. Scarbrough and Frederick M. Hambright
  make oath that they were personally acquainted with Nancy Hambright, dec'd, who was a pensioner of the U.S. at rate of $450
  per annum and that she died 1 Mar 1845 leaving six heirs.
  Frederick, Jane, Elizabeth, John Hambright and /space left vacant
  here_7 "which we are personally acquainted with her only heirs".

HAMBRIGHT, PETER
  WB C 62-63, Will exec. 25 Aug 1838, recorded Nov Court 1838; to
  wife Mary, "land I now live on from the mouth of Atcherson branch
  down the River to the corner of Mr. Wimpie's field"; to sons
  James M., John M., Arthur M., Peter V., and Frederick M. (a
  minor); to the four girls; to Eliza M. Hambright; to Mary M.
  Hambright, a minor; to Nancy Jane and Sarah M. Hambright when
  they come of age; to the three youngest girls as they become of
  age. Execs: Mary Hambright and James A. Haise. Wit: Jesse
  Wimpy, Silas Morgan.
  CR4 399, 5 Nov 1838. Will proven.

HAMILTON
CR9 430, 6 Apr 1868. Susan Hamilton app. Gdn. of her own minor child.

HAMILTON (HAMELTON)
CR10 257, 5 Dec 1870. R.B. Hamilton app. Gdn. of his own minor children: Harriet S., Mary E., Margrett L., Joseph W., James A., and Nancy A.

HAMILTON, JAMES A.
CR2 207, 8 Mar 1827. Margaret Hamilton app. Adminx.; Joab Hill, Tidence Lane, and John Neal app. Comm. to lay off year's support for widow Margaret.

HAMILTON, ROBERT W.
WB F 176, 5 Apr 1858; 266, 5 Apr 1859; 324, 5 Apr 1860; 420, 5 Apr 1861. Sett. by A.C. Robinson, Gdn. to Mary A., N.C., Samuel H., and Jas. H. Hamilton, minor heirs.
WB G 121, 1 Nov 1865. Sett. by Gdn.; receipt in full 5 Aug 1861 from Mary A. Hamilton for her share; receipt in full 22 Jan 1865 from N.C. Hamilton.
CR9 190, 1 Oct 1866. Hugh L. Moore app. Gdn. for S.H. and J.H. Hamilton, minor heirs.
CC 277, filed 16 Dec 1857. Buttram VS Buttram. Robert W. Hamilton died about 1845-47 in Meigs Co., Tenn., leaving widow Rebecca and children: Martha Jane, Mary, Narcissa C., James, Samuel, and Margaret wife of Granville Williams. About 1855 widow Rebecca married Larkin Buttram in Meigs Co.

HAMPTON, WAIDE
WB E 358-359, Will exec. 29 Mar 1851, Codicil 11 Nov 1853; to wife Sarah; to three sons David, Archibald, and George Washington; to daus. Elizabeth, Minerva. Lucinda, Sarah, Martha, and Amanda; $1 each to Frank Presley, Rebecca Shoatman formerly Hampton, Polly Helms formerly Hampton, Catherine Hampton, Nancy Clark formerly Hampton; wife and David Maxwell, Sr., to be guardians of minor heirs. Wit: Wm. C. Porter, O.M. Liner. Signed by mark.
CR6, 6 Mar 1854. Will proven.

HAMPTON, WILLIAM, SR. (WILLIAM DENNIS HAMPTON)
WB A 82-83, no date; 93, 21 Apr 1827. Invt. and Sale by Benjamin Hambright, Adm.; buyers include Morgan, Frances, and the widow Hampton.
WB A 206, no date. Supp. Invt. by Adm.; receipt of arrears of pension of Rev. Soldier.
CR2 193, 8 Dec 1826. Benjamin Hambright app. Adm.
CR2 327, 2 Dec 1828. Petition of Nancy Hampton for dower in land; she is widow of Wm. Dennis Hampton who died in this County on 8 Aug 182 /sic/.

HANEY
CR6, 3 Oct 1853. George W. Haney app. Gdn. to James M. and Wm. C. Haney, his own minor children.

HANEY, EMANUEL
WB F 82, Will exec. 9 Oct 1854; to wife Nancy H.; $1 to heirs of dau. Elizabeth, dec'd wife of Wm. C. Mitchell, "I make this difference between the Legatees for the Ill treatment that I received from Elizabeth and her husband"; balance of estate to son Isaac B. Execs: son Isaac B. and James Buckner. Wit: C.W.

Rice, John Gregory. Signed by mark.
CR7 43, 6 Jul 1857. James Buckner declines to serve as Exec.
WB F 93, no date. Invt. valued by John Murphy and John Gregory.
WB F 286, 11 Sep 1859. Sett. by Isaac B. Haney, Exec.
CR11 22, 27 Oct 1866. Exec. reports that the only remaining
  bequests unpaid are to the Mitchell heirs and that balance goes
  to himself and bro. W.W. Haney if living, if not it all goes to
  him.

HANKS, JOHN
CR8, Oct 1861. Edward Newton app. Adm.
CC 443, filed 30 Oct 1861. John Hanks died 10 Sep 1861 leaving
  widow Elizabeth and children: Alfred, Catharine wife of John
  Scarborough, Mary wife of John J. Dixon, Jonathan, Leavina dec'd
  wife of Wm. M. Scarborough, Elizabeth dec'd wife of Woodson H.
  Weatherly. The children of dau. Leavina, dec'd, are Susan Jane,
  John H., and Hugh Scarborough, all of Polk Co. The children of
  dau. Elizabeth, dec'd, are Margaret wife of _____ McNeel, Sarah
  aged about 15, Henry 18, Jonathan 12, and John Weatherly 10, the
  last three of Bradley Co.
WB F 454-456, 25 Oct 1862. Invt. of sale by Adm.
CC 180, filed 15 Sep 1868. Widow Elizabeth dies between Dec 1865
  and the filing of this Bill; dau. Catherine was 59 in 1869;
  granddau. Susan Jane Scarborough is wife of W. Lafayette Moore
  of Bradley Co., Tenn.; sons-in-law John and Wm. Scarborough are
  brothers; granddau. Sarah C. Weatherly is wife of Greenville
  Baker; grandson Jonathan Weatherly is listed as Jackson; all the
  Weatherly grandchildren are of Henry Co., Tenn.; granddau.
  Margaret J. Weatherly is named in Original Bill as Margaret J.
  McNeel but this is an error as she is Margaret J. McCord, wife
  of P.M. McCord.

HANKS, ROBERT T.
CR5 77, 7 Nov 1842. Peggy Ann Hanks and John H. Eiffert app. Adms.
WB D 109, 29 Nov 1842. Comm. M.C. Hawk, C.P. Owen, and Wm. Rogers
  lay off year's support for widow M.A.W. (Peggy Ann) and family.
WB D 109-110, 5 Dec 1842. Invt. by J.H. Eiffert, Adm.; "property
  belonging to firm of R.T. Hanks & Co. which is under the control
  of Gideon Morgan the surviving partner".
WB D 129, 6 Mar 1843. Invt. of Sale by Adms.
CR6, 6 Jan 1851. J.H. Effort app. Gdn. to minor heirs.

HANTZ, WASHINGTON
CR7 550, 1 Jul 1861. Pauper's coffin and shroud furnished.

HARBERT, N.
CR3 301, 4 Jun 1833. Christopher Bullard, Adm. VS Tidence Lane.

HARDY, SAMUEL
WB E 463-464, Will exec. 15 Oct 1850; to wife Margaret; estate to
  be divided equally between wife and each heir, the wife to share
  as one heir; that part which would belong to son Thomas is bequeathed not to him but to the heirs of his body; to son Samuel
  and dau. Martha the farm on which they live; to dau. Mary. Execs:
  son James and Allen Boon. Wit: D.M. and John Key.
CR6, 5 Nov 1855. Will proven.
WB E 469, 10 Nov 1855. Comm. Wm. H. Ballew, James Gaut, Deman
  Dorsey set apart year's support for widow Margaret and family.
WB E 502-506, 15 Feb 1856 and 507-508, 3 Mar 1856. Invt. of Sale

and Add. Invt. by Allen Boon, Exec.

CC 53, filed 10 Dec 1855. Samuel Hardy died Oct 1855 leaving widow Margaret and children: James with wife Jane of Richland, Green Co., Mo.; Jane wife of Byrum Allen; Thomas of Ala.; Anne wife of Allen Boone; Susan wife of Marcellus Dodson of Oregon; Samuel with wife Elizabeth; Mary wife of Milton Robertson of Mahaska Co., Iowa; Martha wife of W.E. Edgman. The children of son Thomas are William, Susan, Jane, Taylor, Catherine, Angelo, Angeline, Samuel, Martha, and Phenice.

CC 289, filed 13 Mar 1858. Widow Margaret is now of Meigs Co.; son Thomas is dec'd; and Angelo is not listed as a child.

HARMAN

WB F 87, 1 Jun 1857. Report by Wm. Harman, Gdn. to his father Leonard Harman, "Lunatick".

CR11 90, 6 Apr 1867. Report by same, Gdn. to Leonard and Elizabeth Harmon, Lunatics.

HARMAN, MARTIN

WB E 528, 29 Jul 1856. Comm. Henderson Carter, John Small, and Wm. D. Browder set apart year's support for widow and family.

WB E 569, 25 Sep 1856. Invt. of sale; notes on Israel, William, and Leonard Harman; filed by James R. Robertson, Adm.

WB F 186, 2 Jul 1858. Final sett.; balance to Milly Harman.

HARRELL (HARROLD, HERRELD), JOHN, JR.

CR10 234, 5 Sep 1870. J.H. Crockett app. Adm.

CR10 244, 3 Oct 1870. Plat of land assigned as dower to widow Fannie.

CR10 295, Jun 1871. Partition of land: Moses, John, and Matilda Herrell VS James Munds and Ellen Herrell, minor heirs.

CR10 355, Mar 1872. W. Gettys app. Gdn. of James Thomas Munds, minor heir of John Munds, and of Ellen Harrell, minor heir of William Harrell.

CR10 383, Aug 1872. W. Gettys app. Gdn. of Rose Ann and John Herrel, minor heirs of Matilda Herrel.

CR11 266-268, 21 Mar 1873. Sett. by Adm.; unequal payments to heirs: Ellen Harrell by Gdn., James Munds by Gdn., Moses, J.B., Matilda, and John Harrell.

HARRIS, DEBORAH

CR2 418, 1 Mar 1830. John M. and Polly M. Harris, minors over 14, children of Robt. M. Harris by his former wife Deborah McEwen, choose Nathan Harris as Gdn.; Power of Atty. from Robt. M. Harris to Nathan Harris.

HARROD (HEROD), WILLIAM

CR5 442, 3 Apr 1848. Wm. Coats app. Adm.

WB D 530, 1 May 1848. Invt. of sale by Adm.

WB E 40, 5 Feb 1849. Report by Allen Butler, Gdn. to Wm. M. and Lucy Harrod, minor heirs; received warrant for 160 acres of public lands and extra pay due as soldier in service of U.S.

WB E 40, 7 May 1849. Final sett. by Adm.

WB E 43, 111, 177, 265, 338, 378, 430, 523, WB F 86, 177, dating from 31 May 1849 to 31 May 1858. Settlements by Gdn.

WB F 313, 31 May 1859. Final sett. by Gdn.; balance paid to Wm. M. and Lucy Harrod.

HART, BENJAMIN
    WB C 181, Oct 1839 and 217, Feb 1840. Invt. and sale by John Hart, Adm.
    WB D 40, 29 Oct 1841. Sett. by same Adm.; "his own part of sd. estate".
    CR5 15, 1 Nov 1841. John Hart app. Gdn. to Serena J., William J., Caroline Louisa Mary Elizabeth Lewis and Nancy /sic/ Hart, minor orphans.
    WB D 109, 209, 309, 378, 462, dating from 29 Oct 1842 to 22 Jun 1847. Sett. by Gdn.
    WB D 492, 3 Nov 1847. Sett. by same Adm. and Gdn.; receipt of John Hart, Sr., who is the only heir to sd. estate according to his information.

HART, ISAAC
    WB G 50, Will exec. 24 Dec 1864; all property except one red heifer to Jane Lawson and Phebe Snyder if they will agree to keep wife her lifetime; to Jane, my black girl, the red heifer; to Reuben Roddy, $230 if it is ever collected from State Bank of Tenn. at Athens. Exec: E.L. Miller. Wit: C.H. Guthrey, James Coffee. Signed by mark.
    CR9 45, 3 Apr 1865. Will proven.
    WB G 126, 6 Nov 1865. Report by Exec.

HAWK, MADISON C.
    WB E 39, Will, not dated. "County Court May Term 1849. The following is the will of the late Madison C. Hawk who departed this life in said county on the   day of April 1849, and which was made in the presence of the undersigned as witnesses thereto, and of whom to wit, Charles W. Rice felt himself specially called on to have witnesses to the same. Said will was made during the last sickness of the said Madison C. Hawk....."; wills that funds be used to buy a farm for wife and children; not signed. Wit: C.W. Rice and Elizabeth Meigs.
    CR5 529, 7 May 1849. Mrs. Jane Hawk does not appear to contest the noncupative Will.
    WB E 60, 25 Aug 1849. Comm. Robt. Renfrow, John Rice, and Jessee Dodson set apart year's support for widow Jane.
    WB E 109 and 299, 2 Sep 1850 and 30 Dec 1852. Invt. and Sett. by J.W. Gibson, Adm.
    CR8 4, Oct and Nov 1861. Petition to sell slaves: Mrs. B.J. Hawk VS Henry Rice, Jr., and wife M.E., Tim M., Rob. A., G.G., F.J., and M.A. Hawk. John Scarborough app. Gdn. ad litum for G.G., F.J., and M.A. Hawk, heirs.

HAWKINS, BENJAMIN
    WB A 117, Will exec. 28 Dec 1827; to wife Mary; to dau. Polly Hawkins; to granddau. Nancy Templeton; to lawful children; one-half of all property to the one of children who takes care of wife Mary and dau. Polly during their lives. Execs: sons Benjamin and James. Wit: John Walker, Leven L. Ball.
    CR2 262, 3 Mar 1828. Will proven.
    WB B 71, 5 Dec 1831. Invt. by Execs. named.
    CC 46, filed 16 Jul 1860. Mosteller VS Rice. Benjamin Hawkins died about 1827 leaving widow Mary who later married "old man Dodson" and is now deceased, and children: Polly of unsound mind now dec'd; James who moved to Columbus on Hiwassee River and later to Ark.; Benjamin, Jr., who died in Polk Co.; Joseph

and William who went West; Raleigh and John who went to Ala.;
Sally now dec'd, wife of Daniel Newman who died and she moved
West; a dau. who was wife of John B. Campbell, had a large fam-
ily of children, and went West.

HAYMES, DANIEL D.
  CR5 91, 6 Feb 1843. Emanuel Haney app. Adm.

HAYMES, REUBEN
  CR2 24, 7 Sep 1824. Wm. Haymes app. Adm.
  CR2 35, 6 Dec 1824. Terry Walden, Hugh L. Lackie, and James A.
  Templeton app. Comm. to lay off year's support for widow Sarah.
  WB B 188, no date. Invt. of sale by Adm.; buyers include Sally,
  Vincent, Joshua, William, and Caleb Haymes; an acct. against
  David Haymes.
  WB B 242, Apr 1837. Report by Daniel D. Haymes, Gdn. for William
  and Elizabeth Haymes, minor heirs of Reuben Haymes.
  WB C 173, 5 Oct 1839. Report by same Gdn.; receipt from heir Wm.
  Haymes; receipt from Henry and Elizabeth King for equal amount.

HAYMES, WILLIAM
  CR4 219, 2 Mar 1835. Vincent Haymes app. Adm.
  WB B 173-175, Jun 1835. Sale by Adm.; buyers include Daniel, Jane,
  Wm., Vincent, Sally, Caleb, and Pamela Haymes.
  WB B 177, 4 Apr 1835. Report by Comm. A.C. Robeson, George R. Cox,
  Jeremiah F. Strange setting apart year's support for widow Jane
  and family.
  WB B 237, 3 Mar 1837. Comm. Alex. C. Robeson, Jeremiah F. Strange,
  and Henry Walker, sworn by Nicolas P. Dodson, J.P., make settle-
  ment with Adm.

HAYNES, JOHN
  CR4 203, 1 Sep 1834. James P. and Aaron Haynes app. Adms.

HAYS, CARTER
  CR5 202, 3 Dec 1844. Listed as dead in Tax Delinquents for 1844.

HAYS, JOHN
  CR10 173, 7 Feb 1870. L.W. Cate app. Adm. de bonis non.

HEARD, ABRAHAM
  WB A 5-6, Will exec. 29 May 1822; to wife Nancy; to children Nancy
  Abram A. Heard /sic/, Minerva A., John J., George F., and Joshua
  T. Heard; "as my children become of age"; two little grandsons
  Thomas Peter Saffold and James Abraham Heard when they arrive at
  age of 12; execs. to "manage my estate with full power to dispose
  of all my lands in Georgia and elsewhere". Execs: wife Nancy,
  John Coffee, George and Franklin C. Heard, S.J. Saffold, also
  Abraham A. Heard when he comes of age. Wit: Henry Bradford,
  Wm. L. Taylor, James Bolding, Robert Slone, Banner Shields.
  CR1 58, 2 Sep 1822. Chas. McClung and others VS Abraham Heard.
  Plaintiff suggests the death of defendant.
  WB A 19-20, no date. Invt. by Nancy and F.C. Heard, Execs.

HEARD, JOHN D.
  WB B 5-6, Will exec. 27 Nov 1828; John D. Heard of Blount Co.,
  Tenn.; to wife Rebekah; to children Elizabeth, James, Colvin,
  George Washington; little boy of my wife's called Wm. Russell
  Heard to share equally with rest of children; children to be
  educated and supported. Execs: wife and Moses Stalcup. Wit:

Jesse Hannor and John Martin. Signed by mark. Will partly proven
in June Court 1830 by John H. Martin and fully proven Sep 1830 by
Jesse Hannor. Signed by A.R. Turk, Clerk at his office in Athens
Sep 18 1830.

WB C 169, 23 Sep 1839. Report by Moses Stalkup, former Gdn. to
Elizabeth, James, and George Heard, and William Martin, minor
heirs; receipt of Benj. Bond, present Gdn.

HELMS (HELLUMS), WILLIAM

WB C 270-271, Will exec. 6 Jun 1840, returned to Court 5 Oct 1840;
"I William Hellums ... aged and infirm"; to wife Rachel; to son
James; to afflicted dau. Peggy C. Hellums; ten other children:
Elizabeth Fowler, Dorcas Blakely, Salley McCallister, Lydia Max-
well, Polly Hellums, Nancy L. Hellums, Rachel C. Poe, Rebeccah
Hellums, Susannah Burks, and Anne Poe. Execs: wife Rachel and
bro. John Hellums. Wit: John Rogers, Elisha Snider, Robt. W.
McClary. Signed by mark.

WB D 133 and 148, 1 May 1843. Invt. of sale by Rachel Helms, Execx.

HEMPHILL, JOSEPH

CR4 183, 3 Mar 1834. Thomas Hemphill app. Adm.

HENDERSON, JAMES C.

CR4 364, 7 May 1838. Joab Hill app. Adm. and Frances Henderson
app. Gdn. of minor heirs.

WB C 117, Feb 1839. Invt. and Sale by Adm.; Frances S. Henderson,
widow, is a buyer.

WB C 175, 9 Oct 1839. Sett. by Adm.

WB C 234, 2 Mar 1840. Sett. by Joab Hill by Wm. Hill, agent.

HENDERSON, SAMUEL P.

WB G 52, no date. Comm. R.C. Jackson, J.S. Russell, and Raleigh
Chesnutt set apart year's support for widow and children, there
being six in family.

WB G 53-57, 14 Apr 1865. Sale by O.C. Henderson, Adm.; Mrs. Henderson buys 1 Partridge Net, 1 Blind Gray Horse.

WB G 119-121, 27 Oct 1865. Supp. Sale by Adm.; buyers include
Sally and H.S. Henderson.

CC 35, filed 16 Nov 1865. Samuel P. Henderson died Feb 1865
leaving widow Sarah B., who was dau. of Robt. Stephenson, and
children: Robert, Nancy, Samuel, and Anna, all minors.

HENRY, JAMES

CR7 291, 7 Mar 1859. James Wilson app. Adm.

WB F 279, 9 Aug 1859. Final sett. by James Wilson, Adm.; paid to
H.J. and S.M. Vaughn.

HENRY, JAMES G.

CC 8, filed 4 Nov 1867. James G. Henry of McMinn Co. died at
Gallatin, Tenn., on 18 Nov 1865 of smallpox, leaving widow Ellen
and children Wm. A., aged 9, and Elizabeth, aged 11 in 1865.
James G. Henry was conscripted by the Rebels but escaped through
the mountains of East Tenn. and joined Union Army in Ky. Wife
Ellen and two children walked to Ky., finding husband after a
year. Family remained in Ky. until James was discharged in Apr
1865.

HERTT, R.S.

WB E 485, 7 Jan 1856. Report by J.H. Effert, Gdn. to minor heirs;
app. to receive money that was supposed to be due the estate but

has received nothing.

HICKOX
  WB F 254, 11 May 1858. Report by John E. Hickox, Gdn. of his minor
    son.
  CR7 282, 7 Feb 1859. Report by same, Gdn. to his son John H.
    Hickox.
  See also JOSEPH COBB, SR.

HICKOX, HORACE
  CR4 215, 3 Dec 1834. John E. Wheeler, Joseph M. Alexander, and
    Jackson Smith app. Adms.
  CC 18, filed 25 Feb 1845. Dr. Horace Hickox died leaving heirs:
    Mary Elizabeth, wife of Milton L. Phillips, and minors Richard
    Asa, John Elliott, and Lamira Jane Hickox, all of Campbell Co.

HICKOX, JOHN E.
  WB G 125, no date. Invt. by M.L. Phillips, Adm.
  CR9 76, 4 Sep 1865. Geo. W. Ross, W.C. Owen, and James M. Henderson
    app. to lay off year's support for widow Mary Lee and family.
  WB G 197, 3 Sep 1866. Sale by Adm.
  WB G 207, 25 Sep 1866. Comm. A.H. Crowe, George W. Ross, and W.C.
    Owens set apart year's support for widow Mary and family.
  CR16 182, Mar 1867. Bill to sell lot: M.L. Phillips, Adm. VS
    widow and heirs; Campbell Co., Tenn. At a regular term of County
    Court in Jacksborough first Monday of Feb 1867, Court fully satis-
    fied that Mary L. Hickox is a lunatic and David Hart app. Gdn.
    Copy certified by John Peterson, County Court Clerk.
  CR10 441, Jan 1873. M.L. Phillips, Gdn. of minor children J. Horace
    and Melton F.B. Hickox who are the same persons as John H. and
    Melton H. Hickox.

HICKS, DANIEL
  CR9 82, 2 Oct 1865. Comm. app. to lay off year's support for orphan
    children.
  WB G 147-150, 5 Feb 1866. Invt. of Notes and unsettled accounts;
    "for Carding, 1860, 1861, 1862"; Chrisley Foster, Adm.
  WB G 151, 5 Feb 1866. Invt. of sale by Adm.
  CC 53, filed 11 Apr 1866. Daniel Hicks died Jun 1865 leaving as
    his only heirs the following children: William and Artissima,
    minors, and Mary Ann wife of Newton Linn.

HICKS, JAMES
  WB F 101-102, Will exec. 6 Jul 1857, proven Dec 1858; to wife Sarah;
    to infant daus. Mary C. and Jureah M., daus. by Sarah; to sons
    Daniel and Abel P. and to dau. Sarah A. Ragsdale. Exec: Hiel
    Buttram. Wit: Wm. A. Buttram, B.P. Nance. Signed by mark.
  CR7 90, 4 Jan 1858. Will proven.
  WB F 158, no date, and 325, 17 Feb 1860. Invt. and final sett. by
    Exec.

HICKS, LEANDER
  See STEPHEN HICKS.

HICKS, MARY
  CR12 113, 14 Apr 1853. Sterling Ragsdale and wife Sarah Ann,
    Daniel, and John Hicks, heirs of Mary Hicks, dec'd VS Daniel and
    John McPhail, and John S., Neil, Mary M., John A., Martha,
    Caroline, William, and   Hicks, minor defendants by gdn. ad
    litem Thos. Cecil.

CR12 186, 16 Dec 1853. Sterling Ragsdale and wife Sarah Ann, Daniel
and John Hicks VS Daniel McPhail in his own right and as Adm. of
Neil McPhail, Dougal McPhail, and Mary Hicks, and John Leander
Hicks, Neil McPhail Hicks, Mary Margaret, John Alexander, Martha,
Caroline, William, and Abel P. Hicks, infants under 21 by their
gdn. ad litem Thos. Cecil and John McPhail. Partition of land:
to Daniel McPhail, to John McPhail, and to heirs of Mary Hicks
deceased to wit Sterling Ragsdale and wife, Daniel, John, John
Leander, and Neil McPhail Hicks one share to each and the remain-
ing share to the children of Stephen Hicks dec'd to wit Mary
Margaret, John Alexander, Martha, Caroline, William, and Abel P.
Hicks; costs to be paid as follows, 1/3 by Daniel McPhail, 1/3
by John McPhail, and 1/3 by heirs of Mary Hicks, dec'd.

HICKS, NEIL M.P.
See STEPHEN HICKS.

HICKS, ROBERT
CR7 76, 7 Dec 1857. Sett. by Daniel Hicks, Gdn. of minor heirs.

HICKS, STEPHEN
CR6, 6 Feb 1854. Daniel Hicks app. Gdn. to Mary M., John A.,
Caroline, Sarah, Martha A., and Wm. Hicks minors of Stephen
Hicks dec'd and to Neil M.P. Hicks a minor of Neil M.P. Hicks
dec'd and to Wm. Hicks a minor of Leander Hicks dec'd.
WB E 380, 2 Sep 1854. Report by same, Gdn. of minor heirs of
"Stephen Hicks, Wm. Hix Neil M P Hicks Dec'd and Albert P Hicks
minor".
WB E 439, 2 Sep 1855. Sett. by same Gdn.; paid about one sixth
of funds to Elizabeth Hicks and paid same amount to "Abel Hicks
his portion".
WB F 49, 98, 260(1), 358, dating from 2 Sep 1856 to 2 Sep 1860.
Settlements by same Gdn.

HICKS (HIX), WILLIAM
CR6, 4 Sep 1854. Daniel Hix resigns as Gdn. of John L. Hix; Elizabeth Hicks app. Gdn. to John Leander Hix, minor heir of Wm. Hix,
dec'd.
WB E 458, 569, WB F 87, 241, 294, 355, 417, WB G 17, dating from
3 Sep 1855 to 3 Sep 1864. Settlements by Mrs. Elizabeth Hicks,
Gdn. to her son John L. Hicks.

HOGUE, BURREL H.
WB A 149, Will exec. 31 Jan 1829; to wife Patsy; to three children,
John L., Mary Jane, and Amanda Emeline Hogue. Execs: trusty
friends Nathl. Smith and James F. Bradford. Wit: Horace Hickox,
R.J. Meigs.
CR2 346, 3 Mar 1829. Will proven.
CR2 387, 8 Sep 1829. Mary Jane Hogue, minor orphan over 14 chooses
Wm. Hogan as Gdn. and he is app. Gdn. for Amanda M. Hogue, under
14.
CC 192, filed 16 Jul 1853. Burrell Hogue died leaving first wife
Sarah, said to be divorced, and second wife Patsey and the fol-
lowing children by first wife: Amanda Emeline born 25 Sep 1820,
married May 1841 to John S. Benson, living in Lacon, Marshall
Co., Ill.; Mary Jane, married first in Ind. about 1835 to Lawson
Hough who died 1844, married second to Abner Shinn of Lacon, Ill.;
and John L. Hogue who died about 1840 in Smithland, Ky. Sarah
Hogue, age 62, testifies that she and Burrell Hogue were married

in Rutherford Co., N.C., about 1813. Burrell and Patsey were
married soon after he came to McMinn Co. Both wives are still
living.

HOGUE, SAMUEL and MALINDA
  CR13 43, 12 Dec 1860. State of Tenn. VS John L. Bridges, Adm. of
  Malinda Hogue; State sells house and lot in Athens.
  WB F 448, 4 Mar 1862. Final sett. by Adm.; receipt from John F.
  Slover, Clerk of Circuit Court, for the balance, which goes into
  the Common School fund.

HOLEMAN, JEREMIAH
  WB A 31, Will exec. 15 Jun 1823; to wife Sarah; to six children
  living with wife; to dau. Isabella Roberts. Execs: wife and
  James Roberts. Wit: William Heughart, James Gregg, and Rebecca
  Pew.
  WB A 61, 1 Sep 1823. Invt.

HOLT, IRBY
  CR2 440, 3 Mar 1830. Petition of Sarah Holt, widow of Irby Holt,
  dec'd, who died at his usual residence in this county on 12 Jan
  1829.
  WB A 180-191, no date. Sale and Invt. by James H. Reagan and Sarah
  Holt, Adms. /At bottom of last page is written, "And so the
  Chapter ends and I am glad"./
  WB A 212, 8 Jun 1830; B 13, 7 Mar 1831; 85, 4 Jun 1832. Reports
  by James H. Reagan, Gdn. for Robert, Emily, Jane, Fanny, Serena,
  Thomas, and Francis Holt, minor heirs.
  CR2 537, 6 Jun 1831. Heirs of Irby Holt, to wit: Robert, Jane,
  Fanny, Serena J., Thomas W., and Francis A. Holt, Sarah Eliza-
  beth Ragan dau. of James H. Ragan and his dec'd wife Betsy late
  Betsy Holt, and Robert H. Jordan and wife Emily S. late Emily S.
  Holt. Petition of Adms. that Irby Holt died leaving seven chil-
  dren and one grandchild and petitioner Sarah as distributees, and
  all the children are minors except eldest girl who is married.
  WB B 90-114, 31 Mar 1832. Supp. Invt. by Adms.; the share of sd.
  Irby Holt in the estate of his father Robert Holt, dec'd of
  McMinn Co.; sum rec'd from Lewis Cox, surviving exec. of Will of
  sd. Robert Holt; property purchased by Irby Holt at sale of
  residue of sd. Robert Holt's estate on 25 Dec 1828; share of
  Elizabeth Meigs late Elizabeth Holt one of legatees of Robt.
  Holt (share was assigned to Irby); share of Jane Givens dec'd
  late Jane Holt, one of legatees of Robt. Holt, being the part
  of her share belonging to Wm. T. Givens and Nancy Stewart late
  Nancy Givens, two of her children and heirs.
  WB B 146, 2 Jun 1834 and 177, 2 Jun 1835. Reports by same, Gdn.
  for Jane, Frances, Serena, Thos. W., and Francis A. Holt.
  WB B 190, 1 Aug 1836. Sett. by Sarah Holt, present Gdn. to Serena
  J., Thos. W., and Frances A. Holt. Witness: George Horne.
  WB B 191, 29 Jul 1836. Bond. Sarah Holt with Robert S. Holt her
  Security, makes bond before Wm. Lowry, Esq., Chairman of County
  Court, for payment of any debts of Irby Holt, dec'd father of
  Jane Holt, out of money paid by James H. Reagan to Sarah Holt
  as the distributive share of her dau. Jane Holt, dec'd. Wit-
  ness: Hugh Goddard.
  WB B 192, 1 Aug 1836. Bond of Robt. H. Jordan, with A.J. Ballew
  as security. "Whereas James H. Reagan admn. of est. of Irby
  Holt dec'd & Gdn to Jane Holt dec'd has this day paid to Robert

H. Jordan husband of Emily Holt named Emily Jorden heir of Irby
Holt dec'd the distributive share of the personal property of
the sd. Jane Holt dec'd." Witness: Wm. Ballew.
WB B 194, 2 Jul 1836. Bond of Robt. S. Holt with James C. Henderson as Security, for his share of dec'd sister Jane's property.
WB B 195, 2 Jul 1836. Bond of James C. Henderson, with Sarah Holt
as security, for share of wife Frances S. Holt now Henderson in
est. of Irby Holt, dec'd.
WB B 196, 2 Jul 1836. Bond of James C. Henderson for share of
wife in est. of Jane Holt, dec'd, as above.
WB B 197, 20 Dec 1832 /sic7. Bond of Sarah Holt as above.
WB B 258, Jul 1837; WB C 25, Jun 1838; 124, 28 Feb 1839. Report
by same, Gdn. to Serena J., Thos. W., and Francis A. Holt.
WB C 227, 27 Feb 1840. Report by same, Gdn. to Thos. and F.A.
Holt.
WB D 2, 27 Feb 1841. Report by same Gdn.; John L. Kline gives
receipt for share of Serena J. Kline in estate.
WB D 69, 132, and 212, dating from 7 Mar 1842 to 1 Jul 1844.
Reports by same Gdn.
CC 79 and 80, filed 10 Nov 1849. Erby Holt died leaving widow
Sarah, who moved to Mo. 17 Oct 1845 where she died in Mar 1849,
and children: Francis A. of Bradley Co. born 13 Nov 1826; Jane
M. died 1835 unmarried; a dau. who married Franklin L. Yoakum
of Texas; a dau. dec'd who married James H. Reagan; Thomas W.
Holt; Emily S. Jordin; and two more children.

HOLT, MILDRED
CR4 81, 4 Jun 1832. Thos. C. Heniman app. Adm.

HOLT, ROBERT
See IRBY HOLT

HORD, STANWIX
CR2 181, 182, 4 Dec 1826. Thomas Hord, Cary Armstrong, and Wm.
Weaver app. Adms. Robert W. McClary, Joseph Cobbs, Sr., and
Henry Bradford app. Comm. to lay off year's support for widow
Betsey and family.
WB A 76-82, 15 Dec 1826. Invt. by Adms.

HORNSBY, JEMIMA
CR4 277, 1 Aug 1836. Thomas Jefferson Lawson, minor heir of
Jemima Hornsby, of age to choose for himself, chooses Jacob
Lawson as his Gdn.; same Gdn. is app. for minor heirs Berry
and Miller Lawson.
WB B 287, 5 Feb 1838. Report by Gdn.; receipt from Thomas Hornsby
in Clay Co., Ky., for money for sd. minors.
WB C 31, 14 Aug 1838. Sett. by same Gdn.; cash received in Ky. in
1836.

HORTON, DANIEL
CR13 467, 20 Dec 1865. Mary A. McCasland, Gdn. VS Daniel Horton.
The death of defendant is suggested and proven.
CR14 16, 9 Apr 1867. John R. Howard VS Daniel Horton. Scire
facias served on H.M. Roberts and wife Elizabeth A., P.L. Brian
and wife Anna M., William G., H.C., and Joseph Horton as heirs
of defendant.
CR10 63, 5 Oct 1868. O.P. Hall app. Adm.

HOSSY or HOPY
  CR5 26, 4 Jan 1842. Court informed that Jane Hossy a poor widow
  living in McMinn Co. has three small children for whom she is
  unable to provide.

HOUNSHELL, JACOB
  CR5 356, 7 Jun 1847. David L. Hutsell app. Gdn. to Susannah
  Hounshell.
  WB E 67, 1 Nov 1849. Report by same, Gdn. to Susan Hounshell now
  Susan Turner, one of minor heirs; paid Andrew and Susan Turner;
  paid expenses to Va.
  WB E 164, 15 May 1851. Sett. by same, Gdn. to heir Nancy Ann
  Hounshell now Nancy Ann Gamble.
  WB E 400, 1 Jan 1855. Sett. by Geo. M. Hutsell, Gdn. to Jacob
  Hounshell, minor heir; received of James L. Yost, Adm.
  WB E 460, 8 Nov 1855. Final sett. by same Gdn.; receipt of Jacob
  Hounshell for balance.

HOWARD
  CR8, 1 Dec 1862. John R. Howard app. Gdn. of his own minor chil-
  dren.
  WB G 180, 30 Jun 1866. Report by same Gdn.

HOWARD, GEORGE WALTER
  CR6, 5 Jun 1854. Wm. H. Howard app. Adm.
  CR6, 4 Sep 1854. Margaret M. Salle app. Gdn. to Mary Ann and
  Joseph C. Howard, minor heirs.
  WB E 381, 4 Sep 1854; 522, 27 Jun 1856. Invt. and sale and Final
  sett. by Adm.
  WB F 80, 261(1), 356, 425, dating from 1 Aug 1857 to 1 Aug 1861.
  Sett. by John Cunningham, Gdn.
  CR9 332, 5 Nov 1867. Sett. by same Gdn.

HOYL (HOYLE), DAVID
  CR4 377, 6 Aug 1838. James C. Carlock app. Adm.
  WB C 35-38, Sep 1838. Invt. and Sale by Adm.
  WB C 67, 14 Aug 1838. Comm. Robert McClary, William Maples, and
  Green L. Reynolds lay off year's support for widow Nancy.
  WB C 260, 5 Aug 1840. Sett. by Adm.; receipts from T.L., P., and
  Jonas Hoyl.
  CR6, 4 Oct 1852. ⁄The following incomplete entry has been marked
  through in the book.⁄ Petition of James C. Carlock and wife
  Elizabeth M., Caleb R. and John W. Hoyl, Michael C. Reynolds
  and wife Mary C., all citizens of McMinn Co., Tenn., and Jonas
  Hoyl a citizen of Bradley Co., Tenn. - about 1838 David Hoyl
  died in McMinn Co., Tenn., intestate leaving those named and
  Peter Hoyl now of Dade Co., Mo., Sarah who married James S.
  Green of DeKalb Co., Ala., and Andrew F. Hoyl whose residence is
  unknown but is supposed to reside in Chili, South America, as
  his heirs at law.

HOYL (HOYLE), JOHN
  CR7 45, 3 Aug 1857. Thos. P. Wells app. Adm.
  WB F 94, 12 Sep 1857. Invt. by Adm.; slave in hands of Daniel H.
  Hoyl of Atlanta, Ga., who refuses to give him up; a note on John
  Hoyl, Jr.
  WB F 98, no date. Comm. M.L. Philips, Oliver Dodson, and H.P.
  Wilson allot year's provisions to Mary Hoyl.
  WB F 225-227; Sale held 19 Nov 1858.

CC 275, filed 11 Jul 1857. John Hoyl died leaving widow Mary who was not the mother of his children, who are Daniel H. of Paulding Co., Ga. (his wife died 8 Dec 1855 in Ga.); Thomas L.; John; Jemima Hoyl Mastin; Margaret wife of T.P. Wells; Narcissa wife of Williams Mayfield; David and Levi of Miss.; Clark of Texas; and Susan wife of Thomas H. Jones of Ga.

HOYL, MARY

WB G 211-212, Will exec. 8 Dec 1864; I, Mary Hoyl Widow of John Hoyl deceased"; all household furniture to be equally divided among the Negroes and wearing apparel to be given to servant Mary for her to divide among the other negroes and she is to have side saddle for herself; my grave, my husband's grave, the grave of Samuel Love my first husband and his two children who are buried 5 miles above Knoxville, Tenn., on North side of First Creek, the graves of Henry and Margaret Smith buried on McIntosh's reservation two miles north of A. Clag's farm, E Athens and grave of sister Susan who lies close by my last husband - all to be enclosed with posts and paling fence and tombstones at head and feet; $600 to James A.B. Grills; $100 to John B. Hoyl; $100 to Mary dau. of Wm. and Narcissa Mayfield; $25 to Sidney dau. of Wm. and McZainey Smith; $25 to Sarah Jane Allaway; remainder of estate divided among negroes Lawson and wife, Henderson and Mary, Caroline's children, and Bell. Execs: Thos. A. Cass and Milton L. Phillips. Wit: Allen and John R. Ware. Signed by mark.

CR9 241, 4 Mar 1867. Will proven.

CR9 258, 1 Apr 1867. O.P. Hall app. Exec. with Will Annexed.

CC 227, filed 21 Feb 1855. Mary, wife of John Hoyl and widow of Samuel Love, was Mary Smith. Her nine bros. and sisters are as follows: Henry L. Smith, youngest bro., of Benton Co., Ark., with wife Ann L. and child James Henry Smith and another child; Hannah Smith Benson, died before Aug 1852 in Ark., stepmother of Isaac Benson, with no children of her own; Elizabeth Smith who went to Ark. with bro. Henry and died 1853 at his home; Susan Smith who died Apr 1852; Jackson Smith who died about 1851; Stephen Smith who died about 1845 without issue; Nathaniel Smith who died in Texas about 1840-43; Patsey Smith Grills, dead for a long time, who has son James; Umberson Smith died unmarried.

HOYL, NANCY

WB E 261, Will exec. 13 Jul 1852; $1 each to four eldest children, Peter, Jonas, Sarah, and Elizabeth March; to fifth son Andrew Felix, a note I hold on him; to third son Caleb Richardson $110; to fourth son John Wesley $110; to youngest child Mary Cornelia, consort of M.C. Reynolds, the balance of money, etc., to be collected and put on interest for 15 years, to pay her $15 annually and at end of that period to buy farm for her and her heirs and no others. Execs: sons Caleb R. and John W. Hoyl. Wit: David Cantrell, J.A. Long. Signed by mark.

CR6, 2 Aug 1852. Will proven; J.W. Hoyl declines to serve as Exec.

WB E 270, 6 Sep 1852. Invt. and sale by C.R. Hoyl, Exec.

CR6, 6 Sep 1852. Jonas, Caleb R., and John W. Hoyl, James C. Carlock and wife Elizabeth M., Michael C. Reynolds and wife Mary C. VS Peter and Andrew F. Hoyl, and James S. Green and wife Sarah. Petition to sell land. Defendants are all nonresidents.

HOYL, SARAH M.
  See WILLIAM H. COOKE

HUDGENS
  CR7 379, 6 Feb 1860. Jesse M. Hill app. Gdn. to Wm. Hudgens, a
  minor.
  See ELIZABETH MAYFIELD HILL HUDGENS BAKER

HUGHES, JOSEPH E.
  CR9 200, 5 Nov 1866. S.M. Boggess app. Gdn. of George W., P.E.,
  Sarah W., Marthy F., John F., and James Thomas Hues, minors.
  (Hughs heirs).
  CR10 114 and 115, 7 Jun 1869. Sett. by same Gdn. who resigns and
  M.C. Carpenter is app. Gdn.
  CR10 213, 6 Jun 1870. M.C. Carpenter resigns and A.H. Wilson is
  app. Gdn.

HUGHES, WILLIAM
  CR9 300, Sep 1867. Silas Wade app. Gdn. of minor heirs.
  CR10 95, 1 Mar 1869. Gdn. resigns and E.S. Shipley is app. Gdn.

HUMPHREY (HUMPHREYS), JAMES
  WB D 293, Will exec. 9 Jun 1845, recorded 7 Jul 1845; to James
  Baker, a minor; to the heirs of his bros. Hiram and George Hum-
  phrey. Exec: Joseph McCorkle. Wit: R.D. Gaddy, Aaron King.
  WB D 302-306, 4 Aug 1845; 327-331, 6 Oct 1845; 460, 5 Jul 1847.
  Invt., Sale, and Add. Invt. by Joseph McCorkle, Exec.
  CR5 301, 3 Aug 1846. Wm. Coats app. Gdn. to James Baker, infant
  son of Malinda Baker.
  WB D 472, 2 Aug 1847; 555, 4 Sep 1848. Report by Gdn.; has re-
  ceived nothing since his appointment.
  CC 54, filed 17 Aug 1848. Coats VS McCorkle. James Humphreys
  died about 7 Jul 1845 leaving an illegitimate son, James Baker,
  aged about six in Feb 1849, one of the illegitimate children of
  Malinda Baker, housekeeper for Humphreys.
  WB D 475-479, 575, WB E 62, 117, 189, dating from 30 Aug 1847 to
  8 Sep 1851. Settlements by Exec.
  WB E 272, 8 Sep 1852. Sett. by Exec.; paid to W.F. Bang, Editor of
  the Nashville Banner and to John M. McKee, Editor of Knoxville
  Register for publishing for heirs.
  WB F 355, 6 Oct 1860. Sett. by Geo. W. Bridges, Gdn. of Mary Jane
  and Lucy Humphrey, minor heirs of Hiram Humphrey; "having re-
  ceived on the 1st day of March 1854 $1940.42"; receipt for total
  sum from Reuben Humphrey In fact for Lucy and Mary Jane Humphrey
  heirs of Hiram Humphrey who were legatees under the will of James
  Humphrey, dec'd, who died in McMinn Co., Tenn.
  Chancery Record Books A and B; Humphrey VS McCorkle. The children
  of Hiram Humphrey are Reuben, Stephen, Norris, Caroline wife of
  James O. Goodson, Lois wife of John H. Nellis, and Lucy and Mary
  Jane, minors.
  Chancery Record Book B, Feb 1860. Wm. Coats has died and James
  Baker over 14 chooses Allen Butler as his Gdn.

HURST, ELIJAH
  WB D 254-255, Will exec. 12 Dec 1844; to wife Mary; to sons Russell
  R. and John L.; to daus. Jemima Cleage and Sarah Ann Calloway;
  "my four children"; "my executors get my mother and sister
  Delilah to remove from Claiborne County to McMinn County". Execs:
  sons Russell R. and John L. Wit: Justus Steed, Andrew John, and

W.F. Keith.
CR5 217, 4 Feb 1845. Will proven.
WB D 275-277, 7 Apr 1845. Invt. of sale by Lewis R. and John L.
Hurst, Execs.; Mary Hurst gives her consent.
WB D 521, 3 Mar 1848. Sett. by Lewis R. Hurst, one of Execs.

HUSTON (HUSON), WILLIAM M.
CR5 252, 6 Oct 1845. James W. Netherland app. Adm.
CR5 318, 6 Oct 1846. Adm. allowed to resign.

HUTSON, JANE
CR4 442, 6 May 1839. Henry Walker app. Adm.
WB C 142-143, Jul 1839. Invt. by Adm.

INGRAM, GEORGE
CR7 457, 2 Jul 1860. Court pays for coffin for pauper.

IRWIN, PENELOPE E.
WB E 436-437, Will exec. 21 Oct 1852; "having no children and issue
of my body living to give my property to the first object of my
bounty are my negro slaves"; negro slaves to be free and all expenses paid for their removal to the Colony of Liberia and setting them up in that country, with use of her farm, stock, etc.,
until they are so transported; $100 each to Rev. R.E. Tedford
now of Blount Co. formerly of Cleveland, Dr. Charles Dupont, and
Polina Dupont, dau. of Dr. Dupont; $1000 to nephew Thomas T.
Pugh now supposed to be a citizen of La.; balance of property to
the three daus. of deceased niece Sarah Jones who are Mary and
Penelope Jones "as well as I remember and one name not remembered"
all supposed to be of Miss., and who are nieces of sd. Thos. T.
Pugh, and to Elizabeth Ann Keith, dau. of niece Sarah Keith;
these four are all females and of tender years. Execs: Joseph
McCulley and Richard C. Jackson. Wit: Wm. S. Callaway, M.E.
Calaway, John C. Gaut.
CR6, 6 Aug 1855. Will proven.
WB E 443-453, 3 Sep 1855; 474-475, no date. Invt. and Sale by
Execs.
WB F 103, 11 Dec 1857. Final sett. by Execs.; paid $364.45 for
"Carrying negroes to baltimore" and $405 from "baltimore to
liberia"; balance in account distributed to Nancy Fore as Gdn. to
minor heirs of Sarah Jones, dec'd, and A.H. Keith as Gdn. for his
dau.
WB F 194, 6 Sep 1858. Sett. by A.H. Keith, Gdn.
WB F 194-199, 6 Sep 1858. Sett. by A.H. Keith, Adm. of Nancy Fore
dec'd former Gdn. of Penelope, Laura, and Mary J. Jones; paid in
1855 expenses from Bay St. Louis, Miss., to Athens, Tenn.; paid
tuition at Asheville College for Mary J.
WB F 300, no date. Report by Joseph McCully, Gdn. to Penelope,
Laura, and Mary Jones.
CC 46, filed 18 Jan 1859. The mother of Elizabeth Ann Keith is the
only dau. of Nancy Fore.
WB F 349, 2 Oct 1860. Sett. by James Forrest, Gdn. to Mary and
Penelope Jones.
WB F 398, 3 Jun 1861. Sett. by same, Gdn. to Penelope Jones.
WB F 414, 17 Jul 1861. Sett. by Joseph McCully, Gdn. of Laura S.
Jones.
CR8, 2 Dec 1861. D.B. Childress, who has married the sister of
Laura E. Jones and has been app. Gdn. to Laura E. in Jefferson

Co. where they reside, is app. Gdn. in place of Joseph McCully,
and Gdnship. is transferred to Jefferson Co.
CR13 249, 12 Dec 1864. James Forrest Gdn. for the use of Daniel
H. and Penelope Meek VS Timothy Sullins, Lazarus Dodson, and
J.D. Gaston.
CR14 511, 14 Aug 1868. James Forrest Gdn. of Penelope Jones for
the use of D.H. and Penelope Meek VS James Wilson.

ISBELL, BENJAMIN
WB G 232-234, Will exec. 28 Oct 1869, Codicil 3 Jun 1870, probated
Sep 1870; "I have given" dau. Miram Turnley, son Thomas M. in
his lifetime (int. in land on Spring Creek in Monroe Co., Tenn.,
which he owned jointly with Wm. Terry and $100 on his land in
Bradley Co., Tenn.), Martha A. McMilian (to make her equal with
rest of heirs above and her heirs to have her int. in estate),
daus. Francis D. Hughs, Mary L. Hampton, Sarah E. Gaut, Missouria
W. Millian, and son Dennis Isbell; to dau. Francis D. Hughs,
interest in the "Chilhowee Springs" which is 1/3 part of 40
acres, including the mineral spring "they are on the north side
of the mountain near where Wm. Cooper, Esqr. lived and deceased"
and Wm. H. Ballew has the grant in his possession, this bequest
over and above other heirs on account of her living with me so
long and keeping house for me; owns 640 acres in Cherokee Co.,
N.C., and 2 quarters in Polk Co. on Frog Mt., the latter bought
in partnership with Thornton Godard (refused Godard's request
to give Willerson Cunningham and Daniel Lowry an interest, won
resulting lawsuit, received deeds and paid taxes all this time
and Godard has not said any more about it); to son Dennis R.
and dau. Louisa Hampton for living with me, keeping house and
attending to family business for several years; to all children
and their posterity, the "rite of burriel" in Graveyard at back-
side of garden where "my companion Martha Isbell and our two
infants are buried". Execs: Wm. L. Rice, Dennis R. Isbell.
Wit: D.R. Isbell, J.F. Hampton.
CR11 257, 31 Aug 1872; 280, 20 Sep 1873; 288, 12 Nov 1873. Settlements by Execs.; payments to Miram (N.M. or M.L.) Turnley,
F.D. Rice, Missouri (L.M. or M.L.) McMullen or McMillians, J.H.
Gaut and J.H. Gaut as Gdn., M.L. and James Hampton, James B.
and Alice McMullen or McMillians, Mattie (M.J.) Forest, Wm. L.
Isbell, Sarah A. Isbell, J.Y. Maxwell, C.C. Isbell, Jane Isbell,
W.H. Forest, James Forest, D.R. Isbell, and W.L. Rice.
CC 614, filed 22 Mar 1879. Hughes VS McReynolds. J.H. Gaut, at-
torney, is son-in-law of Benjamin Isbell, dec'd. Son Dennis R.
Isbell married a dau. of Saunders Callaway. Dau. Frances D.
Isbell was the widow of John Hughes who died testate about Mar
1855 in Jacksonville, Texas, leaving two children, Benjamin I.
Hughes, born about 1853, who came to live with his uncle and
gdn. Wm. J. Hughes when he was about 16, and Elizabeth (Lizzie)
Hughes, born 25 May 1855, who marries Wallace K. Sheddan during
the lawsuit, Apr. to Jul. 1880. Dau. Frances D. married second
Wm. L. Rice in McMinn Co., 16 Jul 1867. Wm. L. Rice died 22 Aug
1878. His children who testify in lawsuit are Lelia A. Wester,
Cordelia E. Rice, Laura L. wife of David M. McReynolds, and
Mattie L. wife of Dr. Hugh L. McReynolds. The "great financial
panic" was in 1873.

ISBELL, JOHN W.
    CR9 8, 3 Oct 1864. Jesse H. Gaut of Bradley Co. app. Adm.
JACK, JAMES
    CR13 352, 24 Aug 1865. James Jack VS L_____ & Aily; death of plain-
    tiff is suggested and proven.
JACKSON
    CR9 96, 4 Dec 1865. J.C. McMahan app. Gdn. of John Montgomery
    Jackson, a minor.
JACKSON, JOHN K.
    CR8, 4 Aug 1862. J.M. Jackson and T.J. Lowry app. Adms.; Uriel
    Johnson, Raleigh Chesnutt, and C.B. Newman app. Comm. to lay off
    year's support for widow and family.
    WB F 475-478, 1 Sep 1862. Invt. of notes and sale by James M.
    Jackson and T.J. Lowry, Adms.; buyers include Mrs. Jane Jackson,
    Harriet, Sarah, Martha J., Jas. M., and W.D. Jackson.
    CR11 40, 27 Oct 1866. Vouchers paid by Adms. include those to
    Sarah C., J.M., Harriet, M.J., and W.D. Jackson.
JAMESON (JAMERSON, JIMERSON), BENJAMIN C.
    WB F 445, 9 Jan 1862. Comm. S.M. Boggess, Thos. Prigmore, and
    Bogan Cash lay off year's support for widow and family.
    WB F 453, not dated; WB G 46, 15 Feb 1865. Invt., Sale, and Sett.
    by T.L. Farrell, Adm.
    CC 53, filed 21 Aug 1860. Benjamin C. Jamerson died leaving widow
    Mary A. and children: Evalina wife of Joshua Jones; Rebecca E.
    wife of James McCall; Eliza wife of Edward Price; Milton; Jane
    wife of W.R. McConnell; S.Y.; Nancy B. wife of George Fitch;
    Quintine a minor; Thomas P., dec'd, whose children are Kitty and
    Virginia.
JARNAGIN, CASWELL
    CR4 525, 3 Nov 1840. Alexander C. Robeson app. Adm.
    WB C 310, 20 Nov 1840. Comm. John Graham, Martin D. Anderson, and
    John A. Thompson set apart year's support for widow Elizabeth
    and family, being eight in number.
    WB C 314-318, 1 Jan 1841; D 43, Nov 1841. Invt. and sett. by Adm.
    WB D 126, 10 Jan 1843; 227, 5 Sep 1844. Sett. by John McDonald,
    Adm. of Alexander C. Robeson, who was Adm.
    WB D 222, 5 Aug 1844; 334, 5 Aug 1845. Sett. by Elizabeth Jarnagin,
    Gdn. to minor heirs.
    CC 165, filed 3 Aug 1852. Caswell Jarnagin died in McMinn Co. many
    years since, leaving widow Elizabeth and children: Alison Wood-
    ville B., Alfred Houston, Caswell, and John Noah Jarnagin, all
    minors, Amanda M. wife of Morris M. Smith, Sarah L. wife of Henry
    J. Eaton, Mary Ann wife of A.M. Runyon, Hamilton T., and James
    Ahab Jarnagin. The family wishes to sell land and move to Mo.
    File contains letter of authorization from Elizabeth Jarnagin in
    Polk Co., Mo., two original Land Grants issued 1824 to Noah
    Jarnagin, and a copy of deed 1831 from Noah Jarnagin of Grainger
    Co. to Caswell Jarnagin.
JARNAGIN, SPENCER
    CR12 22, 19 Apr 1852. Mary Ann VS Wm. H. Slover and other heirs
    at law.
    CR12 86, 16 Dec 1852. Mary Ann Jarnagin VS Wm. H. Slover and wife,
    John M. Jarnagin, Samuel H. Jorden, Gdn. of the minor heirs;

Judgment pro confesso against Slover and wife Sarah; publication
as to all the nonresidents; answer of Jorden, Gdn. ad litem of
James B., Albert M., Ellen, and Julius Jarnagin, and Martha Colville, minor heirs; Mary Ann is the widow of Spencer Jarnagin
who died intestate possessed of Lots Nos. 112 and 113 in Athens
on which Dr. Jordan now lives, in which said widow is entitled
to dower.
  CR12 108, 14 Apr 1853. Mary Ann Jarnagin VS John M. Jarnagin, Wm.
H. Slover and wife Sarah J., James B., Ellen, Gus H., and Julius
Jarnagin and Martha Colville by their Gdn. ad litem S.H. Jordan.
Widow awarded lots as dower.

JERKINS, ED
  CC 459, filed 24 Apr 1876. Ed Jerkins died 1864 leaving widow
Laura, now deceased, and children: Frances Gibson, Benjamin,
James, Mary C., Lovena wife of S.C. Cannon, Nancy E. Shumaker,
whose husband has long since abandoned her, Lewis B. and Louisa
B., both minors.

JOHN, THOMAS
  CR6, 6 Feb 1854. Ezekiel John app. Adm.
  WB E 362, 23 Feb 1854. Comm. John L. Bridges, Isaiah Smith, and
James Wilson lay off year's support for widow Margaret and family.
  WB E 365, 3 Apr 1854. Invt. of sale by Adm.; "1 half of a wind
mill to the widow 0.50".
  WB E 494, 29 Feb 1856. Sett. by same Adm.

JOHN, WILLIAM
  CR4 516, 5 Oct 1840. Comm. app. to lay off year's support for
widow.
  WB C 293, 2 Nov 1840. Comm. Tandy S. Rice, Justus and Henry Steed,
sworn before J.H. Benton, J.P., set apart year's support for
widow Rebecca and one child, Marcus.
  WB C 294-296, no date; 114, 7 Dec 1842; 132, 3 Apr 1843; 171, 7 Dec
1843; 217, no date. Invt., Sett., Add. Invt., and Sett. by
Thomas John, Adm.
  WB D 88, 4 Jul 1842; 217, no date; 363, 21 Feb 1846; 485, 19 Oct
1847; WB E 50, 7 Jul 1849; 412, 19 Feb 1855. Reports by Ezekiel
John, Gdn. to Marcus B. John, minor heir.
  CR7 78, 7 Dec 1857. Wm. Suthard of Crawford Co., Mo., is regularly
app. Gdn. of Marcus B. John.
  WB F 102, 22 Dec 1857. Final sett. by Ezekiel John, Gdn.; balance
paid to Wm. Suthard, Gdn.

JOHNSON, HENRY
  WB B 136, 3 Mar 1834. Invt. filed by John W. Lide, Adm. app. by
Dec Court 1833; among items listed are a gold watch in hands of
C. Mitchell of Rhea Co., Tenn., who claims it in right of his
daughter, and debts due by persons of State of Ga. where deceased
formerly lived.
  WB B 144, 2 Jun 1834. Acct. of sale by same Adm.

JOHNSON, JAS.
  CR7 536, 6 May 1861. Listed as dec'd in Tax Delinquents for 1860.

JOHNSON, JOSEPH
  CR9 56, 5 Jun 1865. Martha A.E. Johnson app. Adminx.

JOHNSON, POLLY
  CR5 535, 2 Jul 1849. Court pays John J. Dixon for one walnut

coffin for Polly Johnson, a pauper; Saml. Gentry and James C. Carlock paid for taking care of Polly Johnson and furnishing shroud for burial.

JOHNSON, REUBIN
  CR2 116, 6 Dec 1825. Jacob Johnson app. Adm.
  CR4 23, 5 Sep 1831. Andrew Cowan released as Gdn. of minor children.
  CC 97, filed 16 Mar 1850. Reuben Johnson died leaving widow Nancy who afterwards married Wm. McCray and moved to Mo. with children, all infants of tender years when father died: Ester A. wife of Preston Gobin, Martha J. wife of Thomas Austin, and Wm. Johnson, all of Grundy Co., Mo.

JOHNSON, THOMAS
  CR14 398, 13 Apr 1868. G.B. Johnson Adm. VS T.C. and Eldridge Odom. Obtained judgment Feb 1866.

JOHNSTON, JOHN
  CR10 51, 7 Sep 1868. Robert Johnston app. Gdn. of Penelope Johnston, minor child.

JOHNSTON, WILLIAM B.
  CR9 67, 7 Aug 1865. Mary E. Johnston app. Adminx.
  WB G 99-102, 17 Aug 1865. Invt. by Mary I. Johnston, Adminx.
  CR9 185, 3 Sep 1866. E.F. Johnson app. Gdn. of minor heirs.
  CR14 45, 12 Apr 1867. J.E. McElrath VS Isabella Johnson, Adminx.
  CC 408, filed 9 Nov 1874. E.F. Johnston, Gdn. of Martha E., Nannie L., and Mary E. Johnston VS Martha E., Nannie L., and Mary E. Johnston. The defendants are all minors of McMinn Co. and are temporarily in school in Dalton, Ga., and will soon be in Bradley Co., the home of their Gdn.

JONES
  CR1 275, 6 Sep 1827. Margaret Jones, Adminx. VS Wm. Jones.

JONES, THOMAS
  CR4 284, 3 Oct 1836. Elijah Jones app. Adm.

JONES, WILLIAM
  CR5 18, 6 Dec 1841. Will proven by Wm. L. Miller, one of the witnesses.

JORDAN, THOMAS C.
  CR13 216, 4 May 1863. Wm. L. Rice, Gdn. VS Thos. B. McElwee and Thos. C. Jordan - Debt. Plaintiff suggests the death of defendant Thos. C. Jordan which was proven. Cause revived against Robert R. Davis, Adm. of Thos. C. Jordan.

JOURDIN, MARY
  CR7 191, 7 Jun 1858. Sarah M. Jourdin app. Gdn. for Neil Alex Jourdin, minor.

JUDKINS, JAMES
  CR5 214, 3 Feb 1845. Wm. H. Wilson app. Adm.
  WB D 283-287, 7 May 1845; 448, 26 Apr 1847. Invt., Acct. of sales, and Sett. by Adm.

KARR (KERR), JOSEPH
  WB A 15, 31 Aug 1822. Invt. by Wm. Karr, sworn to in court before Wm. H. Cook, appraised 27 Apr and 7 May 1822 by D.A. Cobb, Ezekiel Spriggs, and Henry Gill.

WB C 241, 30 Mar 1840. Sett. by Adm.; "Receipt on Beeson & Nancy
Fields for $112.34 Receipt on James Thomas also an heir for
$112.34".

LANE, ELDRED
CR9 158, 7 May 1866. R.S. Lane app. Adm.
CR9 190, 1 Oct 1866. J.H. Magill, C. Shell, and James Wilson app.
Comm. to lay off year's support for widow Arminda.
CR9 371, 3 Feb 1868. Mathew S. Bryant app. Gdn. of Russel and
Granvel Lane, minor heirs.
CR11 135, 28 Sep 1868. Sett. by Adm.; payments to M.S. and S.F.
Briant, Arminia Lane, and J.M. Lane.

LANE, ISAAC
WB E 225-226, Will exec. 1 Jan 1849; to daus. Betsy Hill, Sarah
Neil, Polly Hurst, Jemima Gibson, and Oliver /sic/ Shults; to
sons Russell, Tidence C., and John F.; to grandchildren: Cole-
man, John, and Semantha McReynolds, and Sarah Gaut, all heirs of
dau. Seleta McReynolds. Wit: David W. Ballew, Wm. L. Rice.
Signed by mark.
WB E 217, 1 Feb 1852. Invt. by Russell Lane, Adm. with Will
annexed; "note on Oliver Shults decsd."
CR6, 2 Feb 1852. Will proven by Wm. L. Rice; handwriting of witness David W. Ballew, who has removed from Tenn. to Texas, is
proven.
CR12 48, 12 Aug 1852. Exparte. Russell and Tidence C. Lane, Mary
Hurst, Sarah and John Neil, Humphrey Shults, George and John
/sic/ Gibson, Logan McReynolds Adm. of Coleman C. McReynolds
dec'd, Elizabeth Hill, John C. and Sarah Ann Gaut, Semantha M.
and John McReynolds, David and Sarah Neil, James McGonigal and
wife on behalf of themselves and all the heirs of Elivia Shults
dec'd. Isaac Lane made Will and thereafter died. Since the
making of said Will, the said C.C. McReynolds has died intestate
and said Olivia Shults has also died intestate leaving the said
Humphrey Shults and others her children.
WB E 353, 6 Feb 1854. Add. Invt.; the only buyers are Mary, Lewis
R., and John L. Hurst.
WB E 383, 30 Sep 1854. Sett.; paid to heir George and Jemima
Gibson; payments to other heirs named.
WB F 260(2), 12 Apr 1859. Sett. by same Adm.; "Left on hand at
death of Sarah Lane dec'd."

LANE, NATHANIEL G.
CR2 177, 6 Sep 1826. Wm. B. Mullins app. Adm.
CR4 199, 3 Jun 1834. Came into Court Elizabeth Lane widow of
Nathaniel G. Lane late a soldier in the Army of the United
States and signified her assent to the app. of Wm. B. Mullins
as Adm.

LANE, TIDENCE C.
WB E 434, 13 Jul 1855. Comm. J.H. Ragain, James Wilson, and
Daniel Lowry set aside year's support for widow Elizabeth and
family.
WB E 455, 1 Oct 1855. Invt. by R.S. Lane, Adm.
WB F 72, 3 Jul 1857. Invt. and sett.; "Wm. C. Lee Receipt Duck
Town"; John F. Lane minor heir, share of personal estate.
WB F 220, 29 Oct 1858. Sett.
WB F 353, 29 Oct 1860. Sett. by R.S. Lane Gdn. of John Lane a

minor.
CC 594, filed 24 Oct 1878. Rider VS Rider. Tidence C. Lane died 1855 leaving widow Elizabeth who died about 29 Oct 1877 and children: Dr. Russell S. Lane, unmarried; John F. Lane, born 6 Mar 1842 and died 4 Oct 1866, unmarried; Sarah Ann, dec'd before her father, wife of James W. Shelton; and Sidney Ann, dec'd before her father, wife of Francis M. Rowan. The children of Sarah Ann, dec'd, are John who died before 1866, unmarried, and William supposed to live in Coffee Co. The child of Sidney Ann is Mary J. Rowan, born 26 Sep 1849, and married 21 Dec 1871 to Robert R. Rider. The Sheriff of Coffee Co. reports that Wm. Shelton, a young doctor, is in Texas, probably Dallas Co.

LANGFORTH, DAVID
CR5 484, 3 Oct 1848. Wm. Langforth app. Adm.

LANKFORD, GIBSON
CR5 457, 3 Jul 1848. Court pays for pauper's coffin.

LANKFORD, JAMES
CR5 205, 6 Jan 1845. Court pays for coffin.

LASATER (LASETER, LASSATER), WILEY
WB F 164, Sale held 26 Mar 1858 by Jonathan and Wm. Lasater, Adms.
WB F 175, 3 Mar 1858. Comm. Robert Cochran, George Reynolds, and Wm. L. Dodson set apart year's provisions for widow Elizabeth and family.
WB F 259 and 299, 1859 and 5 Dec 1859. Sett. by Wm. Lassater, Adm.
WB F 395, 2 Mar 1861. Final sett. by James R. Lasater, Gdn., his ward having arrived at full age; receipt in full from Wm. H. Lasater, ward.
CC 291, filed 11 Jun 1858. Wiley Lasater died 17 Feb 1858 leaving widow Elizabeth and children: Mary, wife of Daniel Robinson of Bradley Co.; Elizabeth, wife of John Smith; Nancy Ann, wife of Wm. McLinn of Collins Co., Texas; Sarah, wife of Justus Campbell Steed of Bradley Co.; Johnathan of Ga.; William; James H. last heard from in Ore. Son Johnathan dies during lawsuit by Feb 1860, leaving widow Mary Ann and children: Margaret J., wife of Henry McKann, and minors James and W.H. Lasater. By Feb 1860 the death of Daniel Robinson is admitted and widow Mary marries Bennett Cooper.

LATTIMORE, JEMIMA
WB A 30, Will exec. 6 Mar 1823; to sons Daniel and John; to dau. Rachael Hoyles. Execs: son-in-law John Hoyles, grandson Samuel Lattimore, Jr. Wit: T.B. Wells, T.L. Hoyles. Signed by mark.
WB A 41, no date. Acct. of sale.

LATTIMORE (LATIMORE), JOHN
WB B 124-125, Will exec. 7 Jun 1833; to wife Soosanny; to children Samuel, Daniel, John, Thomas, Joseph, Rachel, Soos Caroline, and Frances Latimore, Caty Thompson, Sary Firestone, and Jemimy Thompson; to the present living heirs of Sary Firestone and Jemima Thompson. Execs: Samuel Latimore, Wm. Maples, and Joseph Roper. Wit: David Hoyl, John Cobbs, John Ellis. Signed John Latimore.
CR4 166, 3 Sep 1833. Will proven.
WB B 125, 3 Dec 1833. Invt. sworn to by Wm. Maples and Jos. Roper.
CR4 248, 8 Mar 1836. Susan Latimore app. Gdn. to Thomas, Rachel,

Caroline, and Joseph Latimore, minor heirs,
WB B 242, Apr 1837; 269, 6 Nov 1837; C 148, 21 Aug 1839. Report
by Gdn. and Settlements by Execs.

WB C 163, 29 Apr 1839. Sett. by Gdn.; receipt of Thomas Lattimore
and Rachel Queener for one slave each, leaving three slaves in
hands of Gdn. for other heirs.

WB C 288, 29 Apr 1840; D 70, 29 Apr 1842. Sett. by Gdn.

WB D 208, 29 Apr 1844. Sett. by Gdn.; receipt 26 Jun 1844 /sic7
from Caroline Lattimore for her share of estate.

WB E 277; Acct. of sale held 5 Oct 1852 by Thos. and Joseph Lattimore, Agents of the heirs; six of the heirs, namely, Thos.,
Joseph, Daniel W., and John Lattimore, Joseph Cobbs, and G.W.
Queener give their share of an old mare to Sarah Firestone, who
has bought it at sale for $25.

LAUDERDALE
CR2 41, 7 Dec 1824. James Cowan app. Gdn. of Robert, Josephus, and
Almira Lauderdale, minor heirs of   Lauderdale, dec'd. /sic7

LAWSON, HUGH
WB F 397, Will exec. 20 Feb 1858, proven May 1861; to wife Mary Ann
until youngest child comes of age. Exec: John Atkinson. Wit:
A. Barb, Tyra Lawson.

WB F 400. Invt. sold 30 May 1861.

CC 260, filed 8 Sep 1870. Hugh Lawson died leaving widow Mary Ann
who died 1866 in Meigs Co. and children: Elias, David, and Wm.
of Hamilton Co.; John of Meigs Co.; Mary Ann wife of David or
John Powers; Hugh, dec'd, a minor; Tennessee a minor of Meigs Co.
who by 1876 has married Griffin Keith of Hamilton Co.; Cainetta
wife of John Gennoe of Bledsoe; Nathan a nonresident; Louisa,
dec'd, who married first James Snider and second John Howard of
Bledsoe Co.; and Sarah, dec'd, unmarried. The children of Louisa,
dec'd, are William Gilbert Snider a minor and _____ Howard a
minor, both of Bledsoe Co.

LAWSON, ISHAM
WB D 48-49, Will, not dated; to wife Mary; to two youngest sons
Pleasant C. and Alexander A.; to sons Nelson, Houson H. who lives
in Bradley Co., and Wm. M.; to daughters; to five youngest
daughters. Wit: James W. Long and David Cantrell.

CR5 16, 2 Nov 1841. Will proven.

WB D 49, 6 Dec 1841. Invt. by Nelson and Mary Lawson, Execs.

LAWSON, PETER
WB B 157, 5 Dec 1834. Invt. by Nelson Lawson, Adm.

CR3 411, 2 Dec 1834. James Maddy VS Peter Lawson; Isom Lawson
states that sometime before 17 Sep. last Robert Stubblefield
brought Peter Lawson to his house sick and with him brought a
chest and after Peter died he got a key and opened chest, found
$244 in cash and a note on Nelson Lawson executed to George
Smith.

LEE
CR5 465, 7 Aug 1848. Mary Ann Lee app. Gdn. to Mary Jane and John
Lee, minor orphans.

LEE, WILLIAM
CR5 466, 7 Aug 1848. Edward Lee app. Adm.

WB D 554, 18 Aug 1848. Comm. John W. Barnett, Samuel Wilson, and

Joseph Browder set apart year's support for widow Susan and family.

WB D 559-561, 4 Sep 1848. Invt. by Adm.; "note on P.W. Lane in Arkansas for collection".

WB D 592, 4 Dec 1848. Acct. of sale; buyers include Susan, Wm., Pet, Calvin, Zelpha, and John S. Lee.

WB E 96, 31 May 1850. Sett.; paid Calvin Lee, one of heirs.

WB E 120, 4 Sep 1850. Sett. by Susannah Lee, Gdn. to James C. Lee, one of children and heirs.

WB E 127, 7 Sep 1850. Heirs division of property by mutual consent: widow Susannah, Zilpha Lee, James C. Lee, Susan Lee wife of P.N. Lee, Elizabeth Lee now Elizabeth Reynolds wife of H.C. Reynolds, Edward, Wm., and Calvin Lee; Calvin's land is in Monroe Co.; proven 5 Nov 1850 by witnesses Martin M. Hicks and Griffin Lee.

WB E 207, 21 Feb 1852. Sett. by same Gdn.

LEGG, WILEY

WB B 151, 4 Sep 1834. Invt. by Saml. Legg, Adm.

CR4 211, 1 Dec 1834. Jesse H. Benton, Robert Renfro, and Larkin Taylor app. Comm. to lay off year's support for widow.

LEWIS, WILLIAM T.

CR2 34, 6 Dec 1824. Mortgage deed from Joseph Williams to William B. Lewis, Atty. in fact for heirs.

LIDE, JOHN W.

CR5 48, 7 Jun 1842. Alexander D. Keys and Oscar H. Lide app. Adms.

WB D 98-105, 5 Sep 1842. Invt. of sale by Adms.; "Cash due for salary of intestate as President of Bank for three months & ten days ending 10th April 1842 - $111.11"; Comm. John Miller, James S. Bridges, and John McGaughy set aside year's provisions for widow Mary, 4 Jul 1842; Robert Frazier, J.P.

CC 94, filed 22 Feb 1850. Mary E.P. Lide is widow of Dr. John W. Lide, dec'd, and mother of John W. Lide, age 23, and Samuel W. Lide, aged about 21. She is sister to Ann Virginia Netherland, widow of Dr. James W. Netherland.

LITTLE, WILLIAM

WB E 51, 7 Jun 1849. Comm. J. Jack, J.F. Benton, and John White set apart year's support for widow Susannah.

LONG, GEORGE, JR.

CR5 31, 7 Mar 1842. Moses Long chosen Gdn. by Elizabeth, Peggy, and John Long, over 14, and app. Gdn. for Wm. T., Jacob B., and Mary Long, under 14, minor orphans.

WB D 61, Apr 1842. Report by same, Gdn. to minor heirs who are Elizabeth, John, William, Jacob, and Mary Long, and Peggy Long or Ware; widow Nancy Long.

WB D 350, 31 Jan 1846. Sett. by Gdn.; receipt in full from Elizabeth and Pleasant M. Long; Jesse A. Ware sued and has been paid his part in full; expenses for four minors.

WB D 425, 31 Jan 1847 and D 517, 31 Jan 1848. Sett. by Gdn.

WB E 18, 31 Jan 1849. Sett. by Gdn.; paid John S. Long.

WB E 78, 1 Feb 1850 and 90, 2 Apr 1850. Reports by same Gdn.; Nancy Long, Gdn. (appointed) is paid balance in acct.

WB E 191, 6 Aug 1851; 221, 25 Jan 1851 /sic/. Sett. by Nancy Long, Gdn.

LONG, GEORGE, SR.
  WB E 20, Will exec. 25 Mar 1835; to wife Elizabeth; to children:
  Moses, James, John, George, Maples, Isaac, and Ruth Long, Nancy
  Longley, and Elizabeth Morton. Execs: sons Moses and James.
  Wit: Jackson Smith, James D. Sewell, William Crayn, and Thomas
  Atchley.
  CR5 510, 5 Feb 1849. Will proven.
  WB E 35, 2 Apr 1849; 235, 20 Mar 1852. Invt. and sales, and Sett.;
  paid heirs Isaac, John, Moses, and James Long, D. and Rutha Gor-
  man, James and Nancy Longley, Joseph and E. Morton, and P.M. Long
  for M. Long.
  CC 93, filed 8 Feb 1850. George Long, Sr., died 17 Jan 1849 leav-
  ing widow Elizabeth and children: Moses; John and Isaac of Hamil-
  ton Co. and later of Walker Co., Ga.; James; Nancy wife of James
  Longley of Hamilton Co.; Maples of Sevier Co.; Elizabeth wife of
  Joseph Morton; Ruth wife of David H. Gorman of Cocke Co.; and
  George, dec'd, who died 1839-1840, leaving widow Nancy and children: William, Jacob, Mary, Elizabeth wife of Pleasant Long of
  Walker Co., Ga., Margaret wife of Jesse Wear, and John S. Long.

LONG, MAHALA JANE
  CC 307, filed 11 Nov 1870. Mahala Jane Long died leaving husband
  John A. Long and children: Nancy Harriett wife of J.M. Kelly;
  James Robert Dudley; and minors John Barton, Rufus Albert
  Spencer, William Carroll Clinton, Mattie Oury, M.N., and Oscar
  Sissen Long.

LONG, SAMUEL
  CR6, 2 Feb 1852. Isaac Low of Bradley Co. and Wm. R. Long of
  Dalton, Ga., app. Adms.
  WB E 209, and 218, 1 Mar 1852. Invt. and sale.
  CR12 16, 17 Apr 1852. Petition to sell land: Isaac Lowe and Wm.
  R. Long, Adms., Elizabeth H. Lowe, Thomas and Lucy Caldwell,
  Joseph Long, Luke Lea Long by next friend Hannah Long, all
  heirs, and Hannah Long, widow; Samuel Long died about 24 Jan 1852.

LONGWITH, REUBEN
  CR6, 5 Apr 1852. Court pays for coffin for pauper.
  CR6, 5 Jul 1852. Jury of inquest over body, burned to death.

LONIS, CHARITY
  CR6, 6 Oct 1851. Court pays for coffin for pauper.

LORASON, THOMAS J.
  CR5 284, 6 Apr 1846. County paid Coroner for holding inquest over
  body.

LOVE, JOHN
  WB B 163-164, Will exec. 12 Aug 1834, probated 2 Dec 1834; to wife
  Margaret; to daus. Elizabeth Sutton, Loucy R. Reeveley, Sally G.
  Baker; to George A. and Margaret Martin, the children of dau.
  Martha Martin, dec'd; to Hugh M. (W), Mary Jane, Thomas L., and
  Matthew D. Walker, children of dau. Polly Ann Walker, dec'd, as
  they come of age; to son Thos. B.; to John P. Love, son of
  Thomas; family Bible in six volumes and large Bible containing
  family records; Joseph Baker husband of dau. Sally G. Baker.
  Exec: Thomas B. Love, Esq.
  WB E 310-311. "County Court March Session 1853 - Pursuant to the
  last Will and Testament of John Love dec'd it is ordered by the

Court that the following orders receipts and Post Masters Certif-
icates be made a matter of record in the Will Book of McMinn
County (to Wit)"): Order dated 22 Jan 1851 from Wm. T. Walker,
Bowdark Post Office, Green County, Mo., to Thos. B. Love of
McMinn Co., Tenn., directing that he send by mail 12.50 coined
gold, the amount of a legacy left by signer's grandfather John
Love; Certificate of J. McGaughy, P.M. that the gold was deposited
in the post office; identical orders from Matthew W. Walker and
from Wm. D. Renshaw and Mary Jane Renshaw formerly Mary Jane
Walker; receipt of Hugh M. Walker dated 26 Feb 1843 for 12.50, his
legacy from his grandfather John Love; receipt of Lucy R. and
Francis Reevely dated 6 Jul 1841 for $50, her legacy from her
father John Love; receipt of Elizabeth and James Suton dated 16
Jul 1841 for $50, her legacy from her father; receipt of George
A. Martin dated 9 Feb 1838 for $15, his legacy from his grand-
father John Love, dec'd, which will be due four years after the
death of grandmother Margaret Love, witness Hugh Reevely;
receipt of Margaret R. Martin dated 27 Apr 1839 for $35, her
legacy from her grandfather John Love which Thos. B. Love was
to pay her four years after her grandmother Margaret Love's
decease; receipt of Sally G. and Joseph Baker for $50 legacy
from her father John Love.
 CR4 215, 2 Dec 1834. Will proven by Wm. M. Biggs, Robt. W. Mc-
Cleary, and Thos. Gilbreath who identify handwriting as that of
John Love; Will was found among valuable papers of deceased with
his name subscribed thereto.

LOVE, JOHN M.
 CR4 288, 7 Nov 1836. Robartus Love app. Adm.
 CR4 291, 5 Dec 1836. George Reynolds, Alexander Stephenson, and
Wm. Brown app. Comm. to lay off year's support for widow.
 WB B 223-224, Feb 1837. Invt. of sale by Adm.; buyers include
Nancy, Jeremiah, Robartus, John, and Dungens Love.

LOWE, SAMUEL
 CR6, 7 Apr 1856. F.M. Lusk paid for furnishing coffin; Jury of
inquest finds that deceased died 11 Feb 1856 by the visitation
of God.

LOWE, WILLIAM E.
 CR10 242, 3 Oct 1870. J.D. Low app. Adm. and Comm. app. to lay off
dower for widow.
 CR10 256, 7 Nov 1870. Plat of the land assigned to widow Mary E.
as dower.
 CR10 274, 275, 6 Mar 1871. James M. Browder qualified as Gdn. of
minor heirs except John and Julia by last marriage; Mary C. Lowe
app. Gdn. of John W. and Julia R. Lowe, her own minor heirs.
 CR11 290, 11 Nov 1873. Final sett. by Adm.

LOWER, MICHAEL
 CR9 254, 1 Apr 1867. Comm. app. to lay off dower to Amanda Lower.
 CR17 54, 15 Jun 1867. Amanda Lower widow VS S. Houston Jack.

LOWRY, DANIEL
 WB G 7-9, 19 May 1864. Invt. and sale by John D. Lowry and A.A.
Newman, Adms.
 CR9 19, 7 Nov 1864. Susan Lowry widow of Daniel Lowry, dec'd VS
John D. Lowry and Alexander A. Newman, Adms., Margaret A. Newman,
David N. Varnell, Jacob H. and Frances E. Fisher, James R. Lowry,

Francis M. and Virginia M. Pennington, Martha N. Lowry, Daniel C.
Lowry, John N. and Nancy J. Delzell .... it appearing that Daniel
Lowry died on 1 Mar 1864 .... application of widow for dower;
defendants are heirs.
WB G 170, 7 May 1866; 177, 30 May 1866. Settlements.
CC 42, filed 1 Jan 1866. Daniel Lowry's children are as given above.
Margaret A. is wife of A.A. Newman of Bradley Co.; Virginia M. is
wife of Francis M. Pennington and Frances Elizabeth is wife of
Jacob H. Fisher; Nancy J. is wife of John N. Delzell of Richland
Co., Ill,; the children of Mary S. Lowry Varnell, dec'd, are
Susan F. born about 1852, James born about 1855, and Wm. Varnell
born about 1864.

LOWRY, ELIZA EMELINE
WB G 3, Will exec. 6 Jan 1863; to sister Amanda Hall; to nephew
Alonzo P. Hall when he reaches 21; to bro.-in-law O.P. Hall;
their kind attention in all my sickness and troublesome affairs
in life; lawsuit pending in Supreme Court at Knoxville, Tenn.
Exec: bro.-in-law O.P. Hall. Wit: Geo. W. Bridges, P.M. George.

LOWRY, ISAAC
WB D 32-33, Will exec. 3 Oct 1840; to wife Jane until youngest
child comes of age; to children James H., Thomas J., Daniel A.,
John W., William D., David H., Samuel N., Isaac A., Mary J.,
Nancy A., Elizabeth M., Fanny L., Martha M., and Eleanor M.
Execs: James Lowry, Jr., and James Forest. Wit: A. Barb and
Thomas J. Lowry.
CR5 2, 6 Sep 1841. Will proven.
WB D 44, 188, 373, 497, WB E 48, 100, 178, dating from 30 Oct 1841
to 1 Jul 1851. Invt. of sale and sett. by Execs. and sett. by
Mrs. Jane Lowry, Gdn.
WB E 263, 1 Jul 1852. Sett. by Gdn.; received from Execs. of
estate of James Lowry, Sr., dec'd.
WB E 328, 1 Jul 1853. Sett. by Gdn.

LOWRY, ISAAC A.
CR8 148, 6 Apr 1863. Wm. L. Rice, Alex. and Robt. M. Maxwell app.
Comm. to lay off year's support for widow and family.
CR13 215, 4 May 1863; 225, 6 May 1863; 245, 9 Aug 1864. T.J.
Lowry, Adm. VS Manerva J. Lowry, widow, and Isaac R. and Wallace
L. Lowry, minor heirs. Petition to sell land. Isaac A. Lowry
died intestate in McMinn Co., 20 Mar 1863, leaving the widow and
the two minors his only children.

LOWRY, JAMES, SR.
WB E 65-66, Will exec. 5 Mar 1845; to wife Nancy; to children:
James, Jr.; John D.; Daniel; the heirs of Isaac, dec'd; the
heirs of Polly McSpadden, dec'd; Elizabeth Barr; Fanny McGill;
Jane Rebecca Cuningham, "making eight in all". Execs: sons
Daniel, James, Jr., and John D. Lowry and friend Wm. Forrest.
Wit: Tho. J. Campbell, Wm. Lowry, A.D. Keys.
WB E 73. Invt. and sale held 23 Nov 1849, filed by Execs.
WB E 200, 31 Dec 1851. Sett.; paid $630 each to heirs R. McGill
and wife, S.A. Barr and wife, Daniel Lowry, John Cuningham and
wife; paid $105 each to heirs Mathew B., J.T., J.W., J.A., T.A.,

and S.E. McSpadden; paid $45 each to heirs J. Low and wife, Wm.
D., D.H., T.J., D.A., Nancy Ann, Jas. H., John W., and S.A. Lowry;
paid $225 to Jane Lowry, Gdn. of minor heirs.
WB E 211-216. Invt. sold 21 Nov 1851 after the death of widow
Nancy.
WB E 329, 31 Aug 1853. Final sett. by Wm. F. Forrest and James
Lowry, two of Execs.; receipts for $393 each from Daniel Lowry,
Robert Magill, A. Barr, and J. Cunningham; receipts for $123 each
from J.D. and James Lowry; receipts for $65.50 each from M.B.,
J.A., S.E., J.T., J.W., and Thos. A. McSpadden; receipt for
$90.69 from Jane Lowry, Gdn.; receipt for $30.23 each from J.H.,
D.A., F.L., Wm. D., D.H., E.M., N.A., J.W., and T.J. Lowry and
Joshua Lowe.

LOWRY, JOHN
WB A 75, Will exec. 15 Oct 1825; to wife Susanna; to dau. Sarah
Lowry; to son-in-law Jacob Davis; to balance of children. Wit:
Hardy S. Morris, Chapman Stewart, and John Newton.
CR2 119, 6 Dec 1825. Will proven.

LOWRY, JOHN
CR8 139, 2 Mar 1863. R.A. Lowry app. Adm.
CR11 219, 23 May 1871. Sett. by Adm.; book in which sale was
recorded was destroyed during the war; nine payments of $24.77
each to James H., John M., and R.A. Lowry, Eliza P. and John M.
Nealy, Mary Mince, Eliza Keys, Drucilla Campbell, Martha Wasson,
and Isabella Marreset.

LOWRY, MARTHA M.
WB G 44, Will exec. 16 Jan 1865; to two sisters Elizabeth M. and
Fanny L. Lowry "who have waited on me so kindly in my affliction".
Exec: James Lowry, Sr. Wit: Nancy Stalcup, N. Magill, John D.
Lowry, Sr.
CR9 38, 6 Feb 1865. Will proven.
WB G 175, 30 Jun 1866. Sett. by Exec.

LOWRY, SAMUEL
WB C 289. Invt. filed 25 Sep 1840 by Richmond Gaddy, Adm.
CR4 517, 5 Oct 1840. Richmond Gaddy app. Adm.

LOWRY, T.J.
CR10 129, 29 Aug 1869. James C. Lowry and J.M. Jackson app. Adms.
and James Forest, W.L. Burn, and A. Maxwell app. Comm. to lay
off year's support for widow Clarecy and family.
CR11 229, 7 Oct 1871. Sett. by Adms.; receipts from David H.,
J.C., and Mrs. Clarissa Lowry for various amounts.

McADOO, SAMUEL
WB F 90, 15 Sep 1857. Sett. by R.A. McAdoo, Gdn. for minor heirs,
funds having come to his hands from D.L. Campbell and J. Knox,
former Gdns.
WB F 200, 15 Sep 1858. Sett. by same, Gdn. to Elizabeth P., Mary,
and Nancy McAdoo.
WB F 285, 15 Sep 1859. Sett. by same, Gdn. to Mary, Prudence, and
Nancy McAdoo; receipt from Prudence for her share in full.
WB F 348, 15 Sep 1860; 424, 29 Nov 1861. Sett. and final sett. by
Gdn.; receipt from wards for balance.

McAFFREY (McCAFFREY), JAMES W.
CR9 16, 3 Oct 1864. Elias Walker app. Adm.

WB G 24; 4 Nov 1864. Invt. by Adm.; includes "One Stove in Tele-
    graph Office" and "White & Winter Frost borrowed money 400.00";
    list 5 May 1863.
WB G 43, no date. Comm. S.W. Royston, R.A. Love, and J.F. Browder
    set apart year's support for widow Nancy and family.
WB G 175, 28 Jun 1866. Sett.
CR9 151, 2 Apr 1866. E. Walker, Adm., Nancy W., Taylor, John, and
    Alex. McAffrey VS Wm. M. Sehorn et al.

McAMIS (McCAMIS, McCAMISH), D.C.
WB E 45, Dec 1848. Copy of report filed in Anderson Co., Tenn.,
    by J.L. McSpadden, Gdn., certified by John Key, Clerk of Ander-
    son Co.
WB E 115, 303, 369, 405, WB F 58, dating from 1 Sep 1850 to 12 Mar
    1857. Settlements by James W. McSpadden Gdn. to Ann E. and
    David McAmis, minor heirs; paid for their tuition.
WB F 362, 2 Jan 1861. Final sett. by Gdn.; allowed Gdn. for making
    trip from Cass Co., Mo., to Miss. and disposing of a family of
    negroes; paid for tuition for Miss Ann McCamish; receipt of A.E.
    McAmis for one-half of funds.

McBROOM, ANDREW
CR6, 6 Jan 1857. J.S. Russell app. Adm.
WB F 43, 16 Jan /1857/. Invt.
WB F 292, 12 Sep 1859. Pro rata sett.

McCALLIE, WILLIAM T.
WB E 108, Will exec. 31 Aug 1850, proven 1850; the balance of real
    estate after payment of debts and wife's dower to the children
    of son T.H., to dau. Alice H., and to son John H.; $1 each to
    dau. Rebecca J.E. Rowles and to Emma C. and Susan Aldehoff.
    Execs: wife Mary and T.H. McCallie. Wit: Wm. Park Lea, John
    Scarbrough.
CR6, Oct 1850. Will proven.
WB E 131-137, no date; 279, no date; 400, 1 Jan 1855; 413, 19 Feb
    1855. Invt., Acct. of sale, and report by A. Swafford, Gdn. to
    minor heirs.
CR6, 4 Oct 1852. Mary Dixon formerly Mary McCauly petitions for
    dower in land, stating that she is widow of Wm. T. McCauley who
    died leaving the following living children: Rebecca Jane now
    Rebecca Rowles, Henry Theodore, Alice Helen, and John H., the
    two last being minors and children of Mary, the petitioner.
    Mary and the said Henry Theodore were app. Execs.
CC 513, filed 19 Aug 1853 and 119, filed 19 Feb 1851. Wm. T.
    McCallie died 2 Sep 1850 leaving widow Mary who has since mar-
    ried John Dixon, and children as above. The children of son
    Theodore H. are Wm. P., Henry A., James J., and Mary E., all
    minors.
WB E 413, 21 Oct 1855. Comm. Wm. L. McKamy, A.P. McClatchey, and
    A. Swafford set apart year's provisions for Mary Dixon, former
    widow, and her family.
WB E 423, 7 Apr 1855. Sett. by Henry T. McCallie and Mary Dixon,
    Execs.; Firm of McCallie & Scarbrough.
WB E 459, 572, WB F 90, 197, 191, 277, 334, 411, dating from 3 Sep
    1855 to 3 Sep 1861. Settlements by A. Swafford, Gdn.; by H.W.
    Van Aldehoff, Gdn. successor to A. Swafford.
WB G 175, no date. Sett. by James Gettys, Gdn. app. May 1866.
CR7 228, 6 Sep 1858. A. Swafford resigns as Gdn. and H.W.V.

Aldehoff of Bradley Co. is app.
CR8, 5 Jan 1863. Ordered by the Court that H. Van D. Aldehoff Gdn.
of John McCaulie pay to Dr. Wm. J. Johnson $30 and to Dr. J.B.
Smith $34 for the amputation of John McCaulie's arm.

McCALLUM (McCULLUM), THOMAS
WB G 231, Will exec._1 Mar_1870, probated Sep 1870; to heirs
Joseph M., Alley /female7, James F., Margarett E., and Nancy
Tennessee McCallum and to wife Sarah McCallum; Alley to have $50
more than other heirs; wife Sarah to have all furniture she
brought here when we were married and heirs Joseph and Alley to
have furniture I had in my possession at time of our marriage;
all furniture by us since be equally divided among all heirs.
Exec: Chrisley Foster. Attest: John Buttram, Asbery Mains.
CR11 310, 15 Aug 1874. Sett. by Exec.; receipts from Sarah and
Joseph McCullum, Sarah McCullum Gdn., and Moses and Ally Pearce.

McCANN, JAMES
WB E 275-276, Will exec. 4 Feb 1852; to sisters Hannah McCann and
Margaret Roberts; to nephew Christopher T. Roberts; land warrant
to be sold. Exec: nephew Edmund Roberts. Wit: Edmund, E.W.,
and Elizabeth C. Roberts. Signed by mark.
WB E 307, 21 Feb 1853; 337, 7 Oct 1853. Invt. and final sett.
Loose paper in WB E: Letters Testamentary to Edmund Roberts
issued 4 Oct 1852 empowering him to enter upon Execution of the
Will.

McCARTY, JOHN L.
WB F 345-346, Will exec. 17 May 1859, proven Oct 1860; "being advanced in age"; to wife Mary, farm on Hiwassee River; other
lands to be sold at end of 10 years and money divided equally
among the children, with the heirs of deceased dau. Martha Evaline Smith to have her share; younger children to be educated;
if unmarried children should marry, they may live on lands until
the end of the 10 years the same as Johnson Smith Collins and my
son John T. McCarty are now doing. Execs: wife Mary and nephew
Timothy H. McCarty. Wit: S.D. Stout, J.H. Effert.
WB F 381-393, 23 Oct 1860; 461, 26 Apr 1861. Invt. and Add. Invt.
CC 120, filed Apr 1867. John L. McCarty died leaving widow Mary,
now of great age, and children: Mary I., widow of _____ Johnson,
who marries Samuel Workman in 1867; Elizabeth J. wife of J.B.
Collins; Wm. T.; Joseph B.; John T.; Martha E. Smith, dec'd,
(whose children are John S., Wm. G., and Mary J. Smith); and
James McCarty, dec'd without issue, whose widow is Betty.

McCARTY, TIMOTHY
CC 41, filed 27 Dec 1865. John Wallin VS Harrison Dill, et al.
Timothy and Mary H. McCarty were Execs. of Will of John L.
McCarty. Timothy is now dead.

McCARTY, WILLIAM
CR4 550, 552, 5 Jul 1841. Fisher, Rider & Co. paid for making
coffin for Wm. McCarty who died poor. John M. Gibbs, Inn keeper,
paid for taking care of deceased while sick. Chairman of Court
ordered to dispose of property of Wm. McCarty, it appearing that
he has no relatives, unless application be made for same.

McCLATCHY, ADOLPHUS P.
CR8 138, 2 Mar 1863. R.M. and A.P. McClatchey app. Adms.

CR9 25, 5 Dec 1864. Comm. set apart dower for widow Jane R.
WB G 113, 29 Sep 1865. Sale held 28 Mar 1863; records of original
    Invt. and sale returned to Clerk's office were destroyed in 1864.
WB G 128, 18 Nov 1865. Sett.
CC 36, filed 18 Nov 1865. Adolphus P. McClatchey died intestate
    in McMinn Co., 3 Feb 1863, leaving widow Jane R. and heirs:
    Martha E. wife of James R. Lowry; Ellen R.; Minerva J.; James S.;
    Samuel H.; Wm. T.M.; Wiley M.; (last four are nonresidents) and
    Allen B. McClatchey, a minor. The Adms. are Robert M. and
    Adolphus P. McClatchey.

McCLATCHY (McCLATCHEY), JOHN
    CR4 515, 5 Oct 1840. Commissioners (below) app.
    WB C 293, 29 Oct 1840. Comm. John Matlock, Wm. McKamy, and Wm. T.
    McCallie set apart year's support for widow Elizabeth.
    WB D 8-16, no date. Invt.; includes note on Ezekiel Herrien, North
    Carolina; buyers include A.P., W.J., and Elizabeth McClatchey.
    WB D 152, 31 Aug 1843. Sett.; one item is a subscription to Holston
    College, $2.00.
    WB D 209, 1 Jul 1844. Sett.

McCLURE
    CR2 233, 3 Sep 1827. John Love app. Gdn. for Peggy Ann McClure.
    CR2 263, 3 Mar 1828. Gdn. reports receipt of ward's distributive
    share of her father's estate.
    WB A 136, 151, 206, B 11, 80, 139, dating from 3 Mar 1828 to 3 Mar
    1834. Reports by same Gdn.
    WB B 169, 182, 235, C 119, 188, dating from 2 Mar 1835 to 15 Dec
    1839. Reports by Thomas B. Love, Gdn.
    WB C 338, 15 Dec 1840. Thomas B. Love, Gdn. to Peggy Ann Taylor,
    formerly McClure, produced to court a receipt from E.L. (S.)
    Taylor, stating that he had received from Gdn. the full amt. due
    his wife Peggy Ann.

McCOY, JOHN
    CR2 332, 2 Mar 1829. Daniel and Susannah McCoy app. Adms.
    WB A 175, no date. Invt.
    WB C 151, 5 Aug 1839. Final sett. by Susannah McCoy, Adminx.;
    amount paid to the widow for raising the children for many years.

McCOY, WILLIAM
    CR2 119, 6 Dec 1825. John and Daniel McCoy app. Adms.
    CR2 347, 3 Mar 1829. Daniel McCoy, surviving Adm., allowed 12
    months to settle.

McCRARY, ROBERT
    CC 241, filed 3 May 1870. Elizabeth McCrary is the widow of Robert
    McCrary who died 1869 intestate. Land was bought with money com-
    ing to Elizabeth from her brother's estate.

McCROSKEY (McKROSKY), DAVID
    CR13 50, 13 Dec 1860. Phillip Rowland and wife VS David McKrosky
    and others. Petition to sell land. Judgment pro confesso against
    James S. and John A. McKrosky, nonresidents; p. 55 - amended
    petition to include Mrs. Esther Melton as defendant; p. 103 -
    Joseph W., Francis M., Alfred, and Margaret Melton, Celia wife of
    Daniel H. Matthews, Sarah C. wife of Tipton M. Stephenson, and
    May Jane, Peter L., James K.P., George M.D., Amanda H., and Wm.
    J. Melton, the last six minors, Daniel H. Matthews, and Tipton

M. Stephenson made parties defendant to this suit; p. 235, 6 May
1863 - Time granted for Esther Melton, Gdn. of her own minor
children, to file her answer; p. 147, 13 Dec 1865 - Plaintiff
suggests death of defendant John A. McKrosky which is admitted.
CR14 111, 19 Apr 1867. Note of Philip Rowland, J.C. Townsend, and
J.W. Gibson to John F. Slover, Clerk, for benefit of heirs of
David McCroskey.

McCROSKY, WILLIAM
CR4 524, 2 Nov 1840. Will proven by John Scybert, one of the subscribing witnesses. /Will is not in records./
CC 80, filed 4 Feb 1860. Wm. McCroskey died a number of years ago
intestate in McMinn Co. leaving widow Isophene, who has since
married Wm. Emmerson, and children: Sarah wife of Phillip Rowland, Joseph L., James S., of Ark., Pinkney, and John A. McCrosky,
a minor who is temporarily absent in Sevier Co.

McCULLEY, GEORGE, SR.
CR9 189, 1 Oct 1866. Joseph McCully app. Adm.

McCULLY, WILLIAM
CR4 370, 2 Jul 1838. George McCully app. Adm.
WB C 30, Aug 1838. Invt. of sale; buyers include Joseph, George,
and D.G. McCully.

McDERMOTT, COLONEL WILLIAM P. H.
CR6, 4 Sep 1854. Jane E. McDermott and James B. Cooke app. Adms.
WB E 399, no date. Comm. Wm. H. Ballew, R.C. Jackson, and Robt. N.
McEwen set apart year's support for widow Jane and family.
WB E 567, no date. Invt. of sale.
CC 5, filed 8 Aug 1856. Wm. P.H. McDermott died Aug 1854 leaving
widow Jane E. and children: Penelope M. wife of James B. Cooke,
and the following minors: Wm. P.H., Jr., Louisa A., Samuel A.,
Joseph A., John M., Inez C., Elizabeth, and Julia McDermott.

McDONALD, CHARLES W.
CR5 465, 7 Aug 1848. F.P. Pettitt, Nathan Sullins, and Allen
Dennis app. Comm. to lay off year's support for Mrs. McDonald,
widow.
WB D 555, 4 Sep 1848. Above Comm. report.
CC 85, filed about 1849-50. Charles W. McDonald died leaving widow
Nancy Ann and nine children: Virginia wife of James Rucker,
Christopher, Laura, John, Rebecca, Samantha, Isabella, Eglentine,
and Emeline, all minors except Virginia. In the answer of widow
to the lawsuit in Nov. 1850, the minors are listed as A.C., Laura
E., John P., Hariet R., Ollevia E., Samentha T., and Susannah M.

McELRATH, H. McD.
CR9 82, 2 Oct 1865. J.E. McElrath app. Adm.
WB G 164, no date. Invt. by Adm.
CC 68, filed 6 Jul 1866. /There are no papers left in this file.
Information from Record Bks. C and D./ H. McD. McElrath died
leaving widow E.L., who by Nov. 1867 has married W.C. Eblin, and
children as follows: Susan C. who by Nov 1866 has married James
H. Hays; Ellen F. who by 28 May 1867 has become 21 and by 28 Nov
1867 has married James C. Morris; J.E. McElrath; and perhaps two
other children.
CR11 156, 25 May 1869. Sett. by Adm.; estate worth $940,975.50 of
which $936,321.00 is in Confederate bonds and currency.

McEWEN (McEWIN) and McKAMY (McKAMEY, McCAMY)
  WB A 109, no date. Add. Invt. of late firm of McEwen and McCamy.
  WB A 153, Gdn. report, Pumpkintown, Dec 1827. "I Joseph Roberson
    Guardian for the children of James and Polly McKamey both deceased
    acknowledge to have rec'd of Wm. C. McKamey, administrator of
    James McKamey all the property that was purchased by Polly McKamey
    at pumkintown on the 18th of January 1827".....Test: W.T. McEwen
    "saw Robison sign the above in Augt. 1828 but acknowledged to have
    rec'd the property above mentioned in Decr. 1827". 18 Jan 1827
    Polly McKamey, Adminx., and Wm. C. McKamey, Adm. of estate of
    James McKamey. Dec 1827 Joseph Roberson Gdn. for children of
    James McKamey. Comm. John Miller, J.H. Fyffe, and Wm. Hogan cer-
    tify report on 19 Aug 1828.
  WB A 163-171, Aug 1828. List of accounts of McEwen & McKamey; Lot
    No. 7 in Athens where the storehouse stands. Wm. McKamey of
    Anderson Co.
  WB B 62-63, 6 Jun 1831. List of property sold at Athens on 6 Sep
    1830.

McEWING, JOHN
  CR1 329, 4 Jun 1828. Execs. of John McEwing, dec'd, VS Wm. R.
    Tucker and John McAllen.

McGAUGHEY, JOHN, SR.
  CR9 44, 3 Apr 1865. John C. McGaughey app. Adm.
  CR9 50, 1 May 1865. Comm. app. to set apart year's support for
    widow Martha.
  WB G 65, 9 Jun 1865. Comm. David Cleage, Geo. W. Ross, and H.H.
    Rider lay off year's support for family.
  WB G 90-98, 31 Aug 1865. Acct. of sale, list of accts. due, list
    of notes due, and list of Bank Notes, filed by same Adm.
  CR10 76, 7 Dec 1868. R.H. and R.B. McGaughy app. Adms. de bonis
    non.
  CR11 207 to 217, 12 Apr 1871. Sett. by same Adms.; five pages of
    notes and accts. which were returned in Invt. and which are in-
    solvent and uncollectable.
  CR11 295, 27 Feb 1874. Final sett.; nine receipts for equal amounts
    from W.S., G., R.H., Martha, and R.B. McGaughy, R.B. McGaughy
    Gdn., Jane and J.M. Horton, J.W. and V.A. Witcher, and R.A. and
    M. Nelson.

McGAUGHEY, JOHN C.
  CR14 172, 14 Aug 1867. John C. McGaughey Adm. VS A. Cleage; the
    death of plaintiff is suggested and proven.
  CR9 360, 6 Jan 1868. Robert and R.B. McGaughey app. Adms.

McGUIRE, WILLIAM
  CR8 163, 4 May 1863. Eli Dixon app. Adm. Moses Cunningham, J.J.
    Middleton, and A. McRoberts app. Comm. to lay off year's support
    for widow and family.
  CC 179, filed 3 Sep 1868. E.K. Ensminger Gdn. of Thomas McGuire,
    Letitia McGuire and husband Robert McGuire VS Frank M. Rowan,
    Adm. of Eli Dixon et al. Wm. McGuire died Feb 1863 leaving widow
    Letitia M. (whom he married in Oct 1861 and who has since married
    Robert McGuire) and an only child Thomas. Eli Dixon, Adm., died
    and Frank Rowan of Monroe Co. is now Adm. of his estate.

McKAMY (McCAMY), JAMES
  CR2 181, 4 Dec 1826. Wm. C. and Mary McKamy app. Adms. and Special

Execs.; John Miller, Jesse Mayfield, and Moses Stout app. Comm.
to lay off year's support for Mrs. Mary McKamy and family.
CR1 260, 6 Mar 1827. Office of Trustee for McMinn Co. vacant by
death of James McCamy Esq. late Trustee.
CR2 259, 6 Dec 1827. Joseph Robinson app. Gdn. of Isabella C.,
Hannah Manerva, and John M. McCamy, minor orphan heirs.

McKAMY, WILLIAM
WB F 329-330, Will exec. 23 Apr 1860, proven Jul 1860; "I wrote my
will myself"; to wife Polly; to three sons Wm. P., Jasper N.,
and John M.; to daus. Mary C. McKamy when she reaches 21, and
Elizabeth Jane Dodson. Execs: sons Wm. P. and Jasper N. Wit:
J.M. Miller, Daniel Parkerson.
CR7 450, 2 Jul 1860. Will proven; Wm. P. McKamy app. Exec., the
other named Exec. being a minor.
WB F 342, 6 Aug 1860; 356, 12 Oct 1860. Invt. and Add. Invt.
CR7 478, 2 Oct 1860. Resolutions of respect by County Court.
CR9 60, 3 Jul 1865. J.N. McKamy app. Gdn. of minor heirs, John M.
and Mary C. McKamy.

McKELDIN, ANDREW W.
CR9 247, 1 Apr 1867. Comm. app. to lay off year's support for
widow Emily.
CR9 258, 1 Apr 1867. Wm. B. and J.A. McKeldin, and T.L. Farrell
app. Adms.
CR14 13, 9 Apr 1867. Emily McKeldin Petition for Dower; A. McKel-
din died 19 Feb 1867.
CR9 371, 3 Feb 1868. J.S. Matthews app. Gdn. of Hugh, Bell, and
James R.C. McKeldin, minor heirs.
CR11 236, 2 Mar 1872. Sett. by Adms.; Advancements of $3000 each
made to heirs Mrs. E. McKeldin, Wm. B., J.A., and H.M. McKeldin,
W. Gettys and wife, and Gen. Wm. Brazelton, Gdn.

McKINNEY (McKINEY)
CR10 199, 4 Apr 1870. John L. McKinney app. Gdn. for Buford A.
McKiney.

McKINNEY, DAVID
CR1 24, 6 Sep 1821. Catherine L. McKinney, Adminx. VS George
Harlin.

McKINZIE, REUBEN
CR14 327, 16 Dec 1867. James R. Gettys VS Boggess et al. The
death of Reuben McKinzie one of the defendants is suggested.
/This may be in Meigs Co., Tenn.7

McLEAN (McCLAIN), JOSEPH
WB A 94, Will exec. 6 Aug 1827; to father John; to mother Rebecca;
to all bros. and sisters. Execs: father and James Fyffe. Wit:
Benj. C. Stout, Harris D. Thorp. Signed by mark.
WB A 95-103, 14 Aug 1827; 152, no date; 222, 4 Sep 1830. Invt.
and settlements.

McLESTER, W. W.
CR6, 4 Sep 1854. Amelia McLester app. Gdn. to Araminta and Charles
McLester, minor heirs.

McMAHAN, CASWELL
CR4 232, 233, 7 Sep 1835. Caswell Jarnagin, Caleb Haymes, and Geo.
R. Cox app. Comm. to set apart year's support for widow Elizabeth;

Alex. C. Robeson and Elizabeth McMahan app. Adms., and Elizabeth McMahan is app. Gdn. of John McMahan, minor son.

WB B 230-234, 7 Dec 1835. Report of sale; includes note on Washington McMahan.

WB B 243, Apr 1837; C 22, June 1838. Reports by Gdn.

WB C 48-50, 27 Sep 1838. Sett. by Adms.; "Paid John McMahan Sr. and Polly McMahan his wife their claim of support"; paid to James McMahan.

WB C 130, 161, 220, D 82, 134, 187, 189, 308, 369, 512, E 19, 92, 190, 281, 336, 417, dating from Apr 1839 to 26 Mar 1855. Sett. by same Gdn., John C. McMahan minor heir; (1839: 1 bottle of castor oil for the heir 50¢).

WB D 24, 31 Jul 1841. Invt. by A.C. Robison.

WB E 561, 24 Aug 1856. Final sett. by Gdn.

McMAHAN, ESTHER and MARY JANE

CR5 17, 6 Dec 1841. Jury of inquest finds that Peter, a slave of John McMahan's, murdered Esther and Mary Jane McMahan on 15 Nov 1841.

McMAHAN, JOHN, SR.

CR4 338, 7 Nov 1837. Jesse R. Blackburn app. Adm.

WB C 28, 6 Aug 1838; 44, Sep 1838; 167, 2 Sep 1839. Invt., Sale, and Sett.

McMANUS, JOSEPH

CR4 49, 10 Dec 1831. Power of Atty. from John Lambert, Gdn. of minor heirs, to James Standifor is acknowledged.

McMILLIN (McMILLIAN, McMILLION), DAVID

WB A 120-122, Will exec. 26 Jan 1827; to wife Mary; to children Joseph, William, Nancy, Polly, Narcissa; to grandsons David C. and Jonathan P. McMillion when they become of age. Execs: Joseph and Wm. McMillion. Wit: John H. Porter, James Hickey. Signed by mark.

CR2 262, 3 Mar 1828. Will proven.

WB B 158, 28 Oct 1834. Sett. filed by Wm. Lowry, Nat Smith, and Elijah Hurst; "heirs six in number"; finds in hands of executor for David Caldwell, Wm. McDaniel, D.C. and J.P. McMillan, and old Lady McMillan.

McMILLIN, ROBERT W.

CR2 96, 6 Sep 1825. Report by Thos. Parris and Joseph W. McMillin, Adms.

WB A 27-29, no date; 62-64, no date. Invt. and Sale; sold to widow.

WB A 221, 6 Sep 1830. Sett.; Comm. N. Carson, David Roper, and R.W. McClary settle with Joseph Love Gdn. for David C. McMillin and Carson Caldwell Gdn. for Jonathan P. McMillin.

McMINN, JOSEPH

CR4 226, 1 Jun 1835. Wm. J. Johnson app. Gdn. for William C., Nancy G., Reason H., Treacy A., Luisa M., and Elizabeth J. McMinn.

WB B 251(2), Jun 1837. Report by Gdn.; received from Orville Bradley, Exec. of will of Joseph McMinn on 25 Oct 1835.

WB C 24, 143, 145, 262, dating from 4 Jun 1838 to 8 Apr 1840. Reports by Gdn.

McNABB, ELIZABETH

CR5 487, 3 Oct 1848. Wm. McNabb app. Adm. of Mrs. Elizabeth McNabb.

WB E 112, 26 Sep 1850. Sett. by Adm.; received pension money.
CC Record Bk. A, p. 139. Henderson McNabb and James McNabb for
himself and the other heirs at law of Elizabeth McNabb, dec'd
VS Daniel Wammack and Wm. Rivers and his wife Susan Rivers.
Elizabeth McNabb died 20 Jun 1849 leaving heirs James, William,
Henderson, and others.

McNABB, JAMES
WB F 412-413, Will exec. 11 Feb 1861, proven Oct 1861; to wife
Lavista, "having no horse I therefore will her none"; to sons
H.W., Isaac H., Mathew G., Nathaniel B., and Elkany; to dau.
Rhoda T. Robinet; to Lucretia White; "the seven heirs previously
mentioned"; to two sons-in-law Price Ward and John Orton, $1
each; to two granddaus. Mary E. Ward and Mary E. Orton when they
reach 18; Exec. to get a set of tombstones worth $15 to be
placed at head and foot of mother's grave. Exec: James H.
Lowrey. Wit: Robert Mansell, Benj. T. Ziegler, and Robt. A.
Lowery.
WB F 469-471. Invt. of notes and property sold 18 Oct 1861.
WB F 471, 4 Nov 1861. Comm. R.A. Lowry, B.T. Ziegler, and Jas.
H. Lowry lay off year's support for widow.
WB G 32, 5 Dec 1864. Sett.; receipts from N.B. McNabb, J.F.
Robinett and wife, M.G. McNabb, and widow Lavesta McNabb.
WB G 172, 28 Apr 1866. Sett.; receipts from Elkana, H.W., and
Jane (James) McNabb.

McNUTT, JOSEPH
CR10 126, 2 Aug 1869. Report by Daniel Wamack, Gdn. of minor
heirs.

McNUTT, WILLIAM F.
CR8 140, 2 Mar 1863. Boyd Porter app. Adm.
CR9 4, 5 Sep 1864. John B. Porter app. Adm. in place of Boyd
Porter, dec'd.
CR9 30, 2 Jan 1865. John B. Porter, Adm., ordered to deliver all
funds to Gdn. of minor heirs.
WB G 53, 1 May 1865. Report by R.A. Love, Gdn. of minor son
Robert McNutt; has received nothing as yet.
WB G 143, 2 Feb 1866. Invt.
WB G 144-146. Sales held Mar 1863 and Nov 1863 by Boyd Porter,
Adm., filed by John B. Porter; payments for items sold Mar 1863
was in Confederate Scrip.
WB G 147, 2 Feb 1866. Acct. of sales held 29 Oct 1864.
WB G 179, 12 May 1866 and 195, 30 Aug 1866. Sett. by Gdn. and Adm.
CC 48, filed 12 Feb 1866. James McNutt moved to this country in
company with his bro. Wm. F. and his aunt Sarah McNutt in 1861
or 1862. His aunt Sarah married Russell Lane. James McNutt was
away for nearly three years and when he returned his bro. Wm. F.
had died in 1863 leaving an only child represented by Robert
Love, its grandfather. James is the only surviving bro. of Wm.
F. McNutt.

McPHAIL, DANIEL
CR10 90, 92, 1 Feb 1869. John B. Kennedy app. Adm. and Comm. app.
to lay off year's support for widow and family.
CC 199, filed 1 Mar 1869. Daniel McPhail died Dec 1868 intestate
leaving widow Elizabeth and children: Martha J., wife of John
B. Kennedy; Nancy M., wife of James S. Beaver; John P., dec'd,

whose widow is Mary J. and children are Daniel B., age 10, Elizabeth age 8, and John W. age 6, with Stephen Sharitts as their
Gdn.
    CR11 201, 20 Jan 1871. Final sett. by same Adm.; paid equal amounts
    to Stephen Sharrits, Jas. S. and Nancy Beavers, John B. and Martha
    J. Kennedy.

McPHAIL, JOHN
    CR10 69, 2 Nov 1868. Wm. McPhail app. Adm.
    CR10 201, 4 Apr 1870. Stephen Sharits app. Gdn. of minor heirs.

McPHAIL, MARY, NEIL, and DOUGALD
    CR6, 1 Sep 1851. Daniel McPhail app. Adm. of Mary McPhail, Neill
    McPhail, and Dugald McPhail.
    WB E 230-234, 1 Dec 1851; 259, 5 Jul 1852; 275, 4 Oct 1852; 328,
    3 Sep 1853. Invt. and sale at their late residence, Add. Invt.,
    Add. Sale, and Sett.
    CC 199, filed 1 Mar 1869. File contains copy of Circuit Court
    proceedings, 1853, to partition lands among heirs who are as
    follows: Daniel McPhail in his own right and as Adm. of Neil
    McPhail, Doogal McPhail, and Mary Hicks; John McPhail; and the
    heirs of Mary Hicks, dec'd, who are Sterling Ragsdale and wife
    Sarah Ann, Daniel Hicks, John Hicks, John Leonard Hicks, Neil
    McPhail Hicks, and Stephen Hicks, dec'd, whose children are
    Mary Margaret, John Alexander, Martha, Caroline (or Martha
    Caroline), William, and Able Hicks.

MABRY (MABERRY)
    CR5 355, 7 Jun 1847. Sheriff required to bring in William Maberry,
    orphan, to be dealt with as the Court may direct.
    CR5 360, 5 Jul 1847. Wm. Mabry, an orphan aged 9 next Feb, bound
    to Wm. Thompson.

MADDEN (MADEN), WILLIAM
    CR2 485, 6 Dec 1830. John Roberts and James Billingsley app.
    Comm. to settle with James McNabb, Gdn. for Wm. Maden.
    CR2 505, 7 Mar 1831. Report of Comm.; sett. with James McNabb,
    Gdn. for James (William) Madden; received funds from estate of
    Wm. Madden.

MAGILL, JAMES
    CR9 71, 4 Sep 1865. Comm. app. to set apart year's support for
    widow Amanda E. and family.
    WB G 119, no date. Comm. James Willson, James Forrest, and H.L.
    Shults make report.
    WB G 139, 2 Jan 1866. Invt. by J.H. Magill, Adm.

MANSELL, BURRELL
    WB B 7, Will exec. 2 Mar 1825, probated Dec 1830; to wife Martha
    "to raise my children". Exec: wife. Wit: James D. Henly,
    Walter Billingsley.

MAPLES, WILLIAM
    WB F 188, Will exec. 3 Apr 1855, proven Jul 1858; all property to
    be equally divided among Legatees and their heirs; Legatees:
    Mary Ann, Sarah E., Rachel C., James C., Wm. H., Martha M., and
    the heirs of Ailcy J. Pridmore, dec'd /last names not stated7;
    to granddau. Ailcy E. Pridmore. Exec: son Wm. H. Maples. Wit:
    W.C. Vaughan, Jacob Lowe. Signed by mark.
    CC 130, filed 12 Jul 1858. William Maples died about 25 May 1858

leaving children: William H., Mary Ann wife of Wm. Alexander
Carson, Sarah E. Newman, James C. of Texas, Martha M. wife of
Jonathan N. Cate of Ga., Rachel C. wife of Joseph R. Rudd of
Monroe Co. He also left grandchildren Ailcy E. and Wm. M. Prid-
more of Bossier Parish, La., minor children of his dec'd dau.
Alcey Pridmore.
WB F 213-220, no date; 350, 19 Oct 1860. Invt. of sale by Raleigh
Chesnut and report by Wm. S. Chesnutt, Gdn. of minor heirs, A.E.
and W. Pridmore.
WB F 364, 28 Dec 1860. Sett. by Adm.; receipts from heirs Sarah
E. Newman, Rachel Rudd, Wm. Maples, Wm. and Mary A. Carson,
Jonathan and Martha Cate, and Wm. S. Chesnutt, Gdn.
WB F 421, 9 Dec 1861. Final sett. by Gdn.; wards Wm. M. and Alice
E. Pridmore both being of full age.

MARCUM, JOSIAH
CR4 544, 545, 3 May 1841. Eli Sherrill app. Adm.; Wm. Rudd, Nathan
Sullens, and Joseph Gaston app. Comm. to lay off year's support
for widow Barbara.
WB D 19, 7 Jun 1841; 90, 15 Sep 1842. Invt. of sale and pro rata
sett.

MARCUM, PETER
CC 106, filed 5 Jan 1867. Taylor VS Harris. Peter Marcum died
leaving widow Abigail and minor children Frank, William, Thomas,
Alice, and Margaret Marcum, all of Claiborne Co.

MARLER, ALFRED TATE
CR7 479, 2 Oct 1860. Geo. W. Bridges app. Adm.
WB F 359, 22 Nov 1860. Comm. Jas. Gregory, Sterling Lewis, and
John Hart set apart year's support for widow and family, "all
the corn at the widow Coatses and the amt coming from James Mar-
ler".

MARTIN, JOHN
CR4 554, 2 Aug 1841. Thomas N. Clark of Roane Co. app. Adm.
WB D 45, 1 Nov 1841. Invt. by Thos. N. Clark, Jr., Adm. of John
Martin, dec'd, formerly of Arkansas.
WB D 204, 1 Jun 1844. Sett.; Adm. received letter from one of
heirs authorizing him to suspend collection of all notes on Chas.
T. Thornton.
WB D 206, 14 Jun 1844. Sett. by W.S. McEwen, Agent for Thos. N.
Clark, Adm.; receipt from Albert G. Rice for all monies and papers
WB D 206, 5 Jun 1844 and 365, 2 Apr 1846. Sett. by A.G. Rice, Adm.
WB D 468, 2 Apr 1847. Sett.; receipts from heirs John A. Bell,
Joseph M. Lynch, Clement V. McNair, George W. Adair, and Brice
Martin.
WB D 468-472, 21 Aug 1846. Refunding Bonds by above heirs to guar-
antee payment of any future debts; all bonds with Lowry Williams
and Charles T. Thornton as securities and Catharine Lane and Jas.
R. Barnett as witnesses.
WB D 541, 10 Jul 1848. Final sett. by Adm.; receipts of heirs
Nelley, Lucy, Richard F., Elenor, Joseph L., John, and G.M.
Martin, Cicero Martin by Gdn., Samuel and Rachel Bell, Eliza
Wright, William and Nancy Cunningham, B.B. and Paulina Nicholson,
B.F. and Ann Thompson, all receiving equal amounts.
WB D 541-550. Refunding bonds by above heirs, with John A. Bell,
Joseph M. Lynch, and G.W. Adair as bondsmen, and John A. Adair

and C.S. Bean as witnesses; bond of Elenor Martin is by Gdn. Ben
F. Thompson; G.M. Martin signs Gabriel M.; B.B. Nicholson signs
as Braxten B.

MARTIN, JOHN
  CR6, 5 Jan 1852. Coroner paid for holding inquest over body.
  CR6 5 Jul 1852. Jury of inquest over body of John Martin who was
  killed by Daniel Umphrey to be paid by County.

MARTIN, JOSEPH I.
  CR6, 4 Jul 1853. Samuel Vincent app. Adm.

MARTIN, SARAH
  WB D 150-151, Will exec. 24 May 1843; "Being aged and infirm"; to
  Malinda, William, and Sarah, heirs of dec'd son P.H. Martin, each
  $1; to Emaline, William, George, and Thomas, heirs of dec'd son
  Thos. J. Martin, each $1; to two grandsons James and William,
  sons of dec'd dau. Caroline /no last name given7; to dau. Emaline
  Jane E. Wear; to son Zachariah; to son Benjamin F.; to other
  three children, namely, Canzoda Camron, Rebecca Camren, and
  Mariah Jones. Execs: sons Benjamin F. and Zechariah. Wit:
  C.P. Owen, J.D. Chatten. Signed by mark.
  CR5 119, 7 Aug 1843. Will proven.
  WB D 155, 4 Sep 1843. Invt.
  WB D 435, 10 Mar 1847. Sett.; receipts from heirs Martin Cameron,
  Henry Cameron, Jas. and Mariah Jones, Emeline Wear, Zachariah
  Martin, and B.F. Martin.

MARTIN, WILLIAM
  CR10 233, 235, 5 Sep 1870. J.H. Crockett app. Adm.; Comm. app. to
  assign dower to widow.

MASTIN, JEMIMA
  CR7 313, 6 Jun 1859. Urial Johnson and Reuben F. Mastin app. Adms.
  WB F 282. Sale at her late residence.
  WB F 326. Combined report for estates of Thos. W. and Jemima
  Mastin.

MASTIN, THOMAS W.
  WB E 332, 27 Sep 1853. Comm. J.C. Carlock, Uriel Johnston, and
  David Cantrell lay off year's support for widow Jemima and family,
  there being sixteen in family.
  WB E 339-341, 5 Nov 1853. Invt. and Sale by John B. and John J.
  Mastin, Adms.
  WB E 426, 27 Apr 1855. Sett.; paid expenses in Ducktown; paid
  Samuel Boswell for privilege of testing.
  WB F 249, Dec 1858. Sett. by Jemima Maston, widow, Gdn. to minor
  heirs; Sarah Ann Maston arrived at lawful age in June 1854 and
  all her store and other accts. were paid and discharged by Chas.
  A. Proctor her husband; Susan N. Maston arrived at lawful age in
  Mar 1856; Reuben F. Maston arrived at lawful age on 28 of this
  Inst., paid for his schooling at Clear Springs, at Hiwassee Col-
  lege, and at Emory College; Thos. H. Maston now 19 years old,
  paid for his schooling at Emory College; David C. Maston, now
  17; Wm. Wheler Maston now 15; Martha J. Maston now 13.
  WB F 279, 20 Aug 1859. Sett. by John J. Mastin, Gdn.
  WB F 279, no date. Sett. by Wms. Mayfield, Gdn. of David C.
  Mastin; paid for board and tuition at the north.
  WB F 326, no date. Invt. of produce, Thos. W. and Jemima Mastin,

dec'd.

WB F 348, 20 Aug 1860. Sett. by Wms. Mayfield, Gdn.

WB F 431-434, 3 Jul 1861. Sett. by J.J. Mastin, Gdn.; paid for
Wm. W. trip from Tenn. to Mo. and clothing, etc., in St. Louis
1859-60-61; paid board at Benards; paid for Martha J. "cash to
Salem" four times.

CC 43, filed 18 Jan 1866 and 160, filed 20 Jan 1868. Thomas W.
Mastin died 4 Jul 1853 leaving widow Jemima who died 15 Mar 1859
and the following children: eldest son John J. born 14 Dec 1830
and of Jackson Co., Mo., in 1868; Sarah Ann wife of Charles A.
Proctor of Worcester Co., Mass., in 1867 and of Grant Co., Ind.,
in 1868; Susan N. wife of Thomas Jones of Bartow Co., Ga., in
1867 and of Jackson Co., Mo., in 1868 (Thos. Jones dies during
suit Jan 1866 to Feb 1867); Reuben F. of Miami Co., Kan., 1867
and of Jackson Co., Mo., 1868; Thomas H. who was in Rebel Army
and is of Jackson Co., Mo., 1868; David C. of Bartow Co., Ga.,
1867 and Jackson Co., Mo., 1868; William W., dec'd by Feb 1867,
a minor without wife or child; Martha Jemima, youngest child,
aged 7 when father died, wife of David Meriwether of Jasper Co.,
Ga., 1867 and Jackson Co., Mo., 1868. Thomas W. Mastin had bro.
John B. Mastin. Four of Thomas W. Mastin's sons were in Rebel
Army. The Complainant in CC 43, John Caldwell of Sevier Co.,
dies during the lawsuit 1871-72 and suit is revived by A.P.,
Alexander A., George A., John H., and Alfred Caldwell, James C.
Anderson and wife Mary, John C. Douglass and wife Flora Jane,
M.J. Parrott and wife Cynthia, heirs at law.

MATLOCK, CHARLES

WB C 90, Will exec. 27 Feb 1836, registered 7 Dec 1838; to Elizabeth Angeline Rayburn; to Martha Eveline Rayburn; to own bros.
and sisters; the Rayburn girls to be educated, "I leave John
Matlock and John Hayley to see that this strictly complied with";
"N.B. these Two Children lives in Perry County Tennysee six
miles west of Perryville". Execs: John Matlock and John Hayley.

CR4 404, 3 Dec 1838. Will proven by Henry Matlock, Abraham Slover,
and Chas. W. Rice who are acquainted with handwriting and state
that dec'd told them that they could find said Will in his valuable papers.

WB C 125-130, Mar 1839. Invt. of notes due, filed by John Matlock,
Exec.

WB D 535, 15 May 1848. Sett. by same Exec.; vouchers to heirs:
Henry, William, and John Matlock, Elisha Dodson and wife Mary,
John Haley and wife Elizabeth, the heirs of Sarah Forrest wife
of Richard Forrest, Martha Rice widow of Isaac Rice dec'd, Wm.
Rice and wife Elizabeth; all receive equal amounts except Wm.
Rice who receives triple the amount.

MATLOCK, CHARLES

CR4 440, 1 Apr 1839. Noncupative Will presented for probate and
estate did not exceed $250 and same was reduced to writing within
ten days after death of testator; Albartes Arnwine and Henry Matlock were personally present at the making thereof and specially
required to bear witness thereto by the Testator himself in his
last sickness at the house of Charles Matlock where he had been
previously resident for more than 10 days.....Court permitted
the will to be proven. /No will on record./

MATLOCK, CHARLES
CR6, 5 Jul 1852. John Matlock app. Adm.
WB E 262, 2 Aug 1852. Invt.
WB E 311, 26 Feb 1853. Final sett. by Adm.; paid Mrs. Matlock
claim; paid heirs John H. Leuty, A. and S. Arnwine, Nancy Matlock, W.M. and Martha Purcell, Henry Matlock, and J.W. Matlock,
each $247.82 and A. Arnwine, Gdn., $495.64.
CC 162, filed 9 Jul 1852. Charles Matlock died intestate Oct 1851,
leaving mother Nancy, who was widow of Henry Matlock, dec'd, and
bros. and sisters: Sarah wife of Albartis Arnwine, Martha wife
of Wm. Purcell, Elizabeth wife of John H. Leuty, John W. and
Henry Matlock, and George W. and Jane Matlock, infants.

MATLOCK, HENRY, SR.
WB E 159-161, Will exec. 10 Jun 1847; to wife Nancy, the home farm
on Mouse Creek; to sons Charles, Henry, George Washington, and
John W.; to daus. Martha, Elizabeth, Nancy Jane, and Sarah the
wife of Albertis Arwine; "until the coming of age of my daughter
Nancy Jane". Execs: sons Charles and Henry. Wit: Thos. J.
Campbell, Stephen Sharrelts.
CR6, 2 Jun 1851. Will proven by Stephen Sharrets; death of Thos.
J. Campbell, the other witness, is proven.
WB E 238, 6 Oct 1851. Sett.
WB E 335, 12 Sep 1853. Final sett. by Henry Matlock, Exec.; re-
ceipts of heirs Wm. and Martha Purcell, Elizabeth Leuty, the
heirs of Charles Matlock, A. Arnwine and A. Arnwine, Gdn., and
Nancy Matlock.
WB E 366, 1 May 1854; 412, 26 Feb 1855; 418, 15 Nov 1855. Reports
by Albartis Arnwine, Gdn., and Henry Matlock, successor Gdn.
WB E 520, 15 Jun 1856. Report by same, Gdn. to James Matlock.
WB F 74, 6 Jul 1857. Nancy Matlock, dec'd; Henry Matlock surviv-
ing Exec. reports the remainder of estate that was left to widow
her lifetime.
WB F 83, 30 Jul 1857. Sett. by same, Gdn. for Nancy J. Matlock, a
minor; John W. Matlock is successor Gdn.
WB F 83, 30 Jul 1857. Sett. by Henry Matlock, Exec.
WB F 92, 20 Aug 1857. Sett. by Gdn. of Nancy J. Matlock one of the
children.
WB F 187, 25 May 1858. Final sett. by Gdn. to Nancy Jane; paid
"Ear Drops Philadelphia 7.50"; receipt from C.W. Matlock for
balance in acct.
WB F 306, 29 Dec 1859. Sett.
CC 293, filed 29 Jun 1858. Henry Matlock died 1851 leaving widow
Nancy who died Jun 1857 and children: Nancy Jane age 19 who
married James P. Senter in 1858, Charles who died without issue
between 1851 and 1857, Henry, George Washington born 1837, John
W. born 1823, Sarah wife of Albartus Arnwine, Martha wife of Wm.
Purcell, and Elizabeth wife of John H. Leuty of Ga.

MATLOCK, HENRY
WB F 430, Will exec. 2 Aug 1861; "being sound in mind and body....
on account of having enlisted as a volunteer in the Service of
my State and being subject to all the Casualties of war"; all
estate to youngest bro. George W. Matlock. Exec: John W. Matlock. Wit: U.L. York and D.A. Wilkins.
CR8, 2 Jun 1862. Will proven.

MATLOCK, JOHN
WB E 180-181, Will exec. 27 Sep 1848; to wife Mary; to two sons
Henry Harrison and John Clay Matlock; to eldest dau. Sarah
Jane Matlock; to daus. Martha Ellen and Mary Elizabeth Matlock;
"education of my children". Execs: Wm. L. Rice and Wm. F.
Forest. Wit: M.L. Philips, Jonathan Smith.
CR6, 1 Sep 1851. Will proven.
WB E 182-187, 3 Nov 1851. Invt.
WB E 331, 3 Sep 1853. Sett. by Wm. F. Forrest, acting Exec.;
receipts from Wm. L. Rice, Gdn., and from J.W. and Sarah Brown.
WB E 366, 430, 515, dating from 1 May 1854 to 7 May 1856. Sett.
by Wm. L. Rice, Gdn.
WB F 70, 7 May 1857. Sett. by same Gdn.; paid funeral expenses
of Mary E. Matlock.
WB F 176, 7 May 1858. Sett. by Gdn.; "paid Mary Matlock Interest
in the Estate of Elizabeth Matlock Dec'd"; paid for board and
tuition for Martha at Cleveland.
CR7 187, 7 Jun 1858. Wm. L. Rice makes bond as Gdn. to Henry,
John, and Martha Matlock, minors.
WB F 263, 7 May 1859, 322, 7 May 1860. Sett. by same Gdn.
WB F 398, 7 May 1861. Sett. by same Gdn.; paid for tuition for
Martha L. at Winchester.
WB F 431, G 2, 52, 179, dating from 7 May 1862 to 7 May 1866.
Sett. by same Gdn.
CC 263, filed 13 Dec 1856. John Matlock died Aug 1851 leaving
widow Mary and children: Sarah Jane the eldest child who mar-
ried and died after her father's death without issue, Henry
Harrison aged 17, John Clay aged 14, Martha Ellen aged 12, and
Mary Elizabeth who died 8 Nov 1856, a minor about 12 yrs. old.

MATLOCK, JOHN C.
CR9 376, 2 Mar 1868. H.H. Matlock app. Adm.
CR11 249, 24 Apr 1872. Sett.

MATLOCK, NANCY
See HENRY MATLOCK, SR.

MATLOCK, WILLIAM
CR5 212, 7 Jan 1845. Chas. L. King and J.B. Eldridge, of McMinn
and Meigs Cos., app. Adms.
WB D 257, 20 Jan 1845. Comm. Saml. Workman, M.D. Anderson, and
Robt. Rentfroe lay off year's support for widow Sarah.
WB D 258-263, 3 Feb 1845. Invt. and Sale by Adms.
WB D 294, 338, 425, dating from 7 Jul 1845 to 2 Jan 1847. Reports
by Thos. B. McElwee, Gdn. to Charles F. and Nancy Ann Matlock,
two of the heirs.
WB D 466, 479, 488, dated from 9 Jul 1847 to 1 Nov 1847. Sett. by
Adms.; received from John Matlock, Exec. of Charles Matlock, dec'd
$600.
WB D 504, 2 Jan 1848. Sett. by same Gdn.
WB D 537, no date. Add. Invt.; received from Thos. B. McElwee,
Adm. of David Hounshell, dec'd.
WB D 538, 19 Jun 1848. Sett.; receipts from heirs Thomas B. McElwee
and J.B. Eldridge.
WB E 177, 11 Jun 1851. Sett. by same Gdn.; paid C.L. Matlock his
final share leaving balance due to Nancy P. Matlock the other
heir.
WB E 226, 20 May 1851. Sett. by Chas. L. King, one of Adms.

WB E 404, 10 Jan 1855. Final sett. by Gdn.; receipt from Wm. C. and Nancy P. Peake for balance of money.

CC 284, filed 8 Feb 1858. Wm. Matlock died leaving widow Sarah and children: Martha wife of Thomas B. McElwee, Sarah A. wife of Joseph W. Gibson, Sorenda wife of John B. Eldridge of Meigs Co., Nancy wife of Wm. C. Peak of Meigs Co., and Charles Matlock.

MATTHEWS, AARON

CR4 259, 6 Jun 1836. O.G. Murrell, James H. Fyffe, and Solomon S. Bogart app. Comm. to lay off year's support for widow; A.M. Coffey and Uriel Johnson app. Adms.

WB B 205-210, Oct 1836. Invt. and Sale by Adms.; buyers include Mrs. Mary Mathews and Harland and John Matthews.

CR4 293, 6 Dec 1836. Mary Mathews chosen Gdn. by Joseph Mathews, minor heir, who is of age to choose for himself, and is app. Gdn. of minor heirs Asenith Sarah Emily and Jacob Sand Mathews /no commas/.

WB B 287, 1 Feb 1838 and C 81-84, 30 Nov 1838. Report by Gdn. and Final Sett. by Adms.

WB C 164, 7 Mar 1839. Report by Gdn.; paid expenses for 4 minor heirs.

WB C 232, D 1, 97, 147, 214, 310, dating from 2 Mar 1840 to 2 Mar 1845. Sett. by same, Gdn. to Joseph, Jacob S., Asenith, and Sarah E. Matthews.

WB D 372, 2 Mar 1846. Sett. by same Gdn.; has sold farm in Blount Co. to Harlen Matthews.

WB D 493, 551, E 52, 100, 229, dating from 2 Mar 1847 to 2 Mar 1852. Sett. by same, Gdn. to Jacob, Asenith, and Sarah E.

CR5 462, 4 Jul 1848. Mrs. Mary Mathews, Gdn. to her minor children, renews bond.

MAXWELL, ALEXANDER and JAMES (ALLEN MAXWELL and ROBERT MAXWELL)

CR6, Oct 1850. Alexander Maxwell app. Gdn. of Louisa and Cammelia Maxwell, minor children of Robert Maxwell.

CR6, 7 Mar 1853. Ex parte petition to sell slaves: Wm. Maxwell, Nathan Thomas and wife Mary, Sarah, Robert W., Catharine, Alexander, Louisa, and Carmela Maxwell, the latter two being minors by Gdn., children of Robert Maxwell, and George, Mary Ann, Martha Jane, William T., and Sarah L. Maxwell children of Allen Maxwell, dec'd, and grandchildren of the said Robert Maxwell, all minors by their Gdn. Alexander Maxwell, and Elizabeth Maxwell widow of Allen Maxwell, dec'd. Slaves to be valued at residence of Robert Maxwell. /Note that Allen Maxwell is the only person identified as deceased./

WB E 315, 2 May 1853. Report by Alexander Maxwell, Gdn. of George, Mary Ann, Martha Jane, William T., and Noah L. Maxwell, minor children of Allen Maxwell, dec'd; has received their portion of proceeds of slaves devised to them by the Wills of Alexander and James Maxwell. Report by Alexander Maxwell, Gdn. of Louisa and Carmilia Maxwell, minor children of Robert Maxwell; has received two slaves devised to them by the Wills of Alexander and James Maxwell, dec'd.

WB E 323, 380, 435, 529, F 81, 192, 295, 335, 415, G 33, dating from 4 Jul 1853 to 4 Jul 1864. Settlements by same Gdn. for same heirs.

WB G 127, 2 Dec 1865. Sett. by same Gdn.; receipt in full 15 Nov 1864 from Chas. and Mary A. Wyatt; receipt in full 2 Dec 1865 from Geo. W. Maxwell; balance due three heirs.

MAXWELL, ROBERT
WB E 414-415, Will exec. 14 Jun 1854; to wife Elizabeth; to chil-
dren Robert Maxwell, Polly Thomas, Eliza, Carmela, William,
Alexander, and Sally Maxwell, Catherine Wallis, and the heirs of
son Allen, deceased; to granddau. Harriet Maxwell; $5 to heirs of
Elizabeth Hulvy. Execs: Alexander Maxwell and Jefferson Lowry.
Wit: Benj. and B.H. Isbell.
CR6, 5 Mar 1855. Will proven.
WB E 427, 7 Apr 1855. Invt. by Execs.
WB F 60, 28 Mar 1857. Sett. by Execs.; paid about one-fourth of
funds to S.A. Walace, not identified.
WB F 81, 4 Jul 1857; 193, 4 Jul 1858. Sett. by Alex. Maxwell,
Gdn. of minor heirs.
WB F 295, 4 Jul 1859. Sett. by Gdn., paid for care of an idiot.
WB F 335, 4 Jul 1860. Sett. by Gdn.; paid for "Coffin shroud &C
for Lanior".
WB 415, 4 Jul 1861. Sett. by Gdn.; paid for board of an idiot.
WB G 33, 4 Jul 1864. Sett. by Gdn.
WB G 127, 2 Dec 1865. Sett. by same Gdn.; paid for coffin for
Carmelia Maxwell, dec'd, one of the minor heirs.
CR11 335, 14 Aug 1875. Sett. by Alexander Maxwell, Exec.; payments
to N.L., G.W., R.W., W.T., W., and Alexander Maxwell, Nathan and
Mary Thomas, Chris Wyatt, and W.A. Gudger and wife.

MAY, JOHN
CR5 94, 6 Mar 1843. By last Will of John May, dec'd, it is ordered
that Joseph Cobbs, Saml. Firestone, and Thomas Trew be app. to
value two negroes.

MAYFIELD
CR4 178, 4 Dec 1833. Williams Mayfield over 14 chooses his bro.
Jesse Mayfield as Gdn.

MAYFIELD, CARTER
CR16 115, Dec 1850. Thos. B. Mayfield, Adm. VS Joseph Swan and
wife Hulda, David Cobbs and wife Priscilla, John Baker and wife
Elizabeth, Williams Mayfield, Jessee Mayfield, and the children
of Pearson Mayfield, dec'd, to wit, Samuel, Thomas, James, John,
Williams, Standwix, and Pearson, the latter an infant; Subpoena
to Polk Co. for John Mayfield; Subpoena to Bradley Co. for Joseph
L. Swan and wife.
WB E 141, 6 Jan and 3 Feb 1851. Invt. and acct. of sale held 17
Jan 1850 by Thos. B. Mayfield, Adm.
WB E 361, 14 Feb 1853. Sett.

MAYFIELD, ELIZABETH ELVIRA
See ABRAHAM J. and WILLIAM BALLEW

MAYFIELD, JESSE
WB B 127-129, 4 Dec 1833. Invt. by W.T. Mayfield, David A. Cobbs,
and Thos. B. Mayfield, Adms.
CR4 179, 5 Dec 1833. John Miller, Joseph Cobb, and Oliver Dotson
app. Comm. to lay off year's support for widow Penelope.
WB B 170, 20 Dec 1833. Report of above Comm.
CR4 186, 4 Mar 1834. Thos. B. Mayfield app. Gdn. for Carter Mayfield, an Idiot, who will soon inherit part of his father's
estate.

WB B 248, May 1837. Report by same Gdn.

WB C 20, 2 Jun 1838. Last page of sett. by Adms.

WB C 146, 20 Apr 1839. Add. report by Adms.; paid to heirs David
A. Cobb, Thos. B. Mayfield, Elizabeth Hill, Jesse Mayfield,
Mahulda Mayfield, and Thos. B. Mayfield for Carter Mayfield, $50
each.

WB C 228, D 34, 73, 186, 279, 402, 510, E 121, dating from 29 Feb
1840 to 2 Feb 1850. Reports by Thos. B. Mayfield, one of Adms.
and Gdn.

MAYFIELD, PEARSON B.

CR4 74, 6 Mar 1832. Jesse Mayfield app. Adm.

CR4 192, 5 Mar 1834. Nancy Mayfield app. Gdn. of Jesse, John,
William, James, Stanwix, Thomas, Clement, and Pearson Mayfield,
minor heirs.

WB B 141, Jun Court 1834. Sett. by John Bolding and Jos. Cobb,
Comm.

CR4 310, 3 Apr 1837. Widow Nancy requests that dower of land be
set apart.

WB D 486, 10 Oct 1847. Sett. by Nancy Blythe, formerly Mayfield,
Gdn.; receipts in full from heirs T.B., S.H., John G., Samuel M.,
Pierson B., William, James, and Jesse Mayfield, all for same amt.

MAYFIELD, PENELOPE

WB E 129-130, Will exec. 12 Feb 1848; Codicil, same date; to sons
Carter, Jesse, Thomas, and Williams; to dau. Freeda Cobb; to dau.
Huldy Swann and her child now living; to dau. Elizabeth Hudgins
and her heirs now living, viz., Jesse Hill, Eliza Hudgins, and
Wm. Hudgins; to heirs of son Pearson Mayfield; to grandson Jesse
Hill when he arrives at age of 21. Execs: Williams F. Keith
and son Williams Mayfield. Wit: Jas. B. Taylor, Wm. Reynolds.

CR6, 2 Dec 1850. Will proven.

WB E 140, 6 Jan 1851. Invt. by Wms. Mayfield, Exec.; the bequest
to dau. Freeda Cobb is received by David Cobb.

MAYFIELD, WILLIAM T.

/In Index to Will Book C, the Will is recorded on page 1. This
page is now missing./

CR4 356, 5 Mar 1838. Will proven by James H. Fyffe and Williams
Mayfield, the two subscribing witnesses.

CR4 362, 363, 2 Apr 1838. Wm. Ballew and Marshall W. Cunningham
app. Adms.; Joel K. Brown, Wm. Lowry, and Wm. W. Anderson app.
Comm. to lay off year's provisions for widow Nancy C.

WB C 21, Jun 1839; 150, 3 Aug 1839; 229, 29 Feb 1840. Invt. of
sale and settlements by Wm. Ballew, Adm.

CR4 456, 7 Oct 1839. Martial W. Cunningham released as Adm.

WB D 463, 22 Jun 1847. Sett. by same Adm.; "Received from William
Mayfield a son of Peirson Mayfield".

MEIGS, COLONEL RETURN J.

WB A 21-26, no date. Invt. by Return J. Meigs, Adm.; greater part
of Invt. is a list of books of deceased; Y. Colville, Clerk.

WB A 43-53 with pp. 45-46 missing; no date. Supp. Invt.; one item
is "Major Fairchild's Power of Atto. 23 July 1792".

WB A 54-57, no date. Sale of personal property of R.J. Meigs,
Sr., made at Cherokee Agency, 29 Mar 1823.

MELTON, ELIJAH (ELI S.)

WB B 115, Will exec. 16 Nov 1832; to wife Mary; to four children,

Thomas, Alesy, Elisha, and Mahaly. Execs: wife Mary and friend
Thomas Studdard. Wit: Amos Potts, W.C. McMahan. Signed by mark.
CR4 135, 4 Mar 1833. Will proven.
WB B 172, 1 Jun 1835; C 86(2), no date. Invt. of Sale and Sett.

MELTON, ELISHA
WB F 173, no date. Invt. of sale by Easter and Alfred Melton, Adms.
WB F 175, 20 Apr 1858. Comm. lay off year's support for widow and
family of Elisha Melton who died 3 Feb 1858.
WB F 278, 22 Aug 1859; 349, 23 Aug 1860. Sett. by Easter Melton,
Adminx. and Gdn. of her own minor children, to wit, Mary J.,
Peter L., James K.P., George M.D., Mandy H., and Wm. Jones
Melton.
WB F 399, 1 May 1861. Sett. by same Gdn.; receipts for equal amts.
from Caroline Stephenson, Margaret Melton, and Miss Easter Melton.
WB F 418, 22 Aug 1861. Sett. by Gdn.
WB G 126, 22 Aug 1865. Sett. by same Gdn.; receipts in full from
A.T. and M.J. Bayless for one share and P.L. Melton for one
share; four remaining heirs.
CC 40, filed 8 Jan 1860. Amended Bill filed 22 Feb 1868. Elisha
Melton left widow Esther and children: Joseph W., the eldest
son, of Ga., who died after Orig. Bill was filed (his widow is
also dead) and who left dau. Amanda Malissa Melton, a minor;
Francis M. who by 1868 has moved to Ill.; Margaret; Celia wife
of Daniel H. Mathis of Ga. in 1860 and of McMinn Co. in 1868;
Alfred; Sarah Caroline wife of M.T. Stephenson; Mary Jane a
minor in 1860 and married to A.T. Bayless; Peter and Polk
who both reach majority between 1860 and 1868; Dallas; Amanda a
minor in 1868 who has married A. Wilson Glaze; and William Melton. Nathan Melton is bro. to the deceased.

MELTON, JAMES H.
CR10 109, 6 Apr 1869. J.N. Melton app. Adm.
CR10 113, 3 May 1869. Comm. app. to lay off year's support for
widow and family.
CC 218, filed 6 Sep 1869. James H. Melton died about 2 Mar 1869
leaving widow Susan and children: John N., Jr.; Aaron of un-
sound mind; Hulda; Manerva Elizabeth wife of Henry Scybert;
Julia N. wife of Horace Baysinger; Allen Haley Melton; and
Martha Adaline Melton, last three being minors.

MENDENALL (MENDINGALL)
CR4 241, 7 Dec 1835. Isaac Mendingall a minor over 14 chooses
James Atkerson as Gdn.
CR4 281, 5 Sep 1836. Jonathan Thomas, Jesse H. Benton, and John
Grisham app. Comm. to settle with James Atkinson, Gdn. to Isaac
and Elizabeth Mendenall.

METCALFE, GEORGE C.
CR5 494, 4 Dec 1848. Charles W. Metcalfe app. Adm.
WB D 588, 29 Dec 1848. Acct. of sale and invt. by Adm.; buyers
include the widow, Charles and James Metcalfe.
WB E 113, 2 Oct 1850. Sett.
CC 42, filed 23 Nov 1858. G.C. Metcalfe died leaving widow Mar-
garet Jane and minor sons Charles P. and George C. who are now
of Ky., his only heirs.

METCALFE, THOMAS J.
CR5 99, 3 Apr 1843. Chas. Metcalfe app. Adm.

WB D 370, 26 Jun 1846. Sett. by Adm.

MIDDLETON, JOHN
CR6, 4 Dec 1854. Ex parte application to sell land warrant: Addison Lowe, John Bond, Mary Stanton, Benjamin Eldridge and wife Rebecca, John J., Hugh L., James, Alfred K., and Abigail Middleton, heirs; land warrant issued for services in War of 1812.
CR6, 5 Mar 1855. Land warrant for 40 acres sold to Mary Stanton as Agent for Marshall W. Cunningham of Mo. for $5.

MILLER, ANDREW
CR1 6, 6 Jun 1820. Ephraim Walker VS Joseph Cretchfield, Exec. of Andrew Miller.

MILLER, JOHN
WB D 223-224, Will exec. 25 Sep 1835; to wife Jannet; to children Lucien Bonaparte, Luin, Wade H., Vernantis, Parilee C., Armenia Dimoldi Monterria, John Mandaville, and Dallas Hamilton Miller; a horse, saddle, and bridle to be given to each child as he comes of age; "I order that the old horse Billy King be kept on the place as long as he lives". Execs: esteemed neighbor and friend John Crawford Merchant of Athens and sons Lucien B. and Luin Miller. Wit: Saml. Workman, John B. Jackson, and James Newland.
CR5 188, 7 Oct 1844. Will proven by Saml. Workman, who makes oath that witness John B. Jackson now resided in one of the upper East Tenn. Counties and that witness James Newland now resided in Ark.
WB D 230, 2 Nov 1844. Comm. Ch. Metcalfe, Henry H. Rider, and Roberson Snider lay off year's support for widow Jane.
WB D 235-242, 6 Jan 1845; 366, 19 May 1846. Invt. of sale, Invt. of notes, and Sett. by John Crawford and L.B. Miller two of Execs.; received money collected in Ga.; paid T.F. Hoyle of Ga.
WB D 442, 30 Mar 1847. Sett. by same Execs.; receipt from Clerk and Master for total amount in their hands.

MILLER, JOHN
CR5 356, 7 Jun 1847. John Dobbs app. Gdn. to Hiram Francis Miller, minor orphan.
WB D 581, 1 Dec 1848. Sett. by Gdn.; "Cash of Dec'd received from New Orleans"; "Cash of Dec'd three months extra pay as soldier"; "land warrant for 160 acres of land due Estate for services rendered by deceased in the late War with Mexico"; paid for care of ward from 1846.

MILLER, THOMAS
CR4 397, 401, 5 Nov 1838. Wm. McKamy and John H. Miller app. Adms. Jesse Dodson, John McClatchy, and Joseph S. McConnell app. Comm. to lay off year's support for widow Jemima. This day John Miller rendered to the Court the letters of Adm. granted to Thomas Miller as Adm. of Wesley Spearman, dec'd, and it appearing to the Court that the said Thomas Miller has died, John H. Miller is therefore app. Adm. of Wesley Spearman, dec'd.
WB C 94, Dec 1838; 106, 5 Jan 1839. Invt. and Sale by Adms.
WB C 339, 28 Jan 1841. Report by Jemima Miller, Gdn. to minor heirs, Daniel, Nancy, and Thomas. "Pd to Elizabeth Spearman $60 towards her interest in the land and farm whereon Thomas Miller dec'd for the use & benefit of the said Minors". "paid

to Stephen Miller to make him equal in his part".
WB D 17, Feb 1841._ Sett. by John H. Miller, one of Adms.; receipts
to Legatees /sic/: Elizabeth Spearman, Malinda, Elisha E.,
Jemima, Stephen H., and John H. Miller, George G. and Mary
Morris, and to Jemima Miller, Gdn.
WB D 71, no date; 87, Jul 1842. Sett. by same Adm. and by Jemima
Miller, Gdn.
WB D 213, 19 Jul 1844. Sett. by Stephen Miller, Agent for Jemima
Randolph, Gdn.; receipt of Daniel Miller for amount which appears
to be his final share.
WB D 378, 6 Jul 1846. Sett. by Jemima Randolph, Gdn.
WB D 509, 21 Jan 1848. Sett. by same Gdn.; receipt in full from
Nancy Roberts formerly Nancy Miller; balance due T.J. Miller.
WB E 34, 5 Apr 1849. Final sett. by Gdn.; paid heir Thomas J.
Miller balance of acct.

MINATT (MYNATT), SILAS
SB G 216, Will exec. 17 Feb 1864; to wife Sarah; to daus. Sintheann
Hansard and her heirs, Alsy Wamack and her heirs, Norsis herself,
Thersa McNabb, Clerisa Minatt, Silvesta McNabb; to sons D.P.,
G.P., J.L., and C.W.; "if beloved son C.W. should not make his
appearance nor is not heard from in the length of one year of
time after peace between the United States of America and the
People of the South." Exec: James Gregory. Wit: R.A. McAdoo,
B.F. Zeigler.
CR14 301, 11 Dec 1867. Silas Mynatt VS John Gouldy et al. The
death of plaintiff is suggested and admitted.
CR9 352, 6 Jan 1868. Will proven.

MINZE, JOSEPH
WB D 570, no date. Invt. by Ewing S. Minze, Adm.
WB E 58-59, Will exec. 27 May 1848; to wife Margaret; to only dau.
Degenira, wife of Thos. Cecil, and at her death to her two daus.
Mary and Elizabeth Cecil; to son Uen Minze; to Margaret and Nancy,
the twin daus. of son Uen; to grandsons Joseph, William H., and
Granville Cecil and Onslow G.M., Coleman, and Leander M. Minze;
to six granddaus. Margaret, Nancy, Mary J., and Jacenaz Minze and
Mary and Elizabeth Cecil. Execs: my relations. Wit: William
George, Albertis Arnwine, and Chas. Matlock.
CR5 473, 4 Sep 1848. A paper purporting to be the last Will of
Joseph Minze dec'd presented for probate; Thomas Cecill and his
wife De Jenira late De Jenira Minze, make objection; Will and
records sent to Circuit Court.
CR5 474, 5 Sep 1848. Margaret and Ewing Minze app. Adminx. and
Adm. pendente lite.
CR5 548, 3 Sep 1849. Will proven.
WB G 202, 15 Sep 1866. Sett. by Thomas Cecill, Gdn. to Margaret
Minze.
CC 240, filed 22 Apr 1870. Joseph Minze died about Aug 1848 leav-
ing widow Margaret who died 17 Sep 1868 at age of about 80, and
heirs as given in the Will. Mary Cecil is now Mary Fry of Meigs
Co.; Elizabeth Cecil born about 1832, is now Elizabeth Hicks of
Meigs Co.; Margaret Minze is wife of G.B. Harding of Mo.; Nancy
Minze is dead; Mary J. Minze is of Laclede Co., Mo.; Jacenaz
Minze is wife of B. Aaron.

MITCHELL, WILLIAM
CR5 25, 3 Jan 1842. John Jenkins, Thomas W. Smith, and Allen

Haley app. Comm. to lay off year's support for widow.

MONROE, GEORGE, JR.
   CR9 74, 4 Sep 1865. E.L. Miller app. Adm.
   WB G 108, 30 Sep 1865. Invt. and sale by Adm.; S.M. Monroe is
   principal buyer.

MONROE, GEORGE, SR.
   CR10 112, May 1869. A.D. Briant app. Adm.; Comm. app. to lay off
   year's support for widow.
   CR11 218, 1 May 1871. Sett. by Adm.; voucher to widow Elizabeth.
   CR11 324, 1 Mar 1875. Sett. by Adm.; paid for funeral expenses
   for widow.
   CC 293, filed 26 Jun 1871. George Monroe, a minister living about
   8 mi. from Athens, died 13 Oct 1868, aged about 86, leaving
   widow Elizabeth who dies during the lawsuit between 25 Apr 1872
   and Apr 1873, and the following heirs: son Joseph, dec'd, the
   youngest child; dau. Margaret Hardin born about 1818, a widow
   with three children, one of whom is the wife of F.M. Odom; son
   Robert, dec'd; son George Jr., dec'd, with widow Margaret and
   son Sherwood M. born 1846; grandson Millard F. Monroe born Sep
   1852; and the following children or grandchildren: Joseph Wilson and wife Nancy of Mo.; Catherine Dobbs of Mo.; Jesse Monroe
   of Ala.; Robert Monroe of Ky.; Martha widow of Wm. Monroe and two
   children names unknown of Ala. and one child name and residence
   unknown; Jesse S. Monroe; Samintha P. Monroe wife of Wm. M.
   Stanton; James McKeehan and wife Eliza B.; Joseph McCollum;
   Alice Pearce and husband of Ill. W. H. Rothwell deposes that he
   thinks Geo. Monroe had eight children at time of his death. Son
   Joseph died before his father died. Joseph was taken off a
   prisoner in 1863 and never heard from again, so presumed dead.
   Joseph lived with his father and after his death his widow Har-
   riett N. and her family continued to live there for about 20
   yrs. in all. Joseph's children are Mary E.J.B. wife of Wiley
   M. Wallis, Margaret E. wife of John S. McChristian, Wm. M.,
   Louis F., Horace S., Chas. B., Joseph M., Sarah A., Elizabeth
   P., and George N., the last four being minors.

MONROE, JOSEPH
   CR9 82, 2 Oct 1865. Hariet Monroe app. Adminx.; Comm. app. to set
   apart year's provisions for widow and family.

MOORE, DAVID
   CR4 298, 6 Feb 1837. Joseph McConnell app. Adm.
   WB B 246, 3 Apr 1837. Invt. by Adm.
   CR4 315, 1 May 1837. Martha R. Moore app. Gdn. to James A. and
   Mary Amanda Moore, minor orphans.
   WB B 251(1), May 1837. Invt. of sale.
   WB B 253, 5 Jun 1837. Comm. Manuel Parkison, Wm. McKamy, and John
   Camp settle with same Adm.
   WB C 38, 176, 262, D 35, 81, 162, 230, 320, 391, 579, E 66, 119,
   193, 271, 338, 434, dating from Sep 1838 to 21 Jul 1855. Set-
   tlements by same Gdn.; "received from adm. of David Moore Dec'd
   in Iredell County North Carolina" (1841).

MOORE, THOMAS P.
   WB D 128, Will exec. 5 Feb 1843; to wife Margaret T., all estate;
   "if any other persons should come and claim an equal heirship I
   give and bequeath unto each of them one dollar". Execs: wife

and Richard C. Jackson. Wit: Saml. H. Jordan and O.H. Lide.
CR5 93, 6 Mar 1843. Will proven.
WB D 144, 3 Jul 1843. Invt. of sale.

MOORE, WILLIAM
    WB F 438-439, Will exec. 10 Jul 1862; to sons Hugh, Alexander,
    Joseph, William, George, Hamilton, and James; to dau. Mary
    Sweeny; to granddaus. Una and Ibby Basket. Exec: Urial Johns-
    ton. Wit: E. Sawtell and John Hoyl. Signed by mark.
    CR8, 4 Aug 1862. Will proven.
    WB F 472, Invt. sold 22 Aug 1862.
    CR8, 7 Oct 1862. Petition to sell slave. Uriel Johnson, Exec.
    VS William, Hugh, Joseph, Hamilton, George, James, Alexander,
    and John H. Moore, Wm. and Margaret Basket, John and Jane Barker,
    Martin and Mary Sweeney.

MORGAN, GIDEON
    WB E 181-182, Will exec. 22 Aug 1851, proven 2 Nov 1851; to all my
    children, George W. Morgan, Cherokee A. Rogers, Rufus Montezuma
    Morgan, Amanda P. Morgan, M.A.W. Eiffort, Elizabeth L. McElrath.
    Execs: H.M.D. McElrath, G.W. Morgan, A.L. Rogers, and J.H.
    Eiffert or any one or more of them as may be agreed upon between
    them. Wit: Wm. S. Reagan, John W. Griffitts.
    CR6, 5 Jan 1852. George W. Morgan app. Gdn. to R.M. Morgan minor
    heir.
    WB E 207, 2 Feb 1852. Invt. by Andrew L. Rogers, Exec.; received
    "Patent granted to Gideon Morgan for an improvement on Rail
    roads" and "Right of Knowles patent saw for the State of Ten-
    nessee".

MORGAN, JOHN
    CR2 49, 7 Mar 1825. Wm. Ballew, Moses Cunningham, and John Mathews
    app. Comm. to lay off year's support for widow Rebecca and she
    is app. Adminx.

MORGAN, RICHARD
    CR4 23, 5 Sep 1831. Richard Morgan, pauper, died 12 May 1831.

MORGAN, RUFUS
    CR3 109, 8 Sep 1830. A.R. Turk, Clk. VS David Shields, Adm.

MORTON, JOHN
    CR14 393, 13 Apr 1868. The State VS John Morton; Disturbing Pub-
    lic Worship. The death of defendant is suggested and admitted.

MOSS, DAVID
    CR5 199, 200, 2 Dec 1844. Allen Boon app. Adm.; Isham Julian,
    James Gaut, and Dimmon Dorsey, Sr., app. Comm. to lay off year's
    support for widow.
    WB D 244, 6 Jan 1845; 317, 1 Sep 1845; 351, 24 Feb 1846. Invt. of
    sale, Add. invt., and pro rata sett. by Adm.

MOSS, ELI
    CR5 284, 6 Apr 1846. Coroner paid for holding inquest over the
    body.

MOSS, JOHN
    WB F 65-67, Will exec. 10 Jan 1857, proven 6 Jul 1857; to wife
    Rebecca; to dau. Salina wife of Dr. Joseph M. Alexander "my in-
    terest in the store at Benton"; to dau. Queentine wife of James
    T. Lane; to grandchildren Catherine E. and John Moss Taylor,

children of dec'd dau. Rebecca, wife of James B. Taylor; to son-in-law James B. Taylor; "my gold watch and chain" to son-in-law Dr. J.M. Alexander; "my Rifle Gun" to G.W. Price; "my gold spectacles & case" to Nathan Kelley; negro boy Henry to have his freedom at death of wife with privilege of going to Liberia and $200 to pay expenses; "an unsettled partnership business between myself & my friend Richard C. Jackson". Exec: son-in-law Dr. Alexander. Wit: John L. Bridges and Nathan Kelley.
WB F 95, 3 Oct 1857. Invt.
WB F 97, 334, 441, dated from 3 Oct 1857 to 18 Mar 1862. Settlements by Joseph M. Alexander, Gdn. of Catherine E. and John Moss Taylor.

MOSS, REBECCA
CR14 396, 13 Apr 1868. Rebecca Moss VS Moses Cunningham and others. The death of plaintiff is suggested and admitted.
CR9 440, 4 May 1868. Wm. T. Lane app. Adm.

MOUNTCASTLE, GEORGE E.
CR5 512, 5 Feb 1849. Wm. Walsh app. Adm.
CR5 521, 2 Apr 1849. The Adm. reports that no property either real or personal can be found in his county.

MURPHY, EDWARD
CR4 226, 1 Jun 1835. Enoch Wilson app. Adm.

MURPHY (MURPHEY), JAMES
WB A 9-10, Will exec. 15 Jan 1823; estate divided between dau. Elizabeth H. Murphy and son John W. and "my wife's saddle and little wheel be reserved for the benefit of my children and the raising of them". Execs: trusty friend John Walker and bro. Robert Murphy. Wit: Absalom Coxsey, Benjamin Sanders.
CR2 33, 6 Dec 1824. Aaron Haynes, Henry C. Price, and James McNabb app. Comm. to settle with John Walker, Gdn. of Betsey H. Murphy.
WB A 42, 151, 205, B 9, 61. Supp. Invts. for years through 1830 by John Walker, Gdn.
WB B 65-67, 26 Aug 1831. Comm. Saml. Walker and James Gregg settle with John Walker, Gdn. for Elizabeth Murphy, heir; paid to James Walker for "going to Larren County in the western district" on business of the estate.
CC 320, filed 12 Feb 1872 (Enrolled Bills, 1865-75). James Murphy died Mar 1823. Dau. Elizabeth H., now of Bradley Co., married at age of 15 to Wm. S. Stephenson who died 3 Apr 1869. Son John W. Murphy died a few weeks after his father died.

MURPHY, JOHN
CR2 52, 7 Mar 1825. Robert Murphy app. Adm.

MURPHY (MURPHEY), JOHN
WB E 468, Will and Codicil exec. 5 Jul 1855; to son John; to grandson John Murphy $50 and also execs. to pay $29.62½ "that I received from my sons Jeffersons estate and was to pay over to the said John Murphy without interest when he became of age"; "My grave, my wifes grave, and my daughter in law Susan Murphey grave" to be impounded; personal property to be sold and money equally divided among Nancy Coxsey, Rachel M. Huart, William, John, and James Murphey, after paying Rachel M. Huart $18 for a saddle.
Exec: son John. Wit: H.M. McNabb, David L. Boyd.
CR6, 3 Dec 1855. Will proven.

WB E 478-481, Invt. of sale held 24 Dec 1855 by Exec.
WB F 91, 29 Aug 1857. Final sett. by Exec.; receipts for $106 each from William, James, and John Murphy, George Coxsy and wife; receipt for $124 from Wm. and Malinda Hughart; receipt for $79.62½ from Noah Orton, Gdn.

MURRELL
CR5 224, 7 Apr 1845. Onslow G. Murrell app. Gdn. of Emily S., John D., Sophia C., and Manerva R. Murrell.

MURRY, PLEASANT
CR7 451, 2 Jul 1860. Court pays for shroud and coffin for pauper.

NAVE, SARAH
See SARAH KNAVE.

NEAL, CHARLES
WB D 373, Transcript of records 6 Oct 1845 of Van Buren Co. Court at Spencer and recorded 3 Aug 1846 by J.C. Carlock, Clk.; Wm. R. Neal is app. Gdn. to Elizabeth J., Charles W., John A., and Douglass Neal, minor heirs; James F. Thomas and Lemuel Romons are security for Gdn. bond; members of the Court were Uriah York, Chairman, and John Fleming, David Haston, James Right, James A. Haston, Micajah Simmons, Preston Dulany, Wm. L. Mitchell and Thomas Moore, Justices.

NEAL, JAMES
CR9 244, 4 Mar 1867. James Brook, Colored, app. Gdn. of minor heirs.

NEIL
CR7 460, 6 Aug 1860. James Neil app. Gdn. to Margaret L. and Judith L. Neil, his own minor children.
WB F 350, 380, 440, G 141, dating from 11 Oct 1860 to 3 Jan 1866. Sett. by James Neil, Sr., Gdn.

NEIL, JOHN
WB G 220-221, Will exec. 28 Aug 1858; to wife Sarah, interest on $2000; residue to be divided among all children including children of deceased son John R., but Malinda Sherman is to have $200 more than other children; daus. Polly, Nancy, Malinda, Ollivia, and Sarah, their part to them and their heirs and for no other purpose. Execs: sons William, Sterling, and Joseph. Wit: J.H. Reagan, Morgan L. Wallis.
CR9 425, 6 Apr 1868. Will proven.
CC 296, filed 20 Aug 1871. John Neil died Mar 1868 at age 80 odd, leaving widow Sarah (who was sister to Russell Lane and is now living, aged 84, in Monroe Co., with son William), and the following children: Claiborn of Jackson Co., Ore. (started to Ore. 22 Sep 1852 by wagon train and had six children when he went to Ore.); Mary (Polly), wife of George Stephens of Monroe Co. (she has children Parshall Cate and Oscar Cate); Sarah wife of James T. Fitzgerald of Laclede Co., Mo., and later of Jackson Co., Ore.; Malinda wife of John F. Sherman of McMinn Co. (she has children Thomas and Frank Sherman); Nancy, dec'd wife of Roland Burnett of Oregon, Mo.; William, who lived in Ky. in 1852 and is now of Monroe Co.; Joseph, next to the youngest child, of McMinn Co.; Sterling of Houston Co., Ga., and later of Macon Co., Ga. (he married a sister of Russell Hurst); Oliva wife of _____ Burnett of Pope Co., Ark.; Prior who died between 1858 and

1868; John R. who died before 1858. The children of dau. Nancy
Burnett, dec'd, are Isham and Prior of Washington Territory and
later of Boise City, Idaho; William of Kan. in 1871 and of
Boulder Co., Colo., in 1872; Caroline, dec'd wife of _____ Collins, whose children are Mary J. and Carrie E. Collins both of
Oregon, Mo.; Mary wife of Lawson White Lloyd of Kan. and later
of Nebraska City, Neb.; Elizabeth wife of James Ewing of Holt
or Callaway Co., Mo.; Sarah wife of Thos. W. Collins of Holt
Co., Mo.; Malinda wife of Ansel Watrous of Nassau Co., Fla.;
Martha Jane wife of Wm. Hoblitzell of Holt Co., Mo.; and George
of Holt Co., Mo. The children of son Prior Neil, dec'd, are Lea
of Polk Co., Ga.; John C. of McMinn Co.; Mary J., dec'd wife of
James Thomas (whose children are Sarah J., John N., and Franklin
P. Thomas, all minors); Louisa wife of L. Francis Stewart of
Meigs Co.; Mahala wife of Irby Boggess of Meigs Co. (she was
divorced in 1872); Thomas R. and Jerry F. of Meigs Co.; Wm. B.
of Calif.; James Polk and Elizabeth Neil, a minor, both of Meigs
Co. The children of John R. Neil, dec'd, are Eglintine wife of
B. Francis Lillard; Mary A. wife of W. Lafayette Lillard; and
Sterling Neil, a minor, all of Meigs Co.

NEIL, PETER
  WB B 293-294, Will exec. 29 Jul 1835, probated Feb Court 1838; to
  sons William, Joseph, John, Peter, Jesse; to dau. Nancy Southard;
  to dau. Sally Hurst; to son Samuel's heirs; to son Charles' heirs.
  Execs: son William and Joab Hill. Wit: Alexander Keith, Maria
  S. Keith, and Simeon Grisham. Signed by mark.
  WB C 116, 168, 172, 174, dating from Feb 1839 to 9 Oct 1839. Supp.
  Return of sale, Supp. Invt., Sett., and Supp. Invt. by Joab Hill,
  Exec.; receipts from heirs John Hurst, Nancy and Robert Southard,
  John, Joseph, Peter, William, and Jesse Neil.
  WB C 235, 2 Mar 1840. Sett. by Wm. Hill, Agent for Joab Hill,
  Exec.; receipt of Wm. Neil, present Adm. for total sum.

NETHERLAND, DR. JAMES W.
  CR5 490, 6 Nov 1848. James Forrest and Wm. F. Keith app. Adms.
  WB D 583, 10 Nov 1848. Comm. Wm. S. Calloway, T.S. Rice, and
  Daniel Lowry set apart year's support for widow Ann V. and family.
  WB D 584-587, 4 Dec 1848; E 53, 6 Aug 1849; 137, 2 Dec 1850. Invt.
  of sale, Supp. Invt., and Sett. by Adms.
  WB E 202, 13 Jan 1852. Sett. by Ann Virginia Netherland, Gdn. for
  minor heirs; land obtained for services rendered the U.S. as a
  soldier in Mexican War.
  CR6, 3 Jan 1853. James Forrest and Wm. F. Keith, Adms., Ann Vir-
  ginia Netherland, widow, and Virginia W. Netherland VS Cornelia
  V., James W., Catharine R., John P., Josephine T., and Ann Eliza
  Netherland, minor heirs. Since filing bill Virginia W. Nether-
  land has married Wm. M. Heiskell of Monroe Co., Tenn.
  WB E 307, 26 Feb 1853. Final sett. by Adms.
  WB F 323, 9 Jan 1860. Sett. by same, Gdn. of her own minor chil-
  dren; vouchers of Carmelia V., Jas. W., Catherine R., John P.,
  Josephine T., and Ann E.
  CC 319, filed 17 Feb 1872. Dr. J.W. Netherland died many years
  ago, leaving seven children: Virginia wife of Wm. Heiskell,
  Cornelia wife of James Yearwood, Josephine wife of Wm. A. Cannon
  of Madisonville, Annie E. L. wife of Guilford M. Cannon of Mon-
  roe Co., James W., C.R. wife of R.M. Staples, and John P.

NEWMAN
    CR5 49, 4 Jul 1842. Sarah Newman app. Gdn. for John K., Sabra,
    Jesse, and Wm. B. Newman, minor children of Sarah Newman.

NEWMAN, ALFRED C.
    CR4 516, 5 Oct 1840. Comm. app. to lay off year's support for
    widow Susan.
    WB C 291, 12 Oct 1840. Comm. L.L. Ball, Emanuel Hany, and John H.
    Lee make report.
    WB C 313, 4 Jan 1841; D 117, 6 Feb 1843. Invt. and Invt. of sale
    by James Orton, Adm.
    WB D 138, 15 May 1843. Thomas Vaughan, Clerk, makes pro rata
    sett. between Adm. and creditors.

NEWMAN, CLINTON B.
    CR9 2, 5 Sep 1864. Comm. app. to set apart year's support for
    widow Clementine and family.
    WB G 28, 129, 160, 206, dating from 23 Sep 1864 to 21 Sep 1866.
    Sale, Add. Invt. and sale, Sale, and Sett. by James Russell, Adm.
    CR9 284, 1 Jul 1867. Clementine Newman app. Gdn. of her own minor
    heirs, Sarah A., Mary Elmira, Spencer Lee, David M., Robert
    Clinton, Lefaiet C., and John M. Newman.
    CC 64, filed 15 Jun 1866. Clinton B. Newman died Aug 1864 leaving
    widow Clementine and children: Margaret E. who by May 1867 has
    married Wm. Armstrong, and the minors listed above.

NEWMAN, ISAAC
    WB B 75-76, Will exec. 3 Jan 1832, probated Mar 1832; to son
    Samuel; to five sons Joseph, Jared, Samuel, Isaac, and Joshua;
    to son Johnathan; to son Robert; to granddau. Elizabeth Cate;
    negro slaves not to be removed from Counties of McMinn, Monroe,
    or Jefferson and to be emancipated at stated times. Execs: six
    sons Joseph, Jared, Samuel, Isaac, Joshua, and Robert. Wit:
    Chas. Wakefield, John Thompson, H.D. Boid, Obed Patty, and James
    Gaut. Signed by mark.
    CC 87, filed 28 Jan 1850. Isaac Newman died 13 Jan 1832. Sons
    Jared and Joshua have died and son Joseph is of Jefferson Co.
    CC 135, filed 19 Aug 1851. Isaac Newman moved from Jefferson Co.,
    Tenn., to McMinn Co. before 1825; his dau. Rebecca, dec'd, was
    wife of Robert Stephenson and mother of Elizabeth, wife of
    Gideon Cate.

NEWMAN, JOHN
    CR4 292, 5 Dec 1836. Alfred C. and Mary Newman app. Adms.
    WB B 221, Jan 1837. Invt. by Adms.; items include a note on Daniel
    Newman and "estate by the Dec'd John W. Newman coming by his wife
    amount about $100.00".
    WB C 99, 15 Dec 1838. Sett.
    WB C 109, 8 Jan 1839. Sett.; the sum due in State of Virginia was
    found to be not due.
    WB C 230, 29 Feb 1840. Final sett.; receipts from heirs Mary and
    Daniel Newman.

NEWMAN, REBECCA
    CR10 255, 7 Nov 1870. Bird Newman app. Adm.

NEWMAN, ROBERT M.
    WB E 378-379, Will exec. 3 Jul 1854; "Item 1 - I hereby manumit
    and set free all my negro slaves", giving them choice of going to

Liberia with expenses paid or remaining in slavery to be divided
between wife Sarah E. and all the children; to wife Sarah "in
addition to what she had when I married her"; to son Clinton B.;
to five daus. Nancy Buckner, Elizabeth E. Dorsey, Rebecca Dorsey,
Sarah Culton, Mahala Jane Long; to grandson Robert Buckner; to
Hugh Holland. Execs: Raleigh Chesnutt and Milton P. Jarnagin.
Wit: J.N. Cate, John J. Dixon, B.A. Prophet.
CR6, 7 Aug 1854. Will proven.
WB E 385-392, 6 Nov 1854. Invt. of sale.
WB F 28-31, 20 Oct 1856. Sett. by Execs.; paid for negroes to
Liberia $475.00; "the negroes mentioned in the Will elected to
go to Liberia, and after regular emancipation on the 24th October
1855 they were started to Baltimore under the care of Joseph
McCulley of this County to be placed under the care and Trans-
portation of the America Colonization Society whence they were
shipped for the western cost /sic/ of Africa as the Executors are
informed and believe"; legatees signing receipts are C.B. Newman
and the husbands of his five sisters, namely, Burrow Buckner and
wife Nancy, Dimmon Dorsey and wife Elizabeth, McCamy W. Dorsey
and wife Rebecca, A. Culton and wife Sarah, J.A. Long and wife
Mahala.

NEWMAN, SAMUEL
CR6, 4 Aug 1851. Dimmon Dorsey, Jr., app. Adm.
WB E 239-242, 7 Oct 1851. Invt. and sale by Adm.
CC 135, filed 19 Aug 1851. Samuel Newman remained in Jefferson Co.
for some years after his father Isaac moved to McMinn Co. before
1825. Samuel Newman died in McMinn Co. intestate on 25 Jun 1851,
leaving children: William and James G., both married; Elizabeth,
dec'd 1848 or 1849, wife of Levi Smith (who dies 1855 during law-
suit) of Lawrence Co., Mo.; John L., married; Laura S. wife of
George O. Patty; Sarah, Jane, and Rebecca Newman, all unmarried
and living with the father. The children of Elizabeth and Levi
Smith are Sarah Jane wife of Jesse Pigg, Zarah wife of Miller
Martin, Samuel, William Levi, John Thomas, Francis Marion, and
Mary Eliza Smith.

NEWTON, EDWARD
WB G 229, Will exec. 12 Aug 1863, probated Sep 1869; "being ad-
vanced in age"; to Mary A. Grisham, one-fourth of household fur-
niture as her lawful right; equal division among heirs, viz:
the heirs of Wm. Newton, dec'd; Isaac, Jesse D., James A., Ed-
ward M., George W., and Jasper Newton; Mary A. Grisham; Malindy
L. Teague; Rebecky E. Long. Execs: sons E.M. and Jasper. Wit:
James and Daniel Parkerson.
CR10 127, 2 Aug 1869. Will proven.
CR10 139, 6 Sep 1869. Mary D. Newton, widow, dissents to Will.

NICE, DR. WILLIAM G.
WB E 323-324, Will exec. 23 Jul 1853, proven 1 Aug 1853; to wife
Elizabeth R., being now pregnant; to her offspring if born
alive; if not born alive then $800 of its share to niece Mary
Saunders, dau. of sister Mariah A. Saunders of Powhattan Co.,
Va. Execs: wife and Robert N. McEwen. Wit: Milton P.
Jarnagin, Wm. P.H. McDermott.
WB E 349-352, 10 Dec 1853. Invt. by Exec.; includes items found
in Dr. Nice's Medical Office.
WB E 360, no date. Acct. of sale agreeable to notice given in the

Athens Post.

WB F 451, 25 Nov 1859. Final sett.; receipt from Elizabeth R. Nice for all funds for herself and for her son Wm. G. Nice of whom she is natural gdn.

CC 60, filed 6 Aug 1859. Wm. G. Nice died Jul 1853 and his son Wm. G. was born 12 Sep 1853. Widow Elizabeth has bought land in Texas.

NORMAN, GEORGE

CR6, Jul 1855. Court pays for funeral expenses for a pauper.

NORMAN, WILLIAM

WB D 22-23, Will exec. 18 Apr 1840; to wife Hannah; to two youngest sons Flemmin L. and Lafawett; to other children: Mary S. Sutherland, Sally Walker, Betsey O. Shelton, Lucinda Cousins, Belinda Stults, William, Marshall, and Dutton Lane Norman, all of whom receive $1 each in addition to what they have received. Execs: wife and James W. Oakes. Wit: Jonathan Richardson, Terrell Nance, and Anthony Davis.

CR4 555, 2 Aug 1841. Will proven.

NORVAL, MARY

CR9 279, 1 Jul 1867. Report of Jacob Bryant, Adm., received.

CR11 112, 12 Aug 1868. Report by Adm.; eight vouchers of $41.25 each to G.B., G.W., Elizabeth, and F.M. Norvall (Norvell), Emanuel and Sarah Griffitts, J.A. and Elizia J. Henderson, John C. and Cela J. Wilson, and Isam Collinghan Gdn. for John Norvall.

O'DONALD, MAURICE (MORRANCE)

CR2 386, 8 Sep 1829. James H. Fyffe app. Adm.

WB A 217, Invt. 8 Sep 1830 by Adm.

O'NEIL, JESSE

CR2 21, 6 Sep 1824. Rebecca O'Neil app. Adminx.

ONLY, LEVI E.

WB F 358, 22 Nov 1860. Comm. S.S. Morgan, L.L. Ball, and R.D. Pearce set apart year's support for widow and family.

WB F 359, no date. Invt. by John Rogers, Adm.

CC 67, filed 11 Dec 1860. Levi Only has died since Aug 1860 leaving widow Mahala J. and children: Wm. E. of Ill., Mary E. wife of W.J.Y. Bennett believed to be of Ill., Martha E. wife of Benjamin Kibble, Malissa B., Thomas J., Sarah J., Nancy A., and Amanda A. Only, the last four being minors. Mahala Only and family contemplate moving to Ill.

CC 285, filed 18 Apr 1871. Mahala Jane, widow of Levi Only, and dau. of Elizabeth Stafford, executed deed in Williamson Co., Ill.

ORR, JOHN R.

CR9 63, 7 Aug 1865. M.B. Goddard of Monroe Co. app. Adm.

WB G 123, 20 Oct 1865. Invt. and sale by Adm.

WB G 124, 8 Aug 1865. Comm. Wm. M. Edwards, John D. Lowry, and Hugh Goddard lay off year's support for widow and family.

CC 185, filed 10 Oct 1868. John R. Orr died 1861-62-63 leaving widow Edith and heirs: Joseph, Acquilla, James H. of Gentry Co., Mo., Caroline wife of Wm. Weathers of Calif., and seven minors, Sherman, Robert, Elizabeth, Harris, Lee, David, and John.

ORR, NANCY
>   CR8, 2 Nov 1863. Will proven by Jas. H. Reagan and Mrs. M.A.
>   Reagan, the witnesses; J.W. and John R. Orr app. Execs. /No
>   Will is on record./
>   WB G 130-135, 29 Nov 1865. Invt. and sale held 13 Nov 1863 by
>   J.W. Orr, Exec.; buyers include J.B., J.W., J.R., John, and
>   I.H. Orr.
>   CR11 58, 24 Oct 1866. Exec. Sett.; vouchers to Irby H. and J.W.
>   Orr, and Elisha Briant, Gdn.

ORR, WILLIAM
>   WB B 63, 63(2), Will exec. 4 Nov 1830, recorded Sep 1831; to wife
>   Polly; to dau. Jane F. Johnston; to sons John W. and Josiah; to
>   other children; to wife until children shall be schooled and
>   raised. Execs: worthy friends Elijah Walker and John Erwine.
>   Wit: Josiah Rowan, Nealy Chrisman.
>   WB B 70, Dec 1831. Invt. of notes by Elijah Walker and John Arn-
>   wine, Execs.
>   CR4 54, 5 Mar 1832. Deed proven: Chas. Metcalf to Jane F.
>   Johnson, John W., Robert H., Josiah J., Francis G., Lucinda A.,
>   William W., Nancy J., and Hetty Ann Orr, heirs.
>   WB B 120, 5 Jun 1833. Comm. Tidence Lane, Joseph Minzes, and
>   George W. Mayo settle with Execs.

OWEN, DANIEL
>   CR4 509, 7 Sep 1840. Chas. P. and Cloe Owen app. Adm. and Adminx.
>   WB C 273, 5 Oct 1840. Invt. of sale held at Calhoun by Adms.
>   WB C 278, 5 Oct 1840. Comm. John L. McCarty, M.C. Hawk, and Wm.
>   W. Cowan set apart year's support for widow Cloe and family.
>   WB D 50, 6 Apr 1842. Sett. by C.P. Owen, one of Adms.

OWENS, JOHN
>   WB E 84, 1 Apr 1850. Sale held 22 Feb 1850 by Philip P. Owens,
>   Adm.
>   WB E 92, 11 Feb 1850. Comm. Wm. R. Weir, Winston Carter, and Mc.
>   Chambers set apart year's support for widow Elizabeth.
>   WB E 198, no date. Final sett. by Adm.; balance paid to J.R.
>   Witt, Gdn.
>   WB E 301, 7 Feb 1853; 308, 2 Mar 1853. Sett. by James R. Witt,
>   Gdn. of minor heirs.
>   CR6, 7 Nov 1853. Philip P. Owens app. Gdn. to Wm. T. Owens, minor
>   heir.
>   WB E 344, 30 Nov 1853. Final sett. by J.R. Witt, Gdn.; receipts
>   for equal amounts from John and Nancy J. Hale, heir, and from
>   P.P. Owens, Gdn.
>   WB F 41, 30 Nov 1856. Sett. by Philip P. Owens, Gdn.
>   WB F 347, 20 Sep 1860. Final sett. by same Gdn.; receipt for
>   balance from Wm. T. Owens.

OWIN, NANCY
>   CR7 73, 2 Nov 1857. Court pays for coffin for pauper.

PAINE, ORVILLE
>   CR14 349, 18 Dec 1867. F.J. Paine Adm. for the use of Franklin
>   Locke VS A.R. Snyder et al.

PARKISON, MANUEL
>   WB D 450-456, 3 May 1847. Invt. and sale held 19 Apr 1847 by
>   James Parkison and Wm. F. Forrest, Adms.
>   WB D 457, 7 Apr 1847. Comm. Matthew R. Gibson, C.L. King, and

W.J. McClatchy set apart year's support for widow Julian and family.

WB E 22, 15 Feb 1849. Sett. by Adms.; paid L.C. Rentfrow and wife to make them equal with other heirs.

WB E 38, Mar 1849. Add. Invt. of sale by Adms.

WB E 101, 5 Jan 1850. Sett. by Adms.; paid to heirs Mrs. Julia Parkison, Mrs. Mary Camp, Daniel Parkison, L.C. and Nancy M. Rentfrow, John Parkison, Wm. F. and Lear Forrest, all $108.50; paid heirs Nancy Jane and Jonathan Dodson $27.00; paid Jessee B. Dodson Gdn. for _.M., Geo. W., and Daniel T. Dodson minor heirs $81.37; paid Julian Parkison, widow.

PARRIS, LEMUEL J.

WB F 170, Will exec. 17 Mar 1858; to bro. William who is to support aged aunt Elizabeth Gordon during her lifetime; balance to be divided equally among the rest of bros. and sisters, with the share of sister Lucinda Payne to be divided among her heirs and the share of deceased sister Talitha Camran to be divided among her heirs. Exec: bro. John W. Parris. Wit: Joseph Cobbs, Jr., and John Lattimore.

CR7 180, 3 May 1858. Will proven; John W. Paris declines to serve as Exec. and Jas. C. Carlock is app. Adm.

WB F 202-212, 4 Oct 1858. Sale by Adm.; buyers include A.J., R.H., Moses, J.W., and Wm. Parris, Jr. and Sr., E.D. Cameron, James Payne, Uriah Payne, Wm. O. Cameron.

WB F 281, 5 Sep 1859. Invt. of sale of lands.

WB F 332, 25 Jun 1860. Sett.; paid part of legacy to Wm. Parris, Jr.

WB F 400, 28 May 1861. Sett.; paid for tombstones and palings for grave of Elizabeth Gordon.

CC 44, filed 21 Dec 1858. Lemuel J. Paris died leaving bros. and sisters as follows: William, Jr.; Lucinda wife of J.J. Payne of Washington Co., Ark.; Talitha Camron, dec'd; John W.; Robert H.; A.J.; Mary wife of James Hickey of Polk Co.; Elve wife of James Jenkins; Sally wife of John M. Vinzant of Mo.; Jerusha wife of C.H. Ward of Ala.; Nancy Fagan, dec'd. The children of sister Lucinda Payne are Elve, John, William, Jerusha, and perhaps others. The children of sister Talitha Camron, dec'd, are Mary wife of James Corn of Polk Co., Felix, James, Nancy, Caroline, John, and Elve, all minors of Polk Co. The children of sister Nancy Fagan, dec'd, are Mary wife of John Hickey and Nancy a minor. Aunt Elizabeth Gordon, over 85, is sister to Moses Paris.

PARRIS, WILLIAM, SR.

WB G 224-225, Will exec. 7 Feb 1869, prob. Jul 1869; body to be decently interred in burying ground at Coghill; all estate real and personal (except the bedstead with "screns" to it and the bedding and bed clothing belonging thereto bequeathed to wife) to be sold and money divided equally amongst wife and several children and children of those that are dead. Execs: son John W. and C.H. Ward. Wit: W.M. Cass, Joseph Cobb, Sr., and S.W. Payne.

CR10 130, 2 Aug 1869. J.W. Parris and C.H. Ward qualified as Execs. /This entry marked: Null and Void.7

CR10 151, 1 Nov 1869. John W. Parris and C.H. Ward app. Adms. of Wm. Parris who died intestate.

CR10 458, Feb 1873. A. Slack app. Adm.

PARSHALL, ANNA
  CR5 529, 7 May 1849. Samuel W. Royston of Washington Co. app. Adm.
  WB E 54-57, no date; 116, 26 Sep 1850. Invt. and sale, and Sett.
  by Adm.
  See also DR. JOHN PARSHALL

PARSHALL, DR. JOHN
  WB D 566-567, Will exec. 1 Apr 1848 in the City of New Orleans,
  La.; to wife Anna; to children Elizabeth, John R., Jane A., and
  James G. Parshall, and Ann Margaret Stone; none of children to
  be charged for board during their minority; James G. is now at
  school. Execs: James Gettys and wife Anna. "The foregoing was
  read to the testator in our presence we being satisfied from
  conference with him that he was of sound mind", /signed/ Wm.
  Perkins and Abram L. Gammon.
  CR5 482, 2 Oct 1848. Will proven by Abraham L. Gammon who states
  that the other witness is not an inhabitant of State of Tenn.;
  John R. Parshall identifies handwriting of Testator.
  CR5 484, 3 Oct 1848. Mrs. Anna Parshall app. Execx.
  WB E 461, 8 Sep 1855. Sett. by S.W. Royston, Adm.
  CC 73, filed 14 Jan 1861. Dr. John Parshall died on return from
  from Mexican War, leaving wife Anna who died Mar 1849 and children: Ann M. wife of Rufus W. Stone of Texas; Elizabeth who
  married Dec 1848 to Saml. W. Royston, an attorney; John R. now
  dec'd with wife Eva A. and infant dau. Anna Ross Parshall of
  Monroe Co.; Jane A. who died several years ago, a minor unmarried; and James G. of Monroe Co., the youngest child who reached
  his majority in 1857.

PARSONS (PARSON), THOMAS
  CR4 266, 4 Jul 1836. Comm. app. to lay off year's support for
  widow.
  WB B 203, Oct 1836. Invt. by Jont. Couch and Wm. Parson, Adms.
  WB C 57, 1 Nov 1838. Sett. by Adms.; receipt from Nancy Parson,
  heir.
  CR4 407, 3 Dec 1838. Petition for dower in land by Jane Parsons,
  widow of Thomas Parsons who died at his usual residence in McMinn
  Co. sometime during the year 1836.
  WB C 242, 4 Apr 1840. Sett. by Jont. Couch, Adm.; receipts from
  heirs Manvel, John, Jane, and Wm. Parson, Mary Creaghead, and
  from Jane Parson, Gdn. to her son Joseph.
  WB D 3, 15 Apr 1841. Final sett. by Jonathan Couch, one of Adms.

PATTERSON, JAMES E.
  CR6, 1 Dec 1851. James Sloop app. Adm.
  WB E 216, Mar 1852. Invt. and sale by Adm.
  CC 164, filed 31 Jul 1852. James E. Patterson died Nov 1851 leav-
  ing widow Caroline, who is sister to James Sloop, and one child
  Julia Ann, aged less than two years.
  CR6, 6 Nov 1854. Saml. Patterson app. Gdn. to Julia Ann Patterson,
  minor heir.
  WB E 488, F 260(1), 354, dating from 4 Jan 1856 to 4 Jan 1860.
  Sett. by same Gdn.

PATTERSON, ROBERT
  WB A 119-120, Will exec. 7 Jan 1828; to wife Mabel; to sons Samuel,
  William, Robert, James; to daus. Hannah, Anna wife of James

Green, Margret Blackburn, Eda Mcelheren, Martha Moore, Sarah wife of Jonathan Moore, Elizabeth Julian, Mabel Gaston, and Unicy Grigg. Execs: sons Samuel and Robert. Wit: G.R. Cox, Joshu Leonard, Joseph Briant.

CR2 262, 3 Mar 1828. Will proven.

WB B 200, 273, 276, dating from Oct 1836 to Jan 1838. Sett. by Saml. Patterson, one of Execs.

WB C 119, 122, 13 Dec 1838. Sett. by same Exec.; receipts from heirs: Isom Julian, Martha Moore, Jeremiah F. Strange, Joel Gregg, James Green, Richard Moore, John Mcelheran, Margaret Blackburn, Robert, James, and Wm. Patterson.

WB C 171, 27 Sep 1839. Sett. by same Exec.; receipts from heirs John Posten and Samuel Patterson; receipt from Jonathan Moore for equal amt.

PATTY, JAMES M.

WB F 175, 1 May 1858. Comm. John J. Dixon, Wm. Faugerson, and Wm. Newman set apart year's provisions for widow Jathary Jane and family.

WB F 182, 8 May 1858; 193, 1 Nov 1858. Invt. of sale and Add. invt. of sale by Robert Cochran, Adm.

CR7 345, 3 Oct 1859. Mary J. Patty app. Gdn. to Mary Elizabeth Martha Isabella Myram T. Patty, her own minor children. /No punctuation./

WB F 349, 28 Sep 1860. Final sett. by Adm.; receipt in full from Mary J. Patty, Gdn.

WB F 419, 29 Jun 1861. Sett. by Gdn.; vouchers for boarding three minor children.

CR9 42, 6 Mar 1865. Same Gdn. makes bond.

CR9 145, 2 Apr 1866. Mary J. Cockran app. Gdn. of minor heirs.

PATTY, OBED

WB D 136-137, Will exec. 27 Apr 1839; to wife; to son Josiah; sons Benjamin W. and George O. heretofore received their share; to five youngest sons, Obed, William, Robert, James, and Raphael; share of oldest dau. Lucinda Crockett to remain in hands of Execs. and if any remaining after her decease to be given to her youngest child Sarah; to second dau. Mariah Crockett; to dau. Elizabeth, yet single; to dau. Martha Barnett; to youngest dau. Susan Jane Patty. Execs: sons Benjamin W. and George O. and son-in-law James Crockett. Wit: C. Sanders, John Fergurson.

CR5 110, 1 May 1843. Will proven.

WB D 158, 12 May 1843. Comm. Wm. Lee, Robert Gregory, and Alexander Stephenson lay off year's support for widow Sarah.

WB D 158-161, 2 Oct 1843; 215, no date. Invt. of sale and Add. Invt. by Execs.; one note on John Harrel dated 1829, doubtful, if it is on the John Harrel that is dead.

WB D 298, May 1845. Sett.; receipts from heirs Nathaniel Barnett and wife, John Ferguson and wife, Alfred Dodson and wife.

WB D 336, 3 Nov 1845; 436, 5 May 1846; 497, 15 Dec 1847. Add. Invt. and Sett.; receipts from heirs Martha S. Barnett, Susan Jane Ferguson, and Elizabeth Dodson were reported heretofore.

PATTY, WILLIAM H.

WB D 384, 7 Sep 1846; 392, 5 Oct 1846. Invt. and Acct. of sale by Wm. Ferguson, Adm.

WB D 393, 11 Sep 1846. Comm. Chas. T. Thornton, Wm. Newman, and Green L. Reynolds set apart year's support for widow E. and

family。
WB D 415, 4 Jan 1847。 Add. sale.
WB D 492, 6 Dec 1847. Report by Wm. Ferguson, Gdn., to James R.
Patty, minor heir.
WB D 564-565 and repeated 568-569, 19 Sep 1848. Sett. by Adm.;
paid widow Edy.
WB E 19, 82, 528, 571, F 171, 319, dated from 6 Dec 1848 to 26
Mar 1860。 Settlements by same Gdn.
CR8 135, 2 Feb 1863. Wm. Faugerson resigns as Gdn. of Riley Patty
and N。M。 Crockett is app.
CC Record Books A and B。 William Patty, dec'd, (wife Ede and in-
fant son Riley) was son of Obed Patty.

PAYNE, ISAAC
WB E 59-60, Will exec. 12 Jan 1844; to wife Charlotte; $1 each to
children John, James, and Wm. Payne, and Mary Howard; land to
son Uriah; land and dwelling house to son Thomas, and wife to
live with him。 Exec: son Uriah. Wit: T。L. and John Hoyl.
CR5 552, 1 Oct 1849. Will proven.

PEAK, LUKE
CR15 109, 20 Apr 1869. State of Tenn. for the use of Thos. J.
Peak, Adm。, VS A。D。 Briant, Adm。 of J。M。 Yearwood.

PEARCE, DANIEL
WB F 246, Will exec. 5 Sep 1858; to two sons Wiley and Robert;
sister Mary Ann McCasland to handle all property and sales for
best interests of the two children and their education; land in
Gentry Co。, Mo。 Exec: sister Mary Ann McCasland. Wit: James
Pearce and George W。 Bridges.
CR7 256, 6 Dec 1858。 Will proven.

PEARCE, JAMES
CR9 337, 5 Nov 1867. S。M。 Thomas and Robert Pearce app. Adms.
CC 186, filed 10 Oct 1868. James Pearce died intestate Oct 1867
leaving children as follows: Robert D。; Abigail A。 wife of
Samuel M。 Thomas; Margaret Willis; Elizabeth Taylor of Chatata,
Bradley Co。; James H。; Isabella; Mary wife of John F. Larrison
of Bradley Co。; Amanda wife of John Masoner of Meigs Co。; Joriah
wife of Robert S。 Mahan of Monroe Co。; Nancy Ann wife of Robert
Porter of Parker Co., Texas; Sarah Jane, dec'd wife of Merit R.
Ware。 In 1868 the children of dau. Sarah Jane Ware, dec'd, are
James A。, Wm. J., H。P。, Elizabeth L。 wife of Wm. Thornton,
Jesse a minor, and four other minors names unknown, all of Ark.
In 1872 James A。 Ware and Elizabeth L. Thornton are of Pineville,
McDonald Co。, Mo。; Hamilton P。 is of Fannin Co., Texas; and J.B.
Ware is of Perry Co。, Ark. By 1883 there is Power of Atty. from
heirs of Susan Jane Ware, dec'd, as follows: Susan Amanda wife
of Chas. F. Pitman of Benton Co., Ark.; Rutha M. wife of Pleasant
R。 Patterson of South West City, McDonald Co., Mo.; and L.P.
Ware, youngest son and one of the minors whose name was unknown,
of Grayson Co。, Texas. By end of lawsuit E. Grubb and wife I.
/Isabella?/ are entitled to 1/11 of estate.
CR11 271, 30 Jan 1871 and 15 Jan 1880. Sett. by Adms.; equal payments to heirs S。M。 Thomas and wife A。, Margaret Willis, Elizabeth Taylor, J。T. Masoner and wife, J。F. Lorrison, R。D. Pearce,
R。S. Mahan and wife J。, E。 Grubb and wife I., John F. Lorrison
for Robert Porter and wife by Atty。 in fact, and Allen Ware for

M.D. Ware by Atty. in fact.

PEARCE, JOHN
CR5 138, 1 Jan 1844. Court pays for coffin for pauper.

PEARCE, KESIAH
CR4 335, 6 Nov 1837. Court pays Christen Peters for keeping
Sarah Ann Pearce, orphan.
CR4 342, 1 Jan 1838. Above order rescinded and John Rudd paid for
keeping same orphan.
CR4 416, 7 Jan 1839. Elizabeth Rudd paid for keeping same orphan
for year 1838.
CR4 417, 7 Jan 1839. Joseph Rudd admitted to keep same orphan.
CR5 57, 4 Jul 1842. John K. Boyd paid for taking care of same
orphan.
CR5 78, 7 Nov 1842. Sarah Ann Pearce, aged 6 last Jan., bound to
Thomas W. Johnson.

PEARMAN, WILLIAM
CR5 359, 5 Jul 1847. Court pays for shroud for pauper.

PEARSON, DOCTOR
WB B 123-124, Will exec. 4 Sep 1833; to wife Lovy; to youngest son
Charles, a minor; to Maston Pearson; to all lawful heirs. Execs:
wife Lovy and John Foster. Wit: Wm. Dotson, J.W. Pearson.
CR4 172, 2 Dec 1833. Will proven.
WB B 135, 3 Mar 1834; 218, Dec 1836. Invt. by Execs.

PEARSON, GEORGE
WB A 58-59, Will exec. 13 May 1824; to wife Allah; to children
Pleasant Henderson Pearson, Jesse Wilson Pearson, Louisa, George
Washington, William Henry, Christopher Collumbus, and Lusinda
Jane Pearson. Execs: wife and friend James Armstrong. Wit:
Robt. McCleary, Wm. Weaver.
CR2 18, 6 Sep 1824. Will proven.

PECK, ELLIOTT
WB D 139-141, Will exec. 22 May 1843; to wife Nancy; to daus.
Mariah Holston and Adaline Bewly; to sons Washington W., A.
Jackson, and Henry M.C. Peck and to daus. Laura J. and Arutha
Caroline Peck as they arrive at age of 18; youngest dau. Arutha
Caroline; to sons James R., and Wm. F.; to grandson Gilbert, son
of Gilbert Peck, dec'd, whose share is to be placed in hands of
Henry Holston to be used for Gilbert's education. Execs: son-
in-law Henry Holston, sons James R. and Wm. F. Peck. Wit:
Samuel Workman, Hiram Grisham.
CR5 113, 5 Jun 1843. Will proven.
WB D 156, 335, 495, E 151, 459, dated from 1 Oct 1843 to 18 Sep
1855. Sett. by Execs.
CC 299, filed 10 Aug 1858. Elliott Peck died leaving widow Nancy
and eight children /Arutha Caroline is omitted7: Archibald J.
makes affidavit at Sacramento, Calif.; James Russell Peck of Bradley Co.; Washington W. of Murray Co., Ga.; Wm. F.; Laura J. wife
of Wesley Gaston; Henry C. of Gentry Co., Mo.; Levenia A. wife
of W.C. Bewley; and Maria L. widow of Henry Holston of Jefferson
Co., Tenn.

PELLEY, JAMES
CR8, 4 Aug 1862. W.J. Green app. Adm.
WB F 453, no date. Invt. by Adm.

PERRY, HARRY (HARDIN)
   CR7 344 and 426, 3 Oct 1859 and Apr 1860. Court pays for coffin
   and burial clothes for pauper.

PETERS, CHRISTIAN
   CR6, 4 Aug 1851. Jeremiah F. Strange app. Adm.
   WB E 199, 6 Sep 1851. Sale by Adm.; buyers include N.J., Calvin,
   and N. Peters; one side saddle to Caroline.
   WB E 238, no date. Invt.
   CR6, 7 Apr 1856. Newton J. Peters, Gdn. to John Peters, minor
   heir, petitions Court to sell military bounty land warrant.

PETERS, LANDON C.
   CR6, 4 Jul 1853. Jury paid for holding inquest over body.
   CC 174, filed 5 Jan 1853. Moses Sweeney, et al VS Landon C. and
   Newton J. Peters. In 1841 Landon C. Peters was app. Gdn. of
   minor heirs of Joseph Smith, dec'd. Newton J. Peters is son of
   Landon C. Landon C. Peters dies during lawsuit by 30 Apr 1853.

PETTITT, FRANCIS P.
   CR6, 2 Aug 1852. Edmund Roberts and Wm. Rucker app. Adms.
   WB E 266-269, 4 Sep 1852; 299-301, 3 Jan 1853. Invt. of sale,
   invt. of property not sold, invt. of notes, accts., and slaves,
   and Add. invt. of sale, by Adms.
   CR6, 3 Oct 1853. James W. McSpadden and George W. Bridges app.
   Gdns. to George D., Francis A., Carmanda, and Thomas E. McCamron
   Pettitt, minor heirs.
   WB E 485, F 32, 153, 255, 298, 308, dated from 22 Dec 1855 to
   9 Jan 1860. Settlements by Adms. and Gdns.
   CR7 190, 7 Jun 1858. Petition for partition: George D., Margaret
   A., Martha M., and Francis A. Pettitt, and Edmund Roberts and
   wife Elizabeth C. VS Wm. G. Horton and G.W. Bridges, Gdns. for
   Kennedy L. and Thos. E.M. Pettitt; land to be divided into seven
   parts.
   WB F 354, 444, G 194, dated from 9 Jan 1860 to 8 Aug 1866. Set-
   tlements by George D. Pettitt, Gdn. of minor heirs.
   CC 182, filed 12 Apr 1853. Francis P. Pettitt died Mar 1852 leaving children as named in Petition above. His wife, who was sister to Elizabeth C. McCamon, died two or three years before he
   died. Elizabeth C. McCamon, a single woman, lived with her
   mother and father in N.C. in 1825 and her mother died soon after.
   Elizabeth C. McCamon has sister Polly still living in 1853.
   S.S. Glenn, who married a sister of Major F.P. Pettitt, dec'd,
   moved from N.C. to Monroe Co., Tenn., in 1825 and in 1834
   Francis P. Pettitt came from Surry Co., N.C., and lived with
   Glenn one summer, and then moved down to place where he was
   living at time of his death.

PETTITT, NEHEMIAH
   CR2 483, 6 Dec 1830. Petition of widow Susannah for dower in land.

PETTITT, MARGARET A.
   CR9 192, 1 Oct 1866. F.A. Pettitt app. Gdn. of his sister Margaret
   A. Pettitt whom a jury finds in a State of Mania with Paralysis.
   CR9 199, 5 Nov 1866. Invt. filed.

PHILLIPS, CHARLES
   CR5 220, 3 Mar 1845. Wm. Lee, Robt. Gregory, and James Crockett
   app. Comm. to lay off year's support for widow Mary.

WB D 271, no date. Above Comm. reports.

WB D 472, 2 Aug 1847. Report by Martin M. Hicks, Adm.

CC 46, filed 27 Apr 1848. Charles Phillips died 1844 in McMinn Co. intestate leaving the following heirs: widow Mary who is not in McMinn Co.; Elizabeth wife of Wm. Malone of McMinn Co.; Douthit Hicks husband of Hannah Hicks of McMinn Co.; Daniel Casteel of McMinn Co.; Benjamin Phillips of Henderson Co.; William Phillips summoned from Henderson Co. but not found; William Hicks of Henderson Co.; Sarah Jane wife of Chas. B. Lewis summoned from Henderson Co. but not found; Kindrick, Sarah, and John Phillips of Sullivan Co.; Asahel Phillips, dec'd (whose children are John, Jacob, and Henry, all minors); Hannah wife of John Smith of Sullivan Co.; Sarah wife of John W. Malone of Sullivan Co.; Chas. Hicks summoned from Meigs Co. but not found; Margaret wife of Merady Hicks of Monroe Co.; John Casteel of Bradley Co.; Jane wife of Edward Casteel of Bradley Co. but not found there; Hannah_wife of Douthit Hicks summoned in Bradley Co. and_not found /In final decree the name of Hannah Hicks is omitted_7.

PICKENS, JOHN

CR2 243, 3 Dec 1827. Jackson Smith, Robt. W. McCleary, and Henry Bradford lay off year's support for widow Nancy.

WB A 110, 4 Dec 1827. Invt. of personal property, by Nancy, Robert, and Rees Pickens, Adms.

WB A 129-131, 3 Mar 1828. Acct. of sale by same Adms.; buyers include Nancy, Robert, Reese, Rebecca, and Andrew Pickens, and John and Israel C. Smith.

CR2 322, 1 Dec 1828. Andrew, Rebecka, William K., Charles A., Nancy, and Martha Pickens, orphans over 14, choose Nancy Pickens and George Bowman as Gdns.

WB C 46, 12 Sep 1838. Sett. by Nancy Pickens, Adminx.; receipts from heirs Reece, Robert, Andrew, Nancy and Wm. K. Pickens, A.B. Neal, John and Israel Smith.

PIKE, JAMES

CR5 511, 5 Feb 1849. John L. Bridges app. Adm.

WB E 36, no date. Invt. and sale by Adm.; notes on James H. and John B. Pike; Susan Pike is a buyer.

WB E 37, 6 Mar 1849. Comm. James W. McSpadden, James C. Bryan, and Moses Snider set apart year's support for widow.

WB E 194, 10 Sep 1851. Sett. by Adm_.; paid for articles to bury Mrs. Pike Jan 1851; note on John /sic/ H. Pike who resides in Ga. also two judgments against the said James H. Pike.

PIKE, SARAH

CR9 31, 2 Jan 1865. Sheriff ordered to bring forward the three children of Sarah Pike, dec'd, so that they may be apprenticed.

CR9 38, 6 Feb 1865. Martha Pike aged 12 bound to Aaron Matthews; Adam Pike aged 5 bound to C.J. Wright.

PITNER, ADAM

CR4 539, 1 Mar 1841. Adam H. Pitner of Bradley Co. app. Adm.

CR4 545, 3 May 1841. W.J. McClatchy, John Wolff, and W.T. McCallie app. Comm. to lay off year's support for widow Malinda.

WB D 25, no date. Invt. of sale by Adm.

PLANK, CHRISTIAN B. (CHRISLEY B.)

CR7 255, 6 Dec 1858. James W. Plank app. Adm.

WB F 61, 247, 268, 366, dated from 1 Apr 1857 to 24 Dec 1860. Invt. and settlements by Adm.; receipts from heirs Luny Janeway, E. McBee, Thos. Hurst, John, Hiram, and Christian Plank for $41 each and Wm. Plank for $10.

PORTER, BOYD
WB G 20-21, Will exec. 7 Nov 1861; to wife Margaret R.; to two youngest sons James K. and Joseph A.; to daus. Mary F., Margaret J., and Elizabeth M. when they arrive at full age; to heirs of dec'd dau. Amelia McCullie; to grandson G.G. McCully; to sons Andrew J. "but owing to his affliction", Wm. W. ($10, having heretofore been provided for), Benj. J., and John B.; to family for "Summers residence", house and lot at the Chilhowee Springs. Execs: wife and John B. Porter. Attest: S.W. Foster, Wm. George.
CR9 9, 3 Oct 1864. Will proven.

PORTER, HENRY H.
CR5 89, 6 Feb 1843. Elisha Dodson app. Adm.
CR5 547, 3 Sep 1849. John M. Dodson app. Gdn. of minor heirs.
WB E 418, no date. Invt. by Adm.
WB E 460, 21 Sep 1855. Sett. by Adm.; vouchers include 1841 Orphans Court, expense and trips to Ala., moving the family from Ala. and raising them.
WB F 42, 26 Jan 1857. Sett. by Gdn.; receipt 1 Aug 1855 from Harriet A. Turner for about 1/3 of funds; tuition 1853 for Mary Jane Porter; tuition 1855 for Mary J. Turner; tuition for Mary E. Porter.
WB F 267, 26 Jan 1859. Sett. by Gdn.
WB F 443, 30 Nov 1861. Sett. by Gdn.; paid Mary J. Porter in full; receipts from F.L. and J.D. Porter.

PORTER, WILLIAM
WB E 276, Will exec. 27 Sep 1850; slaves to youngest dau. Mary B., wife of Wm. H. Strain, "having otherwise disposed of all my property". Wit: Hillery Patrick, Jabez Henderson, Saml. Kelly.
WB E 277, Will exec. 7 Mar 1851; "in eightieth year of my age"; to two sons Boyd and Wm. B. Porter, "my whole interest in a family of negro,s belonging to the estate of Joseph Sharp Dec'd in the State of Virginia and County of Augusta, the negro,s is in the hand of July Ann Sharp the wife of Joseph Sharp Dec'd as her life time estate"; this interest in said slaves came to him through his wife Fanny who was sister to Joseph Sharp, dec'd; rest of children have received their share. Wit: Pryor N. Lea, Joseph Sharp.
CR6, 1 Nov 1852. Will proven by Henderson, Kelly, Lea, and Sharp.

POWELL, BENJAMIN
CR4 22, 5 Sep 1831. Wm. H. Powell and Doctor W.L. Powell, over 14 and under 21, minor children of Benjamin Powell, dec'd, choose George W. Powell of McMinn Co. as Gdn.
CR4 382, 4 Sep 1838. Sett. by same, Gdn. to Wm. H. and Doctor Willis Powell.
WB C 41, 4 Sep 1838. Sett. by same Gdn.; received funds in July 1833; paid one-half to heir Wm. H. the same month.

POWER (POWERS), HOLLOWAY (HOLOWAY)
WB E 416, Will exec. 30 Dec 1852; to wife Polly; to children John F., Kelsey H., Danl. M., and George H. Power, Scythia McChristian, Articena S. Stanton. Danl. M. and Geo. H. are two youngest sons.

Exec: John F. Power. Wit: Sythia McCristian, John F. Power.
CR6, 1 Jan 1855. Will proven by John F. Powers.
CR6, 5 Mar 1855. Proof given that Sythia McChristian, the other
witness, is and is likely to continue sick, and her handwriting
is proven.
WB E 439, 7 Aug 1855. Invt. of notes by E.L. Miller, Exec.
WB F 34 and 84, 29 Nov 1856. Sett. by same Exec.; receipts from
J.F. Power, D. Morgan Power, Kelsey H. Powers, Geo. Powers,
David McCuistian and wife, and Lewis Stanton and wife.

POWER, JAMES MILES
CC 84, filed 19 Jul 1860. James Miles Power died about 1850, a
minor under 21, leaving bros. and sisters Artie E. wife of Willie
Lowry of Texas, John F., Jr., George H., and Kelsey S. Power.
John F. Power, Sr., is father of James Miles Power, dec'd.

POWERS, MORGAN
CR7 102, 4 Jan 1858. Listed as "died insolvent" in Tax Delinquents
for 1857.

POWERS, SAMUEL
CR9 82, 2 Oct 1865. Carroll Emerson paid for making coffin for
pauper.

PRATHER, WILLIAM
CR9 72, 4 Sep 1865. Benj. Wells app. Adm.
WB G 163, 2 Apr 1866. Report by Adm.
CC 86, filed 29 Jun 1867. William Prather died about May 1861
leaving widow Elizabeth and children: D.W., William M., Martin
T. of Iowa, John A., and James M. Prather, Louiza Jane McMillon
of Bradley Co., Nancy Cassady, Sarah A. Johns, Fatama wife of
Benj. Wells, and Mary A.E. Neil. Son Wm. M. dies during the
lawsuit in Sep 1868 leaving widow Rosselvene and minor children
James H., Maria E., and Ellen M.

PRICE, NANCY
CC 217, filed 6 Sep 1869. Nancy, dau. of Allen Butler and wife of
A.J. Price, died in McMinn Co. about 19 Apr 1869 leaving no chil-
dren, and her next of kin and heirs are T.H. and Isaac Butler;
Louisa Coats formerly Butler, widow of Wm. Coats, dec'd; Lucy
Pearce; Wm. Herrod; and a niece Mary Butler, a minor of Meigs
Co., dau of John Butler, dec'd, who was a bro. of sd. Nancy
Price.

PRIDE, POLLY
CR6, 2 Oct 1854. Court pays for burial expenses for pauper.

PRIGMORE, KIZIAH
WB D 106, Will exec. 14 Jun 1841; $1 each to sons Ephraim and
Thomas; to daus. Margaret Green and Rutha Kelly; to Sally Kelly.
Execs: Thomas Prigmore and Wm. L. Pearson. Wit: Jacob Golden
and John Foster.
CR5 73, 3 Oct 1842. Will proven.
WB D 164, 2 Nov 1843. Sett. by Thos. Prigmore, one of Execs.

PUGH, ANDREW J.
CR5 377, 4 Oct 1847. Hamilton Stewart, James McNabb, and John
Hill app. Comm. to lay off year's support for widow Nancy.
CR5 - Loose paper not dated: Petition of widow Nancy that her
husband died on 3rd day of April last, leaving herself and four

children as heirs; that he left no real estate and little personal property; that Comm. be app. to lay off year's support.

PUGH, FLEMING C.
   WB B 168, Will exec. 16 Dec 1834, probated Mar 1835; to wife Sarah;
   to children Mary Jane, Darky Ellen, and Martha H. Pugh. Execs:
   wife and Jonathan Pugh. Wit: Hamilton Stewart and John Pugh.
   WB D 424, 30 Jan 1847. Sett. by Jonathan Pugh, one of Execs.; the
   widow intermarried with Solomon Smalling about six years ago.
   CR5 389, 6 Dec 1847. James McNabb app. Gdn. to minor heirs.
   WB E 94, 18 Feb 1850. Sett. by Gdn.; paid Mary Jane Pugh, one of
   heirs.
   WB E 210, 18 Feb 1852. Sett. by Gdn.; paid to Dorcas Pugh 29 Jul
   1850; paid to heirs Wm. J. and Dorcas E. Young; paid "Mary Jane
   and Edward J. Grisham Order to Richard Simpson".
   WB E 432, 22 Jun 1855. Final sett. by N.B. McNabb, Agent for James
   McNabb, Gdn.; receipts from Martha H. Pugh and F.C. Pugh for the
   balance.

PUGH, J. F.
   WB F 427, Will exec. 16 Dec 1861, proven May 1862; to children
   Marylin, Manda L., Mahala E., John W., Wm. L., and Henry Thomas
   Pugh, until youngest comes of age. Exec: James W. Plank. Wit:
   Wm. H. Hammons and Thos. Weir.
   WB F 452, no date. Comm. Samuel M. Thompson, Stephen Hill, and
   I.B. Haney lay off year's support for family.
   WB F 452, no date. Invt. of notes and accts.
   WB G 31, 5 Dec 1864. Final sett. by Exec.; receipt from S.M.
   Thomas, Gdn., for balance.
   WB G 137, 5 Dec 1865. Sett. by Gdn.
   CR10 172, 7 Feb 1870. S.M. Thomas resigns and P.L. Dodson is app.
   Gdn.

PUGH, JOHN
   WB F 402, Will exec. 15 Apr 1859, proven Jul 1861; to Johnathan F.
   Pugh, Eliza Reed, Thursa Riggins, Evaline Goforth, James, Josiah,
   and John Pugh; Eliza Reed to have the house where she now lives
   "as long as she conducts herself in a becoming way and Lives by
   herself"; Eliza Pugh wife of Hiram Pugh to have house where she
   now lives; John Pugh when he is 20 yrs. old; land lying on waters
   of Rogers Creek; property and money to be equally divided "among
   my own children". Exec: James W. Plank. Wit: Wm. and F.M.
   George.
   WB F 403, 10 Jul 1861. Invt. by Exec.
   CR8 158, 6 Apr 1863. Thomas Riggins, Jr., and Josiah Pugh VS Jas.
   W. Plank, Exec., et al; Complainants contest the validity of the
   Will; all papers sent to Circuit Court.
   CR13 341, 23 Aug 1865. Complainants dismiss suit to contest Will.

PURCELL (PURSELL), DANIEL
   WB E 179, Will exec. 21 May 1851; to sister Mary McPhail and her
   living children; to the living children of bro. Malcom Pursell
   except Wm. M. Pursell who is to have 25¢ and no more. Execs:
   Dugold McPhail and Crisley Foster. Wit: Wm. Forster, Andrew
   Foster.
   CR6, 1 Sep 1851. Will proven.
   WB E 243-249, 1 Dec 1851; 297, 1 Jan 1853; 327, 1 Jan and 16 Aug
   1853. Invt. and sale, Sett., and Final sett. by Christley

Foster, Exec.; nine receipts for equal amounts from heirs John, Mary, Cynthia, and Martha Purcell by Young A. Purcell, Atty.; Young A. Purcell and Young A. Purcell, Adm. of Daniel Purcell, all of Boone Co., Mo.; James Purcell, Daniel and John McPhail.

PURCELL, DANIEL
  CR6, 6 Dec 1852. Young A. Purcell of Boon Co., Mo., app. Adm. of Daniel Purcell who has departed this life leaving no Will.

PURCELL, WILLIAM M.
  CR9 59, 3 Jul 1865. Geo. W. Matlock app. Adm.
  CC 383, filed 10 Oct 1873. William M. Purcell died 1 Nov 1864 leaving widow Martha and children: Henry, Missouri, Young, Martha, Queen, and William Purcell, all minors except Henry.
  CR11 286, 25 Oct 1873. Sett. by Adm.

PURRIS, ELIZABETH
  WB F 192, 17 Aug 1858. Sett. by Saml. H. Jourdan, Gdn. for heirs and distributees of Elizabeth Purris "Late of the State of Virginia"; receipts in full from heirs and distributees Sarah M. and Jane Jourdan, Mary E. and Sarah P. Gamble (Gamball).

QUEENER, JOHN
  WB D 6, Will exec. 2 Nov 1832, probated Apr 1841; to wife Betsey; to four sons George W., James C., John, and Jacob; to daus. Sally Kline, Polly Pickle, Nancy Iseley, and Peggy Ward, $1 in addition to what they have already received; to little dau. Betsey when she marries or comes of age. Execs: friend Robert W. McClary and son George. Wit: Andrew and Wm. C. Pickins. Signed by mark.

RABOURN (RABURN, RAYBORN), JOSEPH
  WB F 189, Will exec. 2 May 1858, proven Aug 1858; to wife Frances; to sons John, Charley, Octavus, Allen, and Wiley (to live with wife); to sons Jefferson, Henry, William; to dau. Eliza. Exec: A.J. Hill. Wit: John J. Dixon, John M. Monds, and James H. Dixon.
  WB F 221, 26 Oct 1858. Invt. of sale by Exec.
  WB F 257, 17 Feb 1859. Sett. by same Exec. who has resigned and John Jack is Adm. with Will annexed.
  CR7 293, 7 Mar 1859. Petition to sell land: A.J. Hill, Exec. VS Charles, Octavus, Willowby, and John Raiborn; the first three defendants are minors.
  WB F 343, 31 May 1859. Sett. by E.P. Bloom; paid for two coffins.
  WB F 396, 29 Jan 1861. Final sett. by John Jack, Adm.

RAINEY (RAYNEY), JOHN, JR.
  CR4 407, 3 Dec 1838. John Rainey, Sr., app. Adm.
  WB C 112, Jan 1839; 221, no date. Sale and pro rata sett. by Adm.; Wm. Rayney is one debtor.

RANDAL, GEORGE W.
  CR5 249, 6 Oct 1845. Coroner paid for holding inquest over body.

REAGAN, JAMES H.
  CR9 102, 1 Jan 1866. Mira A. Reagan app. Adminx.
  WB G 152, 5 Feb 1866; 159, no date. Invt. and sale by Adminx.
  WB G 160, 21 Feb 1866. Comm. James Willson, James Forrest, and J.F. Lane lay off year's provisions for widow and family.
  .CR11 343, 4 Nov 1875. Sett. by Adminx.; equal payments to W.B.L.,

M.A., and Jas. A. Reagan, and Julia and Jas. R. Love.

RECTOR, DANIEL
  CR4 309, 3 Apr 1837. Sarah Rector app. Adminx. and Gdn. to Sena
  Mary Rebecca and Emma Rector, minor children.
  WB B 255, Jun Court 1837. Invt. by Adminx.; lists land in S. C.,
  house and lot in Ala., and house and lot in Athens, Tenn.

RECTOR, MAXIMILLIAN
  WB E 143, 9 Dec 1850; 281, 6 Dec 1852; 345, 27 Dec 1853. Invt.
  and sale, Add. Invt., and Sett. by Elijah Cate, Adm.; rec'd a
  pension fund.

REDMOND
  CR10 91, 1 Feb 1869. E.C. Redmond app. Gdn. of her own minor
  child, Mary H. Redmond.

REED JEREMIAH
  WB B 152, 4 Sep 1834. Comm. Tidence Lane, Henry Matlock, Jesse H.
  Benton, set apart year's support for widow and family of small
  children.
  WB B 153, no date. Sale by Larkin Taylor, Adm.; Fanny Reed is a
  buyer.
  WB B 234, Dec 1836. Sett. by Adm.

READER
  CR2 385, 7 Sep 1829. Franklin Reader, minor orphan over 14 and
  under 21, chooses Michael Whetsell as Gdn.

REEDER, JOHN F.
  WB D 498, Will exec. 23 Dec 1847; all estate to mother Rachel Kin-
  der; $1 to "each & every of my legal kin that may see proper to
  call on my Executors for the same". Execs: kinsman Stephen K.
  Reeder and friend James F. Bradford. Wit: Wm. Lowry, John King.
  CR5 395, 6 Jan 1848. Will proven.

REEDER, STEPHEN K.
  WB G 9-10, Will exec. 24 Sep 1852; to wife Mary McKim Reeder; to
  all children when they come of age. Testator acknowledges his
  signature before witnesses John D. Alexander and Saml. F. Gettys
  on 8 Jan 1862.
  CR9 1, 5 Sep 1864. M.A. Helm app. Adm. with Will annexed.
  WB G 11-16, 30 Sep 1864. Invt., list of accts., and notes by Adm.;
  invt. includes 1 cork leg; rent of store from 1 Jul 1864; cash in
  Confederate Scrip and bonds in hands of Thos. A. Cleage in Ga.;
  salt and sacks in hands of D.A. Wilkins, Va. Salt Works near
  Abingdon, Va.; Adm. could not classify notes and debts because so
  many of debtors were absent from County in either Army or where-
  abouts not definitely known.
  WB G 22, 26 Sep 1864. Comm. John J. Helm, Wm. H. Ballew, and R.C.
  Jackson set apart year's support for widow Mary M. and family.
  CR9 23, 7 Nov 1864. Mrs. Mary M. Reeder, widow, enters her dissent
  to the Will.
  WB G 61-65, 25 May 1865. Acct. of sales made by Jas. Turner,
  Auctioneer by order of Adms. 15 Mar 1865.
  CR14 112, 20 Apr 1867. Mary M. Reeder, Gdn. of John M., Stephen,
  and William M. Reeder, minor heirs. Stephen K. Reeder died
  5 Jul 1864.

REESER, FREDERICK
 WB A 118-119, Will exec. 27 Apr 1827; to wife Margaret and children; "raising a family"; "those that have married"; land in Rhea Co., Tenn., near Bridwell's. Execs: wife and John Reecer "whom I constitute my son". Wit: John H. Porter, Benjamin Wasson, J.B. Jackson. Signed by mark.
 CR2 266, 3 Mar 1828. Will proven.

REID, CLARISSA
 CR7 377, 6 Feb 1860. Wm. C. Adare app. Adm.
 WB F 323, 5 Mar 1860. Invt. by Adm.

REID, WILLIAM A. G.
 CR8, 7 Jan 1862. Mrs. Loretta Reid app. Adm.

RENOW (REANOW), ANNY
 CR5 370, 371, 6 Sep 1847. Heil Buttram, James Hicks, and John Foster, Sr., app. Comm. to lay off year's support for minor heirs; James W. Christian app. Gdn.

REYNOLDS
 CR2 322, 1 Dec 1828. Henry and Ann Reynolds, minor orphans over 14, choose Henry Reynolds as Gdn.

REYNOLDS, GEORGE
 WB G 222, Will exec. 1 Apr 1868; to wife Susan; to sons Wm. L., Michael C., and the heirs of son James M., dec'd; to daus. Exec: eldest son Wm. L. Wit: H.C. Reynolds, J.H. Crockett.
 CR10 54, 56, 7 Sep 1868. R.J. Patty app. Adm.; Will proven and son Wm. L. declines to serve as Exec.
 CR11 321, 23 Nov 1874. Sett. by Adm.
 CC 18, filed 1 May 1877. George Reynolds died leaving widow Susan who died about 1875 and the following eight children: Wm. L.; Michael C.; James H. dec'd; Lucy wife of A.J. Hill of Murray Co., Ga.; Emaline wife of Wm. Lee of Monroe Co.; Letta Paulina, dec'd wife of R.J. Patty; Nancy Avaline wife of O.W. Patty of Little River Co., Ark.; Hannah, dec'd wife of N.H. Cansellor, dec'd at Rolla, Mo. The children of son James H., dec'd, are S.H.; Susan wife of Richard Wilson, Robert, and Jackson, last three being minors. The children of dau. Hannah Cansellor, dec'd, are Mary Susan wife of Joseph L. Stewart, Martha E. wife of Samuel Bowles, and Millie Cansellor, all of Rolla, Phelps Co., Mo., and James H. Cansellor of Maries Co., Mo. The children of dau. Letta Paulina Patty, dec'd, are Geraldine wife of Thos. P. Duggan, Lucy wife of Geo. W. Carson of Monroe Co., Susan T. wife of D.C. Duggan, W.H. Patty, and James R. Patty, a minor of Texas.

REYNOLDS, GREEN L.
 WB D 430, 11 Dec 1846. Comm. Wm. Newman, John Thompson, and John K. Jackson set apart year's support for widow Tabitha and family.
 WB D 431, 1 Mar 1847; 582, 4 Jan 1849; WB E 265, 28 Aug 1852. Invt. and settlements by James Chesnutt and H.C. Reynolds, Adms.; receipts for equal amounts from Mary, Tabitha, H.C., and Wm. H. Reynolds.

REYNOLDS, HENRY
 WB B 169, 10 Dec 1834. Comm. Urial Johnson, John Morris, and John Jackson set apart year's support for Mary Reynolds.
 WB B 180, 2 Jun 1835. Invt. by David Cantrell and Wm. Grant.
 WB B 238, Apr 1837. Invt. by same as Adms.; cash received of John

Neal and John McDow both of Ala.

WB C 153, 5 Aug 1839. Sett. by Adms.; paid to Wm. Donalson Gdn.
for Ann Reynolds heir of Wm. Reynolds, dec'd; paid Henry Reynolds heir of Wm. Reynolds, dec'd, money due from Henry Reynolds,
dec'd; paid to Mary and Saml. McSpadden heirs of sd. Dec'd cash
received in Ala.

WB C 222, 25 Feb 1840. Sett. by David Cantrell, Wm. Grant, and
Mary McSpadden, Adms.

REYNOLDS, ISHAM

CR10 231, 5 Sep 1870. James S. Russell and Wm. J. Reynolds app.
Adms.; Comm. app. to lay off dower to widow.

CR10 243, 3 Oct 1870. Plat of the land assigned as dower to widow
Nancy.

CR11 260, 29 Oct 1872. Final sett. by Adms.; seven receipts for
equal amounts from W.J. Reynolds for Mary J. Rice, T.J., John
M., D.D., Wm. J., and J.H. Reynolds, and E.A. and A.T. Blair.

CR11, loose paper in book: Donalton, Hunt Co., Texas, 17 Oct 1875;
receipt from Orville Rice, Gdn. of Margaret, Montie, and Robert
Rice, heirs of Mary J. Rice, dec'd.

REYNOLDS, JOHN

CR9 108, 5 Feb 1866. Montreville Reynolds app. Adm.

WB G 165, 20 Mar 1866. Comm. Uriel Johnston, Raleigh Chesnutt,
and E.L. Miller, Surveyor, set apart dower in land for "Margaret
Reynolds former widow of John Reynolds deceased".

CR9 232, 4 Feb 1867. Montraville Reynolds, Adm. VS Wm. H., Manerva
J., Robert H., and Susan Clarinda Reynolds, all minors. J.M.
King app. Gdn. ad litem.

REYNOLDS, TABITHA

WB E 195, Will exec. 29 Jan 1852, proven 1 Mar 1852; Tabitha, widow
of Green L. Reynolds; to second dau. Lucy Jane; to dau. Polly; to
youngest son Samuel; all children to have balance after bequests
paid. Exec: eldest son Hugh C. Reynolds. Wit: Jas. and Raleigh
Chesnutt. Signed by mark.

WB E 254, 7 Jun 1852. Invt. of sale.

WB E 364; 21 Mar 1854. Sett.; paid heirs Lucy J. and Mary M.
Reynolds.

RHEA (RAY), HIRAM

WB D 400, 2 Nov 1846. Invt. by John Cunningham, Adm.

WB D 414, 7 Dec 1846. Acct. of sales by Adm.; Harris Ray is a buyer.

WB D 562, 6 Sep 1848. Sett. by Adm.; "cash balance of his pay due
from US for services under Capt. J.D. Lowry in Mexico"; "cash on
hand at the time dec'd left for Mexico".

RICE

WB E 307, 27 Feb 1849. Sett. by C.W. Rice, Gdn. to J.R., Martha
E., Sarah E., and Susan L. Rice; received of A. Haley.

RICE, ALBERT G.

WB E 120, 4 Nov 1850. Comm. Wilson Chapman, R.M. Newman, and Saml.
Wilson set apart year's support for widow Margaret W., and family.

WB E 122-127, 5 Nov 1850; 142, 3 Feb 1851. Invt. of notes due and
acct. of sale held 17 Oct 1850, and Add. Invt. by James Forrest
and John Scruggs, Adms.

CC 52, filed 15 Apr 1851. Albert G. Rice died leaving widow
Margaret W. and minor children Orville, Albert, Robert, and an

infant not named.

RICE, HENRY
    WB G 66-69, 23 Jun 1865; 84, 22 Jul 1865. Invt. and sale and sett.
    by C.L. Rice, Adm.
    CR9 57, 3 Jul 1865. Invt. filed in lieu of one previously made
    which was destroyed.
    CC 116, filed 4 Mar 1867. Henry Rice died 10 (12) Oct 1862 leaving
    widow Margaret (who was without issue) and children by former
    wife: Charles Lafayette, Henry M., Martha E., and Laura K., the
    last two being minors over 14, his only children.

RICE, ISAAC
    CR1 102, 2 Dec 1823. Martha Rice app. Gdn. for Charles W., Henry,
    Elizabeth, Miller F., and Lucinda Rice, minor heirs; James S.
    Rice app. Gdn. of Tandy and Isaac Rice minor heirs in the settle-
    ment of dower for Martha Rice; Martha Rice Gdn., James S. Rice,
    Gdn., Rubin Walker and wife Susannah all acknowledge that they
    have been notified that John Rice and James S. Rice would apply
    for distributive share of real estate.
    CR1 115, 1 Mar 1824. Report of Comm. app. to divide real estate
    among heirs: to widow Martha Rice; to Henry Matlock Rice and
    Miller F. Rice (land in Roane Co. on N. side Tenn. River); to
    James S., Lucinda, and Isaac Rice, and Reuben Walker (land in
    Roane Co. on S. side Tenn. River); to Elizabeth, Chas. W., John,
    Wm. L., and Tandy Rice (land in McMinn Co.)
    WB A 35, no date. Invt. of sale by Irby Holt and Wm. Lowry, Adms.
    WB A 144, 31 May 1828. Comm. James F. Bradford, Benjamin Isbell,
    and Elijah Hurst make sett. with Adms.
    WB C 56, 26 Oct 1838. Report by Martha Rice, Gdn.; interest due
    from Sep 1823 to Oct 1838; vouchers to heirs Wm. H. Ballew, Chas.
    W., Elizabeth, Miller F., and Henry Rice.
    WB C 73, 4 Jul 1837. Final sett. by Wm. Lowry, one of Adms. with
    Comm. John B. Jackson, Elijah Hurst, and John McGaughy; listed
    are Eavan, John, Isaac, Charles W., Henry, Tandy S., and Martha
    Rice.
    WB C 233, 26 Oct 1839. Add. report by Gdn.
    WB D 157, no date. Sett. by Gdn.; receipts from heirs Wm. L. Rice,
    Allen Haley; receipt from heir Miller F. Rice "filed heretofore
    but he being a minor at the time it is herewith filed again".

RICE, JAMES S.
    CR2 49, 7 Mar 1825. John Rice app. Adm.
    WB D 228, no date. Sett. by Adm.; in 1823 or 1824 he became Adm.
    and filed Invt. of sale, but it can not be found; said J.S. Rice
    was indebted to estate of Isaac Rice; receipts in full from Tandy
    S. and Isaac Rice, Henry Matlock; Adm. has fully satisfied the
    debts and also the heirs of said estate.

RICE, JOHN
    CR4 345, 5 Feb 1838. Jesse Rice app. Adm.
    WB C 113, Feb 1839. Supp. return, by Adm.
    WB C 201, 3 Feb 1840. Sett. by Adm.; paid Wm. Ziegler for his
    wife Lockey.
    WB C 338, 4 Feb 1841. Sett. by Adm.; receipts from Wm. and Locky
    Ziegler, formerly Locky Rice, widow of John Rice, dec'd; Callo-
    way H. Raper and Lancaster Randolph are heirs; the claim of
    Jesse Rice, Adm. in sd. estate.

WB D 56, 12 Feb 1842. Sett. by Adm.

RICE, JOHN
    CR6, 4 Sep 1854. C.W. Rice app. Adm.
    CR6, 2 Oct 1854. Henry Rice app. joint Adm.
    WB E 410, 1 Jan 1855; F 57, 9 Mar 1857. Invt. of notes and Sett.
      by Adms.
    WB F 265, 4 May 1859. Sett. by Jesse C. Rice, Gdn. of James S.
      Rice.
    CC 77, filed 15 Feb 1861 and 279, filed 4 Jan 1858. The ten chil-
      dren of John Rice, dec'd, are Isaac R. of Calif.; Wm. J. of Ala.;
      Letha F. Rice who died without issue; Jesse C.; John; Henry, Jr.;
      Nancy wife of Thos. A. Owens of Ark.; Sarah wife of George Gard-
      ner of Calif.; Charles W., Jr., of Ga. and later of Ark.; and
      James S. who died a minor.

RICE, LEATHA (LETHE)
    CR6, 7 Jan 1856. Jesse C. Rice app. Adm.
    WB F 265, 4 May 1859. Sett. by Adm.
    WB F 272, 4 May 1859. Sett. by Adm.; equal amounts paid to heirs
      Isaac R., John, Chas. W., Henry, Jr., Wm. J., and Jesse C. Rice,
      and George G. Gardener and wife Sarah T.
    CR7 328, 4 Jul 1859. Heirs of Letha Rice and also heirs of James
      S. Rice are C.W., Jr., J.C., I.R., John, and H. Rice, Jr., G.G.
      and Sarah T. Gardener, N.P. and Thos. A. Owens.

RICE, MARTHA
    WB E 130, 3 Dec 1850. Invt. by H. and C.W. Rice, Adms.
    WB E 284, 6 Dec 1852. Add. Invt. by Adms.
    WB E, 7 Nov 1854. Loose paper in book and not registered in book.
      Sett. by Henry Rice, one of Adms.
    WB F 185, 23 Jun 1858. Sett. by same Adm.; amount received from C.
      Matlock's estate; vouchers for presents to grandchildren; receipts
      from C.W., M.F., Wm. L., and Henry Rice, Allen Haley, and Wm. H.
      Ballew.

RICE, TANDY S.
    CR8 162, 163, 4 May 1863. W.L. Rice app. Adm.; Jas. Wilson, Jas.
      H. Magill, and John F. Sherman app. Comm. to lay off year's sup-
      port for widow and family.
    CC 97, filed 30 Dec 1861. Tandy S. Rice dies during lawsuit and
      his adult children are William of Roane Co., Martha, Nancy, James
      H., and Lucinda. James H. is a nonresident of Tenn.
    CR13 230, 238, 6 May 1863. Indiana P. Rice VS Tandy S. Rice. Peti-
      tion for divorce. Plaintiff dismisses suit and death of defendant
      is suggested and proven.

RICHARDS, ADAM
    CR4 112, 120, 3 Dec 1832. Aquilla Leatherwood and Spencer Tillison
      app. Comm. to lay off year's support for widow Jane; Mary Rama
      app. Adminx.
    CR4 246, 7 Mar 1836. James Long, Thos. Marston, and James Chesnut
      app. Comm. to settle with Mary Raimy, Adminx.
    WB B 183, 30 Apr 1836. Above Comm. settle with Mary Rainy (Rany),
      Adminx.

RICHARDS, GABRIEL
    /The Will of Gabriel Richards is not on file in McMinn Co. A copy
      is found in Roane Co., Tenn., Minute Book O/

CR2 160, 5 Jun 1826. Will proven by John W. and James M. Barnett; Richards died 4 Apr 1826; Will contained clause freeing slaves James and Hannah, who present their petition and are freed as James and Hannah Richards.

WB A 143, no date. Invt. by Richard and Asa Richards, Execs.

CR3 9, 3 Jun 1829. John and Mildred Paine VS the Execs.; John Paine and wife Mildred formerly Richards, heir, suggest to Court that Gabriel Richards at time of making purported Will was not of sound mind; Jury to decide issue; process issued to Asa, Richard, Durrett, George, William, and Gabriel Richards, Wm. Everett and wife Nancy late Richards, Lewis Brock and wife Polly late Richards, Rhoda Harvy, and Charles F. Wall, heirs.

CR2 422, 1 Mar 1830. Invt. by Richard Richards, Exec.; receipt from Nancy Richards for total funds.

CR3 77, 8 Jun 1830. Jury finds that "Gabriel Richards devised as in and by the written paper in the Scire facias specified, purporting to be the last Will and testament".

RICHARDS, RICHARD
  WB B 149, 1 Sep 1834; 155(2), no date; 261, no date. Invt., Invt. of notes, and Sett. by Daniel Richards and John W. Blevins, Adms.
  WB B 264, no date. Sett. by Adms.; money spent for Daniel Richards, Heir, D.R., G., Samuel, and Elenore Richards.
  CR4 216, 4 Dec 1834. Daniel Richards app. Gdn. for John, Elijah, Edward, Samuel, Daniel, Elenor, Elizabeth, and Susannah Richards, minor heirs.
  CR4 217, 5 Dec 1834. Elijah L. Richards bound as apprentice to Richard Kelly and John V. Richards bound to Benjamin Ragsdale.
  WB C 55, 10 Oct 1838. Report by Daniel Richard as one of Adms. and as Gdn.; expenses "coming & going to this city" and in margin "White Ct. Sparta".
  WB D 53, 19 Jan 1842. Report by same; boarding and schooling Daniel son of Richard Richards; received from estate of John Vance, dec'd.
  WB E 41, 11 Apr 1849. Sett. by same for years 1843-1848; received cash of John Vance dec'd willed to said heirs $50.

RICHARDSON, JAMES
  CR2 49, 7 Mar 1825. James Bowers and Harriette Richardson app. Adms.; James Cowan, Sr., George Colville, and Jonathan Couch app. Comm. to lay off year's support for widow Harriette.

RICHARDSON, WILLIAM
  CR4 483, 3 Feb 1840. David Richardson of Campbell Co. app. Adm.
  WB C 216, 239, Feb and Mar 1840. Invt. by Adm.

RIDDLE, BENJAMIN
  WB A 7-8, Will exec. 24 Jul 1822; wife Francis to live on land until youngest child Benjamin comes of age; to children Benjamin, Lewis, Dolly, Abraham, and James B. Execs: Wm. Hawkins, John and Harman Riddle. Wit: Jesse H. Vermillion, Daniel Newman, James Hawkins. Signed by mark.
  WB A 13-14, 2 Dec 1822. Invt. taken 23 Nov 1822 by John Riddle and Wm. Hawkins, Execs.
  CR3 192, 6 Dec 1831. Daniel Newman VS Wm. Hawkins and John Riddle, Execs. Defendants not to be found, have removed out of this State and ceased to perform duties of Execs.; Frances Riddle, widow, and John Miller app. Adms.

CR4 74, 7 Mar 1832. Deed proven; Lewis Riddle for his 1/6 undivided part.

CR4 110, 7 Sep 1832. Deed of Trust from Wm. S. Ragan for his share of undivided estate, the share of his wife Mary, formerly Riddle.

CR4 180, 5 Dec 1833. Wm. Rudd app. Gdn. for James and Benjamin Riddle, under 14; Abraham Riddle, over 14, chooses Nathaniel Smith as Gdn.

CR4 181, 6 Dec 1833. Gilbert Crews, Legatee, and Wm. Rudd, Gdn., petition Court to sell slaves.

WB B 247, May 1837; C 97, 15 Dec 1838; 287, 5 Nov 1840. Sett. by John Miller, Gdn. to James and Benjamin Riddle.

WB C 312, Jan 1841. Report, 10 Nov 1840; James B. Riddle reports that he received from John Miller, Gdn., all of his part of his father's estate.

WB D 143, 15 May 1843. Sett. by Gdn.; receipt from Benjamin Riddle for all of his claim.

RIDDLE, MILES
CR10 242, 3 Oct 1870. E.S. Shipley app. Gdn. of minor heirs.

RIDDLE, SAMUEL T.
CR9 171, 6 Aug 1866. A.J. Kyker app. Adm.

WB G 196, 3 Sep 1866. Invt. and sale by Adm.; buyers include Mary A. and John Riddle and Madison McMullin.

CR9 232, 233, 237, 4 Feb 1867. Petition to sell land; Complainants and Defendants are the only distributees; John Riddle, Enoch West and wife Elizabeth, John Inman and wife Sarah C., Jackson C. Dake (Drake) and wife Rhoda VS Martha Dixon, John S. and James W. Dake (Drake), Thomas Dixon, Sarah C. widow of Samuel T. Riddle, Jr., dec'd, Martha and Thomas Moody, James C. and John W. Riddle, Hettie A., Elender, William P. (T.), Mary R., Rhoda E. (C.), and James S. Dixon, Elizabeth Dake (Drake), Phillip M. and Sarah C. Riddle, Jr., Phillip M., Peter, and Hiel Dake, Samuel S. Dixon, James S. and Rhoda Riddle.

CR11 114, 30 Sep 1868. Sett. by Adm.; payments of $15.80 each to John Riddle, James Riddle, Enoch and Elizabeth West, Martha Dixon, John and Sarah Inman, Jack and R. Dake; payments of $2.63 each to James W. and Samuel Dake; balance of $32.04 to be turned over to Gdn. when appointed.

RIGGINS, JANE
CR7 235, 6 Sep 1858. Wm. G. Horton app. Adm.

WB F 201, 4 Nov 1858. Sett. by Adm.; paid to Jane Autery for attendance during Mrs. Jane Riggins last illness and funeral expenses.

RIGGS, ELLIS M.
CR4 537, 1 Feb 1841. Amanda J. Riggs and Jackson Smith app. Adms.

WB C 340, 1 Feb and 25 Feb 1841. Invt. and Sale of personal property.

WB C 341, 15 Feb 1841. Comm. Thomas W. Marston, John Neill, and Jesse R. Blackburn set apart year's support for wife and family, five in number.

WB D 129, 20 Mar 1843; 219, 27 Aug 1844; 352, 23 Feb 1846. Settlements by Amanda J. Riggs, Adminx.

WB D 438, 2 Mar 1847. Sett. by Jackson Smith, Gdn. to minor heirs who are also heirs of Samuel Riggs; land in Hawkins and Jefferson Counties; minor heirs are Samuel L. and Jackson Smith Riggs;

Gdn. has employed Absalem Kyle, T.A.R. Nelson, and R.J. McKinny to file Bill in Chancery in Hawkins Co.

WB D 531, 2 May 1848. Sett. by same Gdn.; support of said children and their mother.

WB E 47, 2 May 1849; 91, 2 May 1850; 192, 1 Sep 1851. Sett. by same Gdn.; Mrs. Amanda Jane Riggs is the widow.

WB E 319, 6 Jun 1853. Report by Wm. D. Smith, Gdn.; paid expenses in prosecuting suit in Chancery Court at Rogersville, Tenn., instituted by former Gdn.

WB E 433, no date; F 63, 1 Jan 1857; 191, 6 Sep 1858. Sett. by O.P. Hall, Gdn.

RIVERS, WILLIAM

CR9 52, 5 Jun 1865. John M. Wright app. Adm.

WB G 88, 14 Jul 1865. Invt. by Adm.; only asset is note dated 15 Apr 1858 on Crepein Miolane.

CC 23, filed 24 Aug 1865. Wm. Rivers died in May 1865. His wife was Susannah and her son-in-law was John Higdon of Polk Co.

CR11 113, 11 Sep 1868. Sett. by Adm.; payments of unequal amounts to Jacob and Robert Rivers.

ROBERTS, EDMUND WATTS

WB G 18, Will exec. 10 Nov 1863; land on North and South of Spring Creek; to wife Mary who was a "widow with children when I married her and I had children also"; to dau. Elizabeth H. Newton; to sons Henry M., Edmund, and Christopher T. Roberts; to granddau. Mary E. Newton; to granddau. Texanna, one purple cream pitcher. Execs: sons Henry M. and Edmund. Wit: John F. Sharp, Boyd Porter, and N.B. McNabb.

CR9 13, 3 Oct 1864. Will proven.

ROBERTS, GEORGE (Colored)

WB D 270-271, Will exec. 7 Jan 1845; to wife Sarah $15; balance to sons James and Daniel but they must care for mother during her lifetime; "son James who is a slave for life purchased by me from John Roberts...refer to register's book...Book C, page 356... should be set free...said James was born the slave of Elizabeth Roberts and became by the division of said estate the property of John Roberts one of the sons of Elizabeth Roberts"; "my said son James being now about 26". Exec: Benjamin Roberts. Wit: Henry M. and Edmund Roberts. Signed by mark.

CR5 223, 7 Apr 1845. Will proven.

WB D 332, 6 Oct 1845; 449, 23 Apr 1847; 496, 6 Jan 1848. Invt., Sale, and Sett. by Exec.

ROBERTS, H. F.

CR5 391, 6 Dec 1847. Listed as "Dead" in Tax Delinquents for 1847.

ROBERTS, JAMES M.

WB E 525, 28 Jun 1856. Invt. of sale by Thomas Roberts, Adm.; buyers include D.W., H.M., Thos. M., and Ed Roberts.

WB F 200, 2 Oct 1858. Pro rata sett. by Adm.; estate insolvent.

ROBESON (ROBISON), ALEXANDER C.

CR5 82, 2 Jan 1843. Comm. app. to lay off year's support to widow Catharine.

WB D 120-124, 6 Feb 1843. Invt. of sale by John McDonald, Adm.

WB D 124, no date. Report of Comm. Henry Rice, Elliott Peck, and Wm. Grubb.

WB D 249, 23 Dec 1844. Sett. by Adm.

WB D 264, 3 Mar 1845. Report by Adm. who is also Gdn. of James M., Calvin, and A.C. Robeson, minor heirs.

WB D 266, 25 Jan 1845. Heirs R.W. Hamilton, W.W. Haymes, James H. Hamilton, Jane Eaton, and Wm. Robeson sign agreement with Adm.

WB D 267, 30 Jan 1845. Sett. by Adm.-Gdn.

WB D 354, 23 Feb 1846. Sett. by Gdn.; receipt from James M. for his share.

WB D 429, 23 Feb 1847. Sett. by Gdn.; tuition paid for Calvin in Decatur.

WB D 494, 3 Jan 1848. Sett. by Gdn.; receipt for balance from Robt. W. Hamilton, present Gdn.

WB E 40, no date; 79, 26 Jan 1850; 148, 26 Jan 1851. Sett. by Calvin C. Robison, Gdn. of Alexander C. Robison.

WB E 165, 5 Jul 1851. Final sett. by same Gdn.; heir A.C. Robison paid in full.

ROBESON, CATHERINE

CR5 300, 3 Aug 1846. Wm. W. Haymes app. Adm.

WB D 385, 7 Sep 1846; 415, 7 Dec 1846; 553, no date. Sales and Sett. by Adm.

WB D 563, 15 Sep 1848. Sett. by Adm.; receipts from heirs James H. Hamilton and wife, Jane M. Gibbs, Rebecca Hamilton, Wm. W. Haymes and wife, and Calvin C., William, Alex. C., and James M. Robison, all receiving equal amounts.

ROBESON, ELIZABETH

CR5 138, 1 Jan 1844. Court pays for coffin for pauper.

ROBESON (ROBERSON, ROBBISON, ROBISON, ROBERTSON), THOMAS

WB D 314, 8 Aug 1845. Comm. Robt. Gregory, Elisha Bryant, and William Terry lay off year's support for widow Eleanor and family.

WB D 315, 1 Sep 1845; 346, 1 Dec 1845; 474, 19 Aug 1847. Invt., Sale, and Sett. by John Grubb and Eleanor Robeson, Adms.

WB D 579, 19 Aug 1848. Sett. by Adm.; paid Samuel Wilson, Gdn. to Wm. S. and T.F. Robison, minors.

WB D 580, 1 Sep 1848; E 60, 1 Sep 1849. Sett. by Gdn.

WB E 67, 6 Oct 1849. Sett. by Adm.; paid heirs John S. and Mary Raper, John and Nancy A. Grubb, John C., N.S., and widow Eleanor Robbison.

WB E 120, 1 Sep 1850; 193, 1 Sep 1851. Sett. by Gdn.; paid Thos. Robison, one of heirs.

WB E 271, 1 Sep 1852. Sett. by Gdn.

WB E 337, 1 Sep 1853. Sett. by John J. Middleton for Saml. Wilson, Gdn.; amount due heirs Wm. S. and Franklin Robeson.

WB E 353, 20 Jan 1854. Sett. by same; receipt from Elisha Bryant, present Gdn. for Franklin T. Robeson.

WB E 365, 3 Jul 1854; 485, 20 Dec 1855; 495, 3 Mar 1856. Sett. by Gdn.; paid Thos. F. Robertson in full.

ROBINETT (ROBBINET), MICHAEL

WB E 59, Will exec. 26 Apr 1849; to wife Margaret; "for purpose of raising my children"; to children Allen, Mc., John F., Margaret A., Hugh B., William G., and Mary C. Exec: wife. Wit: N.T. and James McNabb. Signed Michael Robbinett.

CR5 552, 1 Oct 1849. Will proven.

ROBINETT, WILLIAM G.

CC 203, filed 13 Apr 1869. Wm. G. Robinett died about 23 Apr 1866, unmarried, leaving bros. and sisters: Mary C. Guffey; John F. of Ill.; H.B., dec'd, whose wife is Celia of Mo., and whose children are Wm. A. and James A., both minors.

ROBISON, WILLIAM
CR5 412, 7 Feb 1848. John L. Bridges app. Gdn. to minor heirs.
WB E 46, 9 Jun 1849. Report by Gdn. of James and Nancy E. Robison /all other reference is to Jane and Mary E. Robison7; paid for articles furnished to Mary E.; receipt from A. Henderson who has married Jane.
WB E 145, no date. Sett. by Gdn.; rec'd money from Pension Agent at Knoxville and back pay from Dept. at Washington.
WB E 203, no date. Sett. by Gdn.; balance paid to Alexander Henderson present Gdn. who has been app. by County Court of Polk Co.

ROGERS
CR4 303, 6 Mar 1837. Elizabeth Eliza Rogers, minor over 14, chooses as Gdn. her mother Sarah Rogers.
CR4 500, 4 May 1840. Power of Atty. from Sarah Rogers, Gdn. to Elizabeth Eliza Rogers acknowledged.

ROGERS, W. H.
CR13 230, 6 May 1863. O.P. Hall VS W.H. Rogers - Appeal. Plaintiff suggests death of defendant.

ROLEN, ELIJAH
CR10 216, 4 Jul 1870. Marked "dec'd" in list of Tax Delinquents for 1869.

ROLIN (ROWLAND), WILLIAM
CR6, 7 and 11 Apr 1856. Court appropriated $1050 to arrest and bring to trial a negro boy named Jack who is charged with having murdered William Rolin of McMinn Co.
CR6, 10 Apr 1856. Jury of inquest finds that William Rowland was murdered by persons unknown at his store house on 29 Feb 1856.

ROMACK, MADISON
CR4 237, 8 Sep 1835. James Romack app. Adm.

ROMINES, FANNY
CR5 412, 6 Mar 1848. Lewis R. Hurst app. Adm.
CR5 432, 3 Apr 1848. Coroner paid for holding inquest over the body.
WB D 540, 3 Jul 1848; E 44, 9 Apr 1849. Invt. and Sale, and Final sett. by Adm.; George W. Mayo, Clk., makes pro rata sett. between creditors; note of deceased payable to Wm. Romines and filed by Wm. F. Keith is the only claim.

ROSS
CR10 130, 2 Aug 1869. G.W. Ross app. Gdn. of David L., Wm. W., James E., J.M., Charles B., Mary W., and Lizzie B. Ross, his own minor heirs.

RUCKER, A.J.
CR5 479, 2 Oct 1848. James E. Rucker app. Adm.
WB E 57, 12 Sep 1849; 63, 13 Sep 1849. Invt. and Sett. by Adm.; money due from U. S. for services as soldier in Mexican War.

RUCKER, JAMES, SR.
CR4 336, 6 Nov 1837. Wm. Rucker app. Adm.
WB B 270, Dec 1837. Invt. by Adm.; land lying on Mouse Creek.

WB B 272, no date. Comm. Robert Renfro, Wm. Bryan, and Boyd Porter
set apart year's support for widow Mary (Sarah).

WB B 295-301, no date; C 190, 9 Jan 1840. Invt. of sale and Sett.
by Adm.

WB D 20, 1 Feb 1842. Sett. by Adm.; receipts for equal amounts
from heirs: widow Mary Rucker, Jesse, J.E., John, and Mordecai
Rucker, James Gresham, Matilda Witt, James A. Bates, and Margaret
Rucker Adminx. of son Wilford Rucker, dec'd.

RUCKER, MORDECAI (MORDICA)
CR6, 5 Nov 1855. James R. Witt and H.H. Burk app. Adms.

WB E 469, no date. Comm. Boyd Porter, Allen Dennis, and H.M.
Roberts set apart year's support for widow Miram and family.

CR6, 3 Dec 1855. Mrs. Miram Rucker app. Gdn. for Joseph C. and
Miram M. Rucker, minors.

WB E 495-499, 3 Mar 1856. Invt. and Sale by Adms.

WB E 500, 4 Feb 1856. Comm. M.D. Anderson, J.W. Howard, and J.C.
Barbb, D.C. surveyor, assign dower in land to widow Gemima /sic/.

WB F 59, 108, 154, 263, 318, 393, 442, dated from 4 May 1857 to 30
Jan 1862. Add. Invt. by Adm., Sett. by Gdn., and Sett. by H.M.
Roberts, successor to Gdn.

WB F 157, 27 Feb 1858. Sett. by Wm. Burk, Gdn. of Wm. A. Rucker,
minor.

CR8, 6 Jul 1863. H.M. Roberts resigns and Mrs. Miram Rucker is
app. Gdn.

WB G 105, 9 Jul 1865. Sett. by Miram Rucker, Gdn.

CC 274, filed 8 Jul 1857. Mordecai Rucker died before Sep 1855
leaving widow Miriam and children: Silas N., Rachel wife of
Hamilton Wasson of Mo., Sarah C. wife of Hilton H. Burke, Nancy
wife of Levi Swinford of Smith Co., Tex., in 1854, Mary M. wife
of Pleasant B. Bryan of Smith Co., Tex., in 1854, James C. of
Smith Co., Tex., in 1854, William A., Joseph C., and Miram M.,
minors, John E. a minor, unmarried, who died one week after
father died, Wilford a minor who died about a week before father
died. One statement says that the Swinfords are of Williamson
Co., Ill. Ervine Rucker is bro. of Mordecai, dec'd.

RUDD, HERROD
WB A 177-179, Will exec. 9 Aug 1828; to wife Sarah; to dau. Mary
G.; to youngest son Thomas; to eldest son Joseph; to second son
John; to third son William; to dau. Franky Kindrick and the chil-
dren she had by her deceased husband Robert Kindrick; to grand-
children Sandy, Nancy, Franky, Parker, Sally, and Bryson Hood.
Execs: son William and Moses Stout. Wit: Martin Senter and
Jacob Hoss. Signed by mark.

CR2 383, 7 Sep 1829. Will proven.

CR4 195, 2 Jun 1834. Wm. Rudd, Exec. allowed pay.

WB D 287, 2 Jun 1845. Invt. of sale held 19 Apr 1845 by Wm. Rudd,
Exec.

WB D 487, 15 Oct 1847. Sett. by Exec.; receipts in full from heirs
Joseph, Mina J., John, and William Rudd, John S. O'Neal for R.
Kendrick's heirs, Wm. Cowden, Parker Hood, Alex. Hood, Jas. N.
Haden, and Solomon Kelly.

RUDD, JOHN
CR7 303, 4 Apr 1859. Herrod Rudd app. Adm.

WB F 377, no date; 395, 30 Mar 1861. Sale and sett. by Adm.

CR9 200, 5 Nov 1866. Comm. app. to lay off dower for widow Jane.

RUDD, SARAH
  CR5 231, 5 May 1845. John Rudd app. Adm.
  WB D 288-290, 2 Jun 1845. Acct. of sale by Adm.; buyers include
    Joseph, Wm., Herrod, John, Nealy, and Parker Rudd.
  WB D 413, 24 Nov 1846. Sett. by Adm.; "To paid as security of
    Sarah Rudd on a judgment that John Parshall obtained against
    Sarah Rudd, Mena Rudd, and myself".

RUDD, THOMAS
  CR4 528, 7 Dec 1840. Wm. and Joseph Rudd app. Adms.
  WB C 318-320, Jan 1841. Invt. of sale by Adms.; note on Joseph H.
    Rudd; one gray mare not sold by consent of heirs and was left
    with the mother of Thomas Rudd, dec'd, for her use till her
    death; buyers include Isaiah, John, Meeney, Elizabeth, Joseph,
    and Wm. Rudd.
  WB D 130, 15 Dec 1842. Sett. by Wm. Rudd, Adm.; "Meeny Rudd Heir
    Note lifted".

RUDD, WILLIAM
  CR9 54, 5 Jun 1865. Herod H. Rudd app. Adm.

RUSSELL, JOHN A.
  CR8, 10 Nov 1862. Jas. S. Russell app. Adm.
  WB G 3-4, 4 Jul 1864. Invt. sold by Adm.; invt. consists mainly
    of books; buyers include T.J., G.T., James, W.T., and Elizabeth
    Russell.
  WB G 27, Jul 1864; 170, 1 May 1866. Acct. of sale and Sett. by
    Adm.

RUTHERFORD (REATHERFORD), CALVIN M.
  WB F 221, 9 Oct 1858. Comm. A.D. Briant, I.S. Garrison, and C.L.
    Owens set apart year's provisions for widow Kissiah and family.
  WB F 243, 6 Dec 1858; 357, 9 Oct 1860. Invt. of sale, and Sett.
    by Henderson Carter, Adm.

RUTHERFORD, JAMES
  WB E 74-75, no date. Invt. and sale by A. Winkle and G.P. Owen,
    Adms.
  WB E 76, 14 Dec 1849. Comm. J.H. Reagan, Phillip Fry, and N.C.
    Hood set apart year's support for widow Nancy and family.
  WB E 206, 3 Dec 1851. Sett. by A. Winkle, one of Adms.; paid
    David Whiteside on probate of a lost note sent from Va.
  WB E 297, 16 Dec 1852. Sett. by same Adm.

SAFFELL, JOHN
  CC 627, filed 15 Apr 1879. John Saffell died before 1854 leaving
    widow Clementine A. and children: Richard M. and Samuel, both
    died unmarried minors, Sarah J. wife of W.C. Holland of Dallas
    Co., Texas, and Elizabeth C. wife of J.C.M. Bogle of Blount Co.
    Both daus. were minors in 1854.

ST. JOHN, ARTHUR
  CR9 433, 6 Apr 1868. A.H. Crow app. Adm. of Arthur St. John, late
    of the State of Missouri, dec'd, who had goods, chattels, papers,
    etc., in McMinn Co.
  CR11 248, 4 May 1872. Sett. by Adm.; vouchers of $618.55 each to
    Henry and John St. John, Mary C. Davis, and Susannah Sanders, and
    $661.00 to R.O. and W.H. Bridges.
  CR11 305, 19 May 1874. Sett. by Joseph Neil, Adm. of A.H. Crow who
    was Adm. of A. St. John; four receipts for $61.25 each from

John and Henry St. John, Mary E. Davis, and Susannah P. Sanders;
receipt for $18.81 from W.H. and Rebecca O. Bridges.

SAINT JOHN, NATHANIEL
WB D 561, Will exec. 4 Dec 1841; to wife Sarah, all land and prop-
erty during her lifetime "by her giving to her Daughter Catharine
Saint John two beads & furniture"; at wife's death Catharine Saint
John and Morgan Miller to have $114 to make them equal with James
Matterson Saint John. Wit: Joseph Browder, James Barnett.
CR5 469, 470, 4 Sep 1848. Will proven by Joseph Browder; John L.
Newman makes oath that the handwriting of witness James M. Bar-
nett, who had died since signing, is genuine; Mrs. Sarah St. John
app. Adminx.
WB D 567, no date. Invt. by Adminx.

SAMPSON, SAMUEL
CR5 285, 6 Apr 1846. H.H. Rider paid for making coffin for pauper.

SANDERS (SAUNDERS), CLEMUEL (CLEMENT)
CR5 485, 3 Oct 1848. John M. Cantrell app. Adm.
CR5 491, 6 Nov 1848. Benjamin Marr, Robert Braden, and Jonathan
Floyd app. Comm. to lay off year's support for widow.
WB D 590, Invt. and acct. of sale by Adm.
WB E 204, 2 Feb 1852. Sett. by John Jack, Adm., successor to John
M. Cantrell; creditors take pro rata settlement.
CC 228, filed 25 May 1855. Clement Sanders died leaving widow
Margaret and children: Ellen wife of James M. Hicks, Catherine
wife of James J. Rayburn, Mary Jane Brock, Elizabeth wife of
Calvin Kirby, Wm. T., Arden, John, Nancy J., Margaret, and
Martha.
CC 85, filed 25 May 1861. Clem Saunders died intestate in McMinn
Co., 27 Jul 1848, leaving widow Margaret and ten children, the
youngest of whom is Martha Jane, who has come of age in the past
three years.

SANDERS, WILLIAM
CR2 209, 7 Mar 1827. Robt. Renfroe paid for holding inquest over
body.

SCITES, ABRAHAM
CR2 133, 6 Mar 1826. Margaret Scites app. Adminx.; Abner Lee, Wm.
L. Taylor, and Isaac Carlock app. Comm. to lay off year's sup-
port for widow Margaret.

SCRUGGS, JOHN
CC 52, filed 15 Apr 1851, and reinstated Nov 1867. Scruggs and
Forrest, Adms. of Albert G. Rice, dec'd VS Widow and Heirs.
Nov Term 1867 the death of John Scruggs is suggested.

SEAY
CR6, 1 Dec 1856. Slaves decreed by Supreme Court to be property
of children of Jane R. Seay. In 1852, the mother of said slaves
was sold by the husband of Jane R. Seay to Wm. F. Jackson of
Roane Co., Tenn. The children of Jane R. Seay are as follows:
Laurena Frances wife of Galen B. Gideon, Elizabeth Jane wife of
Thos. S. Kitchen, Silas B. Seay, Hulda A. Lemons, Littleton P.
Seay, Barthena E. Seay, Hesekiah R. Seay who died 18 Sep 1852 a
minor, unmarried, and Bennette F. Seay, dec'd, whose children
are Silas B., Jr., Littleton P., Jr., and Wm. Seay.

SELLERS, JAMES
  CR9 113, 5 Mar 1866. A. D. Briant app. Adm.
  WB G 170, 7 May 1866. Sale by Adm.

SENTER, CALVIN H.
  WB F 457, 10 May 1862. Comm. B.F. Martin, Samuel Workman, and Wm.
  Rogers lay off year's support for family, "we allow her".
  WB F 458-461, 1 Aug 1862. Invt. of notes by Thos. Rogers, Adm.
  CR8 149, 6 Apr 1863. Saml. Workman and Wm. Rogers with County Sur-
  veyor allot Lot No. 51 in Calhoun to widow Sarah as dower; land
  in Gordon Co., Ga.
  CC 377, filed 18 Jun 1873. Calvin H. Senter died early in 1862
  leaving widow Sarah who died 10 Jun 1873 and no children. His
  bros. and sisters are Nancy Senter of McMinn Co.; Preston Senter
  of Polk Co.; Susan M. widow of John Hamilton, dec'd, of Roane Co.;
  Bradford Senter of Haywood Co.; Lewcarena wife of Isham Cox of
  Ga.; Sarah dec'd wife of R.B. Davis of Ark. (whose children are
  Catharine, James, Sarah, Benjamin, Paralee, Leucarena, and Elizabeth Davis, all minors of Ark.)

SENTER, JAMES L.
  CR4 411, 7 Jan 1839. Wm. Bates app. Adm.
  CR4 424, 4 Feb 1839. Elizabeth Senter app. Gdn. of minor heirs.
  WB C 114, Feb 1839. Invt. by Adm.
  WB C 133, Apr 1839. Comm. John L. McCarty, M.C. Hawk, and James
  M. Wallen set aside year's support for widow and family.
  WB C 141, Apr 1839; 191, 6 Jan 1840; 251, 29 Feb 1840. Invt.,
  Sett., and pro rata sett. by Adm.

SENTER, MARTIN
  CR4 457, 7 Oct 1839. A.P. Fore and Isaac Rice app. Adms.
  WB C 202-210, Jan 1840; 244, Mar 1840. Invt. of sale and Supp.
  Invt. by Adms.
  WB D 54, 3 Dec 1841. Sett. by Isaac Rice, surviving Adm.; receipt
  from A.C. Robeson and T.S. Rice, Gdns. to minor heirs.
  WB D 125, 7 Jan 1843. Sett. by Tandy S. Rice, Gdn., and John
  McDonald, Adm. of estate of Alexander C. Robeson dec'd who was
  also Gdn.
  WB D 227, 334, 404, 501, dating from 6 Sep 1844 to 6 Sep 1847.
  Sett. by Gdn.; receipt from James H. Senter for boarding chil-
  dren.
  WB D 515. True copy of Court records of Lincoln Co., Ky.; 3 Jan
  1848; James P. Senter, minor over 14, chooses Hardin M. Weather-
  ford as his Gdn.
  CR5 407, 7 Feb 1848. Petition of James P. Senter of Lincoln Co.,
  Ky., and one of the heirs, who states that in Jan 1843 he was a
  citizen of McMinn Co. and Tandy S. Rice was app. his Gdn.; that
  afterwards he moved to Lincoln Co., Ky., where almost all his
  paternal relations reside; that he is receiving nothing of his
  estate; that it will be to his interest to have his part of
  estate removed to Ky.
  WB E 64, 6 Sep 1849. Sett. by Gdn.; paid heir James Senter; balance due John L. and Wm. T. Senter.
  WB E 229, 230, 322, 336, 402, 509, dated from 6 Sep 1850 to 12 Mar
  1856. Sett. by Gdn.; paid heir John L. 1852 and final sett. 1856.
  CR6, 4 Oct 1852. Petition to sell Bounty Land Warrant No. 17444
  issued 17 May 1852 to John L. and Wm. T. Senter, minor children,
  for services of their father.

SENTER, WILLIAM
  WB G 51, Will not dated, proven 6 Mar 1865; Witnesses make oath
  that Will is a true copy in effect and substance of original
  Will; to mother Polly Neil $5; to wife Elizabeth; to three step-
  children Wm. A. Cochran, Catherine Humphreys, and Martha Jane
  Carson. Exec: Wm. A. Cochran. Wit: Uriel Johnston, James
  Neill.
  CR8, 3 Aug 1863. Will proven.
  CR9 44, 3 Apr 1865. Clerk makes affidavit that original Will
  filed was destroyed by Rebel Army.
  CR9 73, 4 Sep 1865. Wm. Humphreys app. Adm. with Will annexed.

SEWELL, ELIZABETH
  CR2 138, 7 Mar 1826. Wm. Sewell app. Adm.

SHAMBLIN, WILLIAM
  CR6, 6 Oct 1851. Court pays for holding inquest.
  CR12 80, 15 Dec 1852. Grand Jury presents that on 5 Sep 1851 a
  certain Charles J. Price did with malice aforethought strike,
  beat, and kick William Shamblin inflicting mortal wounds from
  which Shamblin died on 6 Sep 1851.

SHARP, ADISON S.
  CR7 225, 6 Sep 1858. Wm. B. Porter app. Adm.
  WB F 244, 6 Dec 1858. Invt. of sale by Adm.; buyers include Mary,
  John, and Alex. Sharp; "one receipt of R.M. Henderson of Ala. for
  eight notes"; "one other receipt on John G. Gillispie of Ala."
  WB F 258, no date. Comm. Wm. S. Calaway, J. Atkins, and John G.
  Hale lay off year's support for widow and family.
  CC 49, filed 7 Feb 1859. A.S. Sharp died 31 Aug 1858 leaving widow
  Mary D. who is dau. of Wm. B. Porter, and children: Mary Eliza-
  beth, Wm. B., Alexander, John B., and Lockey M. Sharp, all under
  age 8. John F. Sharp is bro. to the dec'd.

SHARP, BLUFORD
  WB B 193, Will exec. 14 Oct 1834; probated Dec 1835; "my wife Caty
  and Child if lucky brought forth and lives...if the child dont
  live...be divided equally between my wife Caty and my brothers".
  Exec: Joel Sharp. Wit: James Taylor and Eli E. Sharp. Signed
  by mark.
  CR4 242, 7 Dec 1835. Will proven.

SHARP, JACOB
  CR5 120, 7 Aug 1843. Edward Sharp of Bradley Co. app. Adm.
  WB D 168, 4 Dec 1843. Invt. of sale by Adm.; note on Joel Sharp
  moved to Ark.; note on Eli Sharp moved to Mo.
  CC 2, filed 14 Mar 1844. Jacob Sharp died about 16 Jun 1843 leav-
  ing children: Edward of Bradley Co., Eli, Joel, Hiram, Oliver,
  Nancy Graves, Nelly Matthews, dec'd. Hiram and Joel are of Car-
  roll and Marion Counties, Ark., but now in Meigs Co. Nancy and
  Nelly are "the reputed daughters and heirs". Nelly died before
  her father Jacob.

SHARP, JERRY
  CR15 153, 11 Aug 1869. Grand Jury Indictment: The State VS John
  Wright, John Jackson, and James Perry. On 31 May 1869, defend-
  ants shot with a pistol Jerry Sharp who lived until 5 Jun 1869.
  CR15 283. Nolle prosequi entered.

SHARP, TURNER
    CR6, 6 Jan 1851. Court pays for burying apparel for Turner Sharp
    who died in Apr 1850.

SHEDDAN (SHADDAN), MARY E.
    WB G 38, 87, 180, dated from 2 Jan 1865 to 29 Jun 1866. Sett. by
    James H. Magill, Gdn. of minor heirs.

SHELTON, DAVID
    CR16 78, May 1840. Thos B. Smith VS Saml. Shelton, Adm.
    CR4 546, 7 Jun 1841. Samuel Shelton app. Adm.
    WB D 21, 5 Jul 1841. Sett. by Adm.

SHELTON, JOHN
    CR4 530, 4 Jan 1841. Jeremiah Benton, Thomas Lasly, and Charles
    Hester app. Comm. to lay off year's support for widow Elizabeth.
    WB C 343-347, 1 Mar 1841. Invt. of sale by Thos. K. Napier and
    Josiah Childers, Adm.; report of above Comm.
    WB D 135, 13 Apr 1843. Sett. by Adms.
    WB E 61, 13 Sep 1849. Sett. by Josiah Childers, one of Adms.;
    paid heirs John C. and Joseph Shelton, John McGinly, and T.K.
    Napier.

SHELTON, SAMUEL
    CR5 168, 7 May 1844. Jesse H. Benton, Daniel D. Stockton, and
    George W. Million app. Comm. to lay off year's support for widow.
    CR5 454, 5 Jun 1848. Mrs. Mary Shelton, Widow, consents that her
    two sons Samuel aged about 8 and Wm. C. aged 5 years the 26 Jun
    1848 be bound to Tapley Gregory.

SHELTON, SARAH
    CR6, 4 Jul 1853. James Bonner, Esq., paid for holding inquest
    over the body in year 1851.

SHERMAN, THOMAS
    CR9 95, 4 Dec 1865. John F. Sherman app. Adm.
    WB G 137-139, 1 Jan 1866. Acct. of sale by Adm.; buyers include
    John F. and Thos. J. Sherman.
    CR11 128, 15 Jan 1868. Sett. by Adm.; payments of $97.35 each to
    Isaac, John F., and A.J. Lane, $19.46 each to Armena and J.M.
    Lane, unequal amounts of about one-fourth of funds to Elizabeth
    Lane and Mary Goss, $100.35 to S.C. Lane, $21.25 to S.F. and
    M.S. Bryant, all unidentified.
    CR11 134, 26 May 1868. Sett. by Adm.; payment of $42.75 to M.S.
    Bryant; payment of balance (about one-fourth of funds and same
    amount as paid to Mary Goss) to John F. Sherman.

SHERRELL, ISAAC
    CR6, 6 Jun 1853. Benjamin Wells, Martin D. Anderson, and Elisha
    Williams lay off year's support for widow.

SHIELDS
    CR4 43, 6 Dec 1831. Mary C., Sarah Ann, and Christopher J. Shields,
    over 14, choose their father George A. Shields as their Gdn. and
    he is app. Gdn. to Benj. J. and Fannay H. Shields who are also
    his minor children not old enough to come into court; Power of
    Atty. from Geo. H. Shields to Geo. A. Shields acknowledged.
    WB B 82, 28 Mar 1832. Sett. by Gdn.; list includes amount of cash
    in hands of Sarah Shields, amount going to the widow, amount com-
    ing to eight heirs.

CR4 120, 3 Dec 1832. James Walker and Joseph Bullard released as bondsmen for Geo. A. Shields, Gdn., and David and Geo. H. Shields and Jacob Vinzandt become Security.

WB C 58, 2 Nov 1838. Sett. by Gdn.; receipts on "sd. heirs" as follows: William Murphrey Heir for full amount of his part and same for Mary C., Frances H., Christopher J., and Benj. J. Shealds.

SHIELDS, W. L.

CR13 396, 11 Dec 1865. The State VS W.L. Shields. The death of defendant is proven.

SHIPLEY, CHRISTOPHER

WB A 207, Will exec. 30 May 1830; to wife Elizabeth; to wife's eldest son Uriah; "equally divided between my beloved wife and all my children...above named Uriah shall have an equal part with the balance of my wife's children over and above the said horse above given". Execs: wife and James Rutherford. Wit: James H. Reagan and Philip Fry.

CR2 449, 7 Jun 1830. Will proven.

CC Record Book D 23, 306, 331, 395, 24 Nov 1868 and later dates. Thomas Shipley, Mary and R.B. Smith VS Uriah Shipley, William Shipley, the minor heirs of Randall Shipley dec'd, James H. Shipley, Sarah Shipley, James Shipley, Joseph Shipley, Parlee Shipley, Emeline Shipley, and the minor heirs of Nehemiah Shipley dec'd, Hannah Shipley, William Shipley, Jr., Nancy E. Shipley, Thomas C. Shipley, David R. Shipley, John T. Smith, Nehemiah Smith, Sterling Smith, Elizabeth Smith, Frank Smith, Melton Smith. /There are no papers in the files for this lawsuit and date of filing is not given./ Christopher Shipley died 1830. His Will provided that at the death of his wife Elizabeth his land should be sold and the proceeds divided among his children. Elizabeth has now died. Uriah, James Harvey, James, and Emeline Shipley, Sterling Smith, and the widow of Randal Shipley dec'd whose name is unknown, have all been notified by publication and William Shipley, Sr., Hannah Shipley, John T. and Nehemiah Smith have had notice by subpoena and all have failed to answer. The children of Randal Shipley dec'd whose names are unknown, Sarah, James, Joseph, and Paralee Shipley, minor children of Martin J. Shipley dec'd, also the minor children of Nehemiah Shipley whose names are unknown, William, Mary E., Thomas C., and David R. Shipley, minor children of David Shipley dec'd, Elizabeth, Frank, and Melton Smith are all minors and a guardian ad litem is appointed for them. William Shipley is entitled to one share in his own right as heir and to one share which he purchased from David Shipley in 1856. The share of Elizabeth Smith was deeded to William Shipley, but was not acknowledged according to law. William Shipley also purchased the share of Randall Shipley. Nehemiah Shipley sold his share to William Shipley and also sold the shares of Thomas, Martin J., and James H. Shipley which he had purchased in 1848.

SHIPLEY, ELIZABETH

CR9 458, 6 Jul 1868. R.B. Smith app. Adm.

SHOEMAKER, ELIZABETH

WB D 18, 5 Apr 1841. Invt. of sale by L.L. Ball, Adm.; "part of Turnpike situated on paint mountain in Green County"; "money in hands of James Coulter Agent for Elizabeth Shoemaker from a

settlement made sometime about the middle of September 1837".
WB D 221, 21 Aug 1844. Sett. by Adm.; receipts for equal amounts
from J. Ross, Thomas Ball, H. and M. Holland, James and S.
Coulter, John and Rebecca Gladdin, and L.L. Ball, with latter as
"distributive share".

SHOOK, ANDREW J.
CR4 524, 2 Nov 1840. John Shook app. Adm.

SHOOK, JOHN, SR.
CR2 260, 8 Dec 1827. John Shook, Jr., app. Adm.
WB A 122, no date. Invt. by Adm.

SHORT, SAMUEL
CR2 261, 3 Mar 1828. Mary Short app. Adminx.
WB A 115, no date; 146, no date; 173, 1 Jun 1829. Invt., Sale, and
Sett.

SHULTS, DAVID
WB B 122, 5 Dec 1833; 133, 3 Mar 1834. Invt. and Sale by John Neil
and Russell Lane, Adms.
WB B 141, 19 Dec 1833. Comm. John Arnwine, John Goss, and Henry
Matlock set apart year's support for widow and family.
WB B 246, Apr 1837. Comm. A.G. and John Goss, and Jas. Wilson
settle with Adms.
WB D 192, 1 Apr 1844; 257, 3 Feb 1845; 363, 3 Feb 1846. Reports by
Humphrey L. Shults, Gdn. to Granville, Mary Ann, David, Jacob,
and Sarah Shults, children of David Shults, dec'd.
WB D 439, 3 Feb 1847. Report by Gdn.; the minor heirs receive from
Geo. Shults their interest in estate of Jacob Shults, dec'd.
WB D 523, 3 Feb 1848. Report by Gdn.
WB D 582, 3 Feb 1849. Report by Gdn.; proceeds from farm given to
widow Olivia Shults for schooling of the children.
WB E 82, 3 Feb 1850. Sett. by Gdn.
WB E 153, 3 Feb 1851. Sett. by Gdn.; equal amounts paid to James
and Mary A. McGonigal, Oliver Shults, and Gramble Shults one of
the heirs.
WB E 221, 3 Feb 1852. Sett. by Gdn.
CR6, 6 Apr 1852. Petition to apportion slaves: Humphrey L. Shults,
David Neil and wife Elizabeth A., Granville Shults, and James
McGonigal and wife Mary A. VS Sarah Shults by her Gdn., children
of David Shults.
WB E 317, 3 Feb 1853. Sett. by Gdn. for Sarah Shults; rec'd cash
from estate of Olivia Shults, dec'd.
CR12 119, 16 Apr 1853. David Shults died in McMinn Co. in the fall
of 1833 leaving Olivia his widow who died Nov 1851, and five chil-
dren, to wit, Elizabeth A. now Elizabeth A. Neil, Humphrey L.,
Granville, Sarah, and Mary Ann Shults who married James M. McGonigal and who died intestate in Bradley Co., Tenn., on 29 Oct 1852
leaving John R. McGonigal her son and heir.
WB E 369, 3 Feb 1854; 429, 5 May 1855. Sett. by same Gdn.

SHULTS, OLIVIA
See DAVID SHULTS.

SIMPSON, SAMUEL
CR5 138, 1 Jan 1844. Court pays Fisher and Rider for making coffin
for pauper in 1839.

SISK, JAMES
  CR1 336, 4 Jun 1828. Act of Assembly passed at Nashville on 22
    Oct 1827 entitled An Act for the relief of the widow and heirs
    of James Sisk, dec'd.

SISK, JAMES
  CR5 175, 9 Jul 1844. Court pays for coffin for pauper.

SLACK, EPHRAIM C.
  CR4 256, 2 May 1836. Abram L. Slack app. Adm.
  WB B 183, no date. Invt. by Adm.; includes "Something Expected
    from an undivided part of the estate of henry Lanes deceased
    Virginia amount not known also from that portion due samsun Lanes
    deceased in H. Lanes".
  WB C 59, 189, D 21, 73, 148, dated from 3 Nov 1838 to 6 Jan 1843.
    Sale and Settlements by Adm.; receipt from widow Harret.
  WB D 389, 22 Aug 1846. Sett. by Adm.; "for taking care of three
    children, Abraham, Henry, and John Slack from the year 1836".
  WB D 473, 552, E 48, 113, 166, 265, 334, 380, 440, dated from 22
    Aug 1847 to 22 Aug 1855. Settlements by same Adm.
  WB F 41, 22 Aug 1856. Sett. by A.L. Slack, "Gdn. of Elisha L.
    Slack Deceased"; receipt from Henry I. Slack for about one-half
    of funds.
  WB F 316, no date. Sett. by same Gdn.; John Slack has arrived at
    age of 21 and receives balance of funds.

SLIGER
  CR7 274, 3 Jan 1859. Christopher Sliger app. Gdn. to Elizabeth,
    Joseph, William, Jacob, and Sarah Sliger, his own minor children.
  CR9 198, 5 Nov 1866. Sett. filed by Gdn.

SLOOP
  CR7 555, 2 Sep 1861. Levina Sloop app. Gdn. of her own minor
    children.

SLOOP, HENRY
  WB E 428, 7 May 1855. Acct. of sale by H.P. Wilson, Adm.
  WB E 432, 14 Apr 1855. Comm. James Neill, John Hoyl, and Uriel
    Johnson set apart year's provisions for widow Elizabeth and fam-
    ily, there being seven persons in family.
  WB E 515, no date; 570, 19 Sep 1856. Sett. by same Adm.
  CR7 205, 5 Jul 1858. Petition for partition of land: Elizabeth
    Sloop, widow, Elizabeth E., James C., and John Sloop, Malvinah
    Patterson and husband Samuel, Julietta Hogan and husband Thomas,
    Caroline Gibbs and husband James, Mary Ann Pickering and husband
    John, and George H. Sloop VS Henry M. Sloop. Comm. allot one-
    half of land to Henry M. Sloop and other half to heirs of Henry
    Sloop, dec'd, with widow Elizabeth getting her dower.
  CR10 418, 8 Oct 1872; 428, Nov 1872. Henry Sloop died about 1 Mar
    1855 leaving children as follows: Mary Ann Pickron, Geo. H.
    Sloop, Juliet wife of Thomas Hogan, and Henry M. Sloop, all now
    of Mo., Caroline wife of James Gibbs of Ky., Elizabeth E. Sloop,
    Malvina wife of Saml. Patterson, John Sloop who has since died
    without issue, and James Sloop, who has since died leaving chil-
    dren Henry L., M.L., S.E., and Eliza Sloop who afterwards mar-
    ried A.S. Casey and has since died leaving L.C. Casey her only
    child, all of McMinn Co.

SLOOP, JAMES
  WB F 396, 8 May 1861; 423, no date. Comm. S.P. Henderson, Nathan

Kelley, and R.F. Mastin set apart year's support for widow and family; Invt. by Urial Johnston, Adm.

SLOOP, JOHN N.
   CR9 335, 4 Nov 1867. Petition for dower and sale of land: Elizabeth Sloop widow of John Sloop, dec'd VS Heirs, to' wit, Henry M. Sloop, Absalom Casey and wife Elizabeth, Layfayet, Henry L., and Eliza Sloop, Samuel Patterson and wife Malvina, Elizabeth Sloop, (all citizens of McMinn Co.), George H. Sloop, Mary Ann Picerin, Thomas Hogan and wife Julity, James Gibbs and wife Susan Caroline. Petition states that there are eight heirs. Henry L., Lafayette, and Eliza are minors.
   CC 156, filed 27 Dec 1867. John N. Sloop died in McMinn Co., 3 Nov 1861, leaving widow Elizabeth, formerly Elizabeth Stott, dau. of Elizabeth Stott, and no children. His bros. and sisters are as stated in list of children of Henry Sloop, dec'd, above. Elizabeth Stott came from N.C. with John N. Sloop and wife. Jonas Early also came from N.C. when he was 2 or 3 yrs. old with John N. Sloop and lived with him until he went in Army.

SMALL, WILSON
   WB F 365, 4 Jan 1861. Sett. by Jas. Lamar, Gdn. to minor heirs, Mary E. Lamar, Elizabeth A.F. Small, and J.T. Snider; receipt in full from Mary Lamar.

SMART, A. F.
   CR8, 4 Aug 1862. J.F. Sharp, Wm. B. Johnson, and P.A. Bradford app. Comm. to lay off year's support for widow and family; J.C. Weir and Isabella Smart app. Adms.
   CR8, 3 Nov 1862. Invt. filed by J.C. Weir, Adm.

SMART, BENJAMIN (Colored)
   CR10 104, 5 Apr 1869. George Swafford, Colored, app. Gdn. of minor heirs.

SMART, THOMAS
   WB G 173-174, Will exec. 24 Jul 1862, Codicil 29 Jul 1862; to wife Margret and her three sons; to sons Isaac, John, William, Joseph, Andrew, Archibald F.; to daus. Nancy wife of Henry Goforth, Jane wife of Jacob Whiteside, Margaret wife of G.W. Vinsant; all sons and daus. to be made equal; to grandson Isaac Smart, Jr., when he comes of age (his mother is Ibby); land and negroes to be sold in space of two years after war is over. Exec: son Isaac. Wit: Simeon Graves, Samuel Pearin, Wm. W. Huddleston. Signed by mark.
   CR8, 1 Dec 1862. Will proven by the three witnesses.
   WB G 142, 1 Feb 1866; 168, 16 Apr 1866. Invt. of sale and Invt. of notes by Exec.
   CR9 158, 7 May 1866. It appearing that the Will Book in which the Will of Thomas Smart dec'd was recorded has been lost or destroyed.....it is ordered that said Will as probated at December Session of Court 1862 be again spread of record in present Will Book.
   CC 115, filed 2 Mar 1867. Thos. Smart died 1862 leaving family as given in the Will. Margaret Vinzant and Wm. Smart are of Ark.; Joseph B. is of Ill.; Andrew J., is of Kan.; John B. is of Pulaski Co., Mo.; Jane H. and Jacob Whiteside are of Benton Co., Ark.; Archibald F. is dec'd and his son is Isaac of Mo.

SMITH
   CR6, 4 Apr 1853. Israel C. Smith app. Gdn. to James M., Joseph A.,

Israel O., and Nancy J. Smith his own minor children, and also
to Martha A., Mary M., and Rebecca C. Smith, minor children of
John Smith.

WB E 338, 7 Nov 1853. Report by same Gdn.; Martha A. is not in
list.

WB E 565, 29 Aug 1856. Sett. by same Gdn.; receipt from James M.
Smith "his shear" $60; receipt from Joseph A. Smith for $60;
receipt from Mary M. Smith for $39; receipt from Thomas and
Nancy George for $63.96; leaving balance of $85.57; refers to
sett. in E 338. /This report is entitled "John Smith dec'd"
but is clearly the same gdnship. as in E 338, in which the name
of deceased is not given./

SMITH, DELILAH J.
WB F 344, Will exec. 23 Aug 1860; horse to oldest son James A.
Smith; saddle to oldest dau. Mariah F. Smith; Exec. Elisha Bryant
to take control of all children and all estate and what may be
due from "my mother's estate at her death". Wit: James Denton,
W.H. Hicks.

CR7 477, 2 Oct 1860. Will proven.

WB F 378, no date; G 46, 27 Dec 1864. Invt. and Sett. by Exec.

CR9 276, Jun 1867. Elisha Bryant Gdn. resigns; James A. Smith app.
Gdn. to John W. and Thomas Smith.

SMITH, EDWARD
WB D 224, Will exec. 14 Aug 1844; "being sick and weak in body";
wife Polly to keep all property which she has in her hands; bal-
ance to be sold and money put on interest for children. Exec:
Robertson Snider. Wit: Lewis Stanton, James L. Power, John W.
Knox. Signed by mark.

WB D 225, no date. Invt. taken 5 Oct 1844 by Exec.

WB D 264, no date; 401, 6 Nov 1846. Invt. of sale and sett. by
Exec.

SMITH, ELIZABETH
CR6, 7 Aug 1854. Wm. D. Smith app. Adm.
See also JACKSON SMITH.

SMITH, H. B.
CC 60, filed 5 May 1866, (Incomplete file with Orig. Bill missing)
and Deed Bk. P, page 115. James Forrest, Adm., et al VS Lydia Ann
Smith, widow, and Adaline D., F.M., Mary C., and Christopher C.
Smith, Harriet S. McCuistian, James M., Sarah C., John S., Thomas
R., Missouri C., and Margaret T. Smith, heirs of H.B. Smith,
dec'd. H.B. Smith was heir of Isaiah Smith, dec'd, and heir to
1/11 of his land.

SMITH, HEZEKIAH
CC 214, filed 9 Aug 1869. Hezekiah Smith was killed while in Con-
federate Army in Nov 1863 leaving widow Lucinda and children
Joseph F. aged 16, Martha J. aged 14, Alfred A., aged 12, and
Sarah A. Smith aged 10, all of McMinn Co.

SMITH, ISAIAH (ISAIH, ISAHA, ISAH)
CR7 319, 4 Jul 1859. Coroner's Jury of inquest reports that Isah.
Smith being alone on 4 Jul 1859 in County of McMinn did kill him-
self by drowning hanging.

WB F 277, 23 Aug 1859. Comm. D.W. Ballew, T.S. Rice, and James
Wilson set apart year's support to the children under the age of

15 yrs.
WB F 314, no date. Sale by Jas. Forest, Adm.; buyers include
Henderson, C.C., and Mary Smith.
CC 287, filed 18 Feb 1858. Isaiah Smith, son of Joseph Smith, dies
during the lawsuit, leaving children: Henderson B., Francis M.,
Mary C., Christopher C., James M., Sarah C., John S., Thos. R.,
Missouri E., and Margaret T. Smith, and Harriet D. McCuiston.

SMITH, JACKSON
WB E 250-253, Will exec. 26 Sep 1848, Codicil exec. 27 Sep 1848,
proven 7 Jun 1852; to wife Elizabeth; to daus. Margaret L. Haley,
Harriet W. Grills, Amanda J. Riggs, Sidney R. Haley; to son Wm.
D.; to son Nathaniel D., $50; to the children of Nat. D. "know-
ing that he is a profligate son disposed to waste"; to dau. Eliza
Emeline Lowry, wife of Alexander M. Lowry $50; to heirs of dau.
Eliza Emeline with no control from husband, "he is a profligate
son inlaw"; slaves to be divided into seven equal parts for children except shares of Nat D. and Eliza Emeline to be under con-
trol of Execs. Execs: Wm. D. Smith and Milton L. Phillips.
Wit: John Matlock, J.W. and Jesse Dodson, Isaac Morris, and Wm.
Neill. Codicil No. 2, 22 Sep 1851; the property willed to dau.
Harriet Grills is to be under control of Execs. because Jeffer-
son Grills will not take care of property. Wit: Isaac Morris
and Wm. Neill. Codicil No. 3, 8 May 1852; Wm. Neill to be Exec.
in place of Milton L. Philips. Wit: Joseph M. Alexander, Isaac
Morris, and Clement Eaton.
WB E 281-283, no date. Invt. of sale and allotment of slaves; dau.
Amanda is now Amanda J. Hall; slaves at the request of Maj. Wm.
D. Smith are valued by John Moss and Williams Mayfield, two dis-
interested persons; filed by Wm. D. Smith and Wm. Neill, Execs.
WB E 302, 7 Feb 1853; 319, 2 May 1853. Add. Invt. and sale.
/An account book which deceased mentions in Codicil No. 2 was
found, 1963, in the files of the Chancery Court./
CC 208, filed 31 May 1854. Jackson Smith died 28 May 1852. Widow
Elizabeth died 15 Jun 1854. Dau. Sidney is wife of Wm. Haley.
The first wife of son Wm. D. died and he has small children.
Dau. Harriet Grills dies during the lawsuit. Dau. Eliza Emeline
is divorced from husband Alexander M. Lowry, who is son of Wm.
Lowry. Ellis M. Riggs was first husband of dau. Amanda.
CC 271, filed 1 Dec 1870. Dau. Amanda J. is widow of O.P. Hall.
Son Wm. D., who left this part of the country about Oct or Nov
1865 is now of Benton Co., Ark.; daus. Margaret L. and Sidney
R. Haley are of Roane Co.; son Nat D. is of Ga.
CC 347, filed 23 Oct 1872. Dau. Margaret is wife of Charles Haley
of Roane Co. Son Nat. D. is of Walker Co., Ga. Dau. Eliza
Emeline had child who died an infant before Jackson Smith died,
and no other child. The children of dau. Harriet Grills, dec'd,
are Mary E. wife of Samuel Knox of Adair Co., Mo.; Sidney; William; Emeline; Stark D.; Joseph; and Thomas Grills, all nonresidents; Martha L., dec'd by 1877, wife of Needam Trantham
also dec'd by 1877; Margaret who married first _____ Edmondson,
and married second David L. Baxter of Green Co., Ark.; Amanda who
married first _____ Stroud or Steward and married second Arter
Moore, now dec'd, of Green Co., Ark. Martha L. Grills and husband Needam Trantham left children, Philadelphia Ela, Thomas
Jefferson, Charles F., and Lillie B. Trantham, all minor nonresidents.

SMITH, JAMES
CR2 488, 7 Dec 1830. William, David, and John Smith, over 14, minor children, choose Mary Smith of McMinn Co. as Gdn. and she is app. Gdn. to Israel, Mary, and Morning Smith, minor heirs under 14. Robt. M. Swan and Arch. R. Turk app. Comm. to settle with the Adms. of William Smith, dec'd, who was Adm. of James Smith, dec'd, and Gdn. of minor children of sd. James Smith, dec'd.
CR2 519, 9 Mar 1831. Above Comm. settle with Adms. of Wm. Smith, dec'd, who was Adm. of his son James Smith, dec'd; paid Mrs. Smith widow of James Smith, dec'd, her 1/3 agreeable to the laws of South Carolina.....allowing three years for disposing of said estate since Mar 1824.....find that Wm. Smith, dec'd, was not Gdn. to the children as had been represented to the Court.
CR4 211, 1 Dec 1834. Joseph, John, and Israel Smith, Execs. of Wm. Smith who was Adm. of James Smith.

SMITH, JEHU
CR4 455, 2 Sep 1839. Burden M. Smith app. Adm.
WB C 184, Oct 1839; 297, 5 Dec 1840. Invt. and Sett. by Berden M.C. Smith, Adm.

SMITH, JOHN
CR10 150, 1 Nov 1869. James Dean app. Adm.

SMITH, JOSEPH
CR4 507, 7 Sep 1840. Henderson Smith app. Adm.
WB C 278, 5 Oct 1840. Comm. Nimrod Triplet, Caleb Smith, and Hugh Reavely set apart year's support for widow Margaret.
WB C 302, Dec 1840. Invt. of sale by Adm.
CR5 6, 4 Oct 1841. Landon C. Peters app. Gdn. of Margaret L., Joseph N., and Matilda R. Smith, minor heirs.
WB D 110, 8 Nov 1842. Sett. by Adm.; receipt from heir C.A. Pickens.
WB D 228, 7 Sep 1844; 292, 24 May 1845. Sett. by same Gdn.
WB D 267, 13 Feb 1845; 351, 14 Aug 1845. Sett. by same Adm.; receipts for equal amounts from Jonathan T. and Irby H. Smith.
WB D 403, 5 May 1846. Sett. by Charles A. Pickens, Gdn.; has received nothing from former Gdn.
WB D 512, 5 May 1847; 551, 5 May 1848; E 78, 28 Jan 1850. Sett. by Gdn.; paid heir Nimrod N. Smith; paid W.H. Maples for heir Nelson N. Smith; paid tuition for heir Matilda Smith.
WB E 298, 15 Dec 1852; 401, 2 Oct 1854. Sett. and Final Sett. by Gdn.; receipt for balance in acct. from heir J.N. Smith and from R.A. Stephenson and wife.
CC 287, filed 18 Feb 1858. Joseph Smith died 9 Aug 1840 leaving widow Margaret, who married Landon C. Peters now dec'd, and ten children as follows: Henderson, who died about 1854 in Mo.; Robert B.; Isaiah who dies during the lawsuit; Callaway H. now of Iowa; Malinda now wife of Charles A. Pickens; Jonathan T.; Erby H. and Joseph N., of Ark. or Mo.; Louisa now wife of Newton N. Smith; and Matilda who married Robert A. Stephenson and who by Dec 1858 has died leaving children, names unknown.

SMITH, MAJOR JOSEPH
CR6, 6 Nov 1855. Martin M. Hicks app. Adm.
WB E 483, 24 Nov 1855. Invt. of sale by Adm.
WB E 487, 19 Nov 1855. Comm. W.L. Burns, Eli Dixon, and Elisha

Briant set apart year's support for widow Delila.

SMITH, NATHANIEL
CR5 31, 7 Mar 1842. Thos. J. Metcalf app. Adm. of Nathaniel Smith
who was a nonresident at the time of his death, had made no will,
and had effects both real and personal in this County.
WB D 92, 4 Jul 1842. Report by Adm.
CR6, 4 Dec 1854. /This entry has been crossed out./ John W. Smith,
Mary M. Carr, Wm. Wright and wife Martha, Mark Roberts and wife
Emily, adult heirs, and James C., Laura, and Texana Smith, minor
heirs by Gdn. Mary M. Carr. Petition to sell land.

SMITH, PETER
CR4 547, 7 Jun 1841. Sarah Smith app. Adminx.
WB D 36, Oct 1841. Invt. by Adminx.
WB D 37, 26 Jun 1841. Comm. Willis Wright, Tapley Gregory, and
Thos. Williams lay off year's support for widow Sarah.
WB D 37-39, 4 Oct 1841. Invt. of sale by Adminx. and Richard A.
McAdoo, one of Clerks of sd. sale.
WB D 149, 30 May 1843. Sett.
CR5 224, 7 Apr 1845. Tubal Zeigler app. Gdn. to Catherine Jane
Smith.
WB D 281, 25 Apr 1845. Sett. by Willis Wright, Gdn. to Jane Smith;
he was app. May 1843.
WB D 281, 7 May 1845. Report by Tubal Zeigler, Gdn.
WB D 364, 4 May 1846. Sett. by same Gdn.; he was not app. until
1 May 1845.
WB D 434, 5 Apr 1847. Sett. by same Gdn., one-fourth of rent of
farm belongs to said minor.
WB D 516(1), no date. Order to J.C. Carlock, Clk., from Catherine
J. Smith authorizing him to pay to Willis Wright $2.10 which
Tubal Zeigler paid in for her. Attest: B.T. Zeigler.

SMITH, ROBERT
CR5 458, 3 Jul 1848. Coroner paid for holding inquest over body
on 20 May 1848.
CR5 460, 3 Jul 1848. George Smith of McMinn Co. app. Adm.
WB D 552, no date; 555, 4 Sep 1848. Invt. and Invt. of sale by
Adm.
WB D 569, 16 Aug 1848. Comm. M.W. Cunningham, Henry McGuire, and
Levi Deaton set apart year's support to widow and several minor
heirs.
WB E 191-192, 1 Oct 1850 and 1 Oct 1851. Sett. by Adm.; paid widow
Isabella.
CR16 112, May 1850. George J. Smith, Adm. VS Widow and Heirs;
heirs are Minerva Jane Smith, Margaret Adaline intermarried with
Joseph R. Barnett, Mary Isabella, Elizabeth, Marshall, Elvina,
and Robert Smith, the five last named infants; Isabella Smith,
widow, app. Gdn.

SMITH, SAMUEL A.
CR10 68, 2 Nov 1868. James M. Knox app. Gdn. of minor heirs.
CC 145, filed 25 Oct 1867. Samuel A. Smith, a lawyer, died leav-
ing widow Louvennia who has married J.H. Earnest of Green Co.,
Tenn., and children: John L.M. of Bradley Co.; Isabella and
William, minors of McMinn Co.

SMITH, STEPHEN
WB D 199-201, Will exec. 22 Apr 1844; wife Warnin to remain on

farm and receive suitable maintainance; $15 yearly to be paid to
sister Susan Smith; all estate to lawful heirs of Nathaniel Smith,
late of Republic of Texas, deceased, who are John Williams Smith,
Martha Maria widow of Thos. J. Metcalfe, dec'd, William Pinckney
Smith, Nathaniel Henry Smith, Sam Houston Smith, Emily Jane Smith,
James Coleman Smith, Laura Chitten Smith, Amelia Texianna Smith,
and eldest dau. Mary Myers Carr, with the exception that Mary
Myers Carr is to receive only 25¢; the said heirs are to be
brought - if willing - from Texas and other parts wherever they
may be and live with wife. Execs: Chas. Metcalfe and Henry Mat-
lock. Wit: G.C. Metcalfe, Abner Cunningham. Signed by mark.
Codicil dated 25 Apr 1844: Sarah Thomas Metcalfe, dau. of Thos.
J., dec'd, and Martha Maria Metcalfe, to receive equal share with
other legatees. Wit: Jas. B. Taylor, G.C. Metcalfe, Abner
Cunningham.
CR5 166, 6 May 1844. Will proven; Henry Matlock declines to serve
as Exec. and Court appoints Wm. Burns.
CR5 186, 2 Sep 1844. Warnin Smith, widow, enters her dissent to
Will.
WB D 232-235, 3 Dec 1844. Invt. and Invt. of sale by Execs.
WB D 526, 23 Mar 1848. Sett. by Exec.; pay for services except
trip to Texas.
WB D 554, 15 Aug 1848. Comm. J. McGaughy, S.K. Reeder, and A.
Slover set apart year's support to widow Warning.
WB E 47, 5 Jun 1849; 63, 1 Jun 1849. Reports by Elizabeth Smith,
Gdn. to Susan Smith and John Hoyl, Gdn. to widow Warning Smith.
WB E 118, 2 Oct 1850. Sett. by Chas. Metcalfe, Exec.; "time and
expenses traveling to & from the Republic of Texas in search of
the children of Nat Smith".
WB E 187, 21 Jun 1851. Sett. by John Hoyl, Gdn.
WB E 318, 2 Sep 1850. Sett. by same Exec.; paid J.M. Martin in
right of wife and daughter.
WB E 318, 16 Apr 1853. Sett. by same Gdn.

SMITH, WILLIAM
CR2 172, 4 Sep 1826. Elizabeth Smith app. Adminx.

SMITH, WILLIAM
WB A 193-196, Will exec. 27 Oct 1829; to wife Nancy; to sons John,
Israel, and Joseph; to daus. Patty, Sarah, Mary, and Nancy; to
two unmarried children Joseph and Nancy; to children of dec'd
son James, viz: William, David, John, Israel, Mary, and Mouring;
to Mary Smith wife of dec'd son. Execs: sons John, Israel, and
Joseph. Wit: Geo Bowman, Richard Tankersly.
CR2 395, 7 Dec 1829; 411, 9 Dec 1829; 412, 11 Dec 1829. Will prov-
en and Execs. qualify.
WB A 199-202, no date. Invt. filed by John and I.C. Smith, Execs.;
includes a note in South Carolina.
CR4 211, 1 Dec 1834. Joseph, John, and Israel Smith, Execs. of
Wm. Smith, dec'd, who was Adm. of James Smith.
CC 4, filed 2 Jan 1856. William Smith died leaving widow Nancy, now
age 83, who wants to move West in the Fall, and children: Joseph
who died Aug 1855; John; Israel C.; James, dec'd; Patty Pickens,
dec'd; Sarah wife of Richard Tankersley of Williamson Co., Texas;
Mary wife of Robert Pickens of Bradley Co.; and Nancy Marshall of
Monroe Co. /Mary wife of Samuel Julian and Mourning wife of
George Julian are also listed as children but by all other records

they are the children of son James, dec'd.7 Son Joseph, dec'd,
left widow Delilah Jane who was his second wife, and children:
Mary E. wife of Thos. L. Marshall, Sarah E., Joel C., James A.,
Miriam or Maria F., Louisa Jane, John W., and Thomas Smith, the
last five being children by second wife, and all except Mary E.
being minors. Dau. Patty Pickens, dec'd, left the following
children: Margaret wife of Simeon Rogers of Forsythe Co., Ga.;
W.S.; Robert M.; Martha A.; James M.; and Israel W. Pickens, all
of Anderson Dist., S.C. Son James, dec'd, left children: William of Hamilton Co., David of Bradley Co., and Israel G. of
Green Co., Ala.

SMITH, WILLIAM
  CR5 414, 6 Mar 1848. Joseph Hamilton app. Gdn. of minor heirs.
  CR5 452, 5 Jun 1848. A.G. Rice, Wm. Dodson, and Robert Cohorn app.
    Comm. to lay off year's support for widow Elizabeth.
  CR5 461, 3 Jul 1848. John B., Joseph H., James A., William P.,
    Nancy J., Silina E. Louisa J., Matilda C., and Margaret J. Smith,
    minor children and heirs, choose Elizabeth Smith as Gdn.; she is
    app. Gdn. and Joseph Hamilton who was app. Gdn. for a special
    purpose is ordered to turn funds over to her.
  CR5 462, 4 Jul 1848. Elizabeth Smith makes bond as Gdn. to her own
    children.
  WB D 539, 4 Jul 1848. Report by Joseph Hamilton, Gdn.; received
    on 20 May 1848 of Joseph Smith of Cabarrus Co., N.C., Adm. of
    sd. dec'd; final sett. to "Mrs. Elizabeth Smith, Guardian $147.92
    and to 4 heirs of sd. estate now of age, or their agents, $65.72".
  WB E 51, 325, 429, 565, F 157, 261(1), dated from 26 Jul 1849 to
    21 May 1859. Settlements by Elizabeth Smith, Gdn.; paid heir
    John Smith 1849; paid Nancy Jane and E.W. Brden /sic/ 1853; paid
    James A. Smith 1856; receipt in full from Wm. S. Smith 1859.
  WB F 319, 21 May 1860. Sett. by J.H. Smith for Elizabeth Smith,
    Gdn.; receipt in full from James and Sarah A. Carright.

SMITH, WILLIAM
  CR9 105, 5 Feb 1866. Joseph W. Hamilton app. Gdn. for William
    Benjamin and Sarah Elizabeth Smith, minor heirs.
  See also ELIZABETH (MAYFIELD HILL HUDGENS) BAKER

SNODGRASS, JAMES
  WB A 64, 8 Sep 1824. Invt. by James McKamy and John Miller, Adms.
  CR2 36, 7 Dec 1824. Wm. Cate, James Rucker, and Elijah Grisham
    app. Comm. to lay off year's support for widow Milley.
  CR2 140, 7 Mar 1826. Sheriff ordered to take charge of the three
    eldest children of the late Milly Snodgrass, present wife of
    Nathan Hambrick, until next session of Court.
  CR2 154, 5 Jun 1826. Jeremiah Hambrick app. Gdn. for Nancy,
    Eloner, and Thomas Snodgrass, minor orphans over 14.
  CR2 214, 4 Jun 1827. John Miller, Esq., released as Adm.; Irby
    Holt and Richard Tankersley app. Comm. to settle with said Mil-
    ler; he is allowed $2 per day for 22 days going to and returning
    from Ky. on business for estate.

SPEARMAN, WESLEY
  CR4 370, 5 Jun 1838. Thomas Miller app. Adm.
  WB C 29, 6 Aug 1838. Invt. by Robert Miller, Adm.
  WB C 32-34, 6 Aug 1838. Wm. McKamy, Jesse Dodson, and Joseph S.
    McConnell, Comm. to lay off year's support to widow Elizabeth

and family, make report; Sale by Adm.
WB C 70-71, 15 Nov 1838. Report; John H. Miller, present Adm. of Wesley Spearman, and Wm. McKamy, one of Adms. of Thomas Miller's estate, came into court where Wm. McKamy turned over to John H. Miller "papers and effects so far as the said Thomas Miller former administrator of the sd. Wesley Spearman Dec'd had administered".
WB C 257, 3 Jul 1840. Sett. by Adm. John H. Miller.
CC 42, filed 9 Feb 1860. Wesley Spearman died leaving widow Elizabeth and children: Sarah A.J. wife of Jeremiah W. Davis, John M., Mary wife of Joel Roberts, Robert L., L.M., Susannah wife of Chas. R. Basket, Jemima, Malinda, and Nancy Spearman. Mrs. Spearman and large family of minor children sold land and went West probably to Texas. File contains deed 1861 from the heirs at Grayson Co., Tex.

SPELLMAN, N. J.
CR17 29, 28 Dec 1859. Mary A. Spillman, Adminx. VS Joseph A. Hix.
CR13 56, 14 Dec 1860. M.A. Spellman, Adminx. VS J.J. Elliott.

SPRADLING, RICHARD
CR10 231, 5 Sep 1870. Richard Spradling, Jr., app. Adm.
CC 300, filed 21 Oct 1871. The children of Richard Spradling are: Richard, Jr., Mortimer of Meigs Co., Stanley of Hamilton Co., John residence unknown, Amanda wife of Emberson Sliger of Calif., Louisa wife of Hiram Brandon, and Mary Ann dec'd wife of John Hart whose children are: John, Benjamin, and Elizabeth wife of James Robeson.
CR11 235, 31 Jan 1872; 277, 12 Jun 1873. Settlements by Adm.

STALCUP, MOSES
CR10 175, 7 Mar 1870. Isaac Stalcup app. Adm.
CR10 209, 212, 2 May 1870. Petition of widow Nancy for dower; plat of the dower land.
CC 255, filed 25 Aug 1870 and 311, filed 15 Dec 1871. Moses Stalcup died about Feb 1869 leaving widow Nancy and children: Isaac; Elias; Lee H.; C.C.; F.A.; James H. of Hamilton Co.; Moses of Ind.; W.R. and John W. of Grayson Co., Texas; Joseph C. a minor of Polk Co., Mo.; Sarah E. wife of John H. Wood; and King, dec'd, whose minor son W.K. is of Mo.
CR10 481, Jun 1871. H.H. Raper app. Gdn. in Barry Co., Mo., of Wm. K. Stalcup a minor under 14; funds are in Tenn. with E.M. Stalcup as Gdn.; Court orders transfer of funds to Barry Co., Mo., the present residence of minor heir.
CR11 234, 17 Jan 1872. Sett. by Adm.

STANSBURY, I. N.
WB F 154, 28 Dec 1857. Comm. John Jack, Joseph Rud, and J.M. Burger set apart year's provisions for widow Elizabeth and family; includes $25 for his teaching school.

STEED, HENRY
CR9 445, 1 Jun 1868. Will presented, proven by Claborn M. Howard and John W. Miller the subscribing witnesses, and ordered to be spread of Record. /Will is not in records./

STEED, JAMES
CR8, 7 Jul 1862. Wm. G. Horton and James Steed app. Adm.
CR13 187, 205, 4 Nov 1862. Wm. H. Howard and wife Nancy L., W.G.

Horton and wife P.C., James Steed, John A. Prather and wife
Matilda, H.C.P. Horton and wife Bettie, C.L. Matlock and wife
Louisa, J.S. Riggs and wife Sarah, C.L. Cobb and wife Julia, and
W.H.H. Howard VS J.C. Steed, D.A. Lowry and wife Lucinda, J.M.
Clementson and wife Mary, Henry Steed, Sarah Steed, John R.
Howard, Jr., J.C., Ben, N., and C.L. Howard, last four minors.
Petition to sell land. Publication made as to all the respon-
dents and judgment pro confesso entered to all who are adults
and the Gdn. of minors has answered.

WB G 19, 15 Aug 1864. Sett. by Wm. G. Horton, Adm.; heirs receiving about $32.75 each are J.C., W.H., and James Steed, Wm. H.
Howard and wife, W.G. Horton and wife, D.A. Lowry and wife; heirs
receiving $5.45 each are Sarah, Mildred, and James Steed, Jr.,
Betty Horton, and John A. Prather and wife; heirs receiving $3.64
each are C.L. Matlock and wife, C.L. Cobb and wife, J.S. Riggs
and wife, and W.H.H. Howard; J.R. Howard, Gdn., receives $18.20.

STEED, JOHN
CR5 13, 5 Oct 1841. John R. Howard app. Adm.
WB D 44, 20 Oct 1841. Comm. Wm. Rudd, Nathan Sullins, and A.C.
Robeson lay off year's support for widow Sarah.
WB D 62-65, no date. Invt. of sale; buyers include Sarah, Justus
C., and James Steed.
WB D 156, 4 Sep 1843; 211, 21 Jun 1844. Invt. and Sett. by Adm.

STEED, JUSTUS
WB F 162-163, Will exec. 24 Nov 1851; Codicil dated 21 Nov 1853;
all estate to Lucinda America McNabb, dau. of Wm. and Salina
McNabb; if she dies without issue all estate to children of bros.
and sisters including Louisa Vanderpool and Nancy Hyden dau. of
bro. Henry; Wm. McNabb and wife Salina and C.M. Howard to occupy
lands, supporting in the meantime Lucinda America. Exec. and
Gdn.: particular friend John R. Howard. Wit: Wm. Lowery, J.
McGaughy. Codicil: property to C.M. Howard if he should marry
and have heirs.
CR7 171, 6 Apr 1858. Will proven.
CC 53, filed 1 Jul 1859. Howard VS McNabb. Justus Steed died,
unmarried, leaving illegitimate children Claibourn M. Howard
and Salina, dec'd wife of Wm. McNabb. He also left nieces and
nephews: Louisa Vanderpool; Nancy, wife of Jesse Albert Hyden;
Phoebe Johnson and husband Berry; Lucinda Johnson and husband
Mitchell; Elizabeth Howard and husband John R.; Louisa Howard
and husband Wm.; Phoebe Horton and husband Wm. G.; Matilda
Prather and husband John; Billie, Sarah, Mildred, and James
Steed; Lucinda Lowry and husband Daniel A. of Ga.; Mary Clementson and husband John M. of Ill.; James Steed of Monroe Co.;
Campbell J. Steed of Bradley Co., and Henry Steed a nonresident.

STEED, PHEBE
CR5, on loose sheet of paper, not entered in book: 5 Oct 1846,
McMinn Co., Tenn.; Isaiah Smith and Andrew John on oath say that
Phebe Steed was a pensioner at the rate of $57 per annum commenc-
ing 1 Mar 1839 and that the said Phebe Steed departed this life
Aug 4, 1846, leaving the following named children and only heirs
and legatees at law; viz., Justice Steed, Thomas Steed, Henry
Steed, James Steed, Nancy Johnston, and Polly Steed.

STEED, THOMAS
 WB G 214, Will exec. 27 Apr 186_; to sister Polly Steed and Sarah
  Louisa Vanderpool, the undivided half of land on which I live;
  if Sarah Louisa should survive sister Polly, then she and her
  heirs to have all. Exec: esteemed friend Jessy A. Hyden. Wit:
  David W. Ballew, J.A. Hyden. Signed by mark.
 CR8, 2 Feb 1863. Will proven by Jesse A. Hyden of Knox Co.
 CR9 280, 1 Jul 1867. Will ordered to be recorded as Will Book in
  which it was recorded has been destroyed.

STEPHENSON, ALEXANDER CAMPBELL
 WB F 317, Will exec. 30 Apr 1858, proven Apr 1860; to wife Eliza-
  beth; to two youngest daus. Armindy and Cyntha; to balance of
  children: John, Robert, Edward, William, Daniel Dyre, and Alex.
  Stephenson, Jr., Anny wife of Joseph Walker, Susan wife of James
  Buckner. Execs: sons Edward and William. Wit: John Gardiner,
  C.H. Bogart, John J. Dixon. Signed by mark.
 WB F 334, 7 May 1860. Comm. Joseph Hamelton, John Torbert, and Wm.
  Brown lay off year's support for widow Stephens.
 WB F 373, no date; 449, 14 Mar 1862. Invt. and Sett. by Edward
  Stephenson, Exec.

STEPHENSON, ANDREW
 WB G 117-118, Will exec. 18 May 1854; to wife Catherine; four sons
  Wm. Henderson, John Cannon, Robert Alexander, and Mashie Tipton
  Stephenson to have all land and support "me and my wife" during
  lifetime and to support two daus. Caroline and Arminda as long
  as they wish to live with them; the four sons to pay each of the
  other children $1. Exec: son John Cannon Stephenson. Wit:
  C.A. Pickens, N.N. Smith. Signed by mark.
 CR9 81, 2 Oct 1865. Will proven.

STEPHENSON, FRANCIS M.
 CR6, 7 Jun 1852. Jackson West app. Adm.
 WB E 261, 6 Jul 1852; 266, 11 Aug 1852. Invt. and sale and Add.
  sale by Jackson West, Adm.

STEPHENSON, JOSEPH A.
 CR14 482, 11 Aug 1868. Joseph A. Stephenson VS John Morris; the
  death of plaintiff is suggested and admitted.
 CR15 74, 13 Apr 1869. Jane T. Stephenson has been app. Adminx.

STEPHENSON, ROBERT
 WB E 68-69, Will exec. 27 May 1845; to dau. Elizabeth, wife of
  Gideon Cate, who is dau. by first wife Rebecca; to two little
  daus. by last wife Mary, Sarah B. and Margaret R. Exec: nephew
  Robert C. Morris. Wit: James, Jesse H., and John C. Gaut.
 WB E 85-88, 4 Mar 1850. Invt. of sale by Gideon Cate, Adm. with
  Will Annexed, and report by Dimmon Dorsey, Gdn. to Sarah B. and
  Margaret R.

STEPHENSON, WILLIAM, SR.
 CR4 425, 4 Feb 1839. Wm. S. Stephenson app. Adm.
 WB C 115, Feb 1839; 131, Apr 1839; D 153, 6 Sep 1843. Invt.,
  Invt. of sale, and Sett. by Adm.
 WB D 251, 9 Dec 1844. Sett. by Adm.; Vouchers: John L., Mary E.,
  and W.S. Stephenson, $19 each "for mother's estate" and Henry
  Cameron's receipt for $19 also.
 WB D 271, 7 Apr 1845. Invt. of slave property by Adm.

STEPP
   CR7 321, 4 Jul 1859. Benj. Eldridge, Byrum Allen, and Mount Reynolds app. Comm. to lay off year's support for Sally Stepp.

STOCKTON, JEHU
   CR5 325, 7 Dec 1846. In list of Removals so that Tax for 1846 can
   not be collected is "Jehu Stockton, Dead 30¢".

STOCKTON, JOHN C.
   CR5 368, 2 Aug 1847. Daniel D. Stockton app. Adm.
   WB D 517, Feb 1848. Invt. of sale by Adm.

STOCKTON, SARAH B.
   WB C 271-272, Will exec. 20 Sep 1840, returned to Court 5 Oct 1840;
   to Elizabeth L. Baldwin; to heirs of Catherine Hall Thomas B.
   Stockton Robert Stockton James Y. Stockton /no punctuation7; to
   Mary Callaway; to Joseph and Benjamin Wilson; to Pleasant W.
   Lane for medical services; to Wm. H. Stockton. Execs: Wm. H.
   Stockton and Pleasant W. Lane. Wit: John N. Delzell and A.P.H.
   Jordan.
   CR4 514, 5 Oct 1840. Pleasant W. Lane declines to serve as Exec.
   CR5 1, 6 Sep 1841. Neley Chrisman, Sec. for Wm. Haden Stockton,
   Exec.
   WB D 36, no date. Sett. by Exec.

STOKES, HENRY R.
   CR9 457, 6 Jul 1868. Comm. app. to lay off year's support for
   widow and family.
   CR11 306, 25 May 1874. Sett. by S.S. Morgan, Adm.; receipts from
   John W. Stokes.
   CC 382, filed 9 Oct 1873. Henry R. Stokes left widow Elizabeth and
   children: Martha, wife of John Davis, and John, both of Meigs
   Co.; Wm. of Mo.; and Hixon, residence unknown.

STONE, WILLIAM
   WB A 104-106, Will exec. 24 Jun 1819, proven Jackson Co., Tenn.,
   Feb 1820. Execs. refuse to serve, Edmund Roberts and Uriah
   Stone app. with James D. Hendly and Alexander Ruth as securities
   with Samuel G. Smith, Clk.; Copy of Will from Jackson Co., records, made 29 Apr 1820; to wife Ann; to son Uriah, to grandson
   Asbury son of Uriah; to daus. Jane Roberts and Ann Smith; to son
   Elijah who has no heirs; to granddau. Lucy Ball in place of her
   mother and my daughter who is now deceased; to Edmund Roberts
   husband of dau. Jane; to dau. Jane; Jane's three children Westley,
   Ann, and Thomas Wm. Spearman; dau. Jane has no children by Edmund Roberts. Execs: Archibald Stone, Esq., and James Crawford,
   both of Barron Co., Ky. Wit: Andrew Hibbits and James Fergason.
   CR2 236, 4 Sep 1827. Wm. Stone of Jackson Co., Tenn., made his
   Will, died shortly afterwards, and by one clause in Will he gives
   his black man Thomas his freedom after death of wife; Thomas
   Stone applies for freedom, proving that Wm. Stone's wife is dead.

STOTT, ELIZABETH
   CC 156, filed 27 Dec 1867. Sloop VS Sloop. Elizabeth Stott died
   about 10 Oct 1865 intestate leaving five heirs: dau. Elizabeth
   widow of John N. Sloop; Nancy wife of Andrew Nancy (Nanny, Namy?),
   formerly Nancy Stott, of N.C.; Mary Ann wife of Elijah Hall, formerly Mary Ann Stott, of N.C.; Rebecca Sparks, formerly Stott, of
   S.C.; and Frances wife of Abraham Gross, formerly Stott, of Ill.

STOUT, DR. BENJAMIN C.
  WB A 174(2)-175; Will exec. 4 Aug 1829; to wife Jane and children.
  Execs: wife and Solomon Bogart. Wit: A.D. Keys, Geo. W. Mayo,
  and Saml. M. Gantt.
  CR2 383, 7 Sep 1829. Will proven.
  WB A 213, 7 Oct 1829. Invt. and Sale by Execs.; among the buyers
  are the following doctors: John K. Farmer, Alexander, Morrow,
  Saml. Edmundson, Horace Hickox, and Reid.
  WB B 115-117, Dec 1832. Supp. Invt.
  WB B, twelve pages, not numbered, in back of book, not dated; accts.
  due to Dr. Stout, making an extensive list of residents of McMinn
  Co. and area; also four pages accts of sales, including one tract
  of land in Rhea Co.

STUART (STEWART), HAMILTON
  WB E 79, no date. Comm. Jacob Vanzant, James Buckner, Jonathan F.
  Pugh set apart year's provisions for widow Martha and family.
  WB E 81, no date; 112, 23 Sep 1850. Invt. of sale and sett. by
  Bing Newton, Adm.
  WB E 137, no date. Acct. of sale of rent corn by Nathaniel Barnett,
  Adm.
  WB E 211, 17 Mar 1852; 224, 5 Jan 1852. Sett. by John Whiteside,
  Gdn. to minor heirs; paid heir Margaret Weir.
  WB E 242, 27 Nov 1851. Sett. by Nathan Barnett, Adm., successor
  to Bing Newton; horse sold to heir Henry C. Stuart.
  WB E 263, 26 Jul 1852. Final sett. by Adm.; receipts in equal
  amounts from Mary and Stephen Hill, Henry C. Stewart, Andrew and
  Lydia Goforth, and Martha Stewart, and receipt for triple the
  amount from John Whiteside, Gdn.
  WB E 311, 21 Feb 1853. "Rec'd of John Whiteside guardian of Giles
  Stewart" signed by William Stewart Gdn. to Giles Stewart.
  WB E 312, 21 Feb 1853. Report by John Whiteside, Gdn.; receipts
  from heirs David D. and Margaret Weir and Wm. Stewart; receipt
  from Wm. Stewart Gdn. to Giles Stewart.
  WB E 363, 21 Feb 1854. Sett. by Wm. Stewart, Gdn.
  WB E 364, 21 Feb 1854. Sett. by John Whiteside, former Gdn.;
  "Stephen Hill heir receipt bought of Margaret Ware".
  CC Record Bk. B, page 96. David D., John M.C., and David Weir,
  John and Stephen Hill VS Mourning Isabel Weir defended by her
  Gdn. ad litem Willie Lowry. On 16 Oct 1852 David D. Weir and
  wife Margaret, formerly Margaret Stewart, sold to John Hill one
  child's part or 1/6 of the land which Margaret inherited from
  her father Hamilton Stewart. Margaret Weir died leaving Mourning
  Isabel as her only child.

STUART, JOHN and SARAH
  CR10 55, 7 Sep 1868. Phillip Raulin app. Gdn. of minor heirs of
  John Stuart.
  CR10 156, 3 Jan 1870. Report made by same, Gdn. to minor heirs of
  John and Sarah Stuart.

STUART, SARAH
  CR10 54, 7 Sep 1868. James Steward app. Adm.
  See also JOHN and SARAH STUART.

STUBBLEFIELD, MARY
  WB B 154, Will exec. 29 Aug 1834; to sons Robert and Absalem. Exec:
  Isom Lawson. Wit: Morrison K. Lawson and John Bookout.

WB B 154, 1 Dec 1834; C 45, 7 Sep 1838. Invt. and Final sett. by
Exec.

STUBBLEFIELD, WILLIAM
   CR4 156, 3 Jun 1833. Mahaly Stubblefield app. Adminx.; John Morris, Lewis Triplet, and Wm. _____ app. Comm. to lay off year's
   support for widow Mahaly.
   WB B 120, 3 Jun 1833; 131, 20 Sep 1833. Invt. and Acct. of sale
   by Adminx.
   WB E 270, no date. Sett. by Adminx.; Court allowed her balance of
   property and use of farm until 1853 for her service in raising,
   clothing, and schooling children Pleasant C., Mary Ann, and Martha.

STUDDARD, ABRAHAM
   CR8, 6 Jan 1862. Comm. Allen Haley, F.M. Lusk, and John F. Barton
   app. to lay off year's support for widow and family.
   WB F 444, 21 Jun 1862. Above Comm. report.
   CC 178, filed 19 Aug 1868. Abraham Studdard died Dec 1861 leaving
   heirs: Tabitha Studdard; minors George and Tennessee Studdard;
   minors Matilda and Tilitha Gibson; William, Hugh, Jane, and Mary
   Studdard; and F.A. Dixon and wife Elizabeth.

STUDDARD, NANCY
   WB B 64, Will exec. 2 Jul 1827; to John, Mary, Richard, Abraham,
   Hannah, youngest son Thomas Studdard, youngest dau. Aby (Abby)
   "having seven heirs and five of them having been portioned off
   to wit John Mary Richard Abraham and Hannah". Wit: Wm. Triplet,
   James Patty. Signed by mark.
   CR4 15, 5 Sep 1831. Will proven by Amos Potts and Wm. Triplett.

SULLENS (SULLINS), NATHAN
   WB F 53-54, Will exec. 9 Oct 1856, proven 6 Apr 1857; to son-in-
   law Lazarus Dodson and his wife Rebecca L.; to three children
   Timothy and Morris C. Sullens and dau. Hazy Cardwell; to other
   children, viz, Annis Murry, Elizabeth Myra Street, James Axley
   Sullens, Mary L. Woodward (and her children), Nathan A., David,
   and Stephen Bradford Sullens. Execs: son Timothy and son-in-
   law Lazarus Dodson. Wit: Wm. F. Keith, Wm. H. Briant. Signed
   by mark.
   WB F 74, no date; 320, 30 Jan 1860; 447, 21 Dec 1861. Invt. and
   sale, Sett., and Final sett. by Execs.
   CR7 383, 5 Mar 1860. Hazy Cardwell app. Gdn. to Nathan A., Mary
   R., Eliza H., Jas. H., and Timothy N. Cardwell, her own minor
   children.
   WB F 394, no date. Sett. by Hazy Cardwell, Gdn. /Name of dec'd
   is not given in this entry./

SUTTON, GILBERT
   CR8, 6 Jan 1862. Court pays for coffin for pauper.

SWAGGERTY, JAMES
   CR9 55, 5 Jun 1865. Malinda Swaggerty app. Adminx.
   CR13 412, 13 Dec 1865. Malinda Swaggerty and others VS Henry
   Latham and others; name of Malinda Swaggerty to be changed to
   Malinda Andes and name of Adam W. Andes to be added as plaintiff.
   CR9 257, 1 Apr 1867. Malinda Andes renewed bond as Gdn. of minor
   heirs.
   CR14 419, 14 Apr 1868. Malinda Andes in her own right and as Gdn.
   of Sarah A. Swaggerty and John Andes VS Henry Latham and others.

CR10 51, 7 Sep 1868. Robt. Hackler app. Gdn. of Sarah Ann Swaggerty, minor child.

SWAIN, JOHN
/Name of deceased is not given in the title to these reports./
CR6, 4 Oct 1852. J. William Cullins app. Gdn. to two of minor
heirs and Silas Smith app. Gdn. to four of the minor heirs of
Johnson L. Sims. /Note that Sims is not designated as "Dec'd"./
WB E 314, 2 May 1853. Report by John William Cullins, Gdn. to Wm.
L. and L.J. Sims, minor children of J.L. Sims; total amount in
gdnship. is $286.25 and is received from Jesse Swain, Exec. of
estate of John Swain, dec'd, for benefit of the wards.
WB E 315, 24 Nov 1852. Report by Silas Smith, Gdn. to four minor
children of J.L. Sims, namely, Andrew J., O.J., L.D., and Robert
C.P. Sims; amount in gdnship. is $572.50 and was received from
Jesse Swain, Exec. of John Swain, dec'd, as their distributive
share.
WB E 333, 334, 401, 466, 467, dating from 22 Sep 1853 to 6 Oct 1855.
Reports by the two Gdns.; Luticia J. Sims receives her final share
in 1854; Silas Smith transfers Gdnship. to N.N. Smith in 1855;
Wm. L. Sims receives his final share in 1855.
CR6, 3 Sep and 3 Dec 1855. Wm. Cullins resumed gdnship. of minor
heirs of J.L. Simses Dec. and Silas Smith resigns as Gdn. of min-
or heirs of J.L. Sims Dec., with "Dec." in both entries marked
out.
CR6, 6 Nov 1854. Bond renewed by Silas Smith, Gdn. to Jackson,
Oliver, Lina, and Robert Simms.
WB E 572, 12 Oct 1856; F 99, 12 Oct 1857. Sett. by N.N. Smith, Gdn.
WB F 220, 300, 362, 423, G 184, dating from 12 Oct 1858 to 6 Aug
1866. Sett. by same Gdn.; paid to Andrew J. Sims on Power of
Atty. in 1858; paid to Oliver J. Sims in 1860.

SWINFORD, JAMES
CR6, 3 Jan 1853. Court pays for coffin for pauper.

TALLANT (TALANT), RICHARD
WB B 86, Will exec. 5 May 1832, probated Sep 1832; to wife Sarah;
to son James; to three sons Enoch, John, and James; to William
Talant; to Thomas Talant; to Lidia Wasson, Minty Hankens, Jane
Fisher; land divided among sons Enoch, John, and James, and $1
each to remaining legatees. Execs: wife Sarah and son, not
named. Wit: James McNabb and Robt. Mansell. Signed by mark.
CR4 98, 3 Sep 1832. Will partly proven by Robt. Mansell.
CR4 135, 4 Mar 1833. Will fully proven by James McNabb; widow
Sarah app. Execx.

TALLENT
CR10 215, 6 Jun 1870. Joseph Neil app. Gdn. of Mary A. Tallent.

TAYLOR
CR9 96, 4 Dec 1865. David Cleage app. Gdn. of John M. Taylor,
minor.

TAYLOR, GEORGE W.
CR4 209, 1 Dec 1834. John N. Taylor app. Adm.
WB B 244-245, Sep 1835. Sale by Adm.; buyers include widow Peggy
Ann.

TAYLOR, JABIN S.
WB F 52, Will exec. 9 Feb 1857, proven 6 Apr 1857; "as I have no

children I will my dear wife Minerva C. the entire right" during her lifetime and at her death property to be sold and divided equally among bros. and sisters. Execx: wife. Wit: E.A. Taylor, M.C. Parker.

CC 394, filed 4 Mar 1874. (Enrolled Bills, 1865-75). Bros. and sisters are Louisa Boatright of Ark.; H.W. of Grainger Co.; Emily Witt of Hawkins Co.; E.A. of Monroe Co.; George, dec'd; Rachel Witt; Amanda A. Brickel of Monroe Co.; Elbert E. of Oregon. The children of bro. George, dec'd, are Lafayette, Thomas H., James, Venia wife of _____ Shelton, Mary, Jabin, and George, all of Grainger Co., and last three are minors. /Note: because of lack of punctuation this division of bros. and sisters and their children may be incorrect. All are heirs./ Widow Minerva C. is now of Monroe Co.

TAYLOR, REBECCA
CR7 459, 6 Aug 1860. Report made by Joseph M. Alexander, Gdn. to minor heirs.

TAYLOR, SAMUEL (A man of color.)
CR4 361, 2 Apr 1838. Will proven by Hamilton Bradford and Saml. McConnall, the two subscribing witnesses; Henry Bradford and Wm. Baker app. Execs.
WB C 23, 111, 212, D 4, 73, 149, 151, 208, 294, 377, 463, E 18, 162, 196, 346, 369, F 58, 172, 305, 401, 440, G 59, dating from June 1838 to 14 May 1865. Invt. of sale, and Settlements by Execs.; paid Amy Taylor widow (1840) and paid Aimy Dodson formerly Aimy Taylor (1841). /In later sett. she is listed as Amy Taylor./

TAYLOR, STEPHEN
CR15 186, 13 Dec 1869. James McDaniel Exec. VS James Dennis. Note to Exec. dated 11 Oct 1865.

TEAGUE, JOHN WILLIAM
CR9 244, 4 Mar 1867. W.B. Johnson app. Gdn. of minor heirs.

THOMAS, GEORGE
CR4 130, 4 Mar 1833. Deed proven: Martin Cassaday to Julia Thomas and Heirs.

THOMAS, JAMES, SR.
CR4 376, 6 Aug 1838. James Thomas and J.B. Fitchjerrill app. Adms.
WB C 52, Oct 1838. Invt. and sale by Adms.
WB C 53, 15 Sep 1838. Comm. Elijah Cate, Wm. Dotson, and Joseph Minze set apart year's provisions for widow Mary.
WB D 311-312, 26 Aug 1845. Sett. by Adms.; receipts from heirs T. Lane, Wm. M. Robeson, John C., J.H., D.H., Sam, and James Thomas, Jr., R.W. Jameson, R. Northcross, J.B. Thomas heir of T. Thomas, J.B. Fitzgerald, and heirs of T. Thomas; all paid same amount with J.B. Thomas and heirs of Talbert Thomas receiving as one heir.
WB E 274. See MARY THOMAS.

THOMAS, JOHN
CR9 372, 3 Feb 1868. Robert Cochran app. Adm.

THOMAS, JONATHAN
WB G 4-6, Will exec. 28 Feb 1863; to wife Jane, homeplace and land on north side of Athens and Decatur wagon road; to dau. Harriett

Thomas, the above land at death of wife; to dau. Louisa Wattenbarger, the land on south side of road; to dau. Angeline Arwine; dau. Caroline wife of Marshall C. Owen, and sons James, John L., and Alfred C. have already received their share; to grandson John F. Thomas, infant son of Alfred C. Exec: friend and neighbor Elijah Loughmiller. Wit: Robert Boyd, A.J. Mathis.
WB G 86, 17 Jul 1865; 107, 21 Sep 1865. Invt. and sale, and Sett. by Exec.
CC 16, filed 25 Apr 1877. Jonathan Thomas died 10 Mar 1863. John F. Thomas, son of Alfred C., is now 15.

THOMAS, MARY
WB E 274, 20 Sep 1852. Sale of prop. of estate of James Thomas, Sr., dec'd, and which was in possession of his wife Mary at her death and sold by James Thomas and J.B. Fitzgerald, Adms. of estate of James Thomas, dec'd.

THOMASSON, JAMES M.
CC 305, filed 8 Nov 1871. James M. Thomasson died intestate in Miss. in 1862 on his way home from Vicksburg, leaving widow Nancy J. and children Emma E. now aged about 10 and Louisa V. now aged about 9, all of McMinn Co. Widow Nancy J. is dau. of James C. Carlock.

THOMPSON
CR2 489, 7 Dec 1830. Alfred Thompson app. Gdn. of Amy, John, William, and Sarah Thompson, minor orphans.

THOMPSON, ALEXANDER B.
CR4 72, 6 Mar 1832. Bill of sale proven; from Wm. Ward to Manerva, Stephen, Rachel, William, and John Thompson, heirs.

THOMPSON, ALFRED
CR4 44, 6 Dec 1831. Danl. Lattimore and Jemimah Thompson app. Adms.; Caleb Starr, Wm. Maples, and John Cobb app. Comm. to lay off year's support for widow Jemimah.
WB B 79, no date; 79, 28 Jan 1832; 121, 17 Aug 1833. Invt., Sale, and Sett. by Adms.
CR4 248, 8 Mar 1836. Jeremiah Lillard app. Gdn. to Saml., Merranda, Francis, Katherine, and Alfred Thompson, minor orphans.
WB B 250, May 1837; C 147, 29 Apr 1839. Reports by Gdn.
WB C 304, no date. Report by same Gdn.; he has been gdn. to Samuel, Miranda, Franklin, Catherine, and Alfred Thompson, minor heirs, and one small black boy 8 or 9 yrs. old for four years, supporting them, and has never received any consideration.

THOMPSON, SAMUEL
CR2 261, 3 Mar 1828. Mary and Robert Thompson app. Adms.
WB A 139-140, 4 Jun 1828. Acct. of sale by Adms.

THORNTON
/The following information is contained in two loose sheets of paper, not dated, found in the files of the Chancery Court, entitled "Petition of Mildred B. Thornton & others". The plea is to Hon. Thos. L. Williams Judge which would place the date between 1844 and 1854. In rearranging the files, these papers have been given the number 519. Except as noted there is no indication of the places of residence of persons named or of place of probate of the Will of Mildred Dudley./

Mildred Dudley in her Will leaves slaves to her son Anthony R.
Thornton in trust for Mildred B. wife of son Anthony R. Thornton,
Mary H. wife of her son Benjamin G. Thornton, Ann wife of her son
Wm. F. Thornton, Mariah wife of her son Reubin Thornton, Susan
wife of her son Nicholas C. Thornton, and for Lucy B. wife of her
son Charles T. Thornton. Anthony R. Thornton the Trustee died
recently and the petition is to appoint Reubin Thornton of McMinn
Co. as Trustee. Mildred Ann Grimes Thornton, dau. of Anthony R.
and Mildred B. Thornton, is now dec'd. Mary H., wife of Benj. G.
Thornton is now dec'd and her heirs are Ann W. and her husband
_____ Mirck, Benj. G., Sarah A. and her husband _____ Barnett,
and Anthony R. Thornton. Susan the wife of Nicholas C. Thornton
is now dec'd and her heirs are Richard L., Mildred A., Wm. C.,
and Mary Jane and her husband _____ Kindrick. There are no other
living beneficiaries of the Will.

THORNTON, WILLIAM R.
CR5 489, 6 Nov 1848. A.G. Rice app. Adm.
WB E 1-14, no date. Acct._of sales by Adm.; /this is evidently
sale of a store's stock./
CR5 501, 1 Jan 1849. Coroner paid for holding inquest over the
body.
WB E 15, no date; 35, 6 May 1849; 61, 25 Sep 1849. Invt. of notes,
Add. sale, and Final sett. by Adm.; balance paid over to Wm.
Lowry, Clerk and Master.
CC 73, filed 7 May 1849. Wm. R. Thornton was son of Charles T.
Thornton.

THURMAN, JOHN M.
WB G 10, 4 Jul 1864. Invt. by A. Blizard, Adm.
CR9 9, 3 Oct 1864. Report made by Elizabeth Thurman, Gdn. of Wm.
H. and Mary Lee Thurman, minor heirs.
WB G 185-187, 6 Aug 1866. Acct. of sales at late residence in
McMinn Co. and carpenter's tools sold at Athens; buyers include
Mrs. John Thurman, Mrs. Wm. Thurman, Bettie Thurman.
CR14 212, 214, 19 Aug 1867. A. Blizard, Adm. VS Widow and Heirs.
Mary Lee, William, and James Thurman are minors under 14; sub-
poena served on Malinda Hamilton, formerly Thurman, and her hus-
band Robert N. Hamilton, defendants, and they fail to appear.
Malinda Hamilton, as widow of dec'd, is entitled to dower.

TILLERY, ANDREW
CR9 243, 4 Mar 1867. John Rogers app. Adm.; Comm. app. to lay off
year's support for widow and family.
CR11 172, 29 Dec 1869. Sett. by Adm.; paid to Mrs. M. Tillery,
Margaret Tillery, and M. Tillery, at various times.

TIPTON
CR4 470, 2 Dec 1839. Serene Tipton, of age to choose for herself,
chooses Allen Dennis as Gdn.
WB C 320, 15 Jan 1841. Report by Gdn.; charges for his services
and expense in going to and from Wilson Co., West Tenn. /The
name of the ward is written Serena Tempton, with Tipton inserted,
and Tempton has been changed from Templeton./
WB D 135, 15 May 1842. Sett. by Gdn.; Syrena Tipton gives receipt
in full for her estate.

TRAP (TRAPT)
CR2 140, 7 Mar 1826. Sheriff ordered to take charge of Emeline

Trapt, an orphan child, dau. of Mourning Trap, until next Session of Court.

TREW, GEORGE
CR8, 6 Oct 1862. John A. Goly app. Gdn. of minor heirs.

TREW (TRUE), THOMAS
WB F 435-436, Will exec. 17 Sep 1860, proven Jul 1862; to wife Nancy; to the nine legatees children and grandchildren; children: Eliza wife of James C. Queener, Warner, Perry, Mary Ann, and James C. Trew, Caroline wife of Abraham Slack, Wm. Trew; grandchildren: Isaac N. and Nancy Elizabeth Trew minor children of dec'd sons George and John. Exec. and Gdn. of grandchildren: Wm. Trew. Wit: John A. Gouldy, James Thompson, and John G. Mayfield.
WB G 39, 4 Jul 1862; 154-159, 5 Feb 1866; 178, 11 May 1866. Invt., Sale, and Sett. by Exec.
CR9 283, 284, 1 Jul 1867. John A. Gouldy resigns as Gdn. and Chas. Cate is app. Gdn. to Isaac N. Trew son of Nancy Trew and of Nancy E. Trew dau. of Mary Trew.
CC 85, filed 21 Aug 1862. Thomas Trew died 23 Jun 1862.
CC 167, filed 13 Apr 1868. Son George's widow is Polly and his dau. is Nancy Elizabeth. Son John's widow is Ellen of Monroe Co. and his son is Isaac N. a minor who dies during the lawsuit.

TRIPLETT, LEWIS
WB C 51, Will exec. 29 May 1838; to wife Prudence and children. Wit: Thomas Vaughn, Wm. R. Douglas.
CR4 392, 1 Oct 1838. Will proven by Wm. R. Douglass.
WB C 113, Jan 1839. Invt. by Prudence Triplett, Execx.

TROTTER, ROBERT
CR5 285, 6 Apr 1846. Jacob Hinkle paid for making coffin for pauper.

TROUT, JOHN
CR4 510, 7 Sep 1840. Abraham Slover and James W. Netherland app. Adms.
WB C 272, 5 Oct 1840; D 7, 5 Apr 1841. Invt. and Sale by Adms.
WB D 174, 29 Dec 1843. Sett. by Abraham Slover, one of Adms.; vouchers to heirs Michael, William, and Margaret Trout, and to "Mchail Trout for self Stephen Wood & Mathias Trout".

TUMBLIN (TOMLIN), WILLIAM
CR2 488, 6 Dec 1830. Susannah Tumblin app. Adminx.
WB B 12, 7 Mar 1831; 60, 6 Jun 1831. Invt. and Sale by Adminx.

TUNNEL, ESTHER
CR7 90, 4 Jan 1858. C.A. Proctor app. Adm.
WB F 183, 23 Jan 1858; 261(2), 11 Apr 1859. Invt. and Sett. by Adm.; Jesse Tunnel receipt.
See also JOHN TUNNELL.

TUNNELL (TUNNEL), JOHN
WB B 121-122, Will exec. 19 Sep 1833; to wife Easter; to daus. Sarah and Lydia; to sons James and Wesley; to young children Jesse, Elizabeth, Margaret, Kiziah, Nancy, William P., and Easter Catharine. Execs: wife and bro. William Tunnell. Wit: John Wilson, Absolem H. Doan.
CR4 172, 2 Dec 1833. Will proven.
WB B 139, no date; C 144, 14 Aug 1839. Invt. and Sett. by Wm.

Tunnell, Exec.; paid "Widow Tunnel Troubbles and expenses raising the Children-$50.00".

CC 278, filed 2 Jan 1858. John Tunnell died 1833 leaving widow
Easter who died 30 Nov 1857 and children: Sarah wife of Eli B.
Cate; Lydia wife of Bennett Franklin of Bradley Co.; James; Wes-
ley now dec'd unmarried without issue; Jessee; Elizabeth wife of
Absolum Kegley of Va.; Margaret wife of John M. Hunt of Floyd
Co., Ga.; Kiziah, unmarried; Nancy wife of Augustus Eaton; Wm. P.;
Easter Catherine wife of James F. Roberts. William Tunnell, bro.
to John dec'd, died about 1844.

TURK, ARCHIBALD R.
WB D 252-253, Will exec. 13 Mar 1837; to wife Gincy "earnestly re-
questing that she shall not marry"; at death or marriage of wife,
to Saml. Workman who married niece Rebecca Griffith, nephew James
Griffith, niece Mary Jane Collier, Archibald R.T. Hambright, and
Archibald R. Turk son of bro. Wm. Execs: Alex. D. Keyes and
Saml. Workman. Wit: John F. Amos, Benj. Hambright, and J.W.
Eddington.
CR5 147, 149, 5 Feb 1844. Came Saml. Workman, one of the persons
therein named as an Exec., and produced a paper writing purporting
to be the last Will of Archibald R. Turk, dec'd, and to be proven
as a noncupative will; paper filed and widow and next of kin to
be called to contest the said Will if they think proper; John
Wolff app. Adm. pendente lite and Will contested by Wm. Turk.
CR5 216, 217, 3 Feb 1845. Will proven by Benjamin Hambright, one
of witnesses, who makes oath that the other two witnesses are
not now citizens of this State; the two Execs. named in Will
refuse to serve; Saml. Workman and John Wolff app. Adms.
WB D 255, 3 Feb 1845; 299, 4 Aug 1845. Invt. of sales by Adms.
WB D 314, 7 Aug 1845. Comm. Wm. McKamy, Wm. S. Stephenson, and
Winston Carter lay off year's support for Gincy Douthitt, for-
merly Gincy Turk, widow.
WB D 324, 6 Oct 1845. Add. Invt. by Adms.
WB D 457-460, 7 Jun 1847. Invt. of notes and accts., all of which
are on persons removed from the country or insolvent; included
are the following items: 1 note on Pleasant W. Lane, has runaway
and insolvent; a copy of a note sent to Wm. Fagg of North Carolina
Buncomb Co., on Samuel Smith; 1 note on George Smiley of Virginia;
J.W. Eddington, insolvent and removed from the country.
WB E 80, no date; 98, 5 Feb 1850. Add. Invt. of sale and Final
Sett. by Adms.; paid Gincy Douthitt, widow.
CC 157, filed 16 Apr 1852. Archibald Turk died about 25 Dec 1843.

TURNER, ALEXANDER
CR10 130, 2 Aug 1869. John F. Slover, H.K. Brown, and W.G. Horton
app. Comm. to lay off year's support for widow and family.

UNDERDOWN, GEORGE
WB D 481-482, Will exec. 16 Sep 1847; "being very sick"; to wife
Frances; to son Thomas A.; to sons John W. and Joseph K. when
they come of age; to five daus. Margaret Ann Barker, Jane M.
Swinney, Mary S., Nancy P., and Rebecca E. Underdown, the three
younger named girls when they come of age. Execs: Robt. Gregory,
James D. Henley. Wit: Daniel Pearce, H.K. John, and Thos. C.
Henley. Signed by mark.
CR5 381, 4 Oct 1847. Will proven.
WB D 498, Jan 1848; E 79, 19 Jan 1850; 188, 18 Jul 1851. Acct. of

sales, and Settlements by Execs.

UNDERDOWN, THOMAS A.
CR6, 6 Jun 1853. Isaac Davis app. Adm.
WB E 326, 5 Sep 1853; 433, 29 Jun 1855; 564, 29 Jun 1856. Invt.
of sale and Settlements by Adm. and by W.G. Barker, Gdn. to minor
heir; buyers include Frances Underdown.
CR6, 7 Aug 1854. Wm. G. Barker app. Gdn. to Thos. A. Underdown,
minor heir.

UNDERWOOD, JAMES
CR5 379, 4 Oct 1847. Court pays for shroud for pauper.

UNDERWOOD, WILLIAM H.
CR15 41, 17 Dec 1868. Manerva Hames, Adminx. De bonis non VS
Hilton Humphreys.
CR15 500, 9 Apr 1872. Manerva Hames has married Wm. E. Rucker and
suit is revived in his name jointly with hers.

VANCE, ROBERT
CR8, 5 Jan 1863. H.F. Luttrell app. Adm.
CR8 135, 136, 2 Feb 1863. J.W. Knox, G.W. Hutsell, and S.W. Royston app. Comm. to lay off year's support to widow.
CR9 90, 6 Nov 1865. Subpoena to Hugh F. Luttrell, Adm., to make
sett.
CR11 203, 1 Apr 1871. Final sett. by Adm.; Invt. which was filed
in 1863 was all allowed to the widow; received $55 in Confederate
money and spent $55 for boarding Mrs. Vance for two years.
CC 332, filed 17 Apr 1872. Robert Vance died in McMinn Co. leaving
widow now dec'd and John Vance his only heir.

VANDERPOOL, LEWIS
CR6, 3 Jul 1854. Court to pay for shroud.

VANZANDT, JOHN, SR.
CR4 183, 3 Mar 1834. John and Nancy Vanzandt app. Adms.
WB B 145, 3 Jun 1834. Invt. by Adms.; buyers include widow Nancy.

VANZANT, ANDREW J.
CR5 550, 1 Oct 1849. Jacob Vanzant app. Adm.
WB E 70, 7 Oct 1849. Invt. of sale by Adm.; buyers include John,
Washington, and Jacob Vanzant.

VARNEL (VARNELL, VERNELL), JOHN
CR4 92, 3 Sep 1832. Jesse W. Edington, Saml. Workman, and Isaac H.
Huffaker app. Comm. to lay off year's support to widow Elizabeth.
CR4 98, 3 Sep 1832. Lydia Ann and David Varnell, minor orphans
over 14, choose Elizabeth Varnell as Gdn.
WB B 89, 4 Sep 1832; C 120, 13 Dec 1838. Invt. by Isaac Huffaker
and Elizabeth Vernell, Adms., and Sett. by Isaac Huffaker, one
of Adms.

VARNEL, MARY
CR9 160, 7 May 1866. Jacob P. Bryant app. Adm.

VAUGHAN, MILTON (MELTON, MELLON)
CR4 345, 5 Feb 1838. Thomas Vaughan app. Adm.
WB C 225, 27 Feb 1840. Final sett. by Adm.; vouchers for credit
to ten heirs: William, Allen, Benj. W., Joseph, James Jr.,
John, and Thomas Vaughan, Jas. Donalson, Jacob Harrol, Doswell
Rogers, all "by his agent" except Thomas Vaughan.

VAUGHAN, THOMAS
 CR6, 7 May 1855. Proof offered that Thomas Vaughan, former Court
 Clerk, has died.
 WB E 456, 1 Oct 1855. Invt. of notes due filed by Wm. C. Vaughan,
 Adm.

VAUGHAN, THOMAS J.
 CR6, 4 Aug 1851. Thomas Vaughan app. Adm.

WADE, JAMES P.
 CR9 352, 6 Jan 1868. Wm. McPhail app. Gdn. of Nancy Ann Wade,
 minor heir.
 CC 575, filed 8 May 1878. McPhail VS McNabb. James P. Wade died
 1863 in U.S. Army leaving widow, who married Wm. D. McPhail in
 1867, and only dau. Nancy A. who married Wm. B. McNabb in 1877.
 Nancy A. was born 1861 and received a pension as heir of her
 father.

WAIDE, JAMES
 WB D 106, 3 Oct 1842; 112, 7 Nov 1842. Invt. and Sale by Louisa
 Waide and Richard Spradling, Adms.
 WB D 113, 12 Oct 1842. Comm. Jonathan Thomas, Michael Wattenbar-
 ger, and Wm. Albert lay off year's support for widow Louisa.
 WB D 190, 29 Mar 1844. Report by Richard Spradling, Adm.
 CR8, 4 Aug and 1 Sep 1862. J.W. Blevins and Wellington H. Roth-
 well with the County Surveyor E.L. Miller app. to allot dower for
 Louisa Brannum, formerly Louisa Wade, but now the wife of Hiram
 Brandon.

WALKER, EDMOND E.
 CR4 508, 7 Sep 1840. Bing Newton app. Adm.
 WB C 308, 7 Dec 1840. Invt. of sale by Adm.; one note on James E.
 Walker which Edmond E. Walker, dec'd, paid.
 WB C 311, 3 Oct 1840. Comm. Jacob Womack, Richard Moore, and
 Ezekiel Bonner set apart year's support for widow Sally.
 WB D 220, 27 Aug 1844. Sett. by Adm.

WALKER, HENRY
 CR8, 6 Jul 1863. Charles Staples app. Adm.

WALKER, JAMES
 CR6, 3 Jan 1853. In list of Tax Delinquents for 1851 is "James
 Walker, dead, 9th Dist. .30".

WALKER, JOHN, JR.
 WB B 165-166, Will exec. 31 Oct 1831, proven Dec Court 1834; "I
 John Walker, Jr., of the Cherokee Nation and Dist. of Amoyeh";
 "my interest in Reservations lying in Jackson Co., Ala."; to
 "my family say Emily and three children"; one branch of family
 which will be named in second sheet; children Timothy, Elizabeth, and Jane; to wife Emily; friend and relation Jesse Mayfield, Jr., to carry out terms of wills. Execs: Jesse Mayfield, James McDanniel, Caleb Starr, James Brown, and J.L.
 McCarty. Wit: Jesse Bushyhead and Jesse Mayfield.
 WB B 167, Will No. 2 exec. same date; to young woman by name of
 Nancy Bushyhead and "should she ever bear any children to me
 her children to have an equal share with those mentioned in the
 original". Wit: same as in Will No. 1.
 CR4 216, 3 Dec 1834. Jesse Mayfield one of Execs. app. by Will
 disclaimed all right that he had to execute said Will; Will

proven.
CR4 231, 5 Jun 1835. John L. McCarty makes bond as Exec.
WB C 134-139, 2 Apr 1839. Report by Wm. Lowry, Gdn. to Timothy M.,
Elizabeth Grace, Minerva Jane, and John Walker, minor heirs;
money received from Comm. of Indian affairs.
WB C 240, Mar 1840. Add. Invt. by Exec.; one item is a pony sold
in lifetime of Testator as property of John Walker, Sr.
WB C 249-251, 7 Apr 1840. Report by same Gdn.; heir John is John
Osmar Walker.
WB D 4, 6 Apr 1841. Sett. by same Gdn.; heir Timothy M. has gone
to Ark.
WB D 21, 5 Jul 1841; 74, 12 Nov 1841; 82, 1 Feb 1838; 91, 8 Jul
1842. Add. Invt. and Sett. by Exec. and by Gdn. to Timothy,
Minerva J., and John O.
WB D 218, no date. Report by Gdn.; paid to Timothy M. "on his
first and second visit from Arkansas".
WB D 296, 7 May 1845. Sett. by Exec.; paid to James M. Coleman
and wife; paid to Edward Brown, Jailor (two receipts).
WB D 367, 1 Jun 1846. Add. Invt. by Exec. by A.D. Keys, Agent.
WB D 528, Summer of 1847. Sett. by Dr. John L. McCarty, Exec.;
failed to be recorded at that time and recorded now, 1848.
WB D 528, 1 Apr 1848. Sett. by Exec. by Agent A.D. Keys, and
Final Sett. by Exec.; receipts from P.J.G. Lea Gdn. of John O.
Walker, from Grace Calloway Gdn. of Jane Walker, from J.A. Lea
and wife Jane, Mrs. Emily L. Walker, Timothy M. Walker, and
James M. Coleman and wife Elizabeth.

WALKER, ROBERT
WB C 267-269, Will exec. 24 Jul 1840; to wife Rachel; to two daus.
Elizabeth and Catherine; to son James; to dau. Polly; to dau.
Manervy; to dau. Tabitha; to son Samuel; to youngest sons Wm.
and Joseph; to all daus.; to grandson Wm. son of son Samuel.
Execs: son James and L.L. Ball. Wit: James Gibson and John
Ledbetter. Court members A.C. Robeson, N.P. Dodson, and J.H.
Howard sign.
CR4 511, 7 Sep 1840. Will proven.
WB C 292, Nov 1840. Comm. John L. McCarty, Emanuel Hany, and
Jacob Vanzant set apart year's support for widow and family.
WB C 346-350, 1 Mar 1841. Invt. of sale.
WB D 111, 9 Dec 1842. Sett. by Execs.; receipts from heirs:
Rachel the widow, Tabitha and Catherine Walker, Joseph and
Elizabeth Wilhite, and Burk Priddy.
WB D 191, 1 Apr 1844. Sett. by Execs.

WALLIN, ELIZABETH
CR7 89, 4 Jan 1858. John Wallin app. Adm.
WB F 155, Invt. of sale held 14 Jan 1858 by Adm.; buyers include
Emily and Chas. Wallin.
CR7 169, 183, 223, dated from 6 Apr to 6 Sep 1858. Tax Collector
ordered to refund to John M. Wallin, Adm. of Elizabeth Wallin,
a Revolutionary widow; James and John Wallin VS Thomas, Jesse,
Isaac, and John Wallin, Sarah Igo formerly Wallin, Nancy Wallin
who married Danl. Wallin, Elizabeth McMurry formerly Wallin,
James Jr., Eliza Jane, Nancy, John Jr., Matilda, and Mary Ann
Wallin. All defendants except Elizabeth McMurry are nonresi-
dents; petition to sell land; one-ninth part each to James,
Thomas, Jesse, Isaac, and John Wallin, Sarah Igo, Nancy Wallin,

and Elizabeth McMurry, and the remaining one-ninth to the heirs
of son Stephen Wallin, dec'd, being the last six defendants named.

WALLIN, ISAAC, JR.
  CR5 551, 1 Oct 1849. John Matlock app. Adm.

WALLING (WALLEN, WALDING), JOHN, SR.
  WB B 185, Will exec. 15 Apr 1836, proven 2 May 1836; to wife Elizabeth. Wit: Jos. M. Alexander and John Miller. Signed by mark.

WALLIS, PRIOR
  CR7 536, 6 May 1861. In List of Tax Delinquents for 1860 is "Prior
  Wallis Dec'd."

WAMACK (WAMAC, WAMMACK), DANIEL
  WB F 35, Invt. of sale held 20 Nov 1856 by Isaac Benson and John
  Wammack, Adms.
  WB F 37, 20 Nov 1856. Comm. R.A. McAdoo, James M. White, and
  James Dennis lay off year's support for widow Mary "as she is
  left with a large family of negroes to support as well as her
  own family".
  WB F 223, 30 Nov 1858. Sett. prepared by M.P. Jarnagin for the
  Adms.
  WB F 240, 11 Nov 1858; 306, 1 Jan 1860. Sett. by Isaac Benson,
  Gdn. to minor heirs Jacob, John, William, Mary W., and Joseph
  Wamac; received 5/6 of hire of boy Simon; the real estate oc-
  cupied by the widow and children.
  WB F 363, 1 Jan 1861. Sett. by same Gdn.; wards are receiving
  and paying 5/6 of amounts.
  WB F 426, 1 Jan 1862. Sett. by same Gdn.; in this report the name
  William is written Milam.

WAMACK (WAMMACK), JACOB
  WB D 465-466, Will exec. 20 Jan 1847, probated first Monday in
  Aug 1847; "whereas on 13th day of October 1845 a family of
  negroes which I raised was valued & divided among my children...
  for I had at that time in the above date nine heirs...said valu-
  ation was made by James Lillard, Wm. Lillard, & Emanuel Haney on
  oath to do justice between my children said Family of negroes
  descended to my heirs by a will from their aunt Testimony Wills
  to their Mother & the heirs of her body and they have got them
  or their value...so in addition to what my beloved daughter
  Dessy Moore has already received I will and bequeath to her five
  dollars"; to children Jacob, Jr., John, and Daniel Wammack,
  Susan Rivers, Mary Powel, Sarah Elder, and Narcissus Lucas, all
  personal property. Execs: sons John and Daniel. Wit: R.A.
  McAdoo, James M. White, and James Dennis. Signed by mark.
  WB D 480, Sep 1847. Acct. of sales by Execs.
  WB D 563, 11 Sep 1848. Sett. by John Wamack, one of Execs.
  WB D 571, 2 Oct 1848. Final sett. by Daniel Wamack, one of Execs.;
  receipts from heirs: James and Sarah Elder, Thomas and Narcissa
  Lucas, William and Susan Rivers, Scott and Mary Powell, Jacob,
  Daniel, and John Wamack.
  WB D 572-574. Refunding bonds of heirs.

WAMACK, JOHN
  CR9 54, 5 Jun 1865. Sett. by Peter B. Cate, Gdn. to his own minor
  children.
  WB G 187, 6 Aug 1866. Sett. by same Gdn.

WAMACK, SAMUEL M.
    CR14 489, 490, 11 Aug 1868. The State VS Martha Ball and The State
    VS Richard Knox and Carr Clark. Grand Jury Indictment. Knox and
    Clark on 10 Jul 1868 in McMinn Co., Tenn., murdered Samuel M.
    Wammac, hired and commanded by Martha Ball, who is indicted as
    Accessory before the fact.
    CR10 59, 5 Oct 1868. G.M. Hutsell paid for holding inquest.
    CR10 68, 2 Nov 1868. John Sharp, H.M. Roberts, and Mark Dennis
    app. Comm. to lay off year's support for widow Mary J. and family.

WAMACK (WARMACK, WOMACK), THOMAS
    WB D 430, 8 Feb 1847. Comm. Tapley Gregory, Thos. Spearman, and
    Benj. Roberts set apart year's support for widow Polly and family.
    WB D 445, 27 Mar 1847. Invt. by Mary Warmack, Adminx.
    WB D 530, 1 May 1848. Report by Austin Shifflet, Gdn. to William
    C., Jacob Mc., Mary Ann, Sarah A., Gemima, Narcissa W., Thomas
    L., David, and Samuel M. Wamack, minor children who are living
    on farm with widow.
    WB E 33, 9 Apr 1849. Sett. by same Adminx.
    WB E 34, 9 Apr 1849. Sett. by same Gdn.; paid J.M. White for Wm.
    Wamack, one of the heirs.
    WB E 88, Apr 1850; 90, 25 May 1850. Reports by Mary Wamack, Gdn.;
    paid Paton T. and Polly Ann Nance, heirs, and Jacob Wamack one
    of heirs.
    WB E 153, 163, 254, 322, 382, 429, dated from 29 Mar 1851 to 16 May
    1855. Final sett. by Austin Shifflet, late Gdn., and Sett. by
    Mary Wamack, Gdn.; paid for side saddle for Sarah Adeline 1854.
    WB E 523, 16 May 1856. Sett. by E.W. Roberts and J.M. Wamack,
    Gdns.; paid Thos. H. Smith and wife, P.T. and P.A. Nance, Sarah
    Wamack, and J.M. Wamack, all equal amounts.
    WB F 71, 16 May 1857. Sett. by same Gdns.
    WB F 160, 22 Mar 1858. Sett. by same Gdns.; receipts for $1.11
    each from J.P. Denton, T.H. Smith, J.T. Denton, J.M. Wamack, Thos.
    Smith, Wm. Wamack, P.T. Nance, and $11.15 from Sarah Wamack.
    WB F 264, 22 Mar 1859. Sett. by E.W. Roberts, Gdn.; receipts from
    J.P. and J.T. Denton.
    WB F 319, 27 May 1860. Sett. by same, Gdn. of Thos. L., David, and
    Samuel Wamack.
    WB F 399, 27 May 1861; 443, 23 May 1862. Sett. by same, Gdn. to
    Thos., Daniel /sic/, and Samuel Wamack.

WAMMACK, JOHN
    CR9 247, 1 Apr 1867. Coroner's Jury held inquest 2 Feb 1867 on
    body of John Wammack on the hill East of Miss Smart's in the 9th
    Dist. of McMinn Co. - report that he came to death by violence
    of some unknown person.

WARD
    CR7 456, 2 Jul 1860. John Cunningham app. Gdn. to Mary L____ Ward,
    a minor.

WARE, JOSEPH R.
    CC 129, filed 20 Aug 1863. Joseph R. Ware died 5 Aug 1863 in McMinn
    Co. leaving widow Martha and six children.
    CC 17, filed 18 Apr 1865. Carlock VS Cobb. Joseph R. Ware was
    killed between June 1863 and 5 Aug 1863 and left widow Martha A.
    and minor children David S., Clementine W., Robert R., Samuel B.,
    John W.

WASSOM (WASSAM, WASSAN, WASSON), CORNELIUS
WB C 194, Will exec. 28 Nov 1839; "I Cornelius Wasson...being aged";
to wife Charity; to daus. Rachel Garrison and Patsy Weaver; to
sons Jones and Jacob. Execs: Robt. Garrison and Chrisley Foster.
Wit: John Goss, Jr., and George P. Owen.
CR4 472, 473, 6 Jan 1840. Will of Cornelius Wasson proven; Execs.
make bond. /Wasson changed to Wassom in latter entry./
WB C 255, 258, D 117, 269, dated from 1 Jun 1840 to 1 Mar 1845.
Sale, Add. Sale, and Sett. by Execs.
WB D 437, 13 Mar 1847. Sett. by Execs.; receipt from Robert Gar-
rison for keeping widow Charity Wasson while sick twenty-one
months and for coffin for her burial.
WB D 565, 19 Sep 1848. Final sett. by Execs.; heirs paid are Jonas
Wasson, Polly Weaver, Jacob Wasson by his AF Polly Weaver, Robert
Garrison and wife.

WASSOM (WOSSOM), JONAS
WB G 42, 6 Feb 1865. Acct. of sale by A.D. Briant, Adm.
WB G 43, 21 Jan 1865. Comm. J.M. Burnett, James Magill, and H.L.
Shults set apart year's support for widow Catharine; appointed
Dec 1864.
WB G 205, 2 Oct 1866. Sett. by Adm.
CR9 293, 320, 5 Aug 1867. Petition to sell land: A.D. Briant,
Adm. VS Catharine Wassom widow, Eligah Wassom, John Wassom, Nancy
Sellers, Joseph Sellers, Martha Sellers, Jonas Wassom, Jr., Eliz-
abeth Brandon, Fereby McMillan, John Henry Boofer, Sarah Jane
Wassom, Orpha Paul, Meredith Paul, Mary Wassom, John Wassom, and
the following minors: Jonas T. (P.), Mary C., and Martha E.
Boofer, Eliza Ann, Jackson, Thomas, George, and Cassa Wassom.

WEATHERLY, WOODSON H. and ELIZABETH (FORMERLY ELIZABETH HANKS)
/Entry is headed as given above, but Woodson H. is not dec'd by
records./
CR8, 2 Dec 1861. James H. Melton app. Gdn. of minor heirs.
WB G 106, 25 Aug 1865. Sett. by Gdn.; received funds on 17 Jan
1863; receipt in full this day for 1/5 of funds from Margaret J.
McCord, one of heirs, by W.H. Weatherly, Atty. in fact; receipt
for 1/5 interest from Henry Weatherly.
CC 323, filed 5 Mar 1872. Elizabeth Weatherly, dec'd dau. of John
Hanks, dec'd, and wife of Woodson Weatherly, left five children:
John S., a minor who moved to Henry Co. in 1865 (James S. Rose-
berry of Henry Co. is his Gdn.); Margaret J.; Henry C.; Sarah B.;
and Robert J., all being minors in 1862. Affidavit from Woodson
H. Weatherly, Henry Co., Tenn., 10 May 1873, that he is father of
sd. children and was husband to Elizabeth, dec'd.

WEATHERS, BRACSTON or BRAESTON W.
CR5 478, 2 Oct 1848. Wm. Wright app. Adm.

WEAVER, JOHN
CR13 414, 13 Dec 1865. John N. Taylor, Adm. VS Thos. J. Mastin.

WEIR, ELIAS
WB F 51, 12 Feb 1857. Comm. Philip P. Owens, J.W. Brown, and Wm.
Weir lay off year's support for widow.

WEIR, JAMES N.
WB D 518, Will exec. 13 Nov 1847 "on leave of going to Mexican
war"; to wife Emeline; to two children, dau. Martha and son, not

yet named; interest in balance of Father's estate. Wit: A. Slover, Henry Camron, and Edmund Roberts.
CR5 413, 6 Mar 1848. Will proven; Emeline Weir app. Adminx. with Will annexed.
WB D 532-534, 1 May 1848. Invt. of partnership of dec'd and J.C. Weir, and personal Invt. filed by E.E. Weir, Execx.; "a negro girl named Harriett to come at old Mrs. Weir's death".

WEIR, JOHN M. C.
CC 118, filed 27 Jan 1863. John M.C. Weir died in McMinn Co. in Aug 1861 leaving widow Anna and children: Margaret B. of unsound mind; P.B.; Bella; Savilla who marries Joseph M.C. McMinn during the lawsuit; John H. of Ark.; and Thomas J. who was in Confederate Army.

WEIR (WEAR), WILLIAM R.
WB G 1, Will exec. 23 Jul 1863; all estate to wife Mornon and to Sarah I. Wear who lives with me; at death of wife to be divided equally between daughter Mary E. Mynett and Sarah I. Wear; $100 to granddau. Cordelia Brock and $10 each to balance of Martha's children; has given dec'd dau. Martha Brown her full share. Exec: Wm. B. Porter. Wit: J.G. Hale, David Brown. Signed: W.R. Weir.
CC 516, filed Apr 1866. Wm. R. Wear died 27 July 1863 leaving widow Mornen and children Sarah I., Mary E. wife of J.L. Mynatt of Whitfield Co., Ga., and the children of dec'd dau. Martha, wife of J.W. Brown, who are Cordelia wife of Dock Brock and minors Winfield S., William, Anna R., Robert, Hugh, and Margaret Brown, all of McMinn Co.
CC 604, filed 29 Nov 1878. Second wife Mournen Wear died 10 Jul 1878. Sarah Isabell, dau. by second wife, married W.W. Corley 21 Oct 1869. In 1873 dau. Mary E. and husband Jameson L. Mynatt were living at Chewalla in McNairy Co., Tenn., and now are of Hardeman Co., Tenn. Daughters Mary E. and Martha were children by first wife. The children of dau. Martha Brown, dec'd, are listed as Robert and Scott Brown, and Cordelia Brock.

WELKER, WILLIAM L.
WB B 12-13, Will exec. 10 Feb 1831; to family, according to laws of the State. Execs: Horace Hickox, Jacob Hoss. Wit: Thos. Crutchfield, Russell Hurst, and W.W. Anderson.
CR2 506, 7 Mar 1831. Will proven.
WB B 38-53, 9 Jun 1831. Invt. and Sale by Execs.; Malinda Welker is main buyer.
WB B 53-55, 9 Jun 1831. Invt. of notes.
WB B 78, 6 Mar 1832. Supp. Invt. to correct previous invt.; accts. given as property of Wm. L. Welker are in reality property of firm of Mitchell and Welker.

WELLS, BARNA B.
CR2 279, 5 Mar 1828. George Wells app. Adm.

WELLS, THOMAS P.
CR7 553, 5 Aug 1861. R.H. and D.H. Wells app. Adms.
CC 139, filed 28 Aug 1867. Thomas P. Wells died 1861 leaving widow Margaret who is still living and children: John H. of Bedford Co., Tenn.; Robert H.; Levi C. a nonresident; Mary J. wife of Ewing W. Carlock; Thomas L. a nonresident; and Susan E. Wells.

WEST, JOHN
  CR8 157, 6 Apr 1863. Court pays for coffin for pauper.

WHETSELL, MICHAEL
  WB B 57-58, Will exec. 9 May 1831; one-fourth to wife Angeline;
  request that my family and my brother-in-law Bashergo Ar shall
  reside in the house on the lot whereon I now live...it shall be
  a home for my family and for raising my children; one-fourth to
  mother-in-law Barbera Catron; one-half to son Peter K. and dau.
  Lucinda, both minors. Execs: friends Peter Kinder and Urial
  Johnston. Wit: A.H. Napier, Lewis R. Hurst, and Hilton Humphry.
  WB B 56-57, 16 May 1831. Invt. taken by Execs.
  CR2 533, 6 Jun 1831. Will proven.
  CR4 97, 3 Sep 1832. Angeline Whetsell app. Gdn. of Peter and Lu-
  cinda Whetsell, minor children under 14.

WHITE
  CR4 471, 2 Dec 1839. Elisha White app. Gdn. to Elizabeth, Jessee,
  William, Narcissy, Daniel, Nancy, and Martha White, heirs of the
  said Elisha White.

WHITE, BARTON
  CR5 125, 2 Oct 1843. Elijah Cate, Benjamin E. Blain, and John K.
  Boyd app. Comm. to lay off year's support for widow Mary.
  WB D 175-185, 1 Jan 1844. Invt. of sale by Heil Buttram, Adm.
  /This record is an interesting and informative inventory of a
  general store of the period./
  WB D 192, 1 Apr 1844; 337, 31 Oct 1845; 516, 21 Feb 1848. Set-
  tlements by same Adm.

WHITE, DANIEL
  CR4 284, 3 Oct 1836. David Cantrell, Thomas Mastin, and John
  Good app. Comm. to settle with Elizabeth and John White, Adms.

WHITE, ELISHA
  CR7 440, 7 May 1860. Benjamin Cass, B.A. Prophet, and Wm. A.
  Dugan in connection with E.L. Miller the County Surveyor app.
  Comm. to allot dower including the mansion house to widow Ursula.
  WB F 328, 15 May 1860. Comm. B.A. Prophet, W.A. Daugherty, and
  B.E. Cass set apart year's support for widow.
  CR7 468, 475, 1 and 2 Oct 1860. Petition to sell land: John
  White, Adm. VS Ursula White, widow, Jesse and Wm. White, Mat-
  thew and Elizabeth Mattocks, James F. and Narcissa Benton, Wm.
  A. and Caroline Johnson, Preston and Martha Bates, Daniel J.
  White, and Mary Ann, Henry H., Newton J., and Tempy White, the
  last four minors by their Gdn.; land in Monroe and McMinn
  Counties.
  WB F 446, 13 Jan 1862. Pro rata sett. by Adm.

WHITE, NATHANIEL
  WB B 151, 1 Sep 1834. Invt. by Elizabeth White.
  WB B 158, 25 Sep 1834. Comm. Thomas W. Mastin, Wm. Armstrong, and
  Thos. B. Mayfield set apart year's support for Elizabeth White
  and family.
  WB B 159-161, 1 Dec 1834. Invt. by Elizabeth White, Adminx.; buy-
  ers include Elizabeth, Ann, George, and Comodore White.
  WB B 235, 5 Dec 1836. Comm. Thomas W. Marsten, John Goode, and I.
  Cantrell settle with Adminx.
  WB C 168, 10 Aug 1839; D 72, 30 Apr 1842. Sett. by Adminx.; vou-
  chers to heirs C. White, A.H. Lawson, John White, Martha White,

and James B. Fennell.

WHITE, PHEBE
  CR8, 1 Dec 1862. Will proven.
  WB G 1-2, 12 Apr 1864. Second Invt. and sale by James Parkison, Exec.; also acct. of corn impressed by Confederate Army and Federal Army in 1863-1864; corn taken by Confederate Army, Genl. Wright's forces, was paid for in Confederate money which is and was worthless; vouchers for corn from Col. Long's Command, U.S. forces, at Calhoun; one pair of Cotton Cards taken from the Mansion of deceased by A.J. McMahan who refused to return and "there having been any law for redress"; "See Will". /The Will is not recorded. It was probably in the original Will Book G, which was lost or destroyed./
  WB G 40-41, 24 Jan 1865. Supp. Invt. by Exec.; the original first inventory heretofore rendered believed to have been destroyed by Wheeler's raid in Aug 1864.
  WB G 42, 24 Jan 1865. Invt. by Exec.; "Amt. due as Exec. from Estate of Wm White dec'd (See Will Book F, page 281)".
  WB G 168, 17 Apr 1866. Add. sale of farm produce by Exec.; "The Corn crop raised on the farm in 1864 was taken by Lut. Gilbert and never accounted for".
  CC 78, filed 3 Aug 1866. Copy of Will of Phebe White, exec. 8 Nov 1862; $400 each to servants Isaac, Willis, Matilda, and Mary Athens White, (Mary Athens is minor child of Matilda); $200 to A.J. McMahan; balance to sister Ailsy Tabor of Ala. Exec: Jas. Parkison. Wit: T.F. and T.L. Swaffer. Signed by mark.
  CR11 137, 5 Apr 1868. Sett. by Exec.; vouchers for payment as decreed by Chancery Court at Athens as follows: $450 to Willis White, $200 to A.J. McMahan, $100 each to J.M. Clemenson for Matilda White, Mary Athens White, and Isaac White, and various amounts paid to and for Isaac White.
  See also WILLIAM WHITE.

WHITE, WILLIAM
  WB F 190-191, Will exec. 6 Nov 1857, proven Aug 1858; "being advanced in age"; all negroes to be free at death of wife and to be sent to Colony of Liberia, with all expenses paid and $50 to each one; balance of property to wife. Exec: friend James Parkerson. Wit: E.M. Newton, Wm. Cannon.
  WB F 212, 4 Oct 1858. Invt. by Exec.
  WB F 281, 15 Aug 1859. Final sett. by Exec.; all that has come to his hands is $36.91 and report ends with $20.54 due Exec.
  CC 78, filed 3 Aug 1866. Parkison VS Tabor. Wm. White died about 20 Jun 1858 leaving wife Phoebe but no children. Phebe died 26 Nov 1862. Slaves decline to return to Liberia. This is plea for Court to construe the two Wills.
  CR10 458, Feb 1873. Jas. Parkison app. Gdn. of Mary Athens White, a colored minor.
  CR11 293, 18 Dec 1873. Sett. by Exec.; joint return as Exec. of Wm. and Phebe White.

WHOSER, JEFFERSON
  CR7 344, 3 Oct 1859. Court pays for coffin for pauper.

WIGGINS, JOHN D.
  CR4 378, 3 Sep 1838. Wm. Wiggins app. Adm.
  WB C 54, Oct 1838; D 229, no date. Invt. and sett. by Adm.;

receipts from E.R. and Wm. Wiggins.

WILKINS, REUBEN
CR4 519, 5 Oct 1840. Dimmon Dorsey and Josiah Wilkins app. Adms.
WB C 290, Nov 1840. Comm. Moses Cunningham, David Pearce, and Isom
Julian set apart year's support for widow Mary and family.
WB C 320, 322, D 108, 205, dated from 4 Jan 1841 to 29 Jun 1844.
Invt., Sale, and Sett. by Adms.
CR5 18, 6 Dec 1841. Mary Wilkins app. Gdn. to Elizabeth J., Dem-
mon, and John M. Wilkins, minor heirs.
WB D 356, 5 Feb 1846. Sett. by Adms.; "Additional Inventory re-
turned this day of his Estate from N. Carolina from his Mother's
estate".
WB D 362, 486, 562, E 51, 90, 178, 255, 322, 381, 440, 564, dating
from 4 May 1846 to 1856. Reports by Dimmon Dorsey, Gdn. to Eliz-
abeth Jane, Dimmon Anderson, and John McCamy Wilkins, minor
heirs.
WB F 91, 4 May 1857. Sett. by same Gdn.; receipt in full from
Elizabeth J. Wilkins.
WB F 193, 6 Aug 1858. Final sett. by same Gdn.

WILLIAMS, ELISHA
CR13 345, 24 Aug 1865. The State VS Thomas Jordan, James Cooper,
Stokely Bean, Frank Harrold, Bud Branham, and Jack Brown - Murder. Grand Jury Indictment. About 8 Oct 1863 defendants did
kill and murder in the first degree.

WILLIAMS, FREDERICK or ANDREW
WB B 77, Will exec. 27 Aug 1831, proven Mar 1832; "I Frederick Wil-
liams"; to wife Casandor, to Lavinia Coppehaver, Elizabeth Pra-
ther, Richard Williams, Polly Short, Robert Williams, Daniel Wil-
liams, Sally White, Patience Garner, Shedreck Williams, Casann
Baker; at wife's death estate to be divided equally among others
named. Execs: Richard and Robert Williams. Wit: W.B. Jones,
James Scenter. Signed Andrew Williams.
CR4 53, 5 Mar 1832. Will of Frederick Williams proven.
/Frederick Williams in Index./

WILLIAMS, JAMES
WB B 61, 6 Jun 1831. Invt. by F.L. Williams, Adm.
CR2 533, 6 Jun 1831. Frederick S. Williams app. Adm.

WILLIAMS, NANCY
CR4 391, 392, 1 Oct 1838. Wm. H., Arrena, and Zechious L. Wil-
liams, minor orphans, bound to Silvester Blackwell. Mary E.
Williams, orphan, bound to Joel Grigg. Silvester Blackwell app.
Adm.
WB C 68, 286, D 41, 97, 162, 243, 344, 422, 511, 582, E 71, 148,
197, 309, dating from Nov 1838 to 21 Dec 1852. Sale and settle-
ments by Adm.
WB E 367, 21 Dec 1853. Sett. by same Adm.; receipt from Wm. H.
Williams heir for amount which appears to be his final share.
WB E 417, 21 Dec 1854. Sett. by Adm.; receipts from Z.L. Williams,
and J.A. and Arrena Bryant.
WB E 467, 19 Oct 1855. Final sett. by Adm.; vouchers for total
amount to Z.L. Williams, J.A. and Arrena Bryant, and Frederick W.
and Mary E. Patterson.

WILLITT, THOMAS G.
  WB B 146, 1 Sep 1834; 155, 13 Sep 1834. Invts. by John Beeler, Adm.

WILSON
  CR2 70, 6 Jun 1825. Sarah and Betsey Wilson, over 14, choose James
  Wilson as Gdn. and he is app. Gdn. for John, Polly, and Washing-
  ton Wilson, minors under 14.

WILSON, H. M. (Colored)
  CR9 377, 2 Mar 1868. D.M. McReynolds app. Gdn. of minor heirs.

WILSON, JAMES
  CR5 15, 1 Nov 1841. Thomas W. Marston app. Adm.
  WB D 51-53, 3 Jan 1842. Invt. of sale by Adm.
  WB D 57, 19 Nov 1841. Comm. John Hoyle, John Neill, and Wm. D.
  Smith lay off year's support for widow Dicy and family.
  WB D 189-190, 4 Jan 1844. Report by Adm.
  WB D 230, no date. Report by Dicey Wilson, Gdn. to her two minor
  children.
  WB D 269, 4 Jan 1845. Sett. by Adm.; receipts from heirs Franklin
  and Dicy Wilson, and Sally Glenn; Gdn. receipt for James and Jack-
  son; "And paid Franklin's heirs before the Estate was divided 6.14
  which was coming from James Wilson as Guardian to his daughter
  Betsy from her grand mother McClure. And said administrator further states that he reported as liable as Guardian for the minor
  heirs of E. Franklin 13.06 2/3".
  WB D 350, 28 Jan 1846. Sett. by Adm.; voucher of Levi Long for
  his distributive share.
  WB D 423, 28 Jan 1847. Sett. by Adm.; "Canton, Washington County,
  Indiana, April 4th 1846, to the administrator of my fathers Estate
  or who ever else may have the care of my part of the personal
  property please divide the amount equally that is coming to me,
  let it be more or less & pay it to my sister Mary Long and my
  brother Jackson C. Wilson and this keep for your receipt. John
  M. Wilson."; receipts from Jackson C. Wilson and Levi Long for
  $8.26 each.
  WB D 509, 28 Jan 1848. Sett. by Adm.
  WB D 581, 21 Dec 1848. Final sett. by Dicy Wilson, Gdn. to James
  and J.C. Wilson, heirs.
  WB E 19, 94, 144, dated from 28 Jan 1849 to 30 Dec 1850. Sett.
  and final sett. by Adm.; J.C. Wilson, Gdn. receipt for amount
  in full.

WILSON (WILLSON), JAMES
  CR6, 6 Mar 1854. James Wilson app. Adm.
  CR6, 3 Apr 1854. James Forrest app. Gdn. to James Henry, a minor.
  CR12 207, 221, 268, 270, 10 Apr 1854. James Willson, Adm., Sarah
  Willson widow, W.P. Willson, Russell Miller and wife Jane, James
  Willson, W.W. Peck and wife Dialtha VS Thos. W. Cunningham and
  wife, Wm. Vaughan and wife, and James Henry an infant defended by
  his gdn. James Forrest; partition of lands and negroes among
  heirs. Sarah Willson widow is entitled to 1/3 in all lands, but
  is willing and desires to have only 1/3 in the Home Place. James
  Willson made advance in his lifetime to child Ake Henry and wife
  in her lifetime. Widow Sarah to have 1/7 or a child's part. Wm.
  Vaughan and wife and James Henry shall represent their deceased
  ancestor the daughter of the said James Willson, dec'd. Petition
  of James Henry an infant heir and grandson of James Willson dec'd

for the sale of his 1/12 interest in 5 acres reserved out of
Hicky farm on line of E.T. & Ga. R.R. for a depot.
WB E 367, 14 Apr 1854. Comm. Russell Lane, Humphreys L. Shults,
and John F. Shearman set apart year's support for widow Sarah
and family.
WB E 372-376, 431, 500, 520, F 99, 241, dated from 5 Jun 1854 to
6 Dec 1858. Invt. of notes and sale, Add. invt., and Sett. by
James Wilson, Adm., and Reports by James Forrest, Gdn. to James
Henry.
WB F 257, 7 Mar 1859. Final sett. by James Forrest, Gdn. of "James
Henry Dec'd"; "James Henries receipt for $2278.97". /It is prob-
able that this receipt should be from James Wilson instead of
James Henry. See JAMES HENRY./

WILSON (WILLSON), JAMES
WB G 226-228, Will exec. 3 Oct 1864, prob. 6 Sep 1869; wife Sarah
R. Willson to be gdn. of children; wife to have child's part of
home farm containing 1000 acres in 4th Civil Dist. on headwaters
of Mouse Creek and to include mansion house and all out houses,
at her death to be divided equally among children when youngest
arrives at lawful age or marries; to children, 53 acres lying in
Mouse Creek Valley, 160 acres in Johns River Valley, one-half
interest in 200 acres in Morgan Co., Ala., and whatever money may
be collected upon receipts held on Thomas A. Cleage for $15,000.
Attest: A. Blizard, John F. Shearman. Signed James Wilson.
CR10 135, 136, 6 Sep 1869. James Forest and H.L. Shults app. Adms.
with Will annexed. Sarah R. Wilson app. Gdn. to Hugh M., Robert
S., Ellie, Mary M., and James C. Wilson, minors. Sarah R. Wilson, widow, dissents to Will.
CR10 143, 148, 4 Oct 1869. Sarah R. Wilson VS the Adms. and the
five children, the only children and heirs; petition for dower
of 1/3 in value of all the real estate; James Wilson died in
McMinn Co., 2 Aug 1869; description of real estate and plat of
dower.
CR11 224, 2 Oct 1871. Sett. by H.L. Shults, one of Adms.

WILSON, JAMES C.
CR9 86, 3 Oct 1865. A.J. Shelton app. Adm.
WB G 125, 21 Oct 1865. Comm. Wm. Buttram, J.S. Green, and Adam
Sliger set apart year's support for widow Sarah L. Wilson; all
property on hand does not amount to half of what the law entitles
her.
WB G 126, 6 Nov 1865. Report by Adm.

WILSON (WILLSON), JOHN
WB A 4, Will exec. Aug 1821; to William Mayfield; to Jesse May-
field, Jr. Wit: Da A. Cobb, John Cobbs, James Parkes.
WB A 11, 25 Nov 1823. Invt. by Da. A. Cobb, Adm. of the "Goods &
Chattles of John Wilson Dec'd August 18, 1821 Annexed to Will
made the same day By the Dec'd John Wilson".

WILSON, LEANDER
WB E 143, 309, 521, dating from 15 Jan 1851 to 8 Feb 1856. Invt.
and Sett. by A.H. Wilson, Adm.; vouchers for $12.31 each to the
following: Mitchell Ghaston and wife Jane, Wm. McKowean and
wife Clarissa, S.P., Elizabeth, Margaret E., and Wm. H. Wilson.

WILSON, SAMUEL
WB E 355-357, Will exec. 17 Oct 1853, Codicil 18 Jan 1854, proven

6 Feb 1854; to wife Elizabeth; to two youngest daus. Margaret Elizabeth and Louisa Ann, the Middleton farm and it to be sold when they come of age; to six oldest children, Mary Middleton, Martha E. Middleton, R.B., Joseph C., and Jefferson E. Wilson, and Frances Jane Smith; the farm in Hamilton Co., Tenn., on the river where J.E. Wilson now lives to be divided among J.E. and Joseph C. Wilson and Frances Jane Smith; to Samuel son of Jefferson E. Wilson and to Samuel W. Smith son of Wm. R. Smith, $50 each "for that he was named for me". Execs: Jefferson E. Wilson and John J. Middleton. Wit. to Will: Morgan Miller, Arthur St. John, J.F. Browder. Wit. to Codicil: Benjamin Eldridge, Israel C. Smith, and G.W. Renfro.

CR6, 7 Mar 1854. John J. Middleton of McMinn Co. and Jefferson E. Wilson of Hamilton Co. qualify as Execs.

WB E 411, 6 Feb 1855; F 56, 21 Mar 1857. Invt. and Sett. by Execs.

CC 384, filed 31 Oct 1873. Frances J. Smith, dau. of Samuel Wilson, and her husband W.R. Smith lived in Hamilton Co. 1854 to 1856 on land willed to her by her father.

WILSON, SARAH
  WB F 52-53, Will exec. 1 Jan 1857 at Mouse Creek, McMinn Co., Tenn., proven 6 Apr 1857; property to be divided equally among heirs with following exceptions: $100 only to granddau. Sarah Vaughn, $100 only to grandson James Henry, and son James Wilson to have gray colt before the distribution. Wit: Humphrey L. Shults, J.H. Magill. Signed by mark.
  WB F 70, 4 Jun 1857. Sett. by James Forrest, Gdn. of James Henry; received of James Wilson, Adm. of Sarah Wilson the legacy of $100.

WIMBERLY
  CR5 78, 7 Nov 1842. Jacob Wimberly app. Gdn. to Henry R. Wimberly, minor.

WINCHER, REBECCA FISHER
  CR6, 5 Nov 1855. Chas. Metcalf app. Adm.

WINDER, JAMES
  CR5 194, 7 Oct 1844. Andrew Hankins paid for making coffin.
  CR5 225, 7 Apr 1845. J. and C.H. Spears paid by Court for furnishing burial clothes for James Winder who was recently killed in McMinn Co.

WINDER, NAT
  CR6, 6 Oct 1851. Court pays for coffin for pauper.

WITT, NATHANIEL
  CR2 155, 5 Jun 1826. Wm. Cate app. Adm., the widow consenting.

WITT, SALLY
  WB C 195, Will exec. 9 Apr 1837 /probated about Jan 1840/; "I Sally Witt a widow...being very old"; to son Joseph and dau. Patsey. Wit: Mordaca Rucker, James R. Witt. Signed by mark.

WITT, WILLIAM C.
  WB F 474, 25 Oct 1862. Comm. John L. Bridges, C. Zimmerman, and J.F. Slover lay off year's support.

WOLFF (WOLF)
  CR4 163, 2 Sep 1833. Mary E. Wolf asks Court to examine her son Samuel Wolf for competency.
  WB B 255, 3 Jul 1837. Report by John and Mary E. Wolff, Gdns. for

Samuel Wolf who was found by a jury of inquest to be an "edeott"; proceeds used for support of Samuel Wolf and family; furniture kept for use of Samuel Wolff and his wife.

WB C 47, 24 Sep 1838. Sett. by John Wolff, one of Gdns.

WB C 256, 6 Jun 1840. Report by same Gdn.; Samuel and his wife sold slaves to Mrs. Torbutt of Hamilton Co.; sale not approved by Gdn. and negroes now detained by John Wolff and in his possession.

WOLFF (WOLF, WOLFFE), JOHN

CR6, 6 Nov 1854. Patton A. Bradford app. Adm.

WB E 407-409, 5 Feb 1855. Invt. of sale and list of notes by Adm.

WB E 501, 26 Feb 1856. Comm. James Parkerson, Wm. Mcamy, David Varnell, James Bonner, A. Mckinny, and J.C. Anderson county sur. by J.C. Barbb, D.C. lay off dower to Arrena Workman formerly Arrena Wolf and partition remainder of real estate among the legal heirs, namely, Wm. R. Walker and wife Amanda C. and John L. Michael and wife Martha E.

WB F 311-313, 10 Feb 1860. Final sett. by Adm.; receipts for equal amounts from heirs John L. Michael and wife Martha C., Wm. R. Walker and wife Amanda C., and Arrena and Samuel Workman.

CC 320, filed 12 Feb 1872 (Enrolled Bills, 1865-75). Stephenson VS Workman. John Wolf died leaving widow Rainey (Areny) who married Samuel Workman and she is now his widow, and children: Martha wife of John Michaels and Amanda wife of Wm. Walker. Amanda dies during the lawsuit by April Term 1873 and her children are Martha C., John F., Wm. R., Lawrence, Arena M., Addie, Henrietta, and Joseph L. Walker.

WOLFF, MARY E.

CR5 51, 4 Jul 1842. Coroner paid for holding inquest over body.

WOOD, RICHARD

CR4 148, 5 Mar 1833. Thos. Ireland and wife Hannah to William Wood - Deed for 1/7 part of land which Richard Wood owned at time of his death.

WOODALL, DAVID

CR4 117, 3 Dec 1832. Jesse W. Edington app. Adm.

CR4 178, 4 Dec 1833. Adm. released and Isaiah Woodall is app.

WOODALL, JOHN

CR5 331, 4 Jan 1847. Court pays for shroud for pauper.

WOODS

CR4 288, 7 Nov 1836. Malinda Woods, of age to choose for herself, chooses Vincent Woods as Gdn.

WOODS, JAMES H.

CR7 280, 3 Jan 1859. Comm. James Turner, John Crews, and Benj. Wells app. to lay off year's support for widow and family.

WB F 254, 7 Feb 1859. Above Comm. reports; "agreed to give or allow her all she has and in our opinion she has not as much as the law allows her".

WOOLSEY, JOHN

CC 233, filed 14 Dec 1869. Elizabeth Brock VS John Jack et al. John Woolsey died about Jun 1863 leaving widow Margaret A. and two children, E.S. and D.J.

WRIGHT, PHILANDER
    WB E 165, Will not dated; Philander Wright of York District, S.C.;
    to father George Wright, slaves and property to be sold to pay
    father for borrowed money; "my gold watch" to oldest son George
    Sylvester Wright. Exec: James W. Grisham. Wit: P.K. Whetsell,
    J.M. Yearwood.
    CR6, 5 Aug 1851. Will proven.
    WB E 203, no date. Sale by Exec.

WYATT, SARAH
    CR7 355, 7 Nov 1859. Court pays for coffin for pauper.

WYATT, WILLIAM·
    CR6, 5 Jan 1852. Coroner paid for holding inquest over body.

YEARWOOD, JAMES M.
    CR8 134, 2 Feb 1863. C.V. Yearwood and A.D. Briant app. Adms.
    James Cooper, Joseph Barnette, and Allen Anderson app. Comm. to
    lay off year's support for widow and family.
    WB G 44, 7 Feb 1865. Supp. Invt. and Sett. by A.D. Briant, Adm.;
    original Invt. believed lost in Wheeler's raid in Aug 1864; paid
    Wm. Yearwood on acct.; receipt from H.B. Yearwood.
    CR9 41, 6 Mar 1865. Stephen P. Hale app. Gdn. of James M. Year-
    wood, minor heir.
    WB G 59, 12 May 1865. Report by Gdn.
    CC 45, filed 31 Jan 1866. James M. Yearwood, son of Wm. Yearwood,
    dec'd, died Jan 1863 leaving widow Cornelia V. who has married
    Stephen P. Hale, and one son James M., Jr., 5½ yrs. old who owns
    1/6 interest in lands of his grandfather Wm. Yearwood.

YEARWOOD, WILLIAM
    WB G 111-113, 30 Sep 1865. Invt. and sale by James Forrest, Adm.;
    buyers include H.B., Martha, T., and Nathan Yearwood; one voucher
    on the U.S. Government for $10 executed by E. Woodward Lieutenant
    and 2 M 79th Reg. Ills.; one receipt from Lieut. Daley, Co. I,
    Second Ind. Cavy. for 10 bushels corn; one receipt from Lieut.
    J.M. Baird 2 M 8 Mich. Cavalry for corn and hay, dated 2 Oct 1863.
    WB G 114, 5 Sep 1865. Comm. James Willson, James Lowry, and H.M.
    Simpson lay off year's provisions for widow Martha.
    CC 104, filed 19 Nov 1866. Wm. Yearwood died 5 Jul 1865 leaving
    widow Martha who dies during the lawsuit by 28 Dec 1866, and chil-
    dren: H.B. of Monroe Co.; Thos. of Monroe Co. who was in Mexico
    in 1846 or 1847; Martha J., now dec'd, wife of Samuel B. Haines,
    whose children are Samuel Y. and Walter S. Haines, minors of Brad-
    ley Co.; Sarah D. wife of F.A. Holt of Meigs Co.; James M., dec'd,
    whose widow Cornelia V. has married Stephen P. Hale of Monroe
    Co. and who left a son James M., Jr., aged five; Elijah of Ark.;
    Nancy N., dec'd wife of Robert L. Johnson, whose children are
    James B., Wm. H., Virginia, Thomas, Martha, and Irene Johnson,
    all supposedly of Texas and the last four minors.

YEARWOOD, WILLIAM M.
    WB E 52, 27 Jul 1849. Sett. by Wm. Yearwood, Adm.; received "back
    pay & extra pay for deceased"; paid "expenses bringing remains
    to Stuarts"; paid "Clerk fees promising soldier pay".
    CR5 543, 6 Aug 1849. Sett. made by Wm. Yearwood, Adm. of Wm.
    Yearwood, Jr.

YOUNG, WILEY B.
    CR12 311, 14 Dec 1854. Samuel C. Young, Adm. VS John O. Neal;
    amended to Thos. Cooper for the use of Samuel C. Young, Adm.;
    Jury finds for defendant and case appealed to Supreme Court.

ZIEGLER (ZEIGLER), JACOB
    CR4 329, 4 Sep 1837. Benjamin Zeigler app. Gdn. to Mary S. Newman
    widow of John Newman, dec'd, formerly Mary S. Zeigler, Joseph A.,
    William B., and Jacob Zeigler, minor heirs.
    WB C 160, 26 Apr 1839; 296, 26 Apr 1840. Report by Gdn.
    WB D 18, 26 Apr 1841. Sett. by Gdn.; receipt from Rachel Ziegler
    for boarding sd. minors and receipt of Joseph A. Zeigler for
    amount which appears to be his final payment.
    WB D 76, 26 Apr 1842. Sett. by Gdn.; receipt from Wm. B. Zeigler
    for amount which appears to be his final payment.
    WB D 169, 208, 309, dated from 26 Apr 1843 to 22 Jun 1845. Sett.
    by Gdn.
    WB D 370, 22 Jun 1846. Sett. by Gdn.; receipt in full from Jacob
    Zeigler, he being the only heir yet unpaid.

ZIMMERMAN, JOSEPH
    CR7 529, 1 Apr 1861. James M. Henderson app. Adm.
    WB F 449, 6 May 1861. Invt. by Adm.; the only asset is a bond on
    Cyrus Zimmerman which deceased received 1 Apr 1852.
    CR13 148, 9 Dec 1861. James M. Henderson, Adm. VS Cyrus Zimmerman;
    Defendant moves Court to dismiss suit, plaintiff being an alien
    enemy.

INDEX
WILLS AND ESTATE RECORDS OF
McMINN COUNTY, TENNESSEE 1820-1870

Note: Names in alphabetical order in text have been omitted. Surnames with various
spellings are grouped together in most common form.

WOOD, John H. 167, Sarah
  E. 167, Stephen 177

WOODWARD, E. 193, Mary L.
  172

WOOLSEY, James 53, M.A.
  55, Margaret 53, Mary
  53, Thomas A. 53

WORKMAN, Arrena 192, Mary
  I. 102, Rebecca 178,
  Samuel v,6,35,102,114,
  119,134,154,178,179,
  192

WRIGHT, C.J. 136, Eliza
  110, General 187, James
  124, John 155, John
  M. 148, Martha 164,
  William 164,184, Willis
  164

WYATT, Charles 115, Chris
  116, Mary A. 115

WYRICK, Jane 68, Nancy 90,
  Oscar 68, William S.
  90

YANCEY, Hiram 33

YATES, Samuel 30,47

YEARWOOD, Cornelia 125,
  James 125, J.M. 133,
  193, William 58

YOAKUM, Franklin L. 80

YORK, Mary McK. 45, U.L.,
  Uriah, Uriah L., 45,
  113,124

YOST, James L. 81

YOUNG, Dorcas E. 139,
  Susannah 42, William
  J. 139

ZEIGLER, B.F. 120, Benja-
  min T., B.T. 66,108,
  164, Joseph 31, Lockey
  144, Mary 31, Tubal
  66,164, William 144

ZIMMERMAN, C. 191

* * * * * * *

www.ingramcontent.com/pod-product-compliance
Lightning Source LLC
Chambersburg PA
CBHW072122020426
42334CB00018B/1682